The Angels

ANGEL-MANIA FOR THE ANGELS FAN

The companion scrapbook to The Angels rock book.

theangelsbook.com.au

We have assembled a huge gallery of images that portray the band's illustrious history over the decades. This website is a companion to your book and we invite you to enter and cruise through a kaleidoscope of Angels imagery. There are photos, posters, flyers, gig tickets, handwritten lyrics, letters, music, tour itineraries, diary pages – check out the crazy diamonds in the 'extreme fans' section. Herein lies a gift from The Angels to you, and to their legions of loyal fans.

by BOB YATES with
RICK BREWSTER and JOHN BREWSTER

An Ebury Press book
Published by Penguin Random House Australia Pty Ltd
Level 3, 100 Pacific Highway, North Sydney NSW 2060
www.penguin.com.au

First published by Ebury Press in 2017

Addresses for the Penguin Random House group of companies can be found at global.penguinrandomhouse.com/offices.

National Library of Australia
Cataloguing-in-Publication entry

Yates, Bob, author
The Angels / Bob Yates, Rick Brewster, John Brewster

ISBN 978 0 14378 263 6 (paperback)

Angels (Musical group: Australia)
Rock groups – Australia – Biography
Rock musicians – Australia – Biography
Rock music – Australia – History – 20th century

Other Creators/Contributors:
Brewster, Rick, author
Brewster, John, author

Cover design by Adam Yazxhi/MAXCO
Back cover image by Bitsy Ackland
Internal design and typesetting by Midland Typesetters, Australia
Printed in Australia by Griffin Press, an accredited ISO AS/NZS 14001:2004
Environmental Management System printer

Penguin Random House Australia uses papers that are natural, renewable and recyclable products and made from wood grown in sustainable forests. The logging and manufacturing processes are expected to conform to the environmental regulations of the country of origin.

FOREWORD
BY JIMMY BARNES

I grew up in Adelaide. The home of serial killers and good rock 'n' roll bands. The Angels started out around the same time as Cold Chisel. Originally they were called the Keystone Angels, playing nice old covers of classic rock 'n' roll music, Everly Brothers and Little Richard songs. We did shows all over South Australia together. I used to watch them and I could see that they were very good at what they did but it was always a little nice for me. But I didn't see what was coming. The songs they were playing were beautifully crafted rock 'n' roll songs. I should have spotted that they were serving their apprenticeship. Playing songs written by master craftsmen. This was how they learned to write such great songs. The band learned how to make a chorus pay off. When to drive hard and when to lay back. And they learned all this under the cover of the Keystone Angels.

Then they took a chance and headed interstate, long before we did. I didn't see the band again for a long while. I heard that they had been signed to the legendary label, Alberts. I wondered how that was going for them. One day, coming out through an old AM car radio, I heard a beautiful pop song. 'Am I Ever Gonna See Your Face Again' sounded like a song that I had known for years. Well written and catchy. I waited to see who it was. It was The Angels. Of course it was. They had done really well for themselves. Alberts and the band obviously had good chemistry. I would keep my ears out for more from them.

Next thing I heard was different, though. It wasn't pop. It was fierce and aggressive and driving. It was June 1978 and The Angels had come of age. *Face To Face* was a masterpiece. One of the great rock records made in this country. They had soaked up everything that Alberts had to offer and, together with Mark Opitz, they had produced something very special.

They went on to become one of the bands that changed Australian music forever. Doc was a menacing front-man, Chris and Buzz formed a rhythm section like no other and the Brewster Brothers held it all down. Powerful, aggressive and joyous. If you wanted to show an example of great Australian pub rock, then *Face to Face* and The Angels were it. Especially in a live situation. They filled pubs way beyond capacity and every night of the week audiences were pinned to the back wall.

The Angels went on to make great music for more than thirty years. Players moved in and out of the band but the Brewster Brothers held the sound together. The loss of Doc Neeson in 2014 was a sad day for Australian music but still they kept going. Doing what they know best. Playing rock. Chris Bailey had passed the year before in 2013. We lost a great bass player and a good human being that day. But still the band marched on.

Time has taken its toll on The Angels but it can't stop them and every night the songs come to life on stage thanks to the Brewster Brothers. And every night people walk away shouting, 'This is it, folks, over the top.' I hope they do it for many years to come.

INTRODUCTION

The genesis of this book came many years ago when I helped John and Rick Brewster condense their family story into a mini-biography to grace the centrefold of their first Brewster Brothers CD, *Shadows Fall*, released in mid-2006.

Doc had not performed with The Angels for six years. Accepting that the band's long association with him was over, the brothers invited me to write a book about the extraordinary journey they'd both taken since forming their first band during their university days in the seventies. At the time, I declined the offer – the task was too big for me. Others were asked, but despite a couple of starts, nothing came to fruition.

Fast forward to late 2012 and John and Rick were once again broaching the subject of *the book* with me. During the previous few years, they and Doc, along with original members Chris Bailey and Buzz Bidstrup, had come to an agreement to reform The Angels and they'd toured extensively. However, that line-up had now disbanded and Doc had announced he'd be pursuing a solo career.

While I considered the challenge, news arrived that Doc had been diagnosed with a virulent brain tumour, resulting in him undergoing an operation and months of chemotherapy. Sometime later, with his health improving, I invited Doc and a few mutual friends out for a relaxing day on my old sailing yacht. I told him that I'd accepted an invitation from John and Rick to write their story. He shrugged and it was left at that as we hauled on sails and continued to enjoy a memorable day.

I emailed Doc afterwards, requesting access to the six hours of interviews he'd recently undertaken with journalist Anthony O'Grady for the National Film and Sound Archives. Generously, Doc gave me the written permission I required, in the knowledge that I'd be using the interviews as research for this book. A few months later, he was gone. The insights I gained into his life from those interviews lie between these pages. Rest in peace, Doc, you were a one-off.

A barrister will tell you that when six people witness an incident, there'll be six different accounts. The core of this book was garnered from dozens of interviews with John and Rick; it's essentially their story. But their stories have been overlaid with dozens of other accounts from those whose lives have intermingled with The Angels over the decades: musicians, roadies, promoters, agents, record company executives, fans, friends and, occasionally, the wives who started out with them. Regrettably, the two managers who consecutively handled the band's affairs for thirty years declined to participate.

I was also given full access to boxes of memorabilia and a cabinet of bulging files that Rick keeps locked in a shipping container. Among those records were scores of tour itineraries and a tonne of promotional material. They brought back memories of the late seventies/early eighties years that are now referred to as the golden era of pub rock: an era opened up by The Angels after they released their seminal album *Face To Face* in 1978. What would follow was the phenomenal success of bands such as Cold Chisel, Midnight Oil, Icehouse, Divinyls, Australian Crawl, Mi-Sex, who I managed, and many others. Their legions of fans provided the impetus to hundreds of hotels and clubs in cities and towns to create a thriving circuit, enabling bands to tour the length and breadth of Australia. It was a circuit that also extended to our close neighbour, New Zealand.

Those halcyon times will never return; however, in recent years, with front-man Dave Gleeson, The Angels are once again among Australia's major attractions. They regularly co-headline rock festivals and close doors on their national tours.

Doc once said, 'It's not all hugs and kisses inside a band, you know.' He is no longer with us, and neither are some of the other players who were a part of The Angels juggernaut. Fortunately John and Rick are, and, with the contributions of so many others, here is the story of one of the greatest and most influential rock bands Australia has ever produced.

Bob Yates, 2017

CHAPTER ONE
NEW YEAR'S EVE, 1979

Out of the dark a launch approaches, navigation lights aglow. On the dimly lit wharf a group of young men and women in jeans, leather jackets, short skirts step forward. A solidly built man gripping an aluminium briefcase flashes a torch.

'Mark Pope?' a voice calls from the water.

'That's me.'

The launch comes alongside, ropes are thrown over bollards and it creaks gently against the pylons.

'Everyone here?'

'Yes.'

Other torches flick on, illuminating the rear deck. 'Watch your step.'

Hands reach out to help as they clamber aboard. The crew cast off, the engine picks up and the boat swings back towards the Sydney Harbour Bridge with its rows of lights and arching girders. In the cabin the skipper is on the radio, saying he's collected the group and ETA will be in twelve minutes.

They cruise past Luna Park, under the bridge and the thundering roar of traffic and trains. A warm breeze ruffles a girl's blonde hair and another adjusts her silk scarf. To starboard the city lights blaze into view. The skipper alters course and the bow slices through the wake of a ferry churning out from Circular Quay. Spray splashes aft and there's laughter when it hits the young faces.

Ahead lie the white-tiled sails of the Opera House, shimmering beneath the moon and stars. On the far side, spotlights cut the night and a singer booms out of a massive sound system. His voice echoes back from the city high-rise and the roar of a huge crowd rolls across the water.

The engine throttles back, a crewman with a coiled rope makes his way forward and another takes position astern with a boathook. Torches ashore flicker and flash in their direction. The launch eases up to a concrete landing and a gangplank is thrown across. Hands reach to help everyone ashore. A roar swells as a muffled song comes to an end on the other side. As the group climbs to meet two T-shirted figures with security passes hanging from their necks, a straying spotlight gleams off necklaces and leather jackets.

'How's it going, guys?' one asks, distributing joints and striking matches.

'All good. How's it going, Ray?' The tallest one has a velvety Irish lilt in his voice.

'Mega crowd! Consternation and terror with the Sydney Festival management! My lighting desk is set up stage-side, not good, but not enough cable to put it far enough out front.'

'Natives are restless,' says the other, 'giving all the acts a hard time – they're throwing cans and fruit at them! They've been here all day getting pissed and impatient. Been chanting for the band.'

One of the guys punches the air. 'I'm ready. Let's do it!' There's laughter from the girls.

'Put these on,' says Ray, handing out backstage passes before leading the group through the stage door and past security. High heels clickety-clack as they negotiate flights of stairs and curving concrete-walled corridors. 'Dressing room,' he announces, swinging back a door and standing aside to let them in.

There's a table in the centre with trays of sandwiches, bowls of fruit. In a corner is a kitchenette with glasses, cups, tea, coffee, bottles of wine and a bottle of scotch. There's a fridge with beer, wine, soft drinks, bottles of water. There are guitars on stands, amps lined up behind.

One of the guys picks up a Les Paul, straps it on and begins playing scales. Another lights a cigarette, selects the bass, plucks the strings, adjusts the pegs. Wine is uncorked, handbags and jackets draped over chairs. One of the young men picks up a pair of drumsticks and beats steady patterns on a rubber practice mat. In the kitchen corner, whiskey shots are measured and the roadies roll fresh joints.

'There's a TV monitor up there with the Channel Ten broadcast,' says one. 'You got forty minutes to showtime.'

It's almost midnight as Mark Pope leads them to the side of the stage next to the foldback and lighting desks.

'ANGELS! ANGELS! ANGELS!' The chant rolling up from the vast audience is deafening,

Rolf Harris had stormed off earlier after doing only a couple of songs – dodging beer cans and copping a tomato in the chest. He was last seen swearing all the way back to his dressing-room. Actor Grahame Bond dressed in drag as his Aunty Jack TV alter-ego had done the same, driven off by incoming missiles.

'ANGELS! ANGELS! ANGELS!' All communication onstage is conducted by sign language or shouting into ears at close range.

'ANGELS! ANGELS! ANGELS!'

Out on the stage, the crew are checking equipment, placing bottles of water, laying folded towels on the drum riser, gaffing down stray cables, clearing away the debris being thrown in.

Bang! A can hits the Perspex screen that's been erected between the mixing consoles and the edge of the stage overlooking the audience. Coke dribbles down the screen and mixes with a splash of drying beer where the last one connected.

Ray glances at the group who stare out at the heaving beast; behind them the girls look apprehensive. Roadies stationed each side of the stage periodically run along the edge and push back enthusiastic punters attempting to scramble over, collecting empty cans as they go. Lumps of chipboard sheets that skirt the front of the stage have been ripped off and bits tossed like frisbees at some of the previous performers. People are getting underneath but there are a few security guys down there pushing them back.

Dozens of spotlights along the huge trusses above flash on and off as Ray slides his faders up and down for a final check.

Two of the band are looking meaningfully at each other: '*Should we be going on?*' A white-shirted guy with 'Stage Manager' round his neck comes over. 'This will settle down as soon as you get out there – they're all here for you. The Mayor and the committee are about to do a short welcome speech, then the fireworks, then you're on.'

Tens of thousands are jammed across the forecourt – thronging the paths and lawns snaking around Farm Cove, and thousands more are sardine-packed along the road leading to Circular Quay. Scaffold towers rise out of the audience with dozens of punters hanging off them while the Channel Ten crews perch at the top, swinging their big cameras back and forth across the whole scenario.

The tall one yells into the ear of another, 'Someone's gotta take control – people are going to get hurt!'

At the mixing desk out front, nestled on scaffolding above the audience, ace sound engineer Howard Page eyes a group of drunks among the swaying mob off to one side of the stage. They're chugga-lugging cans and tossing the empties stage-ward. No-one is attempting to stop them. It began during the samba band from Argentina. The Argentineans had the whole place laughing and dancing, but that hadn't stopped a few idiots. After dark more joined in. The cans were empty and light and never going to do much damage, but the cops should have waded in and grabbed the throwers. It hadn't been vicious – they were just bored lobbing up the empties. But as the night progressed, that changed. Now there was fruit, tomatoes and other foodstuff. Someone with authority and balls should be on the mic – singling them out, giving them an ear-bashing.

Howard looks around. From his bird's-eye view he now realises that the police presence, conspicuous throughout the day even though they'd only stood about, has evaporated. Maybe there has been a change of shift, but there are nowhere near enough if things go pear-shaped. He turns to his offsider: 'This could get ugly and we're going to cop the blame! People are gonna get hurt if someone doesn't get onto that mic!'

The Mayor comes on in his suit with his wife, and a group of business straights stand around him as he goes into a speech thanking this and that. The crowd boo and the hurling increases. 'GET THE FUCK OFF! WHERE'S THE ANGELS?' The Mayor dodges and ducks and then he's counting down to midnight, yells 'HAPPY NEW YEAR', and he and his associates are out of there. There are ten minutes of fireworks and the crowd go ooh and ahhh and settle down.

A voice comes through Howard's headphones, 'Fireworks nearly over. Band's ready to go on – do the intros when you're ready.'

'Roger to that,' he says, and switches his mic over to the front-of-house PA.

'LADIES AND GENTLEMEN,' his voice booms, 'THE BAND YOU'RE ALL HERE TO SEE ARE ABOUT TO COME OUT.' A mighty roar goes up but his voice booms on: 'BUT BEFORE THEY COME OUT, WOULD YOU PLEASE STOP THE BEER-CAN THROWING, STOP THROWING CANS AT THE PERFORMERS – SOMEONE IS GOING TO GET HURT! JUST STOP THROWING STUFF, OKAY!' There's more applause and he gives it a minute before drawing breath and then his mighty amplified voice blasts across the audience: 'LADIES AND GENTLEMEN, WOULD YOU PLEASE WELCOME THE GUYS YOU'RE ALL HERE FOR: RICK AND JOHN BREWSTER ON GUITARS, CHRIS BAILEY ON BASS, BUZZ BIDSTRUP ON DRUMS . . .'

The drums and bass come pounding through the huge system, guitar chords kick in and it all throbs through the night as the crowd greets them with a roar. A shaft of light beams down onto Rick Brewster standing rock still, fingers dancing along the frets, peeling off a screaming lead – his face expressionless behind wrap-around shades.

Ray Hawkins slams forward the fader slides, drenching a hundred thousand watts of light across the stage. 'AND LAST BUT NOT LEAST,' yells Howard, 'PUT YOUR HANDS TOGETHER FOR MR DOC NEESON ON VOCALS! WOULD YOU PLEASE WELCOME THE MIGHTY ANGELS.'

The band moves into full flight and the roar is ear-splitting as a tall lean dinner-suited bow-tied figure skips manically out of the wings, whips the mic off its silvery stand, doubles over and snarls, *'Smokers smoking in the smoking room . . .'* and the show is on.

Across the audience, clenched fists punch the sky and mayhem explodes into the midsummer night. Onstage camera crews move in for close-ups, a crouching roadie shadows Doc, feeding his microphone lead as he leaps about. Other crew race in and out, throwing back the debris that's flying in. Doc is in command, prowling along the footlights from one side to the other, dodging the guitarists as they move into the mics for the choruses.

They segue into the next song, 'Who Rings The Bell', Doc staring menacingly into the crowd, oblivious to incoming missiles. Behind, the guitars plough on, a wall of dense concentrated sound. *'It's ringing all over town – tear the big house down . . .'* During the instrumental Doc shrugs out of his dinner jacket, loosens the bow tie. The crowd sings every word of every song, all the phrasing, pauses, choruses.

Out at the mixing desk, Howard's apprehension rises with each beer-can near-miss of a band member. There's now an occasional bottle getting lobbed in. He's muttering to himself about Doc as he works the big sound desk, '*He should step out of character – say something.*'

The opening riffs of another song begin. Right off, the crowd knows it. *'Buy me a box of French cigars . . .'* Thousands of voices chant the words. Guys thrash air guitars, girls dance and wave their arms – the place is going off! *'Take me away to Marseilles . . .'*

Then a bottle sails in and hits Chris Bailey. With blood streaming down his face he stumbles forward – a second later something ricochets off the back of Doc's head and he topples to his knees. With two of the band down, the others grind to a ragged halt and look around, bewildered – except for Rick, who rages on with his solo until John grabs his arm. With debris still arcing over the footlights, the roadies lift Chris and Doc and drag them offstage. Ray dims the lights and in the gloom Buzz climbs out from behind his kit.

Through the PA comes the voice of Howard Page: 'THAT'S IT! ARE YOU SATISFIED NOW? THE SHOW IS OVER, THAT'S IT.

JUST STOP THROWING THINGS. STOP RIGHT NOW. GOOD-NIGHT. THE SHOW IS OVER.'

Doc and Chris are taken by ambulance to St Vincent's Hospital where they both get cleaned up, stitched up and spend the night and next day recuperating. The ambulance officers visit Doc with albums to sign and talk about the dozens of people they'd ferried to the casualty department after the show. 'There were girls' panties and guys' underpants all over the place full of shit because they couldn't get to the toilets,' they said. 'The organisation was pathetic.'

The front pages are dominated by the 'riot'. State Premier Neville Wran is president of the festival board, Mayor Nelson Meers is head of the organising committee. Questions will be asked in Parliament and also at the next Sydney council meeting. It's clear the festival had no idea how to organise a major event of this kind. No one takes responsibility, and none is ever sheeted home to the organisers. No one will acknowledge that keeping tens of thousands of punters waiting for up to twelve hours on a hot day and through a long night, getting pissed and bored, was a recipe for disaster. There were nowhere near enough toilets and there were no station points where water and soft drinks could be bought. The organisers had no concept of who The Angels actually were, only the bare minimum of security staff were rostered on duty and the police presence was totally inadequate for such an enormous crowd.

Despite much official bluster and acknowledgement that there could have been deaths, there was never the promised enquiry into how things got so out of control.

A ban was put on rock performances from the Opera House steps that would remain in place for seventeen years – until Crowded House got permission to stage their career-ending concert there in 1996.

But rock 'n' roll mayhem and large-scale public disorder wasn't the way it had always been for this group of hardy troubadours. Things had been much tamer in Adelaide in the early days, back when it all began.

CHAPTER TWO
MOONSHINE JUG AND STRING BAND

There's no mention of any celebrated rock guitarists on the St Peter's College website list of successful old boys. This is curious because Saints, listed among Australia's top private schools, is where John and Richard Brewster-Jones were educated during the sixties.

St Peter's College is a private school in the South Australian capital of Adelaide. Founded by the Anglican Church, the school is noted for its famous alumni, including three Nobel laureates, forty-one Rhodes scholars, ten state premiers, two Victoria Cross winners, a dozen high-profile sportsmen, an archbishop and an astronaut.

Although not from among the wealthiest of Adelaide's families, nonetheless Rick and John came from a privileged background, and one steeped in classical music. Grandfather Hooper Brewster-Jones had been a concert pianist, composer and founder of Adelaide's first Symphony Orchestra. Their father, Arthur, had conducted the Adelaide Symphony Orchestra and had played as first cellist. Arthur would go on to be Director of Classical Music at the ABC, the national broadcaster, during the years that Rick and John were growing up.

None of this was lost on young Rick, who'd immersed himself in the works of Beethoven, Bach and company since childhood. But Rick's musical taste was broad and at school he once played the ragtime classic 'Black and White Rag' to a rowdy audience, but you could hear a pin drop when he launched into one of his grandfather's compositions, 'Dance of the White Browed Babbler', based on local birdcalls.

Rick and John's grandfather used to spend whole days in the bush around Bridgewater and Hahndorf in the Adelaide Hills with his great friend, artist Hans Heysen. Both were avid bird watchers, and while Hans would set up his easel and paint landscapes that would one day sell for fortunes, Hooper recorded birdsongs on scraps of paper. Hans later presented one of his paintings to Rick and John's father as a wedding gift.

Rick was in the school choir and, on one memorable occasion, sang 'Glory Be To God On High' in St Peter's Cathedral, an Adelaide landmark. The school had an orchestra, but with no call for a pianist, Rick played percussion, a skill that would come in handy in a few years – but more on that later.

His private piano teacher, always encouraging and convinced he'd go a long way, entered him in the state eisteddfod competitions and at sixteen he won the under-21 section, playing Beethoven's Op. 14, No. 1, Sonata No. 19.

Rick was becoming a musician.

Meanwhile, big brother John was spending his spare time with his ear glued to a transistor radio, soaking up pop songs, especially the Beatles. In mid-1964 the Beatles arrived in Adelaide to a frenzied welcome of 200,000 people, the biggest reception they received anywhere in the world. The week before, John, with his friend Julian Goss, had wagged school and queued for a ticket, camping out three days on blankets laid on the pavement among hundreds of others, waiting for the box office to open. His mother regularly dropped off sandwiches and a flask of cocoa.

After seeing the concert he blew his savings on a Yamaha acoustic guitar and then holed up in his bedroom, meticulously learning chords and strums and playing along with every song the Beatles had released.

> **John:** But then I saw Dylan and The Band in '66 and he changed my life, absolutely incredible. I went home and learnt to play his entire recorded repertoire. I loved the Beatles – but Dylan was different.

John graduated from Saints in '66. He'd done well in English and French and played basketball in the A team, but with no idea of what he wanted to do, he took his father's advice and got a job with an accountancy firm. The nine-to-five suited his social life. Lanky with sun-bleached hair, he soon had a ute with surfboards in the back and he and mate Pete Thorpe spent their weekends on the coast surfing Middleton, Trigs Point and Seaford, often staying overnight at his grandparents' beach house at Victor Harbor.

> **John:** We were just teenage guys, me and my friends. Surfing, meeting girls, smoking pot, checking out bands. I'd take my guitar to parties. I was into the Beatles, Stones, Dylan, Byrds, all that. Adelaide city at night was really exciting – there were all these rock 'n' roll places and we were out there discovering. I started going to gigs after I left school. Fantastic bands – psychedelic lighting. There was The Cellar in Twin Street, it was in a basement. Big Daddy's Disco and the 20 Plus club, Pete and I hung out at them all. The Octogen in Elizabeth, the Lord Melbourne Hotel, The Old Lion, Pooraka Hotel, The Arkaba.
>
> The Twilights played at the Caledonian Hall every Friday night, incredible musicians – they did the Beatles and Hollies note perfect, we loved them. Interstate bands came through. Mississippi, The Valentines, The Loved Ones, Procession – what a band Procession were! Fraternity with Bon Scott. Incredible. Masters Apprentices. The scene was about the bands and the music and the clubs and we were just totally into it. Plus surfing, girls, pot, beer – nothing else mattered.

As for Rick, during his final year at school he gave up on his classical piano lessons. He'd never been good at sight reading and loathed that section of the exams. But mainly it was because he'd started playing acoustic guitar with his friends.

Rick: My girlfriend Bitsy and I formed a folk trio with Bob Petchell, a friend who later joined our jug band and played harmonica. We rehearsed a lot and played a lunchtime concert at St Peter's. The repertoire was mainly Simon and Garfunkel, a bit of Donovan and a couple of songs which later made it into the jug band ['Ukulele Lady' and 'I Ain't Gonna Marry'], which Bitsy sang. This was my main period of learning acoustic guitar. I also did a gig for a twenty-first with some friends from school. We practised in my bedroom for days. We did 'Good Day Sunshine', 'Hey Jude', 'Six Days On The Road', some Dylan for sure – and The Rolling Stones. That was my first band gig, and it happened towards the end of my final year at Saints, 1969.

In 1970 Rick enrolled in an Agricultural Science degree at Adelaide University. Tall, gawky, a bit on the nerdy side, he'd always been fascinated by insects, so he specialised in entomology. His idea of a good time was to head out on field trips wearing a straw sunhat and collect specimens. There was a two-week camping excursion to the Snowy Mountains with his friend Greg Baker, hunting for robber flies and setting light traps after dark to collect moths and high-country night insects. They all went into his killing jars to take back to uni.

Uni life exposed him to the band scene. John Mayall and the Bluesbreakers from the UK played the Union Hall; Daddy Cool played a lunchtime concert and Rick was down the front, watching the guitar players, noting everything they did in his studious way; Madder Lake and Spectrum; also Fraternity. Rick gravitated towards new friends who played instruments and there was always a jam happening somewhere. His hair grew longer, clothes of choice from Vinnies: baggy shorts and bright Afghan socks.

John and Pete went to a concert one weekend that featured a Melbourne jug band called the Captain Matchbox Whoopee Band. They were blown away. Adelaide boasted its own Coney Island Jug Band, but they were purists playing it straight and took the music seriously. Nothing like the mad antics Mic and Jim Conway, front-men of Captain Matchbox, got up to, or the show-stopping antics of bassist Dave Flett, holding a huge gramophone speaker to his bum while Mic blew fart noises into his earthenware jug to the melody of 'Hernando's Hideaway'. Hilarious stuff to the young sweat-drenched punters on the dance floor.

The following Sunday, while they were driving back from a weekend of surfing and partying during which John had got up and played his guitar, Pete suggested they start a band.

'Oh, what do you play?' a surprised John asked. 'Nothing,' said Pete, but he reckoned he could learn to play bass like the guy in Captain Matchbox. 'It can't be *that* hard to play that music . . . and looks like a lot of fun!' A couple of days later he'd even come up with a name: The Moonshine Jug and String Band.

> **Mic Conway of Captain Matchbox Whoopee Band:** We first travelled to Adelaide for a folk festival in 1970 – it was in a hall somewhere with a few other folkie acts and groups, held over a weekend. My first hazy memory of Moonshine is probably at the Myponga Pop Festival when we were back in Adelaide a few months later.

John and Pete soon had a bunch of mates rounded up, including brother Rick, and rehearsals got underway. Rick and John fossicked around in second-hand shops and found some pre-war jug band 78 rpm records: Gus Cannon and his Jug Stompers, The Memphis Jug Band and a few others. They'd also bought everything the Jim Kweskin Jug Band (with Maria Muldaur) had recently recorded.

The first line-up was John Brewster on banjo, Pete Thorpe on tea-chest bass, Rick Brewster on washboard, Bob Petchell on jug. John's housemate Leigh Hobba played clarinet and Rick's friend Craig Holden sang and played guitar (although everyone sang to some extent). Rick's girlfriend Bitsy did a few songs too. Graham Harboard played washboard during early rehearsals but decided not to continue, so Rick gave up guitar (Craig was playing guitar anyway) and became washboard player. Graham would move on to being money man – handling door takings or collecting gig fees, and distributing the proceeds among the players.

In October '70, John did the rounds of the pubs, doing a spiel on the band, and eventually landed a Thursday night at the Sussex Hotel in suburban Walkerville for $30.

> **John:** The weekend before, the band did a warm-up at my twenty-first – we had everyone dancing! We spread the word about the Sussex and on the night all our friends showed up. We must have sounded awful but what we lacked in expertise, we made up for in fun and they loved it. The publican was happy and gave us a residency and we were off and running.

At thirty bucks a gig, there wasn't a lot for Graham to distribute, but to have a venue where they could play all night to an enthusiastic crowd was reward in itself. The boys went into rehearsal overdrive, adding to the repertoire on a daily basis, and relentlessly honed their musicianship. Within weeks the tiny venue was crammed tight; punters standing on chairs and tables and singing along.

By Christmas they'd come to the attention of the organisers of a rock festival being promoted as Adelaide's answer to the recently held Woodstock in the USA, and they were booked onto the program.

Originally billed as 'The Australian Festival Of Progressive Music', the festival quickly became known as 'Myponga' due to its location near the village of the same name an hour south of Adelaide.

> **John:** Myponga, that was just a blast and to be there was huge for us. We decided we HAD to have a piano for it, so we borrowed one without asking, from Lincoln College at uni where we used to rehearse down in this little basement. We all carried it up these tiny thin stone steps. Upright piano – weighed a bloody ton. We took it all the way to Myponga, put it up on the stage and Rick played it for one song. I don't know if we were any good, but we went over really well. And the band that followed us was Daddy Cool. I just went 'Arrrggghhh!' They were unbelievable – they'd only been going a few months, but they were hot and really swung. We were very influenced by them. They were performers and really put on a show.
>
> That clip of Daddy Cool doing 'Eagle Rock' was shot during their set at Myponga. People say it was shot at the first Sunbury Festival, but it wasn't. The

audience dancing and getting off on it, that was the vibe at Myponga. It was a full-on hippie event – camping, naked girls, swimming in dams, pot, booze, love the one you're with.

There was this very enthusiastic band that got so carried away with the excitement that they wrote a song about it, right there and then, and performed it. Unfortunately it wasn't quite as good as 'By the time we got to Woodstock we were half a million strong . . .' The chorus went 'My, my, my, my . . . Myponga' to this lame tune. It was just so terrible, but I say that with the greatest affection, cos you know, you had to admire them for the spirit – wonderful. There was a band who lived and travelled in a bus – they wore black clothes, black cloaks and make-up. I can't remember who they were.

The Sons of the Vegetal Mother played – made up of Ross Wilson, Phil Rudd and members of Daddy Cool and Spectrum. They were amazing. Spectrum were something really special because, you know, in an outdoor hippie kind of environment, it was just wonderful stuff . . . and when they did 'Someday I'll Have Money', well . . .

Back at the Sussex things were getting wilder and sweatier. Pete Thorpe on washtub bass developed his own floor show. He'd hand the bass to Rick, step forward as the band swung into 'Mighty Man' and grab the mic. Halfway through the song he'd pour lighter fuel over a leather-gloved hand, set fire to it and – holding his flaming fist aloft – finish off to delirious applause.

The band started picking up gigs on the campuses and occasionally scored a private party; and there were always rehearsals and jams.

Neno Nenadovic was a regular Moonshine punter at the Sussex Hotel:

Neno: My girlfriend Deidre had a pretty good nose for where the action was. We were both busy chasing the vibe post-Woodstock. I was doing an honours degree and Deidre was waiting on tables at a Spanish restaurant, coming home smelling of garlic prawns. She wasn't always waiting on tables – she did work for a bank.

> The future was ours regardless, and this was discussed endlessly in the pubs of North Adelaide. There was plenty to talk about, Whitlam was about to sweep into power and women were on the cusp of equal wages.
>
> One night Deidre announced we had to go to the Sussex in Walkerville, because the band was really pumping every Thursday night. I put my faith in her judgement, after all, she was spot on about Bon Scott in Fraternity, owned the Blind Faith album and gave me Janis Joplin's *Pearl* as a birthday present. The Sussex was packed, punters dancing on chairs and tables! We went every Thursday night for months, and every time it was the same set, but no one got sick of it. We all just danced and grinned at each other for two hours. Stand-out songs were 'Save Me Some', '(You Scream) Ice Cream' and Mungo Jerry's 'Mighty Man'. They finished the night with 'Mighty Man' and the crowd would go wild. We'd go home about midnight, ready for uni, the bank and the garlic prawns.

Eventually the work and rehearsal schedule began getting in the way of Craig Holden's architectural studies. His dream was to get over to Europe and continue his education amongst the classical buildings there and the day came when he put in his notice to quit the band. John's housemate and fellow band member, Leigh Hobba, had played in a group called Southern Union at Teachers College with a tall handsome Irishman who'd just been demobbed from National Service. Leigh had sat in on a gig with him a few weeks back and was impressed at how well he sang. 'There's this guy I know – he'd be good, Bernard Neeson, nice guy. He shares a house with John Woodruff, a guy I used to share with.'

With the blessing of the rest of the band, Leigh rang. 'Hey Bernard, wanna be a star?' he asked.

A time was arranged for Bernard to meet the band and sing a few songs during a rehearsal. His friend Bob Bowes drove him over, and by the end of the session Bernard was in. On the way home he'd fallen silent, staring out the window.

'They reckon I'll be making around thirty to forty dollars a week,' he said to Bob. 'If the National Service Training scheme find out they'll cut my grant back. I think I'll change my name for the band gigs.'

He glanced at Bob. 'And they're calling me Bernie! I told them it was Bernard but they were still saying Bernie when we left.' Looking frustrated, he stared back out the window. 'You know that Wyatt Earp movie . . . *Gunfight at OK Corral*? We used to act it out when we were kids, you know, cowboys. I was always Doc. What was his second name – do you know?'

Bob thought about it, 'Holliday?'

'Yeah, Holliday, yeah that's it.'

When Bob dropped him off he looked back into the car. 'Holliday is naff. How about Doc Talbot?'

Bob shrugged. 'Sure, why not?'

CHAPTER THREE
BERNARD NEESON

Bernard was born in Belfast in early January 1947. He was the first of what would become a family of six kids for Kathleen, a nurse, and his father Barney, a British Army sergeant in the Royal Electrical and Mechanical Engineers – REME for short. At the time of Bernard's birth, his father had been posted to Austria, and soon after, Kathleen and Bernard left Belfast and joined him. Three years later they were transferred to West Germany, then back to the UK, before being sent out to Singapore in 1955. Along the way, another few siblings had come into the world.

During a visit the Neesons made to a local Singaporean family, the father asked his young son and daughter to get out their instruments and sing some songs for the guests.

To Bernard's surprise, they returned with guitars and began singing songs made popular by the Kingston Trio: 'Sloop John B' and 'Hang Down Your Head Tom Dooley'. Bernard was transfixed. During the following weeks he pestered his parents for a guitar until they eventually gave in and bought him not a guitar, but a ukulele with an instruction book. Unimpressed, he nevertheless worked out the fingering for some basic chords and learned to strum along to songs on the radio.

When his father was posted back to Ireland some time later, eleven-year-old Bernard was enrolled in a boarding school where he made friends with a few other lads with musical inclinations. Still playing the uke, he formed a band with them. The family of one of the boys lived near the school and his parents belonged to a skiffle group playing all the songs of Lonnie Donegan, the king of skiffle at the time. Bernard fitted right in, madly playing along with his uke and singing along in the choruses.

In 1958 Barney resigned from the Army and bought a house in Belfast with plans to settle back into civilian life. However, the harsh reality of post-war Northern Ireland soon hit home – the economy was a mess and there was violence and mayhem as a result of the IRA's war against the British; there was tension and fighting between the Catholics and the Protestants too. In 1959 Barney and Kathleen applied for assisted passage to emigrate to Australia: six kids and two adults. He answered an ad for a job at the Holden plant in South Australia and, with his qualifications, was accepted.

On an overcast spring morning the Neeson family pulled away from the bustle of London's Tilbury Docks aboard the 22,000-ton white-painted *Strathnaver*, loaded down with 1250 excited migrants and their crates of luggage.

Bernard, now thirteen, stood at the ship's rail as she slid down the Thames River and into the English Channel. He watched the tugboats break away and return to port as the *Strathnaver* picked up speed, never imagining what destiny had in store for him.

Five weeks later, on Easter Thursday 1960, the ship docked in Port Adelaide. Gazing wide-eyed around, he and his family followed the queue down the gangplank and crossed over a wooden wharf and into a massive corrugated-iron warehouse. While some were greeted by friends and relatives, there was no one waiting for the Neesons. Porters stacked luggage trunks into baggage cars and the families climbed into passenger carriages for the train trip to Adelaide.

For the next hour they clickety-clacked through a heat-scorched barren landscape with barely a blade of grass. The Neesons, used to the teeming streets and cheek-by-jowl tenements of Belfast, stared out the window and wondered what sort of destination lay ahead.

They were taken to a migrant hostel where the Adelaide Festival Theatre now stands. Bernard's father and some of the other men were bussed to the Holden factory to be signed on. The young Neesons joined hordes of other recently arrived kids and played and swam along the banks of the nearby Torrens.

With the money Barney and Kathleen had received from the sale of their Belfast home, they bought a newly built house on Main North Road on the fringe of Elizabeth, an outer suburb 24 kilometres north of the city centre, which had been named after Queen Elizabeth II.

The area was bleak. Across the road were brown paddocks with wire fences where a few gaunt cattle eked out their existence. But migrants were flooding in and new estates were springing up all around them. Workers on the Holden production lines were doing double shifts and the cars were selling as fast as they came out of the factory. Barney, making good money, got in with a circle of friends, many of them Northern Irish, and on weekends there were parties, barbeques and dances at the community hall.

Back at the hostel where people were constantly moving in and moving out, Bernard had managed to snaffle a cracked old guitar that had been left behind. He'd got the hang of the basics of playing it, but, keen to learn more, he now talked his parents into paying for weekly lessons. These were taught above a music shop and it wasn't long before Bernard and his teacher, who also owned the shop, got to work on his mother in convincing her that if her son was to get anywhere with his musical passions, he'd need to have a proper guitar. Within a month Doc was the proud owner of a brand new, semi-acoustic Maton guitar. With a songbook of Chuck Berry hits, he started practising in earnest.

By sixteen, at Elizabeth High School, he was jamming with friends and gaining a reputation for his renditions of Chuck Berry and Rolling Stones songs. He joined the Hideaway Club, part of the St Stephen's youth group, and got in with other budding musicians there. A band formed and played at club parties and barbeques. They were good enough to get invited to open the newly completed Elizabeth Working Men's Club, where their fathers were all founding members.

Bernard matriculated in 1965 and not sure about a career, joined a couple of friends and enrolled for the two-year teacher's diploma at

Wattle Park Teachers College. There, he heard about a battered guitar in the men's locker room that guys would pick up and play during class breaks. The acoustics gave the vocals a nice echo and it was a hang for the musically inclined. With his tall commanding frame, good looks, Irish brogue and repertoire of songs, it wasn't long before a band emerged around him. Called Southern Union, their repertoire included 'Stagolee', 'King Of The Road', 'Chantilly Lace' and a few of Chuck Berry's. All big hits from Bernard's adolescent years.

They also called themselves Dust Bowl, for gigs in which their repertoire included Woody Guthrie and Dylan songs. The great folk revival of recent years was on the wane, but there were still opportunities for an acoustic act to get up, though it was rarely for more than coffee and applause. Dust Bowl performed at Bernard's parents' church, St Anne's in Elizabeth East, during an Easter service, singing the old negro spiritual, 'They Hung Him On A Cross'. It was billed as South Australia's first 'folk mass'.

Bob Bowes was also at Wattle Park College. He fell for Bernard's quick humour and way with words and became volunteer roadie for his band, beginning what would become a lifelong friendship.

Bob Bowes: A few of us used to get together with a guitar or two in the change room at teachers' college. The acoustics were great. Bernard was a Chuck Berry nut and he used to do really good renditions of 'Too Much Monkey Business' and 'Johnny B Goode'. Just him and his guitar. He was tall, handsome, eloquent, talented and much admired by the female students. He was always well mannered with a charming smile. I went into a Catholic church for the first time with Bernard. We'd been at a gig on Christmas Eve and he invited us all to midnight mass at the cathedral in the city. I only went to his family home on a couple of occasions, but his family was very important to him.

We used to busk with Spencer Tregloan – and others who'd join us. There was never any money so we'd sing and play guitars in coffee lounges for cappuccinos and cake. We'd busk customers at the Adelaide pie cart, passing a hat so we could eat – walk city streets on a summer's night sweetly serenading people, and on one occasion, sang for a baker cleaning his shop window at five in the morning for some freshly-baked rolls.

> There was a Saturday night before Mothers' Day, we were ambling home and passed the Botanic Gardens. Bernard suggested we raid their rose garden to get flowers for our mothers. I lowered him over the stone wall until he said he was standing on something so I let go. He instantly disappeared amidst the sound of cracking tree limbs and a lot of profanity. I ran along the footpath and found a section where I could climb over and found him moaning in the dark at the base of a tree. But we got our mothers some beautiful roses that night – and they cost us nothing!

One Friday night Bernard and Bob were in the city, checking things out. Big Daddy's Disco had the house-full sign up and a crowd waiting to get in. The boys hung around chatting to friends and eyeing the girls. Feeling restless, Bernard wandered off to the 20 Plus Club where he decided to invest one of his precious dollars and check out the female action. Casting his eye over the dancing masses, his height giving him a bird's-eye view, he spotted two beautiful, pale-skinned girls shyly taking it all in. He watched for a while, entranced. After making sure there were no boyfriends, he pushed his way over, and summoning every atom of charm in his six-foot-four frame leaned over and asked one of them to dance.

Her name was Dzintra Karklins – he drove her home later and a relationship sprang from there.

He invited her to his twenty-first at the Irish Hall in Elizabeth, proudly introducing her to his family and friends. That night she saw him play Chuck Berry rockers with his band – getting the crowd dancing and cheering.

The party also served as a send-off for Bernard and his friend from teachers' college, Con Brauer – they'd been called up for National Service with the Army. A couple of days later the two mates were on their way to basic training at Puckapunyal in Central Victoria.

The Vietnam War was in full swing and later that year Infantryman Bernard Neeson was three weeks away from embarking with his unit to the battle zone when he was told the Army was looking for recruits with teaching qualifications to go to New Guinea to train the Pacific Island Regiment.

The prerequisite was that applicants had to have infantry training and teacher qualifications, which was a rare combination and qualifications tailor-made for Private Bernard Neeson. He applied and, to his great delight, he was posted to Papua-New Guinea, where he remained as a 'chalkie' for the rest of his time in the Army.

He'd been resentful at having to join the Army, especially with the expectation of going to a war with the Vietnamese, but as it turned out, he had an enjoyable time during his stay in New Guinea. An unexpected bonus was that he and the other teachers were promoted to the rank of sergeant.

Tall, athletic and supremely fit after his months of basic training, he entered the national athletics competition and became New Guinea's high-jump champion, going over the bar at six feet four inches, his own height.

There was plenty of time off and Bernard and some of the other teachers regularly drove into the highlands and trekked about, meeting up with villagers along the way. He also began writing – short stories and dabbling with film scripts. When he was de-mobbed he decided to take up a study grant the Army was offering and enroll in a film-making course at Flinders University.

Settling into civilian life again, Bernard discovered that Leigh Hobba, a mate from his teachers' college days, had joined a jug band and was sharing a house with a rock-band manager called John Woodruff, who smoked cigars and drove a meat truck part-time. Leigh mentioned that he was moving out of Woodruff's share house and moving in with a member of his jug band. Bernard, temporarily back at his parents, wasted no time in securing Leigh's old room.

The Adelaide social scene Bernard had missed out on for the past two years was crackling and he leapt right back in, jamming with old mates again and joining a band to play at a twenty-first on 5 February 1971. The talk amongst the amateur musicians passing joints in the garden was mainly about the Myponga Festival held the previous weekend. Black Sabbath had headlined and blown the place apart. They were also raving about a band called Daddy Cool. Leigh Hobba had played with his new group, the Moonshine Jug and String Band.

They had a regular Thursday gig at the Sussex and were packing it out – the band was happening.

Bernard Neeson, fresh from the Army, tall, fit, short back and sides and about to start his first year doing Drama at Flinders Uni with the elegant Dzintra Karklins at his side, nodded enthusiastically and *yeah yeah*'d and eased into the bubbling band scene with consummate ease.

CHAPTER FOUR
JOHN WOODRUFF

Not long after Doc joined Moonshine, the guys decided to hit the Sussex for a pay rise. They'd already had one, but the publican was still getting the better end of the deal. But that night he told them that was it, he was finishing them up. Stunned, they asked why. 'Too many glasses getting smashed, the crowd's getting way out of control. All the best and thanks, but no thanks.' Soon after the Sussex sacking John Brewster got in his car and drove out Main North East Road, stopping at every pub on the way, seeking a new residency for the band. He was turned away from them all until he arrived at the Modbury Hotel, way out of town, where the manager, John Ryan, offered a Tuesday night residency.

> John: Tuesday night? You've got to be kidding, who's going to come on a Tuesday?! But we took the gig and, soon after we did our first gig, we were selling it out, week after week, around 400 punters. Unbeknownst to me there was a nurses' residence across the road so the young nurses would show up, hence young guys. The fans were so fanatical that they called themselves 'The Transcendental Jug Band'. We played there right up to the last gig for Moonshine. What a blast!

John had belonged to the Adelaide Rowers Club since schooldays, and it had a good social scene. With his job in accountancy, he'd recently been elected honorary treasurer. The club had a spacious bar and Thursday nights were quiet. In double quick time he'd done a deal. The band would put a charge on the door and keep the money, and the club would have a big bar take. Win/win.

The next Thursday Graham Harboard spread the word at the Sussex about what had happened – and that the band would be at the Rowers from now on. Many fans were so incensed they smashed every glass they could get their hands on and then left, never to return.

> **John:** In no time we had a couple of hundred showing up. For a bunch of students we were making good money. The audience were fantastic, it was like the Sussex – berserk. One night someone jumped up and down so hard, his leg went through the floor; you could see the boats stored below. We started getting booked onto outdoor concerts – the radio stations ran them at schools and sports grounds. We did one at the racetrack.
>
> A big highlight was hooking up with Mic Conway from the Captain Matchbox Whoopee Band. They invited Moonshine to Melbourne to play the Much More Ballroom in the First National Jug Orchestra which they organised. It was on April Fool's Day which also happened to be Easter Saturday. We squeezed into a Kombi and drove to Melbourne and stayed at Mic's place. The gig was packed to the rafters. Onstage was a jug orchestra with a massed kazoo section, banjos, mandolins, fiddles, harmonicas, tea-chest basses, washboards, dobros, and an instrument called a 'Throne-A-Phone'. And you never saw so much marijuana smoking in your whole life! That was the first time we played interstate. And it was with Captain Matchbox, who of course were just the greatest jug band! But we held our own. We weren't as good as them, but we were pretty good.

Back in Adelaide, Eddie Young from the Central Booking Agency (better known as CBA) began booking the group into pubs where rock bands got up. Doc had wanted to do some Chuck Berry songs when he joined. They were wrong for the jug band, but John sympathised with him. So now, to win over the rock audiences, they started rehearsing some Chuck and some Bo Diddley numbers. They did the Big Boppa's 'Chantilly Lace' too, which Doc sang well, and of course

Pete Thorpe's burning glove during 'Mighty Man' always sent the crowd nuts. They began to pick up a rock following and Doc started bringing his housemate John Woodruff along.

Woodruff shared a hippie-style house with Doc and a couple of others in suburban Glenunga. Tall and bearded with one droopy eye that made him appear half asleep, he was the son of a wealthy doctor. He'd dropped out of Electrical Engineering at uni to pursue a career as a rock 'n' roll entrepreneur. In Adelaide, that meant getting into any aspect of the business you could find an opening in.

He'd started with a hard-rock band led by Rod Boucher called Buffalo Drive. When they scored a local hit and became a headline act, Woodruff got involved with the people running the CBA booking agency. He set up the Sphere Organisation, working from their office at Lefevre Terrace, North Adelaide. The place was a hive of activity: bundles of posters stacked in corridors, phones ringing, lean young roadies collecting worksheets while their trucks double-parked out the front.

Sphere and CBA did deals with Sydney and Melbourne agencies; bringing their bands into Adelaide for a week at a time. A reciprocal arrangement was made to book CBA's Adelaide acts into interstate gigs. Woodruff was spreading his wings.

> **Rick Brewster:** Doc and Woody's Glenunga house became the place the band went back to after gigs to smoke dope, listen to music and enjoy some crazy times together. We'd sit in a circle on the floor in a trance, amazed at how the milk bottles and other assorted items seemed to have a life of their own. Woody told us how his father had left a $100,000 cheque account in his desk drawer for his wife to find after his death so she had immediate access to funds. He eventually approached us to represent the band and we agreed to that, and from then on the work increased and all dealings with the CBA were handled through him.

Rod Boucher knew Woodruff in earlier days when Woody had dropped out of uni and was trying to break into the music business. Management commissions from an up-and-coming band weren't always enough to cover the bills and he took other work:

Rod Boucher: One time Woodruff got a job labouring on a mining site and a huge tractor had to be moved. He offered to move it knowing nothing about the monster. He climbed in, pulled levers, pushed pedals – and moved it.

Another time he became a television repair man but knew nothing about TV electronics. When called out to a house he'd adjust the horizontal and vertical hold, tune the stations and set the contrast and brightness. If that didn't work, he'd say it had to go back to the factory. If he didn't know something, he'd just have a go, always looking for another way around the problem. He did that with all obstacles throughout his time with Buffalo Drive.

We found it hard later when he created Sphere and managed others – maybe we were jealous? I had so much respect for our wonderful manager who went bare feet and barefaced into *any* situation and made the best of it. The true entrepreneur.

And Woodruff did literally go 'bare foot' – he almost never wore shoes. Woody told John Brewster that he thought it made him stand out at meetings and be remembered as 'that bare foot guy'. This while wearing a suit and tie and smoking a cigar.

John Brewster: By the time Woody got involved we'd begun writing songs. I had this one called 'Keep You On The Move'. It was the first song I'd written: it goes, 'You gotta get up early each morning, catch the bus in your black suit, I just lay round and watch the day dawning, I got nothing to lose – I don't work, you think that I'm crazy, I got better things to do, I see your life, I think it's crazy . . .' It's a silly, banal, young man's lyric.

Woody had set up an independent record label operating under the Sphere banner. When he saw the audience reaction to John's song he booked the band into Derek Jolley's Decca studio and recorded it, along with three other songs, for an EP. On receiving the pressings, he presented a copy to 5KA. To everyone's amazement, they put 'Keep You On The Move' to air, listeners requested they play it again, and it took off.

With the airplay emanating from 5KA, the jug band's following jumped and Woodruff began booking them into mainstream rock venues. New and louder instruments started creeping in. Rick acquired a bass drum and cymbals. An electric bass guitar replaced Pete Thorpe's tub bass. Doc bought an electric guitar and an amplifier. The old-time jug songs started getting rockier, as were the new songs being added to the repertoire. Then Peter Dawkins from EMI Records in Sydney turned up for a few gigs. Dawkins had produced a hit that was riding the charts – Ross Ryan's 'I Am Pegasus' – but it was the next Captain Matchbox Whoopee Band he was looking for. Captain Matchbox were now selling truckloads of albums and Dawkins, spotting the independently released Moonshine jug-band EP in the Adelaide charts, wanted to know who these guys were. He offered them a contract to record a jug-band album, but Dawkins had arrived too late. The Moonshine guys had other plans and, to Dawkins' disappointment, they declined his offer.

Not only was the band moving on from its jug band days, so were the players. Rick had recently married Bitsy, his teenage sweetheart, and Doc and Dzintra were engaged and making wedding plans. John had met Robyn at uni and they too would be married before long. Rick and Doc had completed uni and were about to attend their graduation ceremonies.

> **Rick:** I always intended to finish Ag Science whatever happened. I was majoring in horticulture and entomology. Entomology is insects and that was my main passion at uni. Collecting and classifying insects. There was this outdoor hippie festival somewhere . . . actually a strange mixture of hippies and bikies . . . I saw this beautiful butterfly go across the stage. I couldn't resist. I always carried a collecting net, killing jars, the whole kit, had it right beside me. I whisked the thimbles off from playing the washboard and leapt from stage after this butterfly. I was wearing my baggy Bombay bloomers with a fez on my head – a wonder the bikies didn't kill me!

On the morning of Rick's graduation ceremony John picked him up in his Wolseley and drove him to the uni. Everything was changing. Peter Thorpe was going overseas, Spencer was starting a teaching career. Doc had graduated with honours in Film and Drama but hadn't made up his mind about what he'd do. Driving home in John's car, Rick had his degree in his hand and his graduation mortar-board on his head.

Rick: We were talking about the future. Doc had completed his degree the year before and then been invited to do an honours degree in Film and Drama, which he'd now completed. But all we could talk about was forming an electric band out of the jug band. We'd worked in rock venues and that had got us to put rock songs into the repertoire and to listen to electric bands. The big Australian ones were Skyhooks and Sherbet. Skyhooks we sorta got, but Sherbet we just couldn't, and John said, 'If we put a rock band together, we could knock Sherbet off in a year!' So we decided to go electric and start working towards establishing ourselves in Sydney and Melbourne.

After dropping Rick off, John rang Doc and invited him round to his place for a 'serious talk'. They started talking at six in the evening and wrapped up the conversation early the next morning.

John: We sat up all night talking about how we could do this and that. But really, there is no 'how' to do it, you just do it. And Doc said, 'Yeah I'm in,' and he'd just got his honours degree in drama and I was doing the same course and had another year to go. But I decided the band was more important and dropped out. So I'm an unqualified person, and probably deservedly so.

CHAPTER FIVE
NEW BEGINNINGS

The Modbury Hotel on an autumn night, 1974: sweat-drenched audience manically dance down the front while further back they jostle and drink and smoke. Ceiling fans swirl the blue haze that hovers throughout the room. Tables against the walls bend under the weight of people jumping about, beer slopping onto those below – everyone's roaring along with the musicians. Another wild night with the Moonshine Jug and String Band.

There's a buzz going round that something special is going to happen.

Doc, the tall Irish one, announces that after the next number there'll be a break and then they'll be back with something completely different – a surprise. The washboard player counts in 'One, two, three, four!' and they begin the last song of the set.

It comes to an end, spotlights dim and the musicians head for the dressing room. Sound operator Pud turns up the taped music, grabs a roll of gaffa and pushes through to the stage where he tapes a sheet of black plastic across the front. Behind it, he feverishly sets up for the 'surprise'.

Charlie King: I joined the Keystone Angels when they started. I was introduced by Brian Thorpe who was mates with the Moonshine Jug Band. JB asked him if he knew any drummers as they were going to form a rock band. Brian and I met in Vietnam in the Army. We'd formed a friendship playing music together on leave in Vung Tau. He knew I was handy on the drums.

I had a jam with Doc and the Brewsters, got the gig and we went straight into rehearsals. I was still in the Army, based at Woodside Barracks. I signed up when I was sixteen and now I was twenty. I was ready for something different. My name was Pete Christopoulos, but I changed it to Charlie King after I joined the band. The Charlie 'cos that was my nickname in the Army and the King came out of the phone book. Charlie King – I liked it!

It was agreed that we'd unveil the band at a Moonshine gig, and that would be it, Moonshine would be no more, and it would be the start of the Keystone Angels. So after the jug band did a couple of brackets, we changed into our rock outfits and came onstage as . . . LADIES AND GENTLEMEN . . . THE KEYSTONE ANGELS!

You could have heard a pin drop! The die-hard jug fans couldn't believe what they were seeing! Did not go down well! John Woodruff realised that the Modbury wasn't going to work for the new band – too far out of town for the KA target audience. Soon after we started, he booked us into the Finsbury for a Thursday-night residency. Closer to the young high flyers who worked in the CBD. We started as a fifties and sixties cover band. Chuck Berry, Everly Brothers, Big Boppa. My claim to fame was singing Little Richard's 'Jenny, Jenny' while still playing my kit.

After that first night, rehearsals went full steam ahead at John's Goodwood house as the Keystone Angels.

Doc: We were shithouse when we started as a rock band! I'd been on guitar in the jug band so that's where I stayed.

John: I went onto bass guitar. Rick had been playing washboard so it seemed like he'd be a natural to play drums – but he'd come to Doc and me and said he'd prefer to be a part of the melody side and play lead guitar.

Rick threw himself in the deep end and spent the first couple of years just trying to keep his head above the surface. There was no time for lessons, it was all self-taught. He'd listen to records: Chuck Berry, Angus Young, Clapton. When the band wrote original songs he had no battery of licks to draw from, and improvising was completely foreign and terrifying to him. When he was younger learning to play a Beethoven sonata he'd play the notes exactly as Beethoven wrote them. The only room for improvisation was how he interpreted the expression of those notes. Rick saw no difference with rock 'n' roll. A solo was like a vocal melody, intrinsic to the song, and the best ones could be sung. As his father had instructed him countless times, 'Make the melody sing.' So initially he wrote solos in his head and worked out how to play them. If it was too difficult, he'd change the melody.

Laurie Lever: I was an old Saints friend of Rick's. I won a Saints piano competition in which Rick came third. One day Rick and Doc showed up and said they were forming a rock band and were looking for a keyboard player.

I went to a rehearsal and got told I was in the band if I wanted to be – I mentioned that I was bent on going to Mexico, but John insisted they were going to be big as the Beatles and I'd get my chance to tour over there.

I got stoned with Rick and Doc that evening, all squeezed into the back of John's Wolseley. Doc was such an Irish lad. He had such charm with that lovely gentle manner – listening, leaning forward, attentive. And he spoke with a honeyed voice that ran out of him like smoky Irish whiskey.

Not long after the KA started off, they were about to play a gig when two Army men came in with white armbands – military police.

John Brewster: They walked over to the stage and I said, 'Can I help you guys?' They said, 'We've come here about your drummer.' I said, 'Oh, what's up?' They said, 'We've come to arrest him – he's illegally absent from the Australian Army!' AHH! I said, 'Um . . . well, what are you drinking? Do you mind waiting till the show is over?' They said, 'Sure, that's fine.'

So, they waited till the show was over – then they clapped on the handcuffs and took him off. I had to drive his car home. Doc had been in the Army, so he and I ended up going to see a Colonel Horne and had a series of meetings with him. The last one was a classic, because Colonel

> Horne was sitting at this desk, and he was like a caricature of a colonel: handlebar moustache, large girth and quite a jovial sort of fellow. I'll never forget it because right behind him, through the window, there was Charlie in military prison garb with a broom sweeping the yard. And Colonel Horne said to Doc and me, 'This Private Christopoulos – what do you want him for, he's a ratbag,' and I said, 'Well, if he's a ratbag, why do you want him?' And he laughed, his whole body shook and he said, 'Oh, that's terrific, that's so funny – you make a good point.' Anyhow, they let him go. He got discharged, joined the band and was freed up.

One of the early gigs the new band scored was supporting Canadian comedians Cheech and Chong, whose routines were based on the hippie counterculture – the pot-smoking, free-love movement. The jug band had originally been booked, but Doc, Rick and John refused to perform as Moonshine and stuck to their guns. Woodruff assured the promoter that Moonshine had morphed into a rock band that would slay the Cheech and Chong audience and he'd accepted that.

The night of the concert came round and the Keystone Angels walked onto the Thebarton Theatre stage to an audience of dope-toking hippies and uni students. A haze of marijuana smoke hung in the air and two thousand switched-on eyes checked them out. As they rocked on with 'Little Queenie', Doc threw Minties into the crowd – something he'd taken to doing to the Finsbury audience as a way of breaking down the 'us' and 'them'. But the stoned hippies threw them back and hissed and jeered. The band kept going with Doc giving it his all, but the hippies weren't having any of this fifties rock 'n' roll and just hissed louder. As the set mercifully came near to the end, Doc tinkled his little bell like some demented telephonist, and went into his Big Boppa show-stopper, *'Hello, babe . . .'* After it was over they stumbled off to cat-calls and boos. Cheech stood stage-side as they filed past and gave them a shrug and a rueful smile.

Back at the Finsbury the move Woody had arranged was working out well. The core of the jug band fan-base had loyally followed and pretty soon a new audience developed from the surrounding suburbs and the band's spirits rose, along with their musicianship – and the door takings.

Pud had his eye on one of the few groupie girls who came to see them every week. He was furious when he found Charlie had got off with her and that night the band had to load their own gear out. A few weeks later they played a pub in the outer suburbs. Word went round that Charlie's brother-in-law was there to 'get' him for cheating on his sister. Halfway through a set a guy brandishing a bayonet started climbing onto the stage. Laurie and John jumped forward and managed to kick him back as the band play on.

> **Laurie:** Later that night we heard that Charlie had confronted his brother-in-law in the car park and gave him a 'shot at the title', as he put it. He slapped him around and got the bayonet off him. Charlie had fought in Vietnam – he knew how to look after himself.

Woodruff's next move was to book them onto a big concert that Sphere was promoting with Sydney-based chart-toppers Hush at the Apollo Theatre. The pressure was on to really shine for this one.

> **Laurie:** We practised at John's house every day. I contributed some half-formed songs but got the feeling there wasn't room for more than what John, Rick and Doc were turning out. There was great camaraderie in the group, but John and Rick were a tight unit, in the end controlling things. John set up the equipment, Rick tuned the guitars.

The gig with Hush would prove to be significant for the band, and not just because of Woodruff's outlandish fashion ideas.

> **Laurie:** Woody decided that we needed an identifiable outfit for the Hush gig, rather than the motley leather, jeans and cords we otherwise turned up in. Measurements were taken and he later arrived with satin flared pants and shirts, each in a different colour for the five of us. Dreadful really, but I got mulberry/dark red at least. It was quite an experience – we went over really well and got an encore which I sang: Canned Heat's 'On The Road Again'.

The problem was I had no foldback. I could feel my mouth move but couldn't hear anything coming out. It didn't seem to bother the audience but the next day John had me sit and listen to a recording of the gig. I felt that John, who'd set up the mics and foldback, was criticising me unfairly, almost suggesting I couldn't sing in tune. My singing voice had been an important part of my sense of self from an early age. Like Rick I'd been a choir boy, I'd sung in the cathedral and won a prize – chocolates! – singing Dylan's 'Blowin' In The Wind'. I told John I was leaving the band.

After Laurie left, the band exchanged the white Fender bass that John played for a beautiful blue-and-white Rickenbacker that Doc then took over, while John became rhythm guitarist. The band was now a four piece, with Rick on keys for a couple of songs, but mainly playing lead on a Les Paul Gold Top.

Doc, Rick and John carried the entertainment skills they'd honed with the jug band over to the rock group. Charlie had never played in a regular band, but stripped to the waist behind the Ringo-style pearly grey Gretsch, he totally threw himself into every show.

Charlie: The feel of the band was fantastic and we relayed that to the audience – always made them feel part of the show. Every gig was full-on rock 'n' roll – adrenalin pumped . . . sweat soaked. Raunch. Guts. Balls. Excitement. Sweat-drenched bodies, smoke, beer-soaked. The promise of after-gig depravity in the air. No-bra groupies stirring us up!

CHAPTER SIX
SPREADING THEIR WINGS

The band started getting booked onto high-school lunchtime concerts, 'Rockin' At Your School', promoted by radio 5KA and sponsored by the Savings Bank of South Australia. At nights they continued to rock the pubs.

Doc, John and Rick worked on their songwriting skills: learning the craft of hooks, riffs, middle eights, intros and outros. They studied the lyrical styles of Dylan, the Stones, Beatles, Kinks, and whatever else struck their fancy. Sometimes songs would evolve from an unlikely source.

Woodruff was not only the band's manager, but one of the crazies Doc and his new wife, Dzintra, shared a house with. One night while Woody and Doc were enjoying a bottle of bourbon, Woody told him about a girlfriend he'd had during his university days. He'd arranged a romantic weekend in a country hideaway and each arrived separately, she on her motorcycle, he in his car. On Monday she'd ridden back to the city, but John stayed on for a couple of days to study. On a bend she lost control of her bike, smashed into a concrete and steel telegraph pole and died instantly.

Woodruff, still deeply affected, wondered if there was a life hereafter – if they'd ever meet again. The gentle-natured Doc, moved by Woody's story, was left wondering too. A few days later he showed up at Rick and Bitsy's place with his notebook and a tune in his head. John made minor adjustments and they worked up some harmonies. After an afternoon of rehearsals, a new song entered their repertoire: 'Am I Ever Gonna See Your Face Again'.

The Finsbury was in a rough area but it didn't take long to build an audience that came to see them every Thursday. Because they played so many fifties songs the Hindley Street Rockers started showing up – they had the black ripple sole desert boots and Brylcreem-slicked hair. There were also mods and sharpie gangs in the Finsbury area and they hated each other. Despite the mods riding motor scooters, they were heavy people – they wore bovver boots and carried walking canes.

> **John Brewster:** One night the sharpies and the mods and the Harley Street Rockers were there at the same time, plus a crowd of the Moonshine hippies. And the whole place just erupted into this almighty brawl, it was terrifying. And Doc just went, 'RIGHT, WE'RE STOPPING UNLESS YOU PEOPLE STOP FIGHTING!' And of course no one gave a fuck about what he said!
>
> It was just like this clash of cultures. These tribes in the same venue looking at this band and they just went to each other, 'Ah, fuck you!', and got into it. Some poor bastard was thrown through a plate glass door and lost an ear. There were seven ambulances, ten police cars. We grabbed our instruments and shot up the stairs – we had this sort of boardroom up there as our dressing room and that was it. We didn't go back and the place closed up for the night.

Another time Doc managed to convince some girls to have a wet t-shirt competition.

> **Charlie:** One got caught up in the excitement and peeled off her top and it ended up being a biggest tits competition! Holy shit! The newspapers found out and next day it was splashed across one of the tabloids. KEYSTONE ANGELS' DISGUSTING ANTICS!

With the Keystone Angels' new-found notoriety, they became the target of a surprise drug-squad raid.

Charlie: Doc and Woody and a few others shared this large place and after gigs we'd all go back to unwind and have a few drinks and a smoke and a laugh. On the hallway wall was a big picture of a pig wearing a policeman's hat. One night we'd just got in and suddenly got raided by the drug squad. No one had lit up yet and somehow the ones holding managed to throw it out the window or something. They went through the place like a dose of salts, but didn't find anything. On the way out the head cop stopped and had a close look at the picture of the pig wearing the policeman's hat. Then he turned around to us, 'Nope, don't know him.' *We all cracked up, including the cops.*

With Woodruff working out of Sphere, he was able to do deals with the Melbourne and Sydney agencies and arrange swaps with them – Sphere would take an interstate band for a week, and they'd book his Keystone Angels into Melbourne or Sydney for a week.

In early September '74, the Spirit agency in Melbourne organised a Keystone Angels tour. The band drove over in the EH Holden station wagon followed by Charlie and John in a Transit van with their equipment. Setting up their own gear and operating the small sound desk from side of stage, they played the Hard Rock Café, the Distillery nightclub and the Station Hotel in Prahran, where they were called back for more. There was also a lunchtime gig at La Trobe University where they had the students dancing in the courtyard.

After their final Melbourne gig, the band's EH headed into the night and onto the Hume Highway to Sydney, closely followed by the van with Charlie at the wheel. John Brewster was at his side, with the PA jammed in so tight behind that their heads rested on the speaker cabinets. If they'd had to brake hard, they would have been decapitated. For twelve hours they ground up the old winding highway as streams of semi-trailers thundered past in both directions.

It was late afternoon when they pulled up at their destination: Wallaringa Mansions at Neutral Bay on Sydney's North Shore. The harbourside suburb had just the right-sounding tone for the Adelaide private-school gentlemen. But on arrival they discovered a crumbling old boarding house for the down and out. The carpets stank of vomit and cat piss, armies of roaches lived in every corner and there was no power in the rooms. On the ground floor lurked a bathroom and a kitchen with one small window and a flyscreen so black with grease they couldn't see out. They slowly looked round and shrugged at each other. 'It's more like Cockroach Mansion,' Doc quipped, and the name stuck.

The first gig was a three-night stand at the seedy Chequers nightclub, a basement rock 'n' roll venue near Central Station. Kids from the suburbs would get there via train to Central and then walk up Pitt Street. There was no cover charge on weeknights, a couple of dollars on weekends, and doors stayed open to 3 am. Back in the sixties it had been a flash nightclub – Frank Sinatra, Sammy Davis Jnr, Shirley Bassey and a string of international stars had played there – but now it was worn out and stank of old beer and cheap food.

> **Charlie:** It was raining the first night, hardly anyone there, but we played hard and won them over. It got to closing and it's raining cats, dogs, cows and chickens. Then we noticed from the load-out door that the EH had a flat tyre. We decided to let the rain ease before we changed it, but after half an hour it was worse. We're all buggered after driving up from Melbourne and doing the gig and looking forward to some sleep. So Rick offers to brave the elements and change the tyre. He's out there with the jack under the car and he's drowning, but he changes the tyre over. He undoes the jack and the car comes back down and we all cheer – and then we see the car is still down at one corner. He's changed the wrong tyre!

On Friday night they played a teenage dance in the 'burbs with a couple of other bands. Saturday was an RSL club. The greyhound races were being screened above their heads, poker machines clanged and the bistro kept calling out numbers to let customers know their dinner was ready.

On Monday there was a lunchtime gig at a uni and then they were back at Chequers for two more nights, doing five sets from 9 pm to 2 am for 120 bucks. Thursday they drove up to Newcastle for a couple of nights at the Savoy Club and a gig at the local uni, before driving back, swinging onto the Great Western Highway on the outskirts of

Sydney, over the Blue Mountains, onto the Sturt Highway and across the shimmering Hay Plain. Eager to complete the 1600-kilometre journey home, the EH with Rick and Doc was soon swallowed up in the haze ahead. East of Balranald, with dusk falling, roos on the hop, John snoring beside him in the Transit, Charlie's survival instincts kicked in. He swung onto a scrubby track and parked in a clearing. It was Army bush training. While John got out and stretched and blinked, Charlie foraged for sticks, got a fire going, boiled a billy and they had a fresh cup of tea and a sleep.

After agency commissions the money they'd earned had barely covered petrol, their accommodation bills and pocket money for burgers and beer. But back at the Finsbury Hotel, that didn't stop them telling exaggerated tales of triumphs and encores on their first eastern states tour.

At the end of November they did another run into Sydney, starting with three nights on the trot in Chequers, this time for $150 a night. The manager, Mr Casey, liked them – they were moving up! There were gigs at pubs, another teenage dance, and then the swaying EH followed the rust-bucket Transit down the Hume to Melbourne and into that city's thriving pub scene, beginning with another stint at the Distillery supporting the great Brook Benton direct from the USA.

> **Rick:** The audience gave us an encore which was a surprise. Brook Benton was watching from side-stage and said he wanted me to be his lead guitar player. I felt a flutter of excitement at his flattery, but the feeling was quickly replaced by acute embarrassment with the certainty that he was having me on – in fact, having a good laugh at my expense!

For a second time the Keystone Angels demonstrated their entertainment prowess in front of Melbourne punters, convincing their agency to pitch them to Odessa Promotions, organisers of the Sunbury Festival. Preparations for the next one, to be held over the Australia Day weekend in January '75, were well underway.

Exhausted, they arrived back in Adelaide just before Christmas to get news from Woodruff that they'd been offered a spot at Sunbury. Deep Purple were headlining the festival at a reported $60,000, the highest fee in Australian history. A who's who of local acts had been announced; however, KA, at the bottom of the pecking order, were offered $200 for a one-hour set to close the final afternoon. With previous attendances of over 40,000, this was the biggest and most prestigious event on the Australian rock calendar and the Adelaide boys gladly accepted the gig.

CHAPTER SEVEN
GETTING OUT THERE

The Keystone Angels arrived at the Sunbury Festival the day before their spot. It was raining heavily and the four of them were packed into the EH wagon with their stage gear, windows up, passing joints and sliding all over the muddy road into the property.

> John Brewster: We were free to wander off and do our own thing. Whilst waiting to see Deep Purple, stoned in my Cuban-heeled boots, this guy I'm standing next to passes a joint. I take a long drag and pass it on to the guy to my right. He says, 'No thanks, I'm a police officer,' whereby I freak thinking I'm about to be arrested, at a time when possession of a joint could mean jail. He said, 'But my girlfriend does,' and passed it to her.
>
> I saw Billy Thorpe with Lobby Loyde in the band. They were so fucking loud they sent everyone scrambling up the hill to get away from the pain. The most entertaining part of the whole festival was the entrance of Jim Keays. He had a concept album called *The Boy From The Stars* and he'd gone to great lengths to have a spaceship rigged up on a pulley system with him in it lowered to the stage, while his band played the first track off the album. His spaceship slowly descends and then the pulleys jam and his spaceship is stuck about six feet from Earth. The thing is violently jigging up and down as the band plays on, then it crashes to the stage and rolls along, still with alien Jim inside . . . funnier than Spinal Tap!

While everyone complained about the torrential rain, the Adelaide boys had the time of their lives hanging out backstage. They passed joints with celebrated musicians, rubbed shoulders with the stars and swapped jokes with the roadies. The rock scene on that level was all new to them and like the rain and the mud underfoot, they just soaked it all up.

By Sunday afternoon the black clouds were lifting and the rain, which had fallen all weekend and dampened the crowd's enthusiasm, began clearing. Sunlight shafted through from the western sky as the Keystone Angels were introduced. After swanning about backstage for so long, their time had come. They leapt from the wings full of pent-up energy and went hell for leather.

According to a review in *The Age* the following week, the two 'hit' acts of Sunbury were the band that was arguably the hottest in the land, Skyhooks – and Adelaide's unsigned, unknown Keystone Angels.

On their return to Adelaide, Woodruff announced he'd pulled a big one. Ike and Tina Turner were coming to Adelaide and the Sphere Organisation were organising the concert. The Keystone Angels would be their support for the Apollo on Saturday 1 March.

Things were hotting up for the KA on the home front. Sphere published a press release about the Sunbury encores. How were the Adelaide punters to know that the band only played to the last couple of thousand stayers? They'd played Sunbury *and* got encores. Reviews said they and Skyhooks were the two best bands. They'd toured Sydney and Melbourne. They were supporting Ike and Tina Turner!

Woodruff started pushing up the fees – fifty bucks extra here, a hundred extra there. They were becoming a headline act, despite their dress code that included John in red satin flared pants with a red polka-dot shirt. Rick wore a white top hat with a large blue butterfly pinned to the front and a collarless shirt with a huge medallion hanging from his neck. Not to mention his flared jeans hemmed with red hearts and a second butterfly adorning his belt buckle – a nod to his love of entomology. Doc, at least, sported a leather jacket, while Charlie favoured leather armbands buckled around each bicep and sleeveless muscle-shirts. When it got wild and sticky, he stripped to the waist and showered sweat in all directions.

After seeing Billy Thorpe and Deep Purple at Sunbury, it was becoming clear to them that it was all about the guitars and that to be a rock band they would need to step up the stage volume. British made Marshalls (rock bands' amps of choice) were expensive and out of the question, but the locally built Wasp amps looked and sounded (almost) the part, so they invested in a couple. The transformation was substantial. They were a rock band!

It was around this time that Rick bought an old sewing machine and started making speaker-box covers for their new Wasps, using an old green tarp and army surplus blankets. In true hippie fashion he then progressed to making satin stage cloths and sewing colourful bands around the bottom of his flares.

> **Rick:** The road crew truly hated me through that period. I insisted on having the sewing machine travel in the truck and dropped off at my motel room . . . but that was nothing compared to the trail bike which came soon after. Whenever we lobbed into Melbourne or Sydney, I had instant cheap transport!

Back in Moonshine's Modbury days, John had operated the PA from the stage, but later on Pud had become the Moonshine Man of Sound and he relished the position. Holding down a day job, the extra cash was an added bonus. Pud was, as his name implied, rotund and short of stature. He had long ginger hair and a beard – and an attitude that was perfect one minute, but cooked the next.

His girlfriend, Lyn, had been president of the Moonshine fan club, which involved booking a coach and organising occasional picnics with fans and band members, along with mailing publicity photos and notes to club members. When Moonshine became a rock band, Lyn successfully repositioned the fan club, but Pud struggled to deal with the change. He was not impressed with the larger mixing desks and stage equipment – and, for him, travelling interstate was never on the agenda.

Just before the Ike and Tina show, Pud and the band parted company, but remained on good terms.

Brian Thorpe: In early '75 I was discharged from the Army and the band asked if I'd like to work for them. As I was cashed up after six years' service, I was able to buy a five-ton truck, an eighteen-channel mixing desk and some sound gear. The gear they had from their jug band days wasn't cutting it with the bigger crowds and bigger venues they were moving into. The band invested in some excellent speakers and we were away as a serious professional outfit. I did a deal with them for a rate that covered me and the equipment hire.

The band worked incredibly hard. Rehearsing, doing daytime gigs at high schools, the Finsbury on Thursday nights, weekends at pubs and other venues round town and the state. My roadie assistant was Charlie. We'd formed a close bond during our service in Vietnam. He would help set up, then play with the energy of a marathon runner, have a break, then help pack up and load out. No wonder he was so fit. The first big show I did with the band was supporting Ike and Tina at the Apollo.

Charlie worked as a roadie to make some extra cash. He had a wife and two young kids: Duane and Eddy. But working-class Charlie also preferred hanging out with his mate Brian rather than with the 'silver spoon uni-educated prima-donnas' as he sometimes disparagingly referred to his band-mates – although that never included his manager.

Charlie: Woody was a very astute manager. He always treated me and Brian with respect and always had the welfare of the group as his priority. Mind you, he was getting his cut – he wasn't doing it for free! Because of that droopy eye, a lot of people underestimated him. To their peril!

We did a great gig at this country hotel one weekend and stayed in the rooms upstairs. On Sunday morning Woody informs us the manager had only paid half the fee, making excuses that we weren't as popular as he'd been led to believe. Woody tells us he's going back to see this prick and asked me and Brian to come with him and look tough. So, we put on our tightest black t-shirts, go out to the truck, load the speakers and get the veins standing and get a bit sweaty. Then we follow Woody into the hotel where we confront the manager.

Woody stood in front of him, bare foot as always, poking him in the chest and strongly suggesting that if he didn't pay up the boys behind him wouldn't get their wages – and then he turned and walked out. The manager couldn't get to the safe quick enough to pay us every dollar.

CHAPTER EIGHT
CHUCK BERRY

In January '75 tour promoter Tony Maroney announced he was bringing Chuck Berry to Australia in April. Sphere was contracted to set up the Adelaide concert and Woodruff went into management mode, telling Maroney how well the Keystone Angels had gone at Sunbury with their fifties repertoire and Chuck Berry songs. A week later Maroney came back offering KA the support spot *and* the backing-band gig for the whole tour.

With the Chuck Berry dates in the bag, Woodruff decided to invest in recording a single so the band could promote it during the tour. *Maybe they could pull off a hit like they'd done in Adelaide during the Moonshine era . . .*

Under their relentless workload the band's musical chops had dramatically improved and with the three songwriters spending so much time together, ideas were gelling and new songs were entering the repertoire. A one-day session was booked at Max Peppers Studio in Hindley Street and the two songs getting the best reaction were recorded. Soon after, the first Keystone Angels single, 'Keep On Dancing', backed with 'Good Day Rock 'n' Roll', was released on the Sphere label.

When Rick heard he was expected to play piano for Chuck Berry, he got in touch with Peter Head, Headband's brilliant piano player. He needed to quickly learn some R&R licks – although he had learned to play some basic stuff for a couple of KA songs. After two lessons with Peter explaining the essentials, he practised them every spare minute and by showtime he was ready.

Chuck needed four instruments in his backing band – drums, bass, piano and rhythm guitar. So it was agreed that Rick would play guitar and piano and John the bass. That left Doc performing with the KA for their support set and then standing aside during Chuck's performance. The first show was at the Hordern Pavilion in Sydney. The KA came out and soon had the audience jiggling and bobbing in their seats and wound up their performance with some good-natured applause. But it was Chuck they were there for.

> **John Brewster:** Six thousand people and we didn't do one bar of rehearsal with the man. I was the bass player, and I was only allowed to play one note per chord. I was told he didn't want runs, so that was an easy gig for me. His guitar was always out of tune, so at the last show, Rick snuck into his dressing room and tuned it. But Chuck stopped the band halfway into the first song and said, 'Hold on, man, hold everything, this guitar is outa toon,' and he tuned it back to his kinda funny tuning. But it all worked. You can't knock Chuck Berry because it all works.
>
> He was ridiculously difficult to work with – no rehearsals, no soundcheck. The first time we talked was when he came onstage for the show. He just turned to the band and said, 'Watch my left foot. When I go like that, we start. When I go like that, we stop.' Arrggh! Terrifying!

Night after night Chuck would hold up the shows and nearly cause riots while he demanded more money. The promoter had to constantly slip him more cash or he wouldn't go on. It became dangerous up at Townsville. The show was performed from the back of a semi-trailer parked out in a sports ground in front of thousands. Chuck was not impressed and neither were the punters. An outdoor gig, plenty of booze for sale and the audience got very drunk – resulting in bottles and cans being hurled.

For the Keystone Angels it was one nerve-racking experience after another. Charlie's Greek family was among the thousands at Melbourne's Festival Hall, there to see the black sheep of the clan be a star. Their presence raised Charlie's anxiety even further. Chuck, always attuned to his surroundings, picked up on Charlie's heightened state of terror and sidled over to John during a song. He whispered, 'The drummer's scared shitless, be ready for me,' and then whispered the same to Rick. Suddenly he brought his foot down and stopped the music.

> **Charlie:** He was pointing at me for a drum solo! I don't know how I did it but I did, twice! Scared the crap outa me.
>
> His dislike for agents, managers, hangers-on, was legendary. But to the musos who backed him he was a gentleman and a consummate performer who gave the crowd 150 per cent. He worked the audience brilliantly. Stop . . . start . . . duck-walk . . . solo . . . stop . . . audience singing along . . . start . . . another duck-walk . . . lead break . . . start again . . . drag out the chorus. All controlled by the band constantly watching his left foot.

For Rick, playing with Chuck was inspirational. He was the master and in total control. When he started a song, Rick would put one ear on the grand piano and play a few notes until he had the right key. C# . . . A#. The most boring part was during Chuck's highly successful but worst song 'My Ding-a-Ling'. It had been a huge hit just a few years previously, and to most of the younger ones it overshadowed his masterpieces such as 'Maybellene', 'Roll Over Beethoven' and 'Johnny B Goode'. He would drag it out for fifteen minutes while the band stayed put, not playing a note.

The tour rolled into Adelaide under leaden skies and steady rain. Memorial Drive Stadium was a tennis centre where the stage was set up in the open, facing one of the large covered stands. The Stones had played their 'Exile On Main Street' concert there a few years earlier. The crew erected tarps and the set-up went ahead while Chuck and the promoter watched the clouds come and go. A cancellation would have cost both plenty. As it was, by late afternoon it had eased to a fine drizzle and Chuck gave it the nod.

> **John Brewster:** We couldn't believe it. There were puddles gathering on the stage, despite the roadies mopping them up, and we were plugged into 240 volt electrical equipment! But Chuck loved his money and no way was he going to call a rain day and reschedule. So there you had it: first the Keystone Angels went out and tested the waters. Then the great Chuck Berry did his famous duck-walk through the puddles out by the footlights, playing his guitar over the back of his head! Insane. Us risking our lives behind him. I mean, you can get away with that sort of thing now and then . . . but how many times had he done that in his career?

After the tour was over there were rumours suggesting the promoter had sent a couple of henchmen to Berry's room and 'negotiated' the return of some of the cash he'd been blackmailed into paying. Customs received an anonymous phone call too. They were told that an American entertainer called Charles Anderson Edward Berry was boarding a plane for Los Angeles that afternoon with a briefcase of undeclared cash. Chuck avoided detention by paying his tax and fine on the spot.

As for the Keystone Angels, the tour had given their rock 'n' roll apprenticeship a further nudge and been a master-class in performance skills by one of rock's greatest practitioners. However, their single had gone nowhere despite being plugged to thousands by Doc on a nightly basis. Their debut on *Countdown*, performing 'Good Day Rock 'n' Roll', had also failed to achieve any results.

CHAPTER NINE
AC/DC AND ALBERTS

With the Chuck Berry tour completed, and with their first single as the Keystone Angels having failed to chart, they hit the road for another tour of the eastern seaboard, hoping to consolidate and build on the exposure they'd just received. There'd been some complimentary reviews of their performances, including one that had singled out John's harmonica playing as exceptional. In Melbourne, they supported the likes of Little River Band, Billy Thorpe, Ariel and Kush, then chugged up the Hume in the EH and the truck for some dates in Sydney.

Meanwhile Woodruff had sent a tape of the band's songs to Peter Dawkins at EMI, the most logical A&R manager to initially contact due to his previous interest in Moonshine. However, Dawkins had moved to CBS Records and a young bass player called Rod Coe was the new man in the EMI Artist and Repertoire seat.

Rod Coe: When the Keystone Angels were looking for a record deal I'd already heard of them through Peter Dawkins, who'd seen them in Adelaide as a jug band. So I arranged a demo session at our studios and they brought in some of their material, including 'Am I Ever Gonna See Your Face Again'. This struck me as being their strongest song, and we recorded it. At this stage they hadn't settled on the style they became famous for. I felt the song had country leanings and that's how we recorded it. Needless to say EMI didn't go for it, and they went on to Alberts, with George [Young] and Harry [Vanda].

I remember them as delightfully fresh and enthusiastic and got on well with the Brewster brothers. Doc was on bass then. He was goofy and sweet, and lacked confidence, and the original drummer was still with them. The thing that impressed me was Rick's guitar sound. He had this little Goldentone amp and he overdrove it to get a bagpipe-like tone. That distinctive riff and sound which helped make the Alberts recording of the song such a huge hit over time – it was there on the demo. I always felt their success was well deserved because of their attitude; they were positive and determined.

In October '75 Sphere arranged the South Australian leg of a national tour by a young Sydney band on the rise called AC/DC. Their advance posters announced: 'Lock Up Your Daughters'. With Woodruff's influence, the Keystone Angels scored support spots for three mid-week country dates: Monday 10 to Wednesday 12 November.

John Brewster: We arrived at the Port Pirie hotel in the early afternoon and loaded in our gear. I was still hungover from my twenty-sixth birthday party the night before. We were sitting at the bar when the AC/DC guys walked in with Pat Pickett, who was an infamous roadie of legendary status we'd heard a lot about. They were minus Phil Rudd, who'd broken his hand helping Angus out in a fight with a punter at one of their Melbourne gigs: 'getting beat up, broken boned'. Bon was telling it like it was. We hit it off immediately, a real sense of camaraderie. Angus was drinking a milkshake – he never drank alcohol – and the rest of us were chain smoking, although not Rick and Doc.

The Adelaide boys did their show that night and went over well with the capacity crowd who knew them from previous visits. Then AC/DC came on and commenced to tear the place apart. Angus did his striptease and bare-arse mooned the audience. He leaped onto tables and spun on his back, never fluffed a note on his guitar while knocking beer jugs, glasses, ashtrays to the floor. Up on Bon's shoulders, he was carried into the drunken pack with roadies feeding his guitar lead while Pat Pickett forged ahead. It was like lifesavers with the belt line, reeling it back in when they returned to the stage. The audience went berserk.

On arrival in Whyalla next day, their radio interview was classic Young brothers brashness. The DJ made the mistake of asking them what they thought of Skyhooks. Angus and Malcolm looked at him like he was a complete idiot and said, 'Fuck Skyhooks, we're here to talk about fucking AC/DC!'

Minutes after the interview was over, a dramatic newsflash went to air: Prime Minister Gough Whitlam and the ruling Labor party had just been sacked by the Governor-General. To replace them, Leader of the Opposition Malcolm Fraser and the Liberal party had been appointed to run the country.

The band exiting the building, unaware of the news, signed autographs for the fans and then drove over to the Sundowner Hotel to rest up for the gig that night.

> **John Brewster**: Their gig in Whyalla was even better than the previous one, just amazing – we went over well too. There was much debauchery after the show but that story stays on the road.

Rick was among the crush of punters in front of the stage and got caught up in a fight. Someone spat on Angus and next thing he'd leapt off the stage throwing punches. The punter's mates joined in so Bon jumped off and Pat Pickett appeared and it got ferocious. Fists, blood, ripped shirts, but the rest of the band never missed a beat until Angus and Bon clambered back up and got into it again.

They were all staying in the accommodation above the pub and after the gig Angus took his guitar up to Rick's room. The two of them plugged into Rick's practice amp and, sitting on the two single beds, they jammed on a twelve-pattern blues and talked until dawn.

It was in Whyalla that Angus and Malcolm suggested Alberts as the record company for the Keystone Angels. Doc, Charlie and the Brewsters were stunned as the Youngs said they'd tell George and Harry about them when they got back.

Next day Rick travelled from Whyalla to Port Augusta in their tour coach, an old Pioneer interstater. The back half contained their equipment while the front half retained the original leather seats.

Rick: I sat next to Angus and we spent the trip talking about various guitarists. I mentioned Phil Manning, said what a good player I thought he was. Angus snorted, 'So he fucking should be! He's been playing twenty-five years!' He then got into a rave about his thoughts on performance. He was very taken with the story of Jerry Lee Lewis setting his piano on fire because Chuck Berry was playing after him, saying, 'Top that, n*gger!' Angus thought this was the absolute height of showmanship and proceeded to detail his plan to one day have a giant transparent ball built in which he could run around on stage playing guitar . . . I've always wondered why he never did that.

After the Augusta show, their last together, Bon invited John into the bus parked in the dark around the back of the pub. In the glow of an overhead reading light they shared joints and a bottle of scotch, while Bon talked about the overseas market and how the KA should be aiming for it. It was a conversation John would never forget.

John: He virtually told me what was in store for AC/DC in the big picture, said they'd become one of the biggest bands in the world. There was no argument from me – I could see it too.

I was thinking, 'Yep, okay, so how can we do that too?' Bon said, 'John, you know why we're gonna make it? Because we've got Angus.' I said, 'I agree, but don't sell yourself short, Bon. You *and* Angus are amazing and the band and the songs are just great.'

Two weeks later the Keystone Angels were back in Sydney playing to a small crowd at Chequers, when down the staircase from Pitt Street stepped Bon, Malcolm, Angus, George and Harry. The band played on, acutely conscious that, after their years on the road, the moment of truth had arrived. Vanda and Young and AC/DC were in the house. *Would they cut it?*

At the end of the set Doc, the Brewsters and Charlie tentatively strolled over to their table, stomachs churning. There were intros and handshakes. They lit up and ordered drinks. George looked around the room, aware of the eyes glancing their way. He called manager Casey over and asked to borrow his office. He nodded and they all followed him along a dark corridor in silence. They watched as he unlocked a door and motioned them in.

Crushed around Casey's paper-strewn desk, with George in an old leather chair, Harry leaning against the wall, they smoked and talked about songs, lyrics, melodies, writers, influences. George looked at Harry, downed the last of his scotch, stood up and announced in his Glasgow accent, 'Come to the studio at eleven tomorrow and we'll see what you've got.'

Next day, four anxious young men parked their old EH behind the Alberts building at 139 King Street in the centre of Sydney, loaded their instruments and amps into the lift and travelled up to the studios. George appeared and said, 'Ah, you didna need to bring your gear up. Here's a couple of acoustic guitars – let's hear your songs.'

> **John Brewster:** They must have seen potential that other companies had missed because they handed us a contract. Back in Adelaide with Woodruff, we took it to a lawyer who told us it appeared to favour the record company pretty heavily. But we signed it anyway – it was all too good to be true. We'd been passed over by the others, and now we had Vanda and Young and Alberts wanting to sign us. Are you kidding? If you look at it on face value that solicitor was right, though. But it didn't take us long to realise that being signed to Alberts meant being able to develop our music, develop the show, learn all the tricks of recording and be in a creative environment that was just unbelievable.

The only thing the band insisted on was that a clause be written in to specify that they'd be working with George and Harry. Woodruff met with Alberts boss Ted Albert, along with George and Harry, and they accepted that.

It was at that meeting that Ted Albert took Woodruff aside and suggested that if he wanted to be taken seriously as a band manager in Sydney, he should consider wearing a pair of shoes.

As it was, Woodruff and his wife, Christine, were about to head overseas at this critical point in time. Christine had applied for a one-year teacher exchange program and had accepted a position at a school in Glasgow, beginning in 1976. For his part, Woodruff, a keen skier, had enrolled in a Scottish ski-instructors course in a highland resort.

The contract between the Keystone Angels and Alberts Productions was signed on 26 November 1975, shortly before the Woodruffs flew out. By then he'd come to an arrangement with Peter Rix to manage the band while he was away. Rix managed Hush, Marcia Hines and Jon English. As one of the most successful managers in the country, he had serious clout.

Things moved pretty fast after the contract was signed. George and Harry were taking holidays after Christmas, and before they went they wanted to get the lads into the studio to cut a couple of songs for a single, with the A-side being 'Am I Ever Gonna See Your Face Again'. They'd also used their influence to get the KA a support spot on a summer tour by Alberts' biggest star, John Paul Young.

Brian: The band had returned to Adelaide, but suddenly gigs were cancelled and we headed back to Sydney to record a single. Charlie and I took two girlfriends with us, Jane and Mimi, and we moved into a family flat in Cockroach Mansion where we usually stayed.

Next night we parked in the lane behind Alberts, crammed the guitars and amps into the lift and went up to the third floor.

Studio 1 was where the Alberts acts had recorded the big hits. Stevie Wright had done 'Evie Parts 1, 2 and 3' there, which had gone to #1. John Paul Young's hits came out of Studio 1, Ted Mulry's, AC/DC's as well.

And now Vanda and Young were recording the Keystone Angels there, directing them around the dark atmospheric studio with its blackened walls and low-hanging orange light-shades. Following instructions, Charlie set up his drums in front of a wall of mirror tiles while Brian placed the guitar amps in front of a set of heavy green curtains. The far wall was covered with graffiti and the signatures of artists who'd gone before them. By the time the session was over, four more had been added.

The plan was to record the band live, given that 'Am I Ever Gonna See Your Face Again' had been performed onstage for the past year – and they'd take it from there. On the first few takes they concentrated on getting the drums right. George told Charlie to play dead straight, no fills or cymbal crashes.

During a break Rick had remained in the studio messing around on his Gibson trying to come up with something memorable for the guitar solo. It occurred to him that the song was actually about an accident which had led to the death of a young woman, and his fingers instinctively started fingering the fretboard high up the neck.

> **Rick:** It was just one of those moments – suddenly I was playing the sound of an ambulance siren. George heard it, not even knowing what the song was about: 'Aye, that's hookey – a guid hook there!'

George was a master arranger for hit singles and what he did with 'Face' was no exception: the breakdowns, the whole outro ramming the hook down repeatedly. Rick's ambulance riff was repeated throughout the song – using his little Goldentone amp, the best sound of that riff ever.

> **John:** The rest of the song came together quite easily. I used the Wasp amp I played through every night. There were great vocals from Doc, while I belted out the high harmony and Rick sang the middle harmony. Doc played the bass on the final take but George later replaced it. He did a lot of that in those days – never with Chris Bailey later on, however.

With 'Am I Ever Gonna See Your Face' done and dusted, they then recorded 'Round We Go' for the B-side, a song mainly written by John. As they were packing up, George said, 'Hey, have you guys ever thought about dropping the Keystone thing and just calling yourself

The Angels? It'll stand out better on your records and posters – have a think about it.' They shrugged and said, 'Sure.' By then most of their fans had shortened it to that, anyway.

The band then hit the road with John Paul Young and his Allstars. They played open-air concerts on hot summer nights for holiday crowds thronging the coastal towns. They were now able to announce the imminent release of their new single, while Rick played its catchy new siren hook.

In Coffs Harbour they stayed at a pub where the owner had a pet sulphur-crested cocky that got off on the air out of car tyre valves that he'd learned to depress with his beak. The morning after the gig they got up to find the cocky had undone the caps of all the valves on the EH and deflated the tyres by sticking his beak down the nozzle. Luckily he hadn't got to the truck yet.

The band then returned to Sydney, joined up with the Ted Mulry Gang and headed down the NSW South Coast playing gigs to the holiday crowds in that part of the state. At every show Doc sang 'Am I Ever Gonna See Your Face Again' and Rick kicked in with the siren riff – but to little response. The punters were hanging out for TMG and their big hit 'Jump In My Car', which was getting saturation airplay on its way to the #1 spot for six weeks.

Then it was home to Adelaide to do a run of gigs leading up to a well-promoted farewell Adelaide show to a house-full Finsbury.

With both Alberts Records and Peter Rix based in Sydney, the decision had been made for the band and their wives to pack up and leave Adelaide. By the end of January 1976, the move was complete and they were residents of the Harbour City.

CHAPTER TEN
WELCOME TO SYDNEY

Chris Gilbey, head of Alberts Promotions, had the idea of releasing an all-star compilation album called *Rocka*, made up of tracks from Alberts' roster of artists: AC/DC, Stevie Wright, The Easybeats, Ted Mulry Gang and JPY. With 'Am I Ever Gonna See Your Face Again' due out in April, he made sure the song was also on it. EMI distributed Alberts' records, so EMI's Little River Band would be on it too. To promote the album, he set about organising a short movie for cinemas to play in the lead-up to feature films. Clips of all the acts were available, but as yet the Angels hadn't done one.

Chris Gilbey: The Angels became the actors in a short film we did. They played this group à la the Monkees; running around trying to find the master copy of their promo video, stolen by a mad scientist. Basically it was a whole load of chase sequences where the band acted out these zany roles. I had a number of prints run off and gave them to Greater Union and they ran them whenever they needed some filler. They were played for years.

John Brewster: We were asked – conned actually – by Chris into acting in this movie, which we did so we could get 'Am I Ever Gonna See Your Face Again' in it. We weren't shown performing the song as promised. The other artists had their clips in it – all we got was 'Face' playing under the credits at the end.

Meantime we had to act like The Monkees in a stupid romp. We did scenes like talking on a shoe phone and chasing girls with their underwear on the outside all over Sydney. That part had its moments.

This was our first promo experience with Alberts and it wasn't good! Charlie came across best in the movie – he reminded me of Ringo in *A Hard Day's Night*.

Brian decided not to move to Sydney, but offered to sell his truck and PA to the band for $6000. The guys had paid off a couple of loans and the bank manager was one of those old gems who'd approve a loan if he liked the cut of your jib. With John, Doc and Rick sitting in front of him dressed in their conservative best, he waved it through.

With the departure of Brian, a good-natured twenty-year-old called Ashley Swinfield came on board. Ashley was the son of a parson. He didn't swear, drink or smoke pot and had the strength of Goliath.

Ashley: A guy called John Bee taught me the basics of mixing a band and I was away. I became a one-man show with the help of Charlie. He was living the dream performing with the band but there was nothing pop star-ish about him. They paid me $200 a week, which was pretty good, but I worked for it!

One of the first things John, Rick and Doc did after they'd moved into Cockroach Mansion was visit Peter Rix at his North Sydney office. They were keen to make the acquaintance of their new high-powered manager to discuss tour and promotion plans for the new single. Having been seduced by Gilbey to do the *Rocka* clip, they wanted him to become more involved in their burgeoning career.

After a lengthy wait they were ushered into Rix's office to be told bluntly that Hush had spat the dummy about him taking on their management. 'It's not going to happen,' he said. John, Rick and Doc spluttered in disbelief but Rix raised his hands, said, 'Sorry, guys, can't help you,' stood up and showed the dumbfounded trio the door.

John: Woodruff had disappeared after we signed the record contract and left us in the hands of Peter Rix who, without any warning, now tells us he can't manage the band. We've taken out a loan for six grand for the truck and PA, we've left Adelaide where I was paying $13 a week for a shared house with a beautiful park over the road. We've done farewell gigs and the Adelaide press have written about us going, so we can hardly return! I'm about to sign a lease on a shithole cold-water flat costing $45 a week – and it's the same with the others. Our wives have all left their good jobs and are joining us any day, and now, without the clout and influence of Woodruff and Sphere behind us, we're on our own. Just when we have a new single to promote and a debut album planned! Dropped in the shit!

In desperation, John sought out Jim Towers, who ran the Cordon Bleu agency in a run-down end of town. Towers initially said he wasn't taking on any new bands, but, impressed that The Angels were signed to Alberts and with a single due shortly, he brought them in.

John: We got booked into every shithole from here to Timbuktu, but at least we were working full-time again – and to be fair, there were some good ones too, like the Bondi Lifesaver now and then. I went into Jim's office every few days and would look over his shoulder at his booking book and say, 'You've got a space there – how about putting us into that one?', and he'd um and ah and say he was holding it for someone and I'd say, 'Jim, please,' and he'd write our name in ahead of whoever he was going to put there.

It was do or die for us. Our wives were applying for jobs in their professions, but they immediately got waitressing work and got some desperately needed money rolling in. We wouldn't have survived without those wonderful women.

Meanwhile the songs kept coming, adversity sharpening their pens and focusing skills they'd been acquiring. They'd walk up the hill from Cockroach Mansion to the phone box and call Alberts: 'Hey, George, we've written a new song.' 'Good,' he'd say, 'come in Thursday after lunch, we got some studio time – let's see what you got.'

'Am I Ever Gonna See Your Face Again' was released on 5 April. Despite the band's high hopes of matching the success that AC/DC and TMG's singles had achieved, radio ignored it. When Alberts booked them onto *Countdown*, the ebullient Gilbey pulled the guys into his office. He had four brooms and handed them one each, kept one himself. 'Okay,' he said, 'here's an idea for your *Countdown* appearance to make you stand out.' He dropped the needle onto their single, grabbed his broom and proceeded to go through the step routine that the Shadows had used in the UK fifteen years previously. The four young men stared in disbelief. He lifted the needle: 'Okay. You ready . . .?'

John, in a moment of rage, threw his broom on the floor and stormed out, closely followed by the rest.

Everyone held their breath after the *Countdown* appearance. All the radio programmers watched it, but 'Face Again' remained unplayed. Gilbey drove them to 2UE to wish top DJ Bob Rogers a happy birthday. They took the single which he put on the turntable, listened for three seconds and then declared he'd never play *that* kind of music on *his* radio show. Gilbey grinned awkwardly as they backed out the studio door, humiliated.

> **John Brewster:** Another time we mimed the single on a travel doco starring Barbara Eden, who [on this occasion] *didn't* materialise from a bottle [she was 'I Dream of Jeannie' on TV]. It was filmed in the Rocks area of Sydney around the Old Spaghetti Factory. We often ate there because it was cheap. They got busted for putting dog food in their bolognaise! We also did a thirty-second ad for 7 Up soft drink – we all had to dress as clowns and play our instruments! Another monumental failure for The Angels. At least we got paid for it. It's a wonder we had any credibility left.

Without focused management to plan and execute a strategy, the band was floundering.

Wednesday night at the Bondi Lifesaver was free entry. The fee was an underwhelming $120 but it was where the industry hung and the competition for up-and-coming bands to pull a booking there was intense. Towers offered The Angels the gig only after a last-minute cancellation.

> **Rick:** Angus was there and hung out backstage with us. AC/DC was getting ready to relocate to London and wouldn't be back until they'd cracked the English market. They were leaving their Marshall amps and heads behind – they were picking up new ones in the UK and wanted to know if we were interested in buying them. We had no spare money, but we sold our old gear and somehow found the rest. Marshalls! We'd had Wasps, cheap imitations of the real thing. Malcolm was selling one of his Gretsch guitars as well and John couldn't resist. Funny how we always scraped together money for equipment and instruments.

With the failure of 'Face', Harry and George wanted another single. They weren't too perturbed – it was a good track and would go on the album. They liked a song with a mid-tempo shuffle the guys had brought in called 'No Lies' and a session was booked.

When they arrived, Angus and Bon were there. Bon was putting down a vocal in Studio 1. He did a couple of takes and then George said, 'Ah yeah, that's really good, Bon. The Angels are here, let's leave it at that – come back tomorrow and we'll have another go.'

Rick picked up Angus's guitar and was surprised at how light the strings were.

> **Rick:** I asked him what he used and he said 8 to 42s or something. I'd never used anything that light. Guitarists I knew swore you had to have heavy strings to get the tone. I was thinking, '*Tone?* Show me a better tone than what Angus Young gets!' After that I changed my strings. I didn't go to 8s, I went to 9s. 8s were just a bit too light for me.

The session began but George wasn't content with Charlie's drumming.

> **John:** Charlie didn't make it onto that recording. George played the drums and Charlie sat it out. The song was pretty naff but the drum track was fantastic. George and Harry listened to it later and decided not to release it. They didn't

think it represented the band. Rick and I were really interested in learning how the mixing desk worked and all the rest of the gadgets they had in the studio. We were taking a lot of interest in how they mic'd us up and they were always happy to explain what they were doing. We were learning on every level, bringing in new songs all the time and playing them, demoing them. We'd listen to George and Harry's arrangement suggestions and anything else they had to say – then go away and rework them.

Charlie: I was always nervous and awestruck in the studio. In recording 'No Lies' the band discussed with Harry and George about whether it might be quicker to get session guys in to put down the bass and drum tracks. I didn't mind – it's common practice to get session guys in for studio recordings.

When we made the move to Sydney I drove my chop-top Mini over with my wife and kids. We were staying at Cockroach Mansion where there was nowhere it could be safely parked. George offered for me to park it in his garage. It was a pretty speccy machine and a prime target for thieves. I'd go round to his place to pick it up or deliver it back, and I ended up getting invited to stay for a BBQ sometimes, or a few beers and a rave. George never gave me the feeling that he wasn't happy with my playing. I got pissed there once or twice and slept on the couch.

Since George and Harry had rushed the band into recording 'Face' because they believed it was a hit, the pair had been quietly looking at every aspect of this outfit they'd signed. They could see the potential and there was no question about their work ethic and commitment to *making it.* Work ethic and commitment were everything to George and Harry – they sneered at the Aussie 'she'll be right' attitude.

As working-class immigrants who'd met at the Villawood Migrant Hostel when they were teenagers in the early sixties, they'd worked hard for their success. Everyone they'd signed had similar backgrounds: Thorpe, Wright, Mulry, AC/DC. They understood Charlie, but the three well-spoken, university-educated members were different. George and Harry had watched them closely that first night at Chequers, studied them during the audition, had come to the conclusion that they had something special. There was honesty, creativity and a hunger for success. They knew it was the Brewsters who'd formed the jug band and, like Angus and Malcolm with AC/DC, it was the Brewsters who ran The Angels. They were relentlessly writing and practising and learning the workings of the studio. With Doc and the Brewsters, George and Harry knew the creative engine was running.

Now they set about sorting through the links between the creative input and the commercial output. They were adept at sussing the strengths and weaknesses of a band. If The Angels were to make the big time, there was no room for compromise. George and Harry had been through this with George's younger brothers in AC/DC.

> **John:** George and Harry called me, Doc and Rick into their office. They said that after the 'No Lies' session, they realised they'd have to get a session drummer in to do the album. They said that we could keep Charlie in the band, but that we'd have to use another drummer in the studio.

Rick, Doc and John discussed the situation. No one wanted Charlie to go – he lived and breathed for the band. They considered George's suggestion of hiring a session drummer for recording, but then how would Charlie play the songs onstage? The more they talked, the more they came to accept that if the band was to achieve its full potential, they'd have to find a new drummer, regardless of their feelings for Charlie.

The Angels had always been a loner band. They rarely hung out with other musos and didn't know where to start. Doc suggested they ring one of Woodruff's associates at Sphere in Adelaide. A few days later their man rang back with a name: Graham Bidstrup. He'd recently returned from the UK, was currently rehearsing with a possible band, but keeping his options open.

> **Buzz Bidstrup:** An agent rang and said a Sydney band was looking for a good drummer – was I interested? They'd just signed a record contract. He wouldn't tell me who it was, but he said they'd be in Adelaide the following week and we could talk then. It was only when we met that

I found out it was the guys from Moonshine – I'd seen them years before in a pub somewhere.

We did a rehearsal/audition in a hall at Kensington Park sports ground and kicked a footy around afterwards. Good fun. I didn't know how long I'd be with them but we settled on a wage of $90 a week. They were playing an Adelaide gig followed by some country dates and then heading on to Melbourne and I was able to join them right away.

John Brewster: It fell to me to sack Charlie. We were in Adelaide and Rick and I were staying at our parents. I arranged to meet him at the Sphere office, saying something about things to sign. It was awful really, waiting for him. He got there and I took him out to the car to be private. He was crushed – he didn't see it coming. It was very emotional, me and him sitting in the EH talking it through. Fucking awful. I'll always remember his fierce loyalty, his debts, car repossession, Army arrest, his wife and her brother, the would-be assassin. Charlie was a good guy, one of the boys. Most bands are largely comprised of working-class guys – he was one of them, one of the reasons he was so well liked.

Charlie was highly sceptical of Brewster's reasons and justifications. This had been Charlie's biggest 'shot at the title' and he would forever feel he'd been cheated out of his place in the Aussie rock 'n' roll firmament. As events unfolded for the band over the following years, he would bitterly offer his side of the story to anyone who would listen:

Charlie: John told me this crock-of-shit story that Harry and George strongly suggested to the Brewsters and Doc to get rid of me for a more technical drummer. George and Harry had never mentioned that to me. From the silver-spoon-fed, uni-educated, dope-head, never done a hard day's work in their lives, pissant prima donnas . . .

This was the thanks I received from two years of slogging my guts out for the common good of The Angels, which included a double hernia operation – at my expense – that I needed from lifting heavy sound gear and drumming at the same time. Zilch, kaput, sayonara, au revoir, piss-offski, nothing . . . fuck off, Charlie!

Broke and utterly dejected, Charlie hitched back to Sydney to collect his car and his family. He was picked up by a cattle-truck on the border. Exhausted, he drifted in and out of consciousness. The dream was over, but memories of the wild ride he'd had with the band since leaving the Army would remain for the rest of his long and adventurous life.

CHAPTER ELEVEN
PIVOTAL DECISIONS

Graham set up his blue perspex drum-kit at the Arkaba Hotel the day Charlie was sacked – and the show went on. He'd been given tapes of the songs, and with just a few listens he came through without any mistakes. John thought Graham's kit sounded fantastic. There were a few 'Where's Charlie?' questions but Doc, John and Rick dodged them and they got through.

Next morning the mood in the EH was buoyant as they drove southeast to Mount Gambier with Buzz on board. The band had volunteered to help Ashley with the load-in and load-out for the next few gigs until they got to Melbourne and found a casual roadie.

It was at the Mount Gambier gig that Graham, now confident he could work with these guys, at least until their album was recorded, introduced his stage name: Buzz Throckman. What wasn't mentioned was that he didn't want his mates to know he'd joined the group of amateurs formerly known as the Moonshine Jug and String Band.

Back in Sydney, The Angels began recording demos but it quickly became clear to Buzz that the rhythm section wasn't solid.

He was the only one who had a tape recorder that could play tapes from the studio. Doc had invited him to stay at his place so once they'd got back home they'd listen to what they'd played in the studio and discuss bass, drumming and grooves.

Eventually Buzz suggested to George, and the rest, that a more accomplished bass player was required and George agreed.

But if a new bass player was brought in, where did that leave Doc? Charlie had been made redundant when they'd replaced him with Buzz. If Doc was to be replaced by another musician, was he to be fired as well? Neither Rick nor John for a second entertained that thought, so some reorganisation within the group had to be sorted out first. Maybe Doc could become exclusively the lead singer, but right then that was a duty shared by both him and John.

> **John:** The idea of Doc being the front-man came from George. Doc, Rick, me and Buzz had a conversation with him in which he said that I had a good voice but Doc had a character voice. I was fine with that, no problem.

The chain of events that had unfolded since Buzz joined had now brought about a change that would have far-reaching ramifications for the band's career. At the time, however, the issue was amicably settled with no one, including Doc himself, appreciating the consequences. Doc was plucked from the ranks and appointed front-man, and with that he became the public face of The Angels. The decision would prove to be momentous.

Now, what to do about a new bass player?

> **Buzz:** Chris Bailey and I were in two bands when I joined The Angels. We were also the house rhythm section at a local recording studio, working on various things with ex-Mixtures member Idris Jones. So when I joined The Angels, CB was a bit pissed off to say the least, but we kept in touch when the band played in Adelaide over the following months.

Chris Bailey's parents had owned a pub at Keith, a rural town 220 kilometres southeast of Adelaide. At five years of age they'd packed him off to the pucka Prince Alfred College in Adelaide as a boarder. In 1965 at fifteen years of age, hugely influenced by the Beatles and their bassist Paul McCartney, he began playing bass and went on to be ranked among Adelaide's elite musicians. He'd played in the Mount

Lofty Rangers with Bon Scott and also the acclaimed Headband, in which he'd doubled up on bass and lead vocals. Christopher Mark Bailey was serious talent. When Buzz suggested him for The Angels, Doc, John and Rick's jaws fell open. *Chris Bailey? Are you serious? He won't leave Adelaide to join us!*

> **Chris:** We'd all lived in Adelaide when we were younger. I'd seen them in the jug band but then lost track of them. Buzz sent me a tape of songs they'd been working on and I thought 'Wow, there's something going on here' – that twin guitar attack of the Brewsters and there were some interesting lyrics among those rough demos.

Bailey arrived in Sydney in January 1977. There was no need for auditions. They went straight into intensive rehearsals and then he was onstage with them doing up to ten gigs a week.

> **John:** After Chris joined and Doc became front-man, I stopped lead singing. When we went into the studio and began recording, I sang one song, 'High On You', because the melody was too high for Doc – I also sang the middle eight in 'You Got Me Running' and that was it. We had these songs we'd written over the years and some were a bit country perhaps, but George said, 'Just record them as a rock band.' I'd written 'Shelter From The Rain' and suggested we do it in a certain way to make it more poppy. But George said, 'Yeah, maybe we could have a hit with it if we did it that way – but where would that leave the band? Stick to your guns,' he said, 'don't just write for radio and you'll come through.' Those two guys played such a major part in mentoring us.

Not in their wildest dreams did this group of young men from Adelaide, commencing those sessions together, imagine what destiny had in store for them. But as their Alberts stable mates had said, it's a long way to the top – and they still had a long way to go.

Doc's initial efforts as front-man were embarrassing. He got his moves and stage outfits from studying Rod Stewart and Mick Jagger. Instead of coming across as sexy he just looked tall, skinny and awkward. Friends were telling John and Rick to get rid of Doc but that was never considered. The three had started the band together, they'd struggled for years together, their ambitions remained undimmed and as a brotherhood they were going to make it together.

But it wasn't just Doc who was struggling with his stagecraft. Rick's moves on stage were also underwhelming and he knew it.

> **Rick:** When I was young, learning to play classical piano, my father, whose only experience was the classical world, despised musicians who deliberately used excessive body movements to demonstrate how much they 'felt' the music – like Liberace. He used to say, 'Play with feeling, but let the fingers do the talking – there's no need to move the body.' So I learnt to express myself that way on the piano. After I decided to stand still playing guitar, I felt comfortable on the instrument for the first time.

At Alberts there were important personnel changes going on too. Chris Gilbey left to manage The Saints and Fifa Riccobono took over as Promotions Manager. She decided to have another crack at getting 'Face' onto radio. 'But try as I may,' she said, 'I couldn't give that single away. No one gave a rat's arse about it.' So in April a second single was released, 'You're A Lady Now', written by Brewster/Neeson/Brewster, with a new song on the B-side penned by Buzz and John, 'Can't Get Lucky'.

Meanwhile Buzz was settling into life in Sydney. Initially unsure about how long he'd stay with the band, he lived a gypsy life of camping out in the homes of various band members.

> **Buzz:** The guys' wives were wonderful girls. I lived at each of their houses after I arrived, and I got treated like family. My introduction to Sydney was really cool, and considering I'd been living in the UK a few months earlier, any thoughts of going back to 'join a band' soon faded away.
>
> I was recording an album in the best studio in town produced by the best rock producers in the country: Vanda and Young. We were playing

almost every night of the week up and down the east coast and back to Adelaide. I had my first appearance on *Countdown* and we shot a film clip at Alberts studios.

And so I set out on my life on the road. It was the beginning of a heady time: many laughs, night frisbee games, early morning bakeries, late-night and after-gig frivolity and jocularity – and some songwriting.

Kathy White was a Chequers regular who became a dedicated Angels fan and friend. She lived with her mother in a tumbledown weatherboard in inner-suburban Balmain. It had a store-room dug into the foundations and, after consulting her mother, she offered it to them for a rehearsal space. They'd set up base camp there with some rudimentary soundproofing, amps, speakers, mics and a tape recorder. While the benevolent Mrs White was out of the house at work, the new line-up pounded into action day after day, reworking songs that could now breathe freely with a rhythm section that knew no bounds. By March they were ready to record.

Chris: That album could have been recorded differently, but George and Harry said it should sound the same as the way we were on stage. So we did it pretty much live – with a minimum of overdubs. We went in and put a couple of tracks down. That was mainly to get used to the studio. Then we went out and did a run of gigs. Then it was back to the studio and we did the rest in a few days.

Doc: We went for a live sound – to get the live excitement the new line-up was generating. Especially the rhythm section. We overplayed everything, trying to get more into it.

By the time they wrapped it up, George and Harry had captured the feel of what and who The Angels were and where they'd come from. 'Shelter From The Rain' was a pointer to the future. With the rhythm section redefining the band's sound, George and Harry decided to rerecord 'Face', but this time without Rick's trademark ambulance-siren guitar. However, with all the might of Bailey and Bidstrup, they couldn't capture the magic that Charlie, Doc, John and Rick had found during that first session fifteen months previously. Charlie was no longer in the band, but his drumming would live on in the version of 'Face' that would become one of the band's signature songs.

CHAPTER TWELVE
ON THE BONES OF THEIR ARSE

In May 1977, John Woodruff returned from Scotland. Despite him leaving The Angels for seventeen months on the eve of their recording career – *and* in the hands of Peter Rix, a management relationship that lasted no more than a day – Doc, Rick and John drove out to the airport and picked him up, eager to find out what his plans were and if the band's management was still on his agenda. They desperately needed someone at the helm.

He emerged from customs with a lopsided grin, cigarette in mouth and his usual air of supreme confidence. He stayed at Rick's for a few days and confirmed that he did indeed intend picking up where he'd left off as the band's manager. Easing himself back in, he checked out some gigs and accompanied them to Alberts to discuss the album cover.

John, Rick and Doc explained that they were now living hand to mouth, the principal members taking twenty dollars a week while paying the newcomers survival wages of 120 a week. While their wives kept the home fires burning, the band was sinking into debt. As the bookkeeper, with his finger on the financials, John had been doing most of the worrying. On 4 July, 'You're A Lady Now' was released as the single from the album, complete with film clip shot in Alberts Studio 1. John was hoping that radio would pick it up and give them the visibility required to pull more punters – with the subsequent rise in fees. But as the weeks slipped by, despite a *Countdown* appearance – during which Rick almost fainted and was later diagnosed with hepatitis – airplay had proved elusive.

Woodruff moved into John Brewster's place, resumed taking a management fee and set to work trying to improve things. He took the band out of Cordon Bleu and returned them to Chris Murphy's agency with whom he had a longstanding relationship. However the band's fees remained the same, but with substantially fewer gigs than Cordon Bleu had provided and Woodruff's management commissions now pushed the finances even further into the red.

The 'You're A Lady Now' single died a death, in hindsight probably a good thing. The style and the songs that would make the band famous were yet to come. On 19 September their self-titled album was released. Fifa presented it to the radio stations and Alberts hosted an album launch, followed by another at 2JJ. The rock press gave it mixed reviews but Andrew McMillan at *RAM* magazine gave it a glowing half-page wrap. The LP would eventually achieve gold status, but for now it only dribbled out and the meagre sales had little impact on their live fee structure, and consequently the band's financial woes deepened.

> **John:** We decided that the band would pay for my flight to Adelaide so I could ask Dad to go guarantor on a bank loan. I arrived and surprised him in the kitchen and explained what I'd come for. He listened and then said no. If my mother had been there it would have caused a problem, because she would have badgered him into it. Dad called me a day later to say he was worried that his refusal would affect our relationship. I assured him it wouldn't and that I understood his position. He said, 'Son, you've forced me into giving you my opinion of what you and Rick are doing. I think you've both made a big mistake.'

Rick, John and Doc then approached George and Harry about getting an advance from Alberts. The request was passed on to Ted Albert who reiterated the company's policy of not paying out cash advances. George said, 'Look, we've all been through the hard times – one day you'll thank him.'

Woodruff was still staying at John's place. One morning John told him that they couldn't afford to pay him commissions any longer. At that, he resigned and returned to Adelaide where he drove cabs, then stage-managed Reg Livermore's production of *Ned Kelly* for six months.

In late October 1977 John called a band meeting and gave them cold, hard financial facts. 'We have around ten grand of debt,' he said. 'We own ten grand of equipment and things aren't getting any better.' They discussed disbanding, getting day jobs and even reforming the Moonshine Jug and String Band to play on their nights off. The mood was getting a bit too negative so John hastily pointed out that there was currently a solid block of work booked through to New Year's Eve, albeit at lousy fees – and they were no longer paying management commissions. The meeting broke up with the decision to review their position in the new year. If things hadn't improved, they'd fold the band and sell the equipment.

The following week they were scheduled to play the mid-coastal towns of NSW. On the drive up, the truck blew a tyre, which meant losing the first gig. Doc, Rick and John went to the nearest ANZ branch and applied for bank cards with the basic $250 credit. They were issued over the counter and the three immediately cashed them out to pay for the tyre and plug the hole in the budget from the loss of the gig, thus sinking them even further into debt.

Sometime during this period at a meeting with George, Harry and Fifa Riccobono, George asked, 'Have you guys thought about getting your hair cut? You'd be the first band in Australia with short hair. It might be worth thinking about.' They did think about it – just as they thought about everything else he said.

> **John**: We told George that we'd get haircuts when we had a bit of spare cash. He disappeared and came back with $25, enough for each of us to visit the barber in Pitt Street. Ted Albert had advanced the money against royalties, our one and only advance. Months later when we got our first royalty check, $25 had been deducted! But you know what? With my accountancy background, I respected that. It told me that they weren't casual about money and that everything was done correctly.

John had bought the Sex Pistols album, *Never Mind The Bollocks*, and checked them out in the rock magazines. He loved their roaring energy and now homed in on photos of Sid Vicious in black t-shirt and leather jacket – it created a powerful impression. Doc wore one occasionally – why hadn't that imagery occurred to John before? With Rick and Chris, he drove over to Oxford Street and trawled charity stores and pawn shops. The shades for him and his brother were part of it too – short hair, black t-shirts, jeans, leather jackets. The Angels weren't a punk band, but the imagery was a perfect fit.

CHAPTER THIRTEEN
EMBRACING THE DARK SIDE

One morning at a Brisbane motel, the conversation turned to stage lighting. During the past month Ashley had been helped out by a casual roadie called Phil. Phil owned a small stage-light business hiring modest rigs to bands on a weekly basis. It left him time to do roadie work to bring in extra money. With Phil in the crew, a deal had been done for him to add some extra lights to the rig, which had kicked off ideas for experimenting with what they now had.

John suggested they look at the films and plays of Bertolt Brecht and the German Expressionists. Both he and Doc had studied Brecht during their film-making courses at Flinders Uni. This resonated with Rick, who himself had studied Brecht in German classes at school.

Doc borrowed three books from the Brisbane Library and he and Rick went to a park for the afternoon. They pored over the black-and-white photos of stage and film productions and got excited about the stark minimalist lighting, the angular shadows thrown from floor lamps, the parallel beams, and heavy use of white and black as colours.

They decided Doc should have two floor lamps, one red and one blue. Rick would have a green floor lamp – the only green to be used – to throw shadows of him on the back wall and ceiling. There should be lots of white light, parallel beams and no yellows! A scene should be set and held for a verse, another for a chorus, and for certain solos

Rick should be lit with the green floor light and a white overhead cone, with the rest of the stage left dark. The same for Doc's special moments – light him and no one else. Then have the whole stage explode with white light when the music exploded.

Rick and Doc took the concept to Phil as he set up for the gig.

> **Rick:** He totally lost it when we asked for floor lamps and parallel beams. 'It can't be done! You can't put lights on the floor, you can't use parallel beams. They're theatre lamps – they're delicate. They can't travel in a truck without breaking. I have to use yellow and all the colours otherwise it'll be boring!'

They worked out what could be done with what they were carrying and Phil sullenly agreed to carry out their instructions. However it wasn't long before he'd reverted to his light-flashing ways again. Rick and Doc demanded that he either follow their directions or they'd find someone else. Despite the warnings, the flashing and the multi-colours kept creeping back.

In mounting exasperation as the band toured back to Sydney, Doc and Rick continued to talk it through with him, emphasising their original concepts, but to little avail. When the band returned to the Harbour City, Phil quit. By chance, this paved the way for Ray Hawkins, a friend of Rick and John since they'd arrived from Adelaide, to join the road crew and become The Angels' brilliant lighting guy.

Soon afterwards, when the band did a run of Adelaide gigs, Doc phoned Professor Wal Cherry, head of Drama at Flinders University. Wal was the champion of Bertolt Brecht and would become most animated when discussing him during the lectures Doc had attended while at uni.

Doc explained about being a rock band front-man and how he was struggling to make it work. He said he'd rediscovered Brecht, but, he asked his former teacher, how could he make it work for a band?

Wal invited him to the university for a chat, and they talked for hours. The professor's advice to Doc was succinct: 'Bernard, you must develop a character that you can step into for your performances, just like an actor every time he goes on stage.'

Wal thought he should disassociate Bernard, the nice Northern Irish son of Barney and Kathleen, from Doc, front-man for The Angels. 'Start working on Doc as a separate identity who goes out before an audience and performs a role you've designed for him.'

He suggested Doc come out as a toff in dinner jacket and Ascot tie. *What?* Doc was a bit doubtful. 'Yes, and as he warms up,' continued Wal, 'have him discard the coat, undo the tie, pull out the shirt-tails, undo the buttons. Have him slowly disintegrate until he's a dishevelled mess, and at the end, he staggers off into the night, bloodied, but defiant – undefeated. A very romantic figure – they'll be howling for more.'

It was a bizarre concept and Doc wasn't so sure. The formal dinner suit would be a complete contrast to the leather toughness of the rest of the band and would be a foil to Rick's statue, said the good professor. He had another piece of advice for him: 'When you're performing to your audience, pull back at dramatic moments, bunch your hands into tight fists and breathe deep, focusing all your energy within. Then, at the right moment, fling your hands wide open at the audience, fingers splayed and stare right into their eyes, their heart and soul! This releases pent-up energy and flashes it out like electricity. Getting it exactly right is an elusive skill, but when you've mastered it, everything else will fall into place.'

As it was, Doc took on board many of Wal Cherry's ideas and suggestions. But he couldn't see the band accepting the concept of him performing in a formal dinner suit! In fact, he couldn't see it himself but he liked the idea of adopting a 'look' that Elvis Costello had: tailored jacket, a shirt and loosened tie. He thought about it for a while before scouting through the thrift shops. Eventually he appeared in blue jacket, white shirt and an old school tie – and it worked.

All the visual components were falling into place. Rick the agricultural scientist had nailed it during a magazine interview: 'Four elements came together like chemistry: the songs, the statue, the character of Doc and the light show.'

Another breakthrough came a few days after they returned from the Adelaide dates. John had worked up a new song with a punk feel he hadn't used before.

The song was 'I Ain't The One'.

John: Most of the lyric was written in a car in an Adelaide suburban street. Rick added the line 'well dressed waxwork wound up to walk'. What a line! When we got back to Sydney, we did a demo in Studio 2, using a series of quick downstrokes which had everyone leaping around.

Mark Opitz: . . . we instantly started jumping up and down and yelling, 'That's it, that's it!' We all knew at that point that we had a sound.

Rick: Jumping is right. The control-room lounge seat became a trampoline and we were literally jumping in the air, punching to the ceiling – the whole band and Mark. The downstroke style was immediately branded the 'nic nics'. It sounded like a toy name when you said it, but what soon became apparent was it provided a wonderful rhythm with your guitar without interfering with the vocals.

It meant that with a mid-range vocalist like Doc, we could play the guitars pretty hard without getting in his way. If you're going to thrash the guitars, you need a singer who's right up there like Bon Scott. We learnt to use nic nics for the verses, then thrash the guitars in the chorus.

John: We floated out of there at nine in the morning about five inches off the ground, got coffees and finger buns from the café across the road and went home. We finally had a picture, we'd cracked the puzzle, had an identifiable sound, something tough that fitted with everything else we were doing.

The newest member of the road crew, Ray Hawkins, remembered the moment – 'the tipping point', he calls it – when everything seemed to change for The Angels.

Ray: The thing about a 'tipping point' is that, at the time, it's just another moment in life, and especially so if you're young, stoned and checking out the chicks at Chequers on a wet Tuesday night surrounded by twenty disinterested punters. It's afterward, and in this case decades later, that I realised what I'd witnessed – the moment where the destiny of a young rock band radically altered its course.

I had met The Angels in Sydney when they had just arrived from Adelaide. They were on a mission to break Sydney, which appealed to my sense of adventure. I got to help out taking money on the door as they gigged around town. That was far from an onerous job because no one came, and no one came because they were shithouse. On stage, Doc's party trick was to turn his back to the audience, as his head swivelled coquettishly around to them, and wiggle his bum. Not good. I remember, and don't resile from, my suggestion to the Brewster brothers that they 'ditch the fucking lead singer'.

Back to Chequers. It happened in a flash. The band suddenly launched . . . no, attacked . . . no, blitzkrieged, into a new song – 'I Ain't The One'.

Doc spat out the incendiary lyrics of the first verse as a stunned crowd looked on.

Ray: In the audience, where I stood shell-shocked, it was a musical miracle. While the blind didn't suddenly see, those few observing the band rushed the stage and those ignoring them became riveted and every head performed an incipient version of what would become the characteristic Angels head thrust. It was pure magic, the epiphany when a band discovered its own unique identity. The Angels sound would be forever determined by the characteristic 'nic nics' of 'I Ain't The One', and its stage persona framed by the menacing and evocative lyricism.

The new band arrived that night at Chequers, an alien creature suddenly plonked into the middle of the room, fully formed and demanding attention, rudely aborted from a body of work that still had its origins rooted in the jug band. No place for stupid arse-wobbling now.

That same night, backstage, Rick wrote a new song, 'Take A Long Line'.

The inner-city new wavers began picking up on the band's metamorphosis, arriving early and dancing manically in front of the stage in white shirts and thin black ties. They were soon joined by tough out-of-work kids from the suburbs. They identified with the dark lyrics, Doc's developing persona and the aggression of the music.

With no airplay it was word of mouth and it wasn't happening in a rush – but it was happening. Once the audience had a taste they were hooked and kept coming back.

On New Year's Eve the band's agent Chris Murphy and offsider Richard McDonald came to see them at the Stagedoor Tavern, near Central Station. The wall of sound smashed into them as they entered. Onstage, among criss-crossing white beams and black shadows Doc hurtled about, arms thrashing, demonic visage, mesmerising. They stood dumbstruck. This was a fun band no more – this was a serious rock 'n' roll outfit extracting very serious audience response.

Murphy and McDonald spoke to the band during their break. Openly gob-smacked at the changes and audience reactions, they announced they'd immediately commence booking them into more prestigious venues and start pushing up their fees.

Using their big bands as leverage ('*We'll give you Dragon if you'll take an Angels date at $500*'), they got to work in January. It was a narrow escape, but The Angels' hard-scrabble days would soon be over.

CHAPTER FOURTEEN
ALBERTS' STUDIO

It was during this period that I first came in contact with The Angels. I'd recently begun promoting gigs at the Stagedoor Tavern. It was a new venue and it was slow going, but the numbers had gradually lifted until there was a regular hundred and fifty or so most Friday and Saturday nights at a two-dollar door charge. There were a lot of deep-cushioned lounges scattered around the bar area in those days and with a dance floor in front of a low stage, it was a nice place to go to for a night out.

I had a friend who was a weekend DJ at 2JJ. He'd seen The Angels somewhere and began championing them. He told me that if I put them on at the Stagedoor, he'd plug the hell out of it. So, sight unseen I booked them, and their first Stagedoor gig was in November 1977 for $250. For that they played four forty-five minute sets from eight to midnight. Two roadies did the load-in – one was called Ashley, the other called Doc, nice guys. I was surprised later on when one of them turned out to be the singer.

Three months later, I was driving through the empty city after visiting some friends. Heading along Market Street I came up behind a four tonner slowing to the red lights at George Street. A Blondie song came on the radio. I was turning it up when a massive shudder shook through the ground and a roar slammed down George Street, followed by a billowing cloud of smoke and dust.

The driver of the truck ahead leapt out of his cab and raced to the corner. I did the same and, when I got there, realised the truckie was Ashley from The Angels. Halfway up the block we saw debris strewn across the empty street and shattered glass smashing onto the footpath. Through the dust and falling rubbish loomed the back of a wrecked garbage truck. 'What the fuck . . .?' People staggered through the haze and then uniformed men poured out of the building. Two came our way yelling, 'Keep clear, keep clear, get back!' On the ground were three inert bodies. Coincidentally, we'd both arrived at the scene of the Hilton Hotel bombing at the same time. Australia's first terrorist attack, it was 13 February 1978.

> **John:** Rick and I were in the studio working with Mark Opitz when that bomb went off. We felt the vibration through the building and heard the bang. Mark raced down to George Street and came back in shock . . .

Ashley and I parked our vehicles against the curb and stood at the corner watching police cars, ambulances and fire-engines arrive with their sirens and flashing lights. As a crowd gathered, asking what had happened, we found ourselves repeating what we'd seen. Blocked by police cars and unable to get any info from the noncommittal cops, we gradually drifted into talking music business. I told him I was no longer promoting the Stagedoor, but now running the band room at the Civic Hotel, which was going gangbusters, and I hoped The Angels would do some gigs there.

He told me the boys had recently played the Bondi Lifesaver to a huge crowd headlined by Billy Thorpe. People were bringing the album up to get signed. Ray Hawkins had become the band's full-time lighting trog. He'd added extra lights to the rig and a fancy lighting desk that could fade or brighten each spotlight. And Woodruff was coming back to Sydney, now that they could afford to pay him again.

Ashley had just come from Alberts where he'd lugged in the instruments for an all-night Angels session. They were working on a new song called 'Comin' Down', to be released as a single in a few weeks. 'There's a young bloke called Mark Opitz helping out,' he said. 'He sorta crept in a few months ago, helping around the place making the coffee, adjusting mics and sitting with George and Harry. He's been watching them working, learning about the mixing console and taping.' He also mentioned AC/DC were back in town recording a new album, and The Angels had to juggle their studio time around theirs.

It was getting late and Ashley had to get some sleep before going back to Alberts in the morning to pick up the band's gear, so we shook hands and went on our way.

Doc was having trouble singing some of the new songs they were recording. He wanted to know more about his vocal range and what he could do with it, how to improve his tone, learn how to warm up his voice, improve his breathing technique. The mentor he chose, John Forest, wasn't your typical vocal coach but had been highly recommended by a friend.

> **Rick:** John Forest invited Doc, me and JB over for a jam and we ended up going there a few times after gigs. We smoked dope and jammed. It was like the old Glenunga days after Moonshine gigs. John Forest was an aging eccentric with a thin lined face and long straggly hair. He bordered on being a dero. He played the ukulele and busked up at the Cross. His voice was shot but he could still hold a tune.
>
> He had a fish tank and knew all his fish by name. We'd get ripped while he talked to them and explained their relationship problems. 'Cyril has been in a bad mood and completely antisocial ever since Milly started hanging out with Adrian . . . he feels inferior because Adrian has those long rainbow fins. Now he spends most of his time under that rock in the corner . . .'
>
> We wrote 'Open That Door' after an all-nighter when Joe the milkman joined us. He was a friend of John Forest's. JB started playing a chord progression on John's Fender Rhodes piano and Joe began singing, 'Open that door, let me in, you got the key . . . baby.' The lyrics just floated in through the window and we all took up the chant. He had a great voice and we jammed on it for hours.

Rick and John's grandfather Hooper Brewster-Jones at the piano, with their father, Arthur. The family legend is that Hooper had perfect pitch and a photographic memory. He could look through an unseen manuscript, close the book, go to the piano and play it note perfect. He was also known for playing simultaneous games of chess blindfolded.

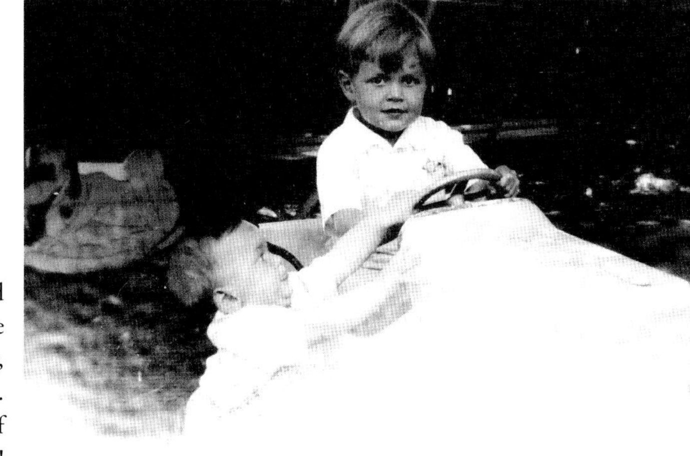

John (on the right) and Rick. After forty-five years of touring together, nothing has changed. John has never let go of the wheel!

The only known photo of the Brewster-Jones family. Left to right: Mem, John, Arthur, Rick and Anne.

John and Rick with their first 'guitars'.

Young Bernie Neeson, as Doc was known then, was keen to play his guitar every chance he got. In 1965, he belonged to the Hideaway Club, a group that used to meet up at St Stephen's church in Elizabeth North. (ALAN HALE)

Moonshine Jug and String Band.
Left to right: Doc (guitar and vocals), Rick (washboard), John (banjo and vocals), Spencer Tregloan (mandolin and vocals) and Pete Thorpe (washtub bass).

Ah, the things a young and ambitious rock band will do to be noticed!

Keystone Angels *TV Guide* pin-up: Rick, John, Doc and Charlie King, the band's first drummer.

Doc, Rick, John and Chris in the dressing room before a gig in 1979. Bitsy, Rick's wife at the time, came to hundreds of gigs and her sharp eye produced many remarkable shots. (BITSY ACKLAND)

Above: Dinner with George Young, Mark Opitz, Fifa Riccobono and Harry Vanda in 1979. 'It hurts to look at this photo,' says John. 'We had the dream team! And we threw it away.' (RICK BREWSTER)

Left: Doc and Mi-Sex singer Steve Gilpin in the dressing room, Council Club, Melbourne, 1979. (RICK BREWSTER)

Doc in Alberts Studio 1 recording the *No Exit* album. (RICK BREWSTER)

Right: John in the control room of the famous Alberts Studio 1, where the band recorded their first three albums, *The Angels*, *Face To Face* and *No Exit*. An unforgettable experience for them. (RICK BREWSTER)

Below: Cloudlands Ballroom, Brisbane, 1980. The front lighting truss gave way during 'Comin' Down On Me'. Rick ran up into the gallery with camera and tripod to shoot the scene. (RICK BREWSTER)

New Year's Day, 1980 – Doc performing to the out of control, rioting crowd at the Opera House. (BITSY ACKLAND)

Doc and Rick at the Opera House. (BITSY ACKLAND)

New Year's Day, 1980, 3 am. Rick and Bitsy return to the scene. The stage is empty, the silence eerie; roadies, ambulances, police and council workers long gone; over 100,000 people melted into the night; a few unconscious bodies sleeping it off; some couples still making out in the bushes. Rick set up his tripod and photographed the carnage left behind. (RICK BREWSTER)

Rick at Strata Inn with Karen and Petra, Sydney's most famous groupies. (CHRIS BAILEY)

Above: Chris and Buzz with girls backstage, Whisky a Go Go, April 1980. (RICK BREWSTER)

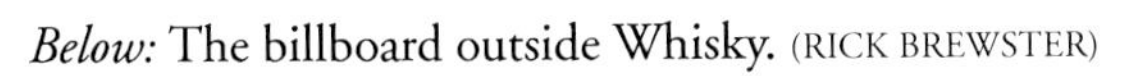

Below: The billboard outside Whisky. (RICK BREWSTER)

Above: John tuning his SG, Whisky a Go Go, with Rick's beloved Epiphone Sheraton in the background. Just two days later, all of John's and Rick's guitars and Chris's basses were lost forever when the truck was stolen in Chicago.
(RICK BREWSTER)

Left: Rick the statue, wearing the 'Walter why have you been lion to me' shirt. It became so well known that fans had it copied and wore it to gigs.
(BITSY ACKLAND)

The queue outside the Paramount Theatre, Seattle, for Angel City, 1980. (RICK BREWSTER)

The band went to see AC/DC in Madison, Wisconsin, September 1980, and met up with Rick Nielsen from Cheap Trick. (RICK BREWSTER)

Rick and Doc take the London Tube, West Brompton, 1980. (BITSY ACKLAND)

Above: Posters at the Bataclan, Paris, 1980. That's John on the right. (RICK BREWSTER)

Left: Chris frisbeeing in Paris. The band (except Doc) used to stop wherever there was a car park, oval or park to frisbee. The rules of etiquette became very complex. (RICK BREWSTER)

Below: Dinner with the record company in Paris – Chris and John soaking it up. (RICK BREWSTER)

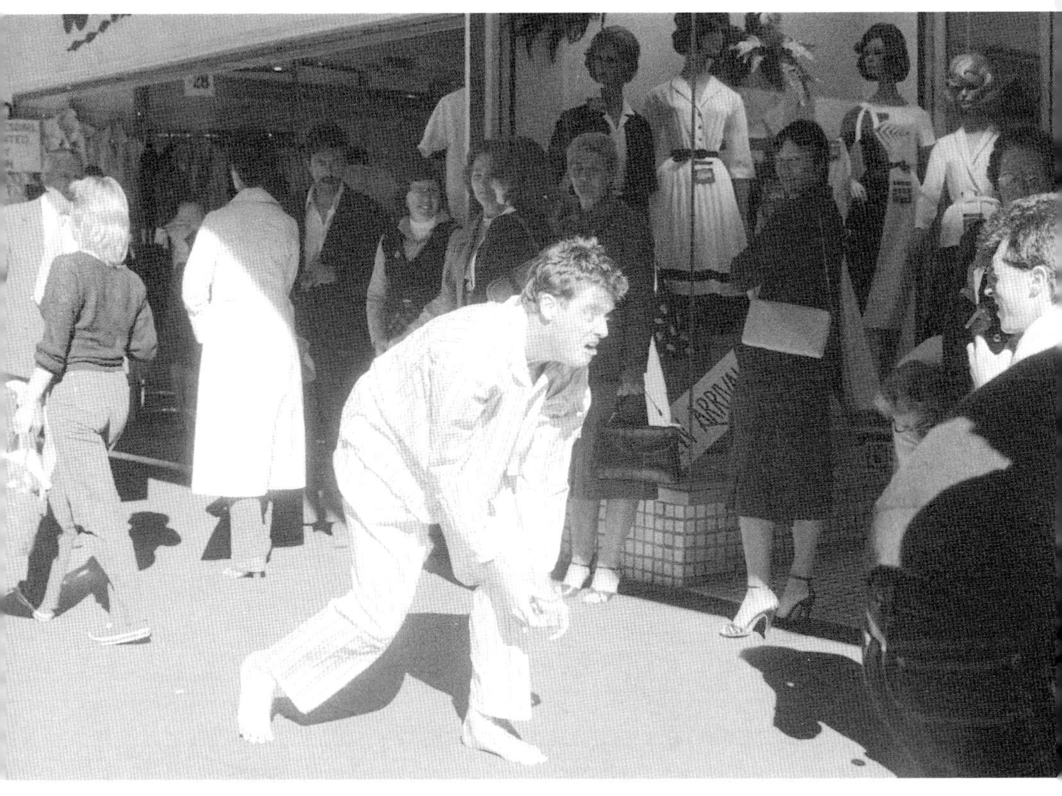

Doc menaces the crowd on George Street, Sydney. 'Face The Day' film clip, 12 August 1980, 9 am. Cameraman Peter Levy on the right. (RICK BREWSTER)

The band later that day. Director Peter Cox on the far right. (BITSY ACKLAND)

Ray Hawkins and John fixing rain lights in the motel room, Detroit, 1980. Ray was dedicated to putting on a theatrical, moody light show and Rick and John often helped him assemble the rain lights, a feature of the No Exit tour.
(RICK BREWSTER)

Doc in Rotterdam with his Super 8 camera.
(RICK BREWSTER)

Above: Rick in the dressing room, Top 10 Club, Hamburg.
(BITSY ACKLAND)

Left: John on the tour bus, Portland Paramount Theatre.
(RICK BREWSTER)

In 1989, the band played at the Whisky a Go Go. Members of Guns N' Roses turned up and joined them onstage for 'Marseilles'. Angry Anderson happened to be there on the night and jumped up for this shot.

Doc busking outside a record store in Rundle Mall, Adelaide, in 1992. (NEWS LTD/NEWSPIX)

2008 – the reunion of the original line-up. (CRAIG PEIHOPA)

2010 – the original line-up gathered for a photo around the grand piano. (CRAIG PEIHOPA)

Symphony of Angels – the original line-up playing with the Adelaide Art Orchestra at the Festival Theatre, Adelaide, April 2010. (CRAIG PEIHOPA)

18 April 2013 – Cold Chisel members join the band onstage at the Chris Bailey benefit concert, Thebarton Theatre, Adelaide. Over $100,000 was raised to help Chris's wife and son. (GARY BRADSHAW)

The current line-up take a bow at Wentworthville Leagues, Sydney, 2015. Left to right: Nick Norton, Rick, Dave Gleeson, John and Sam Brewster. (CRAIG PEIHOPA)

Above: Big Red Bash, Birdsville, 2016. (NICK NORTON)

Left: Rick, John and Sam Brewster at the Bridge Hotel, Sydney, 2017. (TANIA SMITH)

John with sons Tom, Harry and Sam.

John and Sue at
Sam and Lara's wedding.

Rick with his family.
(RICK BREWSTER)

> We went into Alberts that day and finished it. George and Harry loved it. We recorded it but it didn't really fit with where the band was heading. So it got shelved but used later.

All through January, February and March, Ashley lugged the backline up to Alberts' studios after gigs so they'd have it for the next day's writing and demo session. Whenever the band played the Lifesaver, Vanda and Young were prowling around, checking reactions. They could see it was finally underway. They knew that even without radio support the first album was steadily selling. They read the gig reviews appearing in the rock press.

The songs for the new album were coming along well. One night John and Rick were jamming on an A chord and got a groove going. When they took a break, the two non-smokers, Doc and Rick, went into the junk room with an acoustic guitar and started singing 'Looks like it's comin' down on me' over and over on the A chord groove, going full pelt. Rhythm guitarist John yelled, 'Try changing the chords to D on "down on me", then C on the next "down on me".'

After the break the band kept at it and then a chant was added, 'For big brother,' and the rest of the lyrics soon followed. They played the tape to George and Harry a couple of days later. 'Think we've got a hit here,' said George and booked in a date for a full-scale recording.

'Comin' Down' was released on 28 March, but, as with the previous two, it sank without trace.

Mark Opitz had now put in a solid half-year working as an apprentice recording engineer under Vanda and Young. There'd been John Paul Young's international smash hit 'Love Is In The Air', Flash and the Pan's 'Down Among The Dead Men', and he'd been part of the team on AC/DC's just-completed fifth album, *Powerage.*

John and Rick, who had also come through an apprenticeship of sorts under Vanda and Young, had taken a keen interest in the way their first album was recorded and produced, and since then they'd been producing The Angels' demos under George and Harry's guidance.

The Brewsters had a handle on the new style of punter that George and Harry saw flooding into the Lifesaver in Sydney and the cavernous

Bombay Rock in Melbourne, the premium venues in those cities. It wasn't hard to see that a new wave of rock was rolling in. George and Harry hadn't missed the Brewsters' ambition and drive either. The brothers had a work ethic that the migrant lads greatly admired. One afternoon the band was in the studio listening to demos they'd recently recorded. George and Harry motioned to John and Rick to step into the corridor.

John: It was after the failure of 'Comin' Down' to get airplay that George and Harry took Rick and me out into the corridor and announced they wanted us to produce the band. I said, 'How do you do that?', and George said, 'Don't worry, we're just down the hall. Knock on our door any time you need a bit of help.' My heart sank because I thought they'd lost interest and maybe they had. Everything was on a knife-edge after our records had all flopped. George thought we had good ideas and that we should be free to develop them without the constraints of the Vanda/Young sound. He chucked us in at the deep end and I'm eternally grateful!

Back in the studio George officially announced the new arrangement to the rest of the band. Mark Opitz was rostered on as engineer.

John: The feeling of being part of a family at Alberts was overwhelming, particularly through Fifa Riccobono. Fifa was incredible for The Angels. But it was impossible to not be influenced by all the goings-on in that place. We were often in there with AC/DC, and there was the Tatts, JPY and George and Harry.

Having a key to the studio became a major plus for us. Rick and I did a lot of our best work through the night in there. We'd play a gig, then go to the studio, and go home when the sun was up, and do it all again the next night. We were trying out ideas: experimenting, looking for that certain something to give us an edge, to set us apart, creating a style that was distinctively Angels – the way you could instantly recognise the Pistols or AC/DC, Beatles, Stones.

CHAPTER FIFTEEN
BEYOND A SUPPORT BAND

Woodruff arrived back in Sydney in early April 1978, and moved into John and Robyn Brewster's place. He was stunned at the crowds now showing up, and especially at Doc's stage metamorphosis from the gentle Irishman Woody once shared a house with to the manic and intriguing front-man he now portrayed. He was just as stunned to find that the band's fees were lagging way behind their increasing drawing power and made an appointment to see Chris Murphy.

Waiting to be ushered into Murphy's office, he could overhear agents booking Angels dates. He was delighted to hear them pushing up the band's fee (but nowhere near enough in his opinion), but appalled to realise that while one agent was talking to a pub in one suburb, another was booking a date at another pub just up the road for the following weekend. There was no strategy about geographical placement so as not to overexpose them in any one area.

During the meeting with Murphy, it became apparent the agents were just out to make hay while the sun shone. Bands became popular, it was explained, but it only lasted a couple of years before audiences moved on to the next hot favourite. Woodruff came away unsettled and began thinking about how he could do things in a more strategic and business-like manner.

Early in March had come news that 2JJ wanted the band for one of their Tuesday-night studio concerts before a live audience. The station would be giving 'Am I Ever Gonna See Your Face Again' and 'Comin' Down' some serious airplay to promote the gig. Airplay – *finally*!

George Wayne, one of JJ's most popular jocks, dropped into the Bondi Lifesaver to check The Angels out, became an immediate fan, and began playing more tracks from their first album. He managed to get hold of Doc's home phone and rang him every few days for the latest news on recording the new LP.

Two weeks later, when the band arrived at the 2JJ studio for their performance, they discovered hundreds waiting for the doors to open.

The show was broadcast live as they always were. This time, however, the response was so overwhelming that during the following months the station played songs from the concert on a daily basis, most of which were currently being recorded for the new album.

One night Doc was telling George Young about his stage persona and performance ideas he was working on. George said, 'The main thing is to be different and to give the audience something to remember you by.' He laughed, 'You can throw a bucket of fish at them – but whatever you do, make the performance memorable!'

A few days later, taking him at his word, Doc dropped into the Sydney Fish Markets and bought a bucket of fish off-cuts. That night they were playing their first headline with a support band at the Lifesaver.

Doc brought in his bucket wrapped in a black garbage bag, and placed it by the stage. He waited until Rick started into the solo on 'Comin' Down', now a crowd favourite, before reaching down and throwing the fish off-cuts at the audience. Punters recoiled and, unimpressed, began throwing them back. One piece landed on Chris's bass and a few seconds later a fish head splattered between John's guitar strings. The band ground to a halt while John and Chris, equally unimpressed, cleaned up their instruments and the others dodged the rest of the muck being hurled back.

> **Doc:** It didn't go down the way I expected . . . but there was a journalist from one of the papers there and next day he wrote the whole thing up. George was right – it got us noticed!

On Sunday 28 May, The Angels assembled in the wings of the stage at St Leonards Park for a 2JJ outdoor concert. The station was recording the gig on sixteen-track tape to play the live tracks on-air after the show. Cold Chisel, yet to record their first album, had opened the concert and received polite applause from the estimated eight to ten thousand sitting quietly on the grass out front. George Wayne strode to the microphone and asked the audience to put their hands together for the hottest new band in Sydney – and as one, they cheered and whistled. By the end of The Angels' set the whole crowd were on their feet, and for their last song, 'Am I Ever Gonna See Your Face Again', to the band's amazement, some sang along to the chorus.

> **John Brewster:** The JJ airplay we got in the lead up to that concert was what really got the ball rolling. We were arriving at gigs to find a queue waiting to get in – to see us! And then we did the concert and just brained them. Doc was incredible that day on the big stage. He'd discarded the leather jacket and bought a second-hand blue sports jacket and was wearing a white shirt and a loosely tied tie. Some of the English new wave bands had that look; Elvis Costello for one. The reaction we got was the best yet. And Keith Walker did such a great job recording the set that we mixed one of the songs down, 'Live It Up', and put it on *Face To Face* as a live performance track.

Three weeks later, on 17 June, they hit the road with Meat Loaf, opening for him at Sydney's Hordern Pavilion. Earlier in the year promoter Paul Dainty had announced he was to tour Meat Loaf – and offered The Angels the support slot for every concert in the country. Meat Loaf had released *Bat Out Of Hell* the previous year and it had been a runaway success in Australia.

The Angels were now so popular in Sydney it was ludicrous to consider them a support band. But as the tour moved on to other cities, it gave swathes of new punters the opportunity to see what the fuss was all about, and they won over new fans by the thousand.

The headliner might have been jealous of the reaction they were getting, but Meat Loaf was doing a roaring business with his own fabulous show and had nothing to worry about. He'd spent years on the road playing every shithole across America before recording *Bat Out Of Hell.*

Meat Loaf was a gentleman, embracing The Angels as fellow musicians, and the backstage camaraderie ran high. In Adelaide the boys unwittingly moved into his dressing room, happy to see the promoter had laid on a bowl of fruit and a fridge of drinks for the hometown band. As they started into the goodies, the tour manager arrived and demanded they get the fuck out, they were in Meat Loaf's room. As it happened, the big man was chatting with someone in the corridor and came sailing in. 'Hey, you listen, Mister! Don't you talk to these guys like that! If they wanna be in here, you leave 'em alone, ya hear me. I'll change out in the corridor.' He winked at them and closed the door as he left.

> **John Brewster:** Meat Loaf did two sold-out concerts everywhere we played. We got back to Sydney and it was completely crazy. It was a month before the release of *Face To Face*, and every gig we did was a sellout. It didn't matter what night of the week it was.

On 3 July 'Take A Long Line' was released. 2JJ had now been playing Angels songs for months, but Sydney's commercial stations, including the biggest, 2SM, still refused to touch them. No other major radio station in the country was playing them either. In a cunning move, Fifa had a 'white label' single made up, with the name of the song the only information available. She arranged an appointment with Barry Chapman, 2SM's program director, and took in a couple of other artists' releases as well. Fifa pulled out The Angels' single and asked if he'd like to give her an opinion on the song. 'It's by a new band,' she said. Chapman put it on, leaned back and grinned, 'It's AC/DC! This one goes straight onto high rotation!' It was only when she'd got him to confirm he'd put it to air that she revealed the name of the artist. But Barry was 'in', and the song exploded onto Sydney's airwaves and went straight into the local charts.

CHAPTER SIXTEEN
CHANGING THE GAME

I was about to sit down to dinner with my wife when there was a knock on the door. Standing in the dusk were four guys who had never paid me a visit before: John Woodruff, who I'd only recently met; Rod Willis, an agent at Solo-Premier who also managed Cold Chisel; Richard McDonald, another agent from Solo-Premier; and Ray Hearn, manager of Flowers, who had a Wednesday night residency at the Civic Hotel and were also regulars at the two other venues I was running. The four of them shuffled around and said they'd like a chat – it wouldn't take long. And so I became the first pub promoter to be briefed by the men behind the newest management and booking agency, Dirty Pool Management Pty Ltd.

The company had been conceived by Hearn and Woodruff a couple of months previously after Woodruff realised he'd have to take control of The Angels' bookings if he was to manage their soaring career effectively. Ray had big ambitions for Flowers and wanted to take control of their fee structure and bookings too. Willis was invited onboard due to his and Chisel's old Adelaide connections – and because the band was gaining a loyal following and had recently signed to WEA Records. Along the way, the managers had head-hunted Richard, offering him the job of in-house booking director.

They explained that they'd left Solo-Premier, and from now on they'd be booking direct. They produced contracts with their new letterhead covering the dates I had with their bands. We all shook hands and they were on their way to the next promoter.

The era of Dirty Pool Management had begun. Over the next few years it would become a powerhouse in the music industry, developing a multi-million-dollar business, representing The Angels, Cold Chisel, Mental As Anything, Divinyls, Icehouse (formerly Flowers) and INXS, among others. Dirty Pool would singlehandedly change the way band business was done in Australia.

> **Doc:** We were finding ourselves in situations where agents were not getting the best deals for the band, they were getting the best deal for themselves. Sometimes ripping us off. And there were constant stuff-ups. We were getting sent along to dinner dances – we'd play all our soft songs in the first half hour and then we'd have to go home, because we'd have blown the walls out. Other things like the agent offering three bands to a promoter, even if he only wanted The Angels. Tricky stuff. So John Woodruff, Ray Hearn and ourselves set up an organisation that changed all that, booking the band into the right venues that would best showcase us in front of our kind of audience.

Dirty Pool was the first to introduce legally binding performance contracts. Up to then, an agency simply sent a confirmation of a booking made with a venue organiser. If the band was lucky, the agency would provide a worksheet, with access and technical details for the crew, and performance times for the band. Sometimes there might be additional info such as other bands on the bill and contact details. But it was rarely a contract legally committing a venue to the band's performance. Last-minute cancellations, or gig 'blow-outs', would happen and the band had no recourse.

One of the last of Solo-Premier's bookings Dirty Pool honoured after they established themselves was a three-night stand at Cronulla Leagues Club for The Angels. The fee per night was $400, less $40 agency commission, a net $360 to the band per night.

Fresh off the Meat Loaf tour, The Angels did three huge nights and the club made a multi-thousand-dollar killing while the band, now one of the most popular in Sydney and comprising five members, four crew, truck, tons of equipment, plus a manager, ended up with $1080 after agency commissions.

Things had to change, and they certainly did, but not before the Dirty Pool foursome had endured high drama and serious threats from vested interests, who were determined to keep the old status quo.

The Melbourne scene had been the worst, often with three layers of fees being skimmed off a band's fee before they got what was left. As Dirty Pool's agency front-man, Richard McDonald was regularly threatened.

> **Richard McDonald:** I got sent an elaborate funeral wreath by one mafia type in Melbourne. I was regularly threatened with having my kneecaps smashed and often had heavies who'd been dealt out of the equation come up to me at gigs where our bands were playing and push me around. Others would try to get me to step outside for a minute to 'talk things over'.

Pub promoters were threatened by the major agencies that had once represented the Dirty Pool bands, that if they dealt with Dirty Pool they wouldn't get any more bands from them. That caused a few problems, but it wasn't very effective. The good promoters ran venues that everyone wanted to play, and a phone call to the bands concerned soon brought that behaviour to a finish.

It was the big licensed clubs that continued to be a problem. Dirty Pool introduced the concept of door deals. They started selling the Angels for a guaranteed fee against 75 per cent of the door takings, whichever was the greater. It was a fair way to do business and most of the pub managers went along with it. If the band pulled a big crowd, they were rewarded for it. But the boards of the licensed clubs couldn't get their heads around the possibility that they'd be paying out thousands of dollars to some rock band they regarded as a bunch of no-hopers.

> **Richard:** Some of the meetings I had with club boards were unbelievable. I wanted to book The Angels back into the Cronulla Leagues Club after they'd sold out three nights at a $400 fee per night previously. At a new deal of three bucks out of four to the band, the club were looking at paying them something like two grand per night. That was big bucks for a band that they'd paid $400 a night for only months previously and they wouldn't come at it. Eventually their own club manager brought to their attention the massive money the bar had taken the last time Angels played there and they came back with a counter offer.
>
> I spent hours arguing with those idiots and eventually they began caving in. But then it got petty and they said they'd only agree to the new deal as long as the crew wore clean white overalls when they were setting up so as not to disturb the regulars with the t-shirts and dirty shorts and jeans they usually wore. I rang Ashley right there in front of them. The directors could hear the laughter and derision coming out of the phone.

A funny thing happened with that gig. To make as much as they could, the club management packed in as many as they could. Dirty Pool had a guy on the door with a sheep counter making sure there was no funny business with the final number count, so that was okay.

The next night they packed even more in. During the show, the punters were jumping so hard that it was estimated the centre of the room was moving up and down eighteen inches. The venue was on the first floor, and down below, chandeliers started breaking loose and one fell onto the board-room table where a meeting was taking place. Staff had to evacuate the poker-machine gamblers out to the car park. The manager of the club raced up to the room where The Angels were playing and pulled the power. Naturally the audience went berserk. John Brewster came offstage yelling at him to switch it back on or the place would be destroyed. The manager eventually agreed to, provided they only played 'slow songs'.

They got back up and in fury blasted out 'Take A Long Line', followed by 'Comin' Down', which almost literally did bring the house down on them. Richard, Woody and the roadies ended up holding the manager back while he was trying to throw the switches again.

Everyone was praying for the band to finish, and when they did they went back out for an encore which took the place right off the chaos scale. The manager could see that his club would be taken apart if he pulled the plug now. When it was over, they found him sprawled back in a chair, a shaking emotional wreck.

Needless to say the band was barred from ever playing there again, but that didn't matter – everyone else wanted them.

Cronulla Leagues Club wasn't the only one reluctant to sign a Dirty Pool contract. Many was the time that the person at the venue responsible for signing couldn't be contacted – of course, this before the era of mobile phones and email – or they made themselves uncontactable, due to not wanting to take responsibility. Richard would ring the venue on the morning of the show to tell them that, as a signed contract hadn't been received, the band's road crew had been told not to leave for the gig until further notice.

Dirty Pool introduced another tweak to the Aussie rock 'n' roll biz: the sheep counter. Available at sports stores it was a small, chrome, hand-held clicker that counted up to 1000. The observer only had to stand at the door with clicker in hand and click it each time someone went in, then match it up with the numbered stubs the venue's ticket-seller had at the end of the night. Sometimes it might be a few counts out, but in most cases it effectively stopped the rorting.

One infamous publican who ran a big venue near Sydney's Central Station got up to all sorts of tricks with door deals. He'd get friendly with the clicker person early in the evening and ply them with free drinks and chat with them incessantly. It wouldn't be long before they were half-pissed and getting confused about who was going in and who was coming back out. And then they'd need to take a toilet break. The good-natured ticket-selling door girl would offer to keep clicking the sheep counter as each new punter bought a ticket. Unbeknown to the clicker person, she was the publican's girlfriend and only clicked in half a dozen while the observer was away. Those tricks would go on throughout the night. It was just a game and he'd often brag about it, so the word got out. He was a rogue, everyone knew it, but he was always generous with his high-quality marijuana and liberally passed it around among the bands and their crews. When the roadies finished loading out at dawn, he'd often shout them breakfast at Sweethearts up in the Cross.

As Dirty Pool's bands grew in drawing power, so did the amount of cash taken over a typical weekend. By the early eighties, with every band in the stable drawing capacity audiences, Richard often found himself with a fortune in cash under his bed ready for banking on a Monday morning.

Richard: What is truly amazing is that there was never a robbery of a hotel or club during any of our bands' gigs. A criminal gang only had to look up where The Angels, Cold Chisel, Divinyls, INXS or Icehouse was playing and they'd know that the place would be awash in cash. All they had to do was mingle with the punters and watch. They'd soon work out where the office was.

It was normal to just step into the manager's office afterwards, count the money, sign for it and walk out. Meanwhile the bar managers would be walking in with their takings, and we're talking serious money for the times. All they had to do was walk in, point a gun, and we'd have given it to them. But it never happened. I guess we were just lucky – we didn't have armed guards watching out for us.

John: We played at the Manly Vale Hotel after the band had hit the big time. Dirty Pool called the publican and advised him to take out all the tables and chairs, because the audience would be over the top. He said, 'Don't tell me how to run my hotel.' After the show to nearly 2000 punters I was standing on the stage surveying the carnage. There wasn't a table or chair in one piece, the false ceiling over the bar was wrecked because fans had climbed onto it and fallen through, and the floor was a bed of broken glass and blood-soaked thongs. Then the publican made a bee-line to me and I said as he got close, 'Sorry about the damage.' Holding up a cash register print-out, he said, 'Damage, what damage? This is my bar take. When can I get you guys back?'

CHAPTER SEVENTEEN
FACE TO FACE

12 August 1978. Exactly a year after the first album came out, Alberts released *Face To Face*. This time every star and planet in the universe was aligned for The Angels. The single 'Take A Long Line' went racing up the 2SM charts and into their top ten. Nationally it went to #29 and remained in the national charts for twenty-nine weeks. Radio loved the entire LP and right from the start, most tracks received heavy airplay. When *Face To Face* finally dropped out of the national charts, it had been in there for a year and a half.

During that time, every song would etch itself deep into the psyche of a whole generation of young Australians. They'd become so familiar with the lyrics that audiences of thousands would sing along word perfect at every gig. They'd study Peter Ledger's artwork for which he'd win the *TV Week* award for 'Best Album Cover Design' the following year. Fans would read the liner notes, hoping to dig deeper into this mystery group of young aliens in tight black t's and jeans and wraparound shades, whose front-man wore formal suits and performed like a man possessed. They'd gaze at Doc stepping out of the mirror on the cover with a hand outstretched – then they'd turn it over and stare at his back receding into the mirror and wonder about him, where he'd come from, where he was going to. Inside were photos taken by celebrated rock photographer Philip Morris that were closely scrutinised.

The songs were listed as Brewster/Neeson/Brewster, an agreement that the core of the band had made between themselves way back, no matter who actually wrote the song. Much of the essence of the B/N/B lyrics came from the influence of Bob Dylan's work: they wanted lyrics and melodies that would remain timeless. It was a conscious strategy they'd all agreed on since the beginning of the songwriting partnership.

Buzz Bidstrup would debate with them about how The Angels could be made more radio friendly and get more airplay. This created tensions within the band during recording sessions. Doc, Rick and John wanted airplay, but only on their terms. They wanted to go with their gut feelings and write for themselves.

It would be decades before the credits were rewritten to reflect how the album actually came about, but production credits on *Face To Face* remain as: Mark Opitz and The Angels. However, it was actually produced by John and Rick, with Opitz engineering, as per the agreement they had with Vanda and Young, who remained as executive producers.

CHAPTER EIGHTEEN
DAVID BOWIE TOUR

When promoter Paul Dainty signed up David Bowie for his first Australian tour, he put forward a number of bands to open the shows. After watching film clips and listening to albums, Bowie picked The Angels. He then insisted they be billed as 'special guests' and it was Bowie who instructed his crew to give them every assistance with lights and sound and stage space.

The gates opened for the start of the tour at the Adelaide Oval on a sunny afternoon and thousands raced across the grass to grab a spot as close to the stage as possible. There were no seats, just standing room only.

As it got close to show-time, a golden sunset threw shadows across the jostling crowds and into the backstage bustle where The Angels had a furnished marquee of their own.

> John Brewster: During our soundcheck Bowie was sitting on the lawn watching us. I didn't recognise him, but as we left the stage he came round and met us and said, 'Welcome to my tour . . . I really like your music. Please join us for dinner.' Bowie paid us a compliment for our music – wow!

At 7.30 the hometown boys opened the hottest concert to hit Adelaide since the Stones had played Memorial Drive in 1973. Doc confidently prowled along the lip looking like a riverboat gambler in Ascot tie, puffed white shirt, elastic armbands and waistcoat. Behind, three desperados in wraparound shades and black leather jackets toted guitars like cut-down shotties and Buzz pounded along like the cavalry behind them. Even though the audience were there to see the Thin White Duke, The Angels went over a storm – hardly a surprise because *Face To Face* was by now double platinum (platinum = 50,000 units) and the band was now the number-one drawcard at their own gigs all over the country.

James Ivens was there and became a lifelong fan.

> **James Ivens:** After thirty-seven years, I can still visualise standing on the oval close to the front of the stage on that balmy night. I guess I was young, impressionable and twenty years old, and travelling in from the country to see this concert was really exciting. The smell of marijuana drifted through the air as Lou Reed's 'Take A Walk On The Wild Side' blasted out of the sound system just before The Angels came out. They were the consummate professionals – tight and punchy. It was the first time I saw them and I don't remember half the songs they played, but they were so cool and belonged on that home-crowd stage.

Bowie's drummer, Dennis Davis, played the first gig using his full drum set-up – he had fifteen drums and nearly as many cymbals – but after watching Buzz play his modest kit, Dennis had his stripped down to basics for the remainder of the tour.

> **John Brewster:** We watched David Bowie from side of stage every night. What a superb artist – what a band! The camaraderie between us and Bowie's band on that tour was amazing.

David and his band repaid the compliment and came early to each show to watch their support act. They even went to the Bondi Lifesaver to see The Angels the night after the first Sydney Showground concert, rocking down the front with the rest of the punters. Rick watched Bowie's shows too. He singled out guitarist Adrian Belew for special attention, in awe of his playing.

Rick: I spied Adrian before one of the Sydney shows and told him how much I admired his playing: 'How the fuck do you do that?' He said, 'It's easy. Come and I'll show you.' I followed him into a small caravan and sat next to him on a single bed. He grabbed his guitar and played a few licks, 'None of it's mine. It's just tricks and Jimi Hendrix did it all before me. I don't believe in being protective about knowledge and techniques – it should be shared. No one else will use it the same way as me . . .' It was a valuable lesson and I've never forgotten it when I get asked, 'How do you play that riff?' As soon as I got home that night I set about writing 'Save Me' and applying my newfound technique into the solo. We recorded the song soon after for the *No Exit* album.

The tour finished with two open-air concerts at the Sydney Showgrounds – 20,000 attending each one. The Angels were on home territory. The ground-swell roar of welcome when they came on could be heard in every suburb surrounding the grounds. 'Take A Long Line' was getting saturation airplay and *Face To Face* was now on its way to triple-platinum sales. For the encore both nights, the band returned to do a beautiful rendition of 'Be With You'.

Next day – and the following three – The Angels were back at Alberts working on demos for the new album. There was to be no let-up in the forward trajectory of this band.

John: As summer came on that year you could step outside on a warm still evening and you'd hear *Face To Face* being played at someone's suburban backyard barbecue. What a huge year 1978 was for us, with much more to come . . .

CHAPTER NINETEEN
RECORDING *NO EXIT*

In a period of eighteen months The Angels had emerged from relative obscurity and become the biggest band in the country. The well-oiled Dirty Pool machinery had been a vital part of the equation, allowing the band to concentrate on the creative side. Band members believed that the business side was best left to management, albeit with regular band/ management meetings. At the heart of the success were the original songs, the musicians' virtuosity and the performances they delivered night after night.

At the time *Face To Face* was released and Dirty Pool established, industry gossip was that they'd have a good year or two and then begin to fade from overexposure and lack of staying power – as so many before them had. As it was, things had just kept snowballing.

Face To Face had now reached triple-platinum status. With the widespread taping of albums onto cassettes to be played in cars, it was estimated that over 250,000 copies were in circulation. You'd only have to stand in the car park after an Angels gig to hear *Face To Face* blast off every tape-deck to be aware of that. There were also reports that a couple of thousand had been shipped over to a chain of Los Angeles record shops but no one would confirm that one.

With the airplay *Face To Face* was getting, Alberts wanted new product on the market as soon as possible. John and Rick moved into Studio C, the small demo studio on one of the lower floors. Compared to the months it took to record *Face To Face*, this time they had their nic-nics, and their confidence and ease in the studio was well established. But they'd been so busy on the road that there weren't enough completed songs, although they had plenty of musical ideas to try out.

> **Rick:** Alberts made their demo studio available and it became a home away from home for a while. First up, John and I started messing around with chords and phrasing on 'Save Me', which was only half-completed, and one of us started doing that 'dooten bah!' 'dooten bah!' 'dooten bah!' riff, while the other one held the chord 'bah!' 'bah!' 'bah!' . . . 'bahbup!' And you get this shift every time it comes up – which was pretty cool and a jump forward for us.

It became another distinctive aspect of the band's style.

The Angels were still slotting in gigs between these sessions. While in Adelaide playing two nights at the Arkabah Hotel and holed up in their rooms one rainy afternoon, Doc presented John with lyrics for 'Can't Shake It'. John got out his acoustic guitar and started strumming chords as the two of them chanted the lyrics. Later, with the rest of the band, they worked it up in the empty venue downstairs and performed it that night for the first time. Next morning they flew back to Sydney and recorded it. The funny noise ('mee-op') at the beginning is Mark Opitz switching on the tape a few seconds after the guitars began playing. The take had so much magic that it was kept.

Since Rick had suggested 'No Exit' as a name for the album, ideas began occurring to John for a song of the same name as he was playing onstage at gigs. Back in Studio C one night, he spliced together some words, along with a few lines from Doc's notebook. Rick came up with the music and a new Brewster/Neeson/Brewster classic was created.

> **John:** We were using a loop of George Young playing a simple rock beat on the drums. We would speed it up or slow it down to the tempo we wanted, then write the song, usually words and music.

A guitar jam on a chord progression and melody with Rick on a Hammond organ using his classical training morphed into the beautiful 'Out Of The Blue'. As he was playing, Doc and John jostled phrases and words into lyrics for it.

Another song that got its finishing touches in Studio C was 'Mr Damage'. After a gig at the Comb and Cutter hotel in Sydney's western suburbs, Rick was talking to a group of fans when a huge tatt-covered and heavily scarred bikie pushed in and thrust his hand out to be shaken. 'G'day, mate, Damage. How ya goin'?'

Driving home that night he couldn't get the dangerous image of Damage off his mind.

> **Rick:** There was a hit by Plastic Bertrand that I really liked, sung in one note at a punk-style pace with chords moving around beneath it. I really wanted to write something similar for The Angels. As I drove, I had this one-note melody running through my head and I'm belting a beat on the steering wheel and the lyrics started to form around the guy: 'dadada with the king and queen, trying dadada with their regime . . . waiting for . . . Mr Damage!' I stayed up till morning on it and presented it to the band next night at the Stagedoor Tavern.

After more work with John and Doc in the studio, the band rehearsed it, Chris and Buzz adding their own flourishes as it was recorded. 'Ivory Stairs' was another that came out of a session in Studio C. The music was written mainly by John, with lyrics from Doc's notebooks. John thought it needed an extra section and added the 'You found the door' breakdown in the middle. Once the recording session started, Rick came up with the fluid and unforgettable solo.

The single 'Shadow Boxer' was released on 28 May ahead of the *No Exit* launch and began a steady climb up the national charts. The song came about after John had watched a drunk throwing punches at a 'No Standing' sign in Kings Cross one night. Next day, Doc was at John's house and, between them, they completed the lyrics.

With *No Exit* recorded and in the system for manufacture, Alberts and their distributor EMI sprang into action with pre-publicity. Advance orders soon topped 20,000, guaranteeing gold status on release.

*

There was another aspect to the *No Exit* sessions that the band didn't mention in interviews: nitrous oxide. They'd got into laughing gas through a medical student friend. He used to lie in bed on his days off wearing a mask attached to a cylinder of nitrous, and flick it on and off from time to time. Rick bought a box of cream whippers from a supermarket. They came with small cylinders of nitrous and he'd been passing them around backstage at gigs.

He came to grief one night when he, John and Ray Hawkins and their ladies attended a puppet play. It was at a small theatre and they sat along the back row. The lights went down, the show commenced and Ray and Rick started passing the nitrous cylinders.

> **Rick:** You could hear a pin drop and the hissing of the cream whippers throughout the first half drew outraged glares. It also drew the attention of the management, and in the interval Ray and I felt a tap on the shoulder. We turned to see two cops who invited us to join them in the foyer with our cream whippers. I explained that it was just a cheap thrill, a harmless gas and legal. I told them that the whippers were normally very quiet and the noise was because one of the seals was leaking. They made a call and to their disgust were told that we couldn't be arrested for using nitrous oxide. They let us return for the second half – 'But no more sucking on those things!'

Once the recording sessions got underway, Rick rang CIG, the gas company, and ordered an industrial bottle of nitrous. When he showed up to collect it, the guy said, 'We need to register what you want it for.' Rick had been given a heads up on this one. 'We're working on a drag-racing engine,' he explained. 'We need to run it and get it tuned.' 'No worries,' said the guy and wrote it into his book.

Back in the studio the musos would line up at the start of a session taking turns at cradling it. 'Oh mighty bottle,' they'd say, put their lips around the rubber teat and release a lungful of pure nitrous oxide. Doc chipped a tooth when trying to get a hit one night.

> **Rick:** Nitrous oxide is an inert gas. If taken straight it fools the brain into thinking it's getting oxygen, but in fact you're basically suffocating yourself. All

> of a sudden things start to go dark, and for about ten seconds you experience some sort of revelation and the answer to everything is revealed. Then you recover and return to normal.

It was a good studio drug. It wasn't like marijuana, which could affect you for hours; with nitrous, your clarity came back immediately. They started treating it a little more warily when they found themselves sometimes face down on the far side of the room after a few too many hits.

CHAPTER TWENTY
NO EXIT SHOOT

The cover of *No Exit* was photographed by rock shutter-man Philip Morris. Rick watched him at work, deftly going about his craft with innate artistry. Picking up on his interest, Philip invited him back to his studio and darkroom to observe the process of bringing the shoot to fruition.

As he had with Vanda and Young at Alberts, Rick soaked it all up, eventually taking Philip's advice and buying a Nikkormat FT2, a top-of-the-range single-lens reflex camera, and launched himself into what would become a serious lifelong hobby.

> **Philip Morris:** I'd done all the photos for the inside sleeve of *Face To Face*, which the band were very happy with. So John Woodruff asked me to come up with a location to illustrate the 'trapped-no-way-out feel' of one of the songs on *No Exit*.
>
> I remembered a recent Aussie movie *Newsfront*, produced by David Elfick, that really impressed me. The actor Bill Hunter is seen walking down a long tunnel that to me was very claustrophobic. I thought it was perfect and, after a few enquiries, found it was the tunnel leading to the morgue at Royal Prince Alfred Hospital, Sydney.

The shoot had to be late at night, when the tunnel wasn't in use. To add to the trapped-no-way-out feel, Philip hired a Hasselblad

Superwide, a camera with an extremely wide-angle lens. This camera featured no distortion, which meant Doc could be placed close in the foreground, with the other band members spaced out behind. Two nights were planned to get the shoot done. On the first, the band arrived at midnight. Polaroids were shot and discussions held on how to improve the look of the tunnel, and the best ways to position the band. The 'look' the Superwide gave was distinctive and one the band was pleased with.

Philip had enlisted lighting tech extraordinaire Brian Bansgrove, who'd also worked on *Newsfront*. With great disruption to staff and public, they hosed the walls and ceiling of the tunnel to give it a gleam. Brian then lit the tunnel from behind, using wooden makeshift bars, and shone a huge spot from the ceiling covered in blue gels. From time to time patients who hadn't made it would be wheeled past to the morgue, which only added to the sombre mood of the final photo.

Philip: With a little retouching on Doc's eyes to make them stand out more, the cover was produced and became my most loved album jacket.

In late June, a week after *No Exit* was released, The Angels performed its official release at a two-night stand sponsored by 2SM at the stately old Elizabethan Theatre in inner-city Newtown. It was an 'all-ages' event, and tickets were given away on-air via competitions. Both shows would be recorded by Mark Opitz and then spliced into a single tape featuring the best of the performances. A few nights later, 2SM and thirty affiliate stations would broadcast it around the country.

The band's original plan was to open the shows with Doc descending to the stage on a trapeze wire from the ceiling, but theatre management vetoed that one. He then discovered a trapdoor in the centre of the stage and made arrangements with staff to have him rise up through it after the band had come on and begun playing.

All afternoon before the first show, punters, mainly young girls, queued for the standing-room tickets the theatre had agreed to release. There was a petrol strike on but that wasn't affecting demand. A convoy of coaches was making its way down from Newcastle full of ticket winners from radio 2NX, where 'Shadow Boxer' was top ten and advance sales of *No Exit* had sent it straight to #1 on release.

The band got off to a nervous start. This was not a raging alcohol-fuelled audience in a pub and it took a while to adjust, but they soon found their pace. Many were too young to have experienced 'Angelmania' in the pubs and were overawed by the ferocious energy coming off the stage. For the mostly younger fans in the theatre, this was nothing like the Sherbet concerts they'd seen in their teenybopper years.

There was a reception at the Argyle Tavern after the show, where a whole lot of media people who weren't in the seats allocated to them miraculously arrived to guzzle the free booze. The Angels lined up under the lights to be awarded platinum records for *Face To Face* and gold records for *No Exit,* a rare feat for an album in the shops for just a week.

Doc made a gentlemanly speech, then popped a balloon of helium gas and inhaled a lungful. It made his voice go squeaky and everyone laughed.

A few days later they were on tour again and rumbling into the north-coast towns of New South Wales and onwards to Queensland, as *No Exit* moved to number eight on the album charts, drenching the airwaves with a new batch of Angels songs.

The punishing 'Closing In' tour of over seventy dates arrived in Melbourne and the band prepared for the gig at La Trobe University on 13 September. It would be a major promotion – and another opportunity to continue consolidating the southern market. A lot of money had been spent on extra staging, and a gigantic concert PA – usually reserved for the top overseas acts – was being erected.

Ross Stapleton, writing in Adelaide's *Roadrunner* magazine, had this to say:

> The effect of the special staging before 3000 hysterical punters at La Trobe was to provide an awesome aural and visual feast. I have never seen a more professionally mounted show by an Australian band. The lights performed their

> usual magic under the guidance of Ray Hawkins. He has perfected a standard of lighting against which all other local acts must now compete. The same for the sound by maestro Ashley Swinfield.
>
> The red-hot set by the band made it the most stimulating and satisfying gig I've yet encountered with The Angels. As the power rhythm exploded into 6000 ears, the might and control of those crackling riffs had people shaking their heads and raising fists. If there are any die-hard Angels knockers still left after seeing the band that night, they should hang their heads in shame!

With *No Exit* poised to take The Angels to a new level, Angus Young's parting words to Rick when AC/DC had left for the UK fifteen months before were beginning to ring true: 'We won't be back till we've cracked it overseas – it's all clear for you guys now!'

CHAPTER TWENTY-ONE
LEAVING ALBERTS

Since his return, John Woodruff had been voicing his displeasure with the deal the band had signed with Alberts. He'd approached Ted Albert on numerous occasions about renegotiating but Ted's answer was always the same: John, let's talk about it after we're ahead in the investment we've made.

Ted had been unimpressed when he'd discovered that Woodruff had left the country right at the time Alberts had signed The Angels. He knew the band had been left in the lurch after the loose arrangement with Peter Rix fell through, and he hadn't forgotten John Brewster asking him for the $10,000 advance so they could pay their bills.

As Ted saw it, Woodruff had re-emerged only after The Angels had completely reinvented themselves. Without any help from him, they'd scrabbled out of near annihilation and built an audience generating enough income to pay him a management fee and pick up where he'd left off. Their breakthrough while he was away was a direct result of talent, hard work, Albert Productions and the canny mentoring of George Young.

After setting up Dirty Pool and the successes that quickly followed, Woodruff became more emboldened: 'I went to see Ted a million times but he intimidated me – he reminded me of my father.'

Part of his gripe with Alberts was understandable. They had no international release plan in place for The Angels, and it was only when Woodruff suggested he'd go to LA and work on getting one that Ted offered to do what he'd done for AC/DC's manager Michael Browning: fund an apartment and phone for him in America.

> **John Woodruff:** To me, the US was the be all and end all. We didn't have a release anywhere outside of Australia and New Zealand. Alberts seemed to be far more interested in getting AC/DC heard overseas than The Angels, so I went over and lived in LA until I got a deal.

What Woody didn't acknowledge was that AC/DC were two albums ahead of his band. Alberts' masterplan, of which he was aware, was to funnel The Angels into the same pipeline that Browning was adroitly opening for AC/DC – first in the UK and Europe, and then into the States. But Woodruff was too impatient for that.

Arriving in LA, he started calling every record company in the book and eventually landed a deal with CBS/Epic that included financial tour support and a hefty advance. Of course, Epic first rang CBS Australia to get the lowdown on The Angels in their home market. CBS Australia's recently installed boss was the ambitious Paul Russell, a rising star in the company, who'd previously been based in the head office in New York. He'd been sent out to Australia to gain experience prior to his next big promotion.

'The Angels?' Russell had yelled down the line. 'Are you kidding me? They're the hottest act in Australia!' He immediately went to work pulling strings to ensure that any deal the American label offered to the band included the proviso that they also sign to CBS Australia.

The Angels had one more year left on their Alberts contract, with one more LP to deliver. Recording sessions were already being planned for early 1980 for an album release mid-year. They'd then be free to sign with Epic, collect their advance and begin recording for them.

But Woodruff couldn't wait that long. He discussed with the band the benefits of doing a worldwide deal with the Americans and the higher royalties on offer. He also mentioned he'd be taking a 20 per cent management fee out of the advance – as per the agreement he already had with the band.

> **John Brewster:** We'd had a long relationship with Woody, and despite the fact that he'd abandoned us at such a critical time we held him in awe in many respects. Certainly since he'd set up Dirty Pool he'd had an incredible impact on the band's business, and hadn't put a foot wrong. At the time we were flat out holding our end up being the creatives and performers, and he'd been flat out looking after our management and business. We trusted him implicitly with that side of our career. So when he laid it on us that Alberts were short-changing us and we should go with the much better deal that Epic offered, well, we didn't feel good about leaving, but he presented the whole scenario in such a way that we said, 'Yeah, okay, John, if you think this is the way to go, then let's do it.'

With the Epic deed of understanding in his briefcase, Woodruff marched into Ted's walnut-panelled office one morning accompanied by high-powered American music-biz attorney Owen Sloane, over from Los Angeles especially. Before tea and biscuits were served, Woodruff took a deep breath and announced that The Angels were breaking their contract with Alberts.

Absolutely gobsmacked, Ted's first reaction was to call in George and Harry.

> **John Woodruff:** I was intimidated by them and I didn't handle it as well as I could have. I went in on the attack, which in retrospect wasn't the right thing. I did offer them a scenario where they could have an interest in the Epic deal, but they were offended and felt snubbed, as I probably would have been.

Ted Albert felt utterly shafted. As did Harry and George. After all, Alberts had provided funding and contacts for Woodruff's American record-deal mission. Ted left the room to discuss the matter and returned to say he had no further interest in continuing his company's relationship with The Angels. It would be the last time Albert spoke to Woodruff.

Fifa Riccobono was astounded by the way her genial boss spoke about Woodruff after the incident. 'Ted said to me that he never wanted to make that man feel welcome in our company. And that's when I realised there must have been something pretty heavy that had gone down.'

George tracked down John Brewster, then in Melbourne. 'I hear you're leaving us,' he said. His Scottish accent was thicker than usual and there was deep sadness in it. John told him that Woodruff was convinced this was something they had to do – to stay in Australia without striking out overseas would see the gradual decline of the band – and that if they were to accept Epic's offer, it came with the proviso that Epic/CBS had to have Australasia too. George told John that Ted held Woodruff personally responsible for the decision. While they were all deeply disappointed that the band had gone along with it, they'd always be welcome back as visitors. John hung up with tears rolling down his face.

Ted rang Rick and John a few days later and asked them to come and see him. Both now in their late twenties, they felt like errant schoolboys as they were ushered into Ted's plush, old-world office where portraits of his illustrious forebears graced the walls.

Stony-faced, Ted announced that he was going to rescind the verbal agreement he'd made with them to pay a producer's royalty for *No Exit.* He said that he had nothing against the band at all but couldn't forgive John Woodruff. The Brewsters nodded and quietly apologised for what had happened.

> **John:** Mark Opitz wrote in his book [his memoir, *Sophisto-punk*] that we were grown adults and should have stood up to Woodruff at the time. He shows no understanding of what it is to be in a band and how much influence a manager can have. He can be forgiven, I guess, as he's never been in a band to my knowledge.

CHAPTER TWENTY-TWO
POOLED RESOURCES TOUR

Cold Chisel, managed by Dirty Pool director Rod Willis, brought out their second album *Breakfast At Sweethearts* in February 1979. By November there'd been three hit singles, and the album had spent thirty-two weeks in the charts and gone to #4 nationally. Backed by relentless touring, Chisel had finally broken through and become a major drawcard.

Flowers, managed by Ray Hearn, had been getting plenty of exposure supporting The Angels and Cold Chisel, but were still a lower-order act. However, they were shifting from being a note-perfect cover band to playing self-penned gems. Rejected by the major labels, they'd signed with independent Regular Records, with their first album due out in months. Ray had boundless faith in Flowers and was looking into touring strategies to create a national profile ahead of the album release.

Hot on the heels of *No Exit*, Alberts had released The Angels' EP *Out Of The Blue*, featuring the third studio version of 'Am I Ever Gonna See Your Face Again' in three years. Within the inner sanctum of Dirty Pool, the scene was set to make an end-of-year statement by flexing the company's muscles.

A plan was put into action to bundle their three core acts onto a bill and call it the Pooled Resources tour, playing major concerts with a full-blown sound and lights production supplied by Jands. Since the early seventies Jands had supplied top-flight concert equipment and crew for most of the international tours that came to Australia. Their services came at a price and had been beyond the budgets of local bands.

The costs and risks would be high and meant that ticket prices would have to be set at $10, a premium for an all-Australian show.

The tour kicked off at the Apollo in Adelaide on 23 November. There'd been doubts about The Angels having the drawing power in their home town on the level required, and it was deemed that Chisel had the stronger following there. In every other city, The Angels were the undisputed first choice.

As the three band managers walked about the crowded Apollo that Friday night, there was little doubt in their minds they'd made the right decision. The number of Chisel t-shirts being worn suggested they'd drawn the larger portion of the crowd.

The show opened with locals Lemmie Caution, followed by Flowers, who had to put up with constant chants of 'Angels, Angels', but gamely soldiered on and eventually won through.

Then The Angels appeared. Pandemonium broke out as the opening riff of 'Take A Long Line' rang through the stadium and Doc came lurching across the stage and grabbed the microphone. He swan-dived, hurled himself about, hung off lighting gantries, reached beseechingly out to the enraptured audience, hands splayed, eyes blazing. Smoke machines billowed, follow-spots shafted and the songs roared out of the gigantic speakers with bruising power.

During 'I Ain't The One', as the guitar solo approached, Ray Hawkins cut all the lights apart from a single spot on Doc. At that moment Rick stepped behind a curtain while still playing, and in the dark a roadie replaced him with a life-size photographic cardboard cut-out of himself, standing legs spread, playing his guitar in typical statue position. The lights came up and Rick played the solo from behind the curtain while a dimmed green spot lit up his cut-out. As the solo howled to its finale, every light blazed on. Doc pulled his right arm back and swung a karate chop to the stomach of cardboard 'Rick'. As the cut-out doubled over and crashed to the floor, behind the curtain

Rick brought his solo to an abrupt end and Ray killed every light, shrouding the stage in darkness.

'*Whoawa!*' The audience roared – which turned to cheers as Rick, expressionless, sauntered back out for the next song and ripped into the intro.

By the end of their encores the audience was completely used and abused but still screamed for more. Off to one side of the stage, Bernard Neeson's mum and dad, standing alongside Rick and John's parents, could only gape. Doc's mentor from Flinders Uni, Professor Wal Cherry, was also there, applauding.

Thirty minutes later the members of Cold Chisel took to the stage for the closing set, knowing that anything they did would be anti-climactic. They'd already been upstaged.

CHAPTER TWENTY-THREE
DARK ROOM

Bernard Neeson sat in the kitchen with his first tea of the day, sun slanting through the window, scanning the front page of the last edition of the *Sydney Morning Herald* for 1979. The names of sixteen new knights and two new dames were in the New Year's honours list and the truce in Rhodesia was holding. Misha, the big gangling Afghan hound who held centre-stage in the Neeson household, loped in and nuzzled his hand – a couple of pats were never enough for Misha.

Suddenly, an article at the bottom of the page caught his eye. Rock band The Angels were playing a concert on the Opera House steps that night. Bernard grinned: 'Hey, Dzintra, we're on the front page of the *Herald*!'

He gazed out the window to the rolling fairways of the Concord Golf Club. His thoughts wandered back over the last two crazy years since that New Year's Eve at the Stagedoor Tavern, playing to a small crowd of enthusiastic punters for peanuts. The night their booking agent arrived and discovered how much they'd changed and the reaction they were getting. Doc was shaking his head as the phone rang. Rick was inviting everyone round to his and Bitsy's newly bought house for a barbeque before they headed off to the big gig. 'It's New Year's Eve. Let's celebrate ten years together before we go to the Opera House.'

Things went ballistic after the Opera House show. Agent Richard McDonald had negotiated the whole thing with the Sydney Festival organisers. Right up to the day of the concert the organisers had little concept of who the band were, other than they were popular with the *young people*. Eric Robinson, boss of Jands, who supplied the festival's sound system, had become a friend of the band since the Pooled Resources tour, and saw to it there was a full concert PA in place. Otherwise they would have had the small sound system that was originally allocated to the show.

> **Richard McDonald:** We got the festival to build a stage walkway for Doc, but they probably thought it was for dancing girls or something. By now they knew that a lot of people were coming, but they thought it was for the family orientated acts on earlier. They still didn't realise the power of The Angels to pull a massive rock 'n' roll crowd.

The punters knew what was happening, though. A free Angels concert! They'd been arriving from eleven in the morning, waiting in the sun and getting pissed. When the band finally came on at midnight, the sheer excitement and frustration that had built up had exploded. Photos of Doc going down and Chris with blood all over his face were plastered across the front pages of the Sydney papers and all over the TV news.

And so began the eighties for the boys from Adelaide.

The day before the first tour of the year, Woodruff called a meeting with some bad news. There was a band in the States working under the registered name 'Angel', so The Angels would have to come up with something else to work under. Various names incorporating the word 'Angels' were suggested, but the only one they could live with – albeit reluctantly – was 'Angel City', a nod to Los Angeles, which would be their nominal base. It was another unhappy compromise.

Woodruff then passed around a wad of worksheets covering the twenty-five-date tour around Australia. Once back in Sydney, they'd have ten days of rehearsals preparing songs for the next album. They would then move into Paradise Studios in Kings Cross to record it, followed by a couple of large-scale concerts. They'd then board a plane to LA for a two-month North American tour, followed by showcase gigs in London and Europe. After that they'd return to Australia for the release of the new album backed up with another national tour. At the completion of that there was another USA tour pencilled in to promote the new album and consolidate the ground-work of the first tour.

The relationship with Epic didn't get off to a great start when Woodruff revealed that they'd be releasing songs from *Face To Face* and *No Exit* as one album in the USA, and the songs would also be remixed for the American market. The Brewsters in particular were incensed: both albums had been runaway successes with their current production. Surely that's what had attracted Epic to signing them?

Woodruff told them that the production was fine for Australia, but wasn't up to international standards. American John Boylan, who'd produced Boston's debut album, which had sold 17 million units and spawned the hit 'More Than A Feeling', was in line for the job. After a heated meeting where Woodruff pointed out that Epic contractually had the right to release greatest hits albums, and this came under that clause, the band accepted the inevitable. Eventually a compromise was struck wherein Epic would fly John Brewster to LA to co-mix the American version of *Face To Face* with Boylan.

While all the big radio songs would be included, it meant that 'Be With You', 'Love Takes Care', 'Outcast', 'Dawn Is Breaking', 'Skid Row After Dark', 'I Ain't The One', 'Straightjacket', 'Save Me' and 'Ivory Stairs' were to be left off. Songs that had given those albums depth.

John arrived in Los Angeles and met up with Boylan at Westlake Audio, a top of the range studio near Sunset Boulevard. Because the American album would be a hybrid of the two Aussie albums, the aim was to work on mixing the songs to make them sound like they were from the same album.

John: We had a great engineer who would get the sounds and basic mix in the ball park, and then I was very hands on with the levels. The main difference from the Australian mixes is that Boylan added reverb to the guitars, which I wasn't keen on. I loved the dry guitars on our Australian mixes but Boylan wanted more of the US sound, more slick. I'm not saying he was wrong, but I still prefer the Oz mixes.

Whatever, we did a good job, I wound up enjoying the camaraderie, and we produced a great sounding album. But we should have had the two albums released one after the other – big mistake in my view!

Soon after the split from Alberts, Woodruff had rung Mark Opitz. He told him that Epic wanted Boylan to produce the next album. In addition to his work with Boston, Boylan was vice president of Epic for the West Coast and had also produced an album for Little River Band, so, according to the American label, it made sense for him to fly to Sydney and produce The Angels.

Woodruff understood the merit of having a 'name' producer to get radio interest, but after they'd produced the band's last two albums, Rick and John weren't wearing being dumped. A compromise was struck: Boylan would be 'production consultant' and the Brewsters would be the hands-on producers. Woodruff made a financially generous offer to Opitz to be recording engineer that he couldn't refuse. With Vanda and Young's permission, he accepted.

Ten spare days had been set aside for writing and working up new songs. Nowhere near enough. It felt like they'd only just done all this for the previous album. Life had been crazy since then with little time for songwriting – although their notebooks were full of ideas and Doc had most of the lyrics for a song:

Doc: 'No Secrets' came about when I was driving through Sydney one morning. I saw a young woman running for the bus but she missed it, so I pulled up and said, 'Do you want a lift into the city?' During the fifteen-minute drive she told me her life story. They say we talk best to strangers and she told me some very personal stuff. I was so overwhelmed that when she got out, I pulled over and wrote it all down.

Buzz was living at Doc's place and came up with a tune for 'No Secrets'. When the pair brought the song into the studio, it seemed obvious to John and Rick that it was off the mark for The Angels. Doc's lyrics were strong, but Buzz's country-rock tune was reminiscent of an Eagles track: long and dreamy – 'Sheeee keeps no see-e-crets . . .' Rick chopped it around and rewrote it, while John came up with the signature verse riff. The changes were profound and transformed it into a rock song with an Angels feel. Doc strongly suggested that John and Rick should be credited as co-writers and the royalties split four ways. However, the Brewsters, completely missing the future significance of the composition, consented to Buzz being 50/50 songwriter with Doc. 'After all,' said John, 'our names were on just about every other song.'

Doc's notebook was full of lines and phrases which the Brewsters trawled through to complement lyrics they had, and it didn't take long for 'Wasted Sleepless Nights' and 'Dark Room' to emerge. While the others jammed on the bluesy genesis of 'Devil's Gate' one afternoon, John and Doc collaborated on lyrics for a riff John had composed. With Doc pulling lines from his notebook and Rick and John throwing in bits from the darker side of their imaginations, a song about paranoia took shape – fighting an imaginary enemy, 'black visions and danger signs' and being choked up in the city. They rejoined the others with a new song: 'Face The Day'.

It was an inspired and creative period, but there was perspiration too – twelve-hour sessions the norm. After ten days they had a store of songs ready for recording at Paradise.

Cold Chisel had just recorded *East* there and praised the place. Now it was The Angels' for two-and-a-half weeks – not a lot of time. They were used to the laissez-faire of Alberts, where time limits didn't exist and the key to the studio lay in their pocket.

> **Mark Opitz:** On the first day at Paradise, Boylan sat us all down and issued his production-consultant instructions: 'What I want you to do is exactly what you have done before.' What? He's out here to produce and now he wants us to do things the way we always have!

Which is pretty much how it worked out. Jet-lagged, Boylan went upstairs, found a comfy couch and dozed off, waking occasionally to continue the book he was reading before dozing off again. Having worked with John during the mixing sessions in LA two months before, he had complete confidence in him. Boylan would show up now and then, ask what was happening, offer advice, then wander off and make calls to the States.

The first song to be recorded was 'No Secrets'. Later, when the others disappeared for lunch, Rick stayed back and wrote the searing solo that had his fingers spidering to the top of his fretboard and tremolo-ing out as Doc's voice came screaming in for the final verse. A&R manager at CBS Peter Karpin presented a rough mix to the company's troops who went nuts for it.

Despite his misgivings, John Brewster allowed Buzz to talk him into letting him do the mix. Next day John apprehensively checked in to see how it was going, only to be casually told it hadn't been completed.

'When can I get it? The record company are on my back.'

'Tomorrow morning,' said Buzz. 'I'll finish it tonight.'

JB arrived the next morning to find Buzz inebriated and still up after an all-night drinking session – with a mix that was unlistenable. During an angry exchange, Brewster grabbed the tape, stormed out and rang Alberts (who had publishing rights for Angels songs for another year). Ted Albert granted permission to come straight in and use Studio 3. Within hours it was mixed and John delivered the tape to CBS that afternoon.

At the end of a long session on Sunday 2 March, The Angels packed up and bid a happy farewell to Paradise. They had ten new songs on an album that would be called *Dark Room*. It still needed to be mixed – but that would happen in LA. Flights were booked for John to do the job, with production consultant John Boylan riding shotgun to ensure its appeal to American ears.

When John arrived in LA, he stayed in a hotel on Sunset Boulevard, with the Comedy Club next door. He'd look up at the massive billboards promoting albums by Bob Seger, Bruce Springsteen and Fleetwood Mac.

> **John:** When we first played Sydney it felt slightly Americanised to us, but you get to America in a rock 'n' roll band and, of course, this really is America, the heart of where it all started! 'Wow, we're signed to an international record company and we're about to tour this place.' Stretch limos. I'd never seen one before: 'What movie star's in that one?' Petrol was cheap and everyone was driving these floating living rooms. When I'd go to eat – Taco Bell, Denny's – if I ordered a steak this huge plate would come out with a steak covering most of it. You could feed a family on it. 'What's this all about?'

At nights, John was alone and missed Robyn and the camaraderie of the band and crew. The day he turned thirty, feeling old, he rang home to discover she and the guys were having a birthday party for him in absentia. She put Rick on who told him that 'No Secrets' had been released and radio stations all over the country were playing it. Peter Karpin had rung to say they had a national smash hit in the making.

He wasn't lonely for long, though. A couple of weeks later the band and crew arrived and preparations for a two-month tour of North America got underway.

CHAPTER TWENTY-FOUR
AMERICA

Doc's personal life had become more complicated during the previous twelve months. He'd fallen for Coe Uttinger, the twenty-three-year-old daughter of an American military attaché based in Canberra. Doc had met her after a gig at the Bondi Lifesaver in mid-1979. Short blonde hair, slight build, red-lacquered nails, a strange attractive face and a seriously intense demeanour. A graphic artist at a boutique agency, she'd recently designed what would become the famous Weiss clothing logo. Coe was into many of the things that fascinated Doc: symbolism, metaphors, surrealist philosophy. She was well read and, for Doc, inspiring to be with.

She had stood right in front of him during that gig and never taken her eyes off him. Punters – both men and women – often did that, but never with Coe's intensity. Their eyes locked and telepathy crackled as rivulets of sweat rolled down his face and dripped from his jaw. As soon as he came off he sent a roadie to bring her to him and it effortlessly went from there.

Bjarne Ohlin was keyboardist for Divinyls and a friend of Coe's:

Bjarne: As well as being an artist, Coe was a singer, musician and songwriter, always alive to the possibilities of making new things. She had a big impact on

Doc in that she inspired him to add more stylistic theatre and greater depth and dimension to his many personas on stage, as well as suggesting methods to enhance the mystique of the band with the media.

But it was Coe's messing with the band's mystique through Doc that infuriated the others. Her influence on him in changing the unique image he'd cultivated since adopting the German Expressionist theories put her totally offside with them. Coe's influence was at work in Doc's insistence that his stage persona needed to constantly evolve. She persuaded him to abandon the Ascot tie and dinner suit in favour of a loose-fitting grey suit: *'like David Bowie'*.

Bjarne: Coe had an 'old soul' vibe. She looked at and responded to life in a classically fascinating way that empowered the creative journey to take you anywhere, connecting you to everything that had gone before.

When Coe's influence moved from Doc's wardrobe to the recording studio, John quickly put a halt to it.

John: Back in 1979, when I was mixing 'Shadow Boxer' one afternoon at Alberts, Coe came into the control room. She stood listening for a while, tapped me on the shoulder and told me to turn down the backing vocals and raise the level of Doc's voice. I got up off my chair, opened the door and said, 'Coe, this is a door. It's time for you to go through it.' That was the last time she came into the studio.

Doc kept Coe a secret from Dzintra by explaining away the nights spent at his new girlfriend's Kings Cross flat as working hard in the studio. Things came unstuck for the singer when the band gathered at Sydney Airport to go to the US. As the band hugged and farewelled their loved ones, Coe came rushing up to Doc wailing, 'Doc, Doc, I love you,' and, oblivious to Dzintra, wrapped her arms around him. A stunned Dzintra demanded, 'Who's this?' As the others hastily disappeared through the departure door, Doc extricated himself and followed them out of sight.

During the first weeks in America, those who had rooms next to Doc's could hear his deep voice resonate through the wall at night, assuring his wife on the phone that the woman was just a fan, nothing more.

While Doc's flight from Sydney to the States was probably less than comfortable, tour manager Mark Pope was extremely impressed by the luxury he experienced.

Mark Pope: Woody had somehow pulled off first-class flights to America for the price of economy. Seated ahead of me was Sir Edmund Hillary and on the other side was [future Prime Minister] Bob Hawke. I'd had two dreams. One, to work for a rock 'n' roll band, and two, to work in America. They were two very different dreams and there I was, flying across the Pacific on my way to LA. It was Easter, a cloudless night, a full moon reflecting on a calm sea five kilometres below, and Fleetwood Mac's 'Sara' playing, and to this day every time I hear that song, I remember that night.

On 12 April everyone gathered beside the Beverly Laurel's pool. In the unseasonal heat they ordered drinks and settled into cane chairs. Woody gazed round with his one good eye and gave a lopsided 'well, here we are again' grin. It was the first time they'd all been together since filming the clip for 'No Secrets' a month before.

The Australian crew – Pope, Ashley and Eric Robinson – had arrived the previous evening and were now joined by Ricky, an American who would drive the truck and provide local knowledge. Robinson, boss of Jands, wanted to look at the USA touring business close-up, so he'd joined the crew at his own expense for a look-see and for the adventure.

Rick: To us it was: 'Eric Robinson! He's the man!' To have him as production manager and foldback operator was, well, you can't get better than that. It was something Woody arranged – he and Eric were thick as thieves. Ray Hawkins was left behind, though. Without him there was no way we could present the same show we'd been doing in Australia.

Mark Pope: Eric had decided not to trust any of the foldback systems at the clubs we'd be playing – he'd heard most of them were shit. If the guys didn't get a good sound on stage, they'd be fucked. So he brought over a Jands foldback rig which he understood, and we hired a row of good foldback speakers.

That night they all went out for dinner, apart from Doc, who rarely participated in those things. An upmarket diner had been recommended. The waitress put down a jug of ice water, a custom unknown in Australia. Chris Bailey, the suave one, looked around appreciatively: 'Oh America. They just do it right!' Later, he pointed to 'Perrier Water' on the menu: 'What's that?' The waitress brought a little bottle, poured his glass and he had a sip: 'Oh my God, this is the best water I've ever drunk.' It cost a fortune. He checked the label, 'Ah yes, it comes from France!'

Rick: We got up to go without leaving a tip and the waitress came over. 'Is there something wrong?' I said, 'No, it was great.' 'Well, where's the tip?' Someone explained that they rely on tips for their wages. It's obligatory, whether the service is shit or not. Which, of course, we objected to strongly at some of the dumps we ate at on the road. But when in America, you know. The first time we caught a domestic flight, I got out of the car and put my suitcase on the ground. It was immediately picked up by a six-and-a-half-foot black dude built like a refrigerator. I said, 'It's okay, I'm just going to the check-in.' But he insisted – and then held his hand out. I gave him two bucks and he just left his hand there. I kept going until I hit ten dollars. Then he said, 'Thank you.' Fucking hell, ten bucks!

A few days later the Angel City convoy headed out of town for a two-hour drive south: destination, the art deco Roxy Theater in San Diego for the band's first American gig – and a headliner at that. 'Marseilles' had been getting airplay on local radio KGB. With Epic reporting respectable album sales in the area, the guys were hot to get on stage and play to an American audience. The date was a last-minute booking by the promoters who'd bought the album and become fans.

They came close to filling the club and scored their first encore. 'You did a whole lot better than Rachel Sweet did last night,' said the promoters, insisting they do a return date. They drove back to LA in high spirits.

The next night was off and then the crew set up for a weekend at Hollywood's infamous Whisky a Go Go – two shows a night. There were queues for every session and closed doors before each performance.

> **John:** We'd been getting airplay on the LA rock stations, plus Epic had taken out a lot of press ads. Doc did heaps of media so there was a vibe out there. Record shops had been importing our Australian albums for months, and the American version of *Face To Face* was steadily selling.

Regardless, the songs were little known except for 'Marseilles' and 'Long Line', which were getting airplay. In the first show Doc went into the audience and pretended to punch people during 'Shadow Boxer' and everyone recoiled. By the fourth show they'd got it and joined in. They were also singing along on 'Be With You' and punching the air in 'Comin' Down'. The LA crowd was picking up on things pretty quickly.

After it was all over, the convoy of truck and hire cars headed out of the city to Denver, a thousand miles away. They pulled into truck-stop gas stations, ate at dusty roadhouses, slept in cheap motels, were asked about their accents, studied road maps and began soaking up middle America.

> **John:** You'd lob into town and it felt like you were on a production line. You're greeted at the hotel by the record reps. The publicist comes in: 'Hey, I love your shit!' She's a hot-looking girl. Sometimes it felt like Spinal Tap. Then there's the guy managing the photo sessions: 'Hey, get rid of that cigarette. Stand over there. Here's the photographer.' We were processed. There'd be filming for a TV show or a news break, interviews with the radio, newspaper journos, magazine columnists, stuff going on all the time. But it was exciting. They'd drive you into the local Epic office for a meet and greet and a few photos. Maybe a quick lunch with a radio jock or entertainment writer.

That happened all round the States. There was never a time to relax before a show. At the record stores there'd be a queue as a result of radio promos announcing that Angel City from Australia were signing records. Sometimes the station was playing a track or two, so there was a vibe. And the band was the support act on the big show in town that night. Or maybe they'd be headlining a club.

> **Doc:** After each show the dressing room filled with people. Shaking hands, meeting this person, smiling for the camera, people shuffling in line to say hello. Record store people, radio jocks, journos. That's what these tours were about – meeting those in the music business and having a chat. You do one show onstage and another in the dressing room.

By 23 April, they were in the Poison Apple club in another Midwest town, supporting the Romantics.

> **Mark Pope:** They had a hit with 'What I Like About You' and they were pretty arrogant about us. Their crew set up their drumkit about a metre from the front of the stage because their drummer was also the lead singer – and so refused to move it. Eric says, 'Fine, if you won't move your drums, you ain't using our foldback.' Eventually they moved it. Eric was great at taking people on, he didn't care who they were – he had the most acerbic tongue in the business!

The Australian road crew were quietly pleased that, after The Angels came off, half the audience left.

They were now getting airplay on 130 stations and the album was in *Billboard* as the twenty-seventh highest rotation airplay in the country. They were in good spirits when, in Michigan, they opened for The Joe Perry Project. Until the previous year, Joe had been lead guitarist and sometime singer of Aerosmith. It was an excellent fit for The Angels. They received a convincing encore, followed by a visit to their dressing room from an impressed Joe Perry who invited them to do more shows with him.

Then it was on to their biggest show yet, supporting Cheap Trick in a sold-out concert at the 14,000-capacity Joe Louis Arena in Detroit.

John: When they toured Australia, Robin Zander and Rick Nielsen [Trick's singer, and their lead guitarist] had struck up a friendship with us, even showing up at a gig we did in Melbourne. The night before the Detroit concert they drove eighty miles to see us supporting Joe Perry – and we'd heard that when Rick Nielsen did radio interviews he'd wind up talking about us and getting them to play an Angels track.

But opening for Cheap Trick turned out to be an anti-climax. Despite full co-operation from Trick's road-crew, Angel City's timeslot had them taking to the stage as people were still filing in and the house lights were on. Despite the circumstances, with the Trick musicians applauding from side of stage, they pulled out all stops and, by the end of their set, received a respectable response.

Back in the dressing room all focus was now on the following night when they'd be headlining a sold-out show at Chicago's premier club, the Park West, with local band Survivor opening for them.

They were getting solid airplay in Chicago and Epic had set up important interviews and store appearances. Rather than stay in Detroit for the night and leave early next morning, they hopped into their cars and swung onto Route 94 for the 280-mile drive with the truck following. As they sped through the night they made jokes about the city where Al Capone and his mafia had reigned supreme during the twenties. Woodruff told them the owner of the Park West was Arny Granat.

'Arny Granat? Jeez, what sort of name is Arny Granat?'

'Arny Granat is a Chicago name.'

It was Woodruff who received the call from Mark Pope at 9 am next day to say the truck had been towed away from where he'd parked it at 4 am. Ricky, the American roadie, was right now calling the police to find out where they could collect it and how much it would cost. Woodruff brusquely told him to sort it out and hung up. *RAM* magazine back in Sydney was about to ring for an interview and Woody had the task of waking Doc and John to do it.

As it turned out, the equipment truck hadn't been towed away by any legal authority. It had been stolen, along with all the hired sound and light equipment, plus the band's instruments – including Rick's Epiphone, which had produced some of the most distinctive lead breaks in the band's recorded repertoire.

At the police station things got weird. Ricky, their driver, and Ashley explained the situation – Australian band, signed to Epic, hire truck full of equipment, stolen in the night. But then the cop stopped him.

'Sir, how did you ascertain that your vehicle has been stolen?'

They told him that it was no longer where it had been. It hadn't been legally towed away, so presumably it had been stolen.

'Presumably? Sir, nothing you say proves your vehicle has actually been stolen.'

Nonplussed, they insisted that it had indeed been stolen because it was no longer where it should have been. Rick then produced the hire agreement with the truck's registration details.

The cop gave it a cursory glance. 'Sir, that registration number isn't for a truck – it's for a pick-up. You're wasting my time.'

An exasperated Ashley searched for a public phone box and rang Woodruff. It was now getting close to set-up time.

Woodruff rang Arny Granat. A deep slow voice right out of *The Godfather* came down the line. 'We have a house PA you can use and I'll call Survivor – you can use their gear. Which police station is your guy at?'

Back at the station Ashley and Ricky observed an officer coming out from a back room and telling the duty cop, 'Hey, Dino, just got a call from our other boss about this band truck. Looks like we gotta take on the case.'

Ashley is ushered into the office and told that someone will need to come over with a grand in cash and they'll then get started on the case. Ashley is confused so the officer slowly repeats it, then summarily dismisses him.

The enormity of the loss is hitting the band and they pour out the story to a DJ at the radio station promoting their gig and he goes to air with it. Minutes later Rick Nielsen is on the line – he's heard the bad news. He's three hours away but he'll meet them at the club and bring a bunch of instruments.

Later that afternoon he arrives with a dozen guitars, including a couple of basses for Chris to choose from. He's brought Paul Hamer along. Hamer makes Nielsen's guitars, including his famous five-neck special, and he's brought along a selection for The Angels to try out. Support band Survivor are helping the roadies with the set-up. Other local musicians have arrived offering help. Despite the crushing loss, the Australians are buoyed by all the generosity and spirits lift. Rick tries one of Hamer's guitars and falls in love with it. John spots a Les Paul amongst Nielsen's offerings. (Which he was unable to part with and eventually bought.)

Nielsen is sticking around for the gig – he knows Arny Granat. 'In that case,' says John, 'how about getting up with us on "Can't Shake It"?' The Cheap Trick guitarist accepts with a grin.

After the day's well-publicised dramas, the band get a roaring welcome as they take the stage. Joe Perry and a couple of the guys from Aerosmith are in the audience, along with Nielsen and Robin Zander. By the time the show comes to a close, the sweat-drenched crowd is going berserk. Then Nielsen appears for the encore. It's mayhem and the gig becomes part of the Park West's illustrious history.

Rick: Paul Hamer – that was a significant meeting. He invited me to his factory next day. My first experience of a guitar factory, and the first time I'd seen a Floyd Rose tremolo bridge. I had to have one! Heavily using a traditional tremolo arm ('dive-bombing') can leave the guitar out of tune after the strings return to normal tension. The Floyd Rose bridge locks the strings at the nut and at the bridge and ensures that the pitch remains true, no matter what you do with the tremolo arm.

Paul generously gave Rick two Hamer guitars, a custom-made one fitted with a Floyd Rose bridge, and a mini-guitar he could take on a plane and practise with. He used them for years.

Rick Nielsen: The Angels' 'Great Chicago Robbery of 1980'. The Angels, whose music I'd discovered, heard and purchased, were on their very first US tour and for their Chicago debut arrived a day early, parking their loaded equipment truck, naively or unwittingly tempted and successfully encouraged an overnight robbery – Al Capone-influenced – by thieves, in a downtown Chicago parking lot, locally known for such activities. Oops! Bad move . . .

After playing the Park West Club, because the band had to buy new equipment and the police report hadn't reached the insurance company, the next four shows had to be cancelled – radio-sponsored club gigs in Milwaukee, Pittsburgh, Washington and Philadelphia, all sold out and a huge blow. They stayed in Chicago for a day or so then moved on to New York.

John and Buzz were keen to see America from a different perspective and decided to do the next leg 'riding the rails', as depicted in Woody Guthrie's old songs.

John: My introduction to New York was by train. Buzz and I booked a sleeper and we left late afternoon and arrived next morning. The last few hours we glided alongside the Hudson River while it was getting light. As we entered the outskirts we were struck by the derelict buildings. Entire suburbs just ghost towns. Then you see New York laying before you and it's like, 'Fuck, that's big.'

They checked into the old Gramercy Park Hotel, where the Stones had stayed on their earlier tours. It was cheap accommodation for actors, artists, writers, other creatives.

John: We entered this wonderful old foyer. It was steeped in history. The desk clerk said: 'Ever been to Noo York before, Mr Brewster?' I said no. He got a map out. 'Well, these are the areas you don't go into day or night. This area here, you can go into in the daytime, but don't be there after dark.' It was like mapping out a war-zone.

A police report arrived, clearing the band of involvement with the theft, and with insurance issues sorted out they were looking forward to playing two headline nights at Great Gildersleeves, a famed punkish club in The Bowery.

John: That was in a really tough area. We had to walk through all these street bums and very weird people. You got the feeling that if you looked the wrong way, said the wrong thing, you'd be in a lot of trouble. But those two gigs were hot ones for us. We had a few celebrities coming backstage to say hello – including Ian Hunter from Mott The Hoople and Karla DeVito, who we'd met on the Meat Loaf tour when she was singing back-ups and duos with him.

Mark Pope: The first gig after we left New York was a club in Newhaven. As usual the band blitzed the joint, left them standing on chairs and tables yelling for more. Next night we were booked at the Paradise Club in Boston. Epic had lined up a full day of media so we jumped in the cars, lit up a few numbers and drove on to Boston. After midnight we stopped at a Wendy's and ordered steak and stuff.

JB had earned a reputation as a hypochondriac, especially when he was stoned. We were halfway through the meal and he suddenly said, 'I'm having a heart attack – I'm having a heart attack. We have to go!'

Woody by now was getting pissed off with JB's constant ailments and said, 'Well, if you're having a heart attack, does it matter if you have it here or in the car? Can't we eat our steak first?' 'No, no', said JB, 'we really have to go, we've really got to go.'

He created such a fuss that we all got up, left our meals, and we were driving along and there was silence for half an hour. Then Woody went, 'How's that heart attack going, John?' And you know, John was sitting in the back all quiet, and he said, 'Ah yeah, ah, much better, thanks.'

You know, none of us could eat because he had to have his heart attack!

They crossed the Canadian border into Toronto where number-one rock station 1050 CHUM was giving 'Marseilles' plenty of airtime. They were booked to headline the El Mocambo nightclub, which had made international headlines a couple of years earlier due to a Rolling Stones performance after which Mick Jagger had an assignation with Margaret Trudeau, wife of the prime minister. He then ran off with her for a week. The Mocambo had hosted gigs by Blondie, Ramones, Devo, Talking Heads, and now Angel City. After delivering a killer show to a packed room, they were immediately offered a return gig.

Then it was back into the States. The promoter of the Cheap Trick concert at the Joe Louis Arena had been so impressed that he'd booked them to headline at his Detroit club Center Stage, and had promoted it hard over the intervening two weeks, selling out two shows. The tour continued on, playing club gigs in Cincinnati, Columbus, Minneapolis, Seattle and Portland. All presented by radio stations playing tracks off the American version of *Face To Face*. They wound up in San Francisco at promoter Bill Graham's Old Waldorf club, where AC/DC had played on their first American tour three years earlier.

> **Mark Pope:** We got back to LA and Woody and I were working on the Dark Room tour being arranged in Australia for when the band got back home. We had a big show booked into the Hordern Pavilion in Sydney, capacity 5000-plus. I'd been checking ticket sales every day, and it had sold out. Woody and I were on the balcony at Glenn Wheatley's Little River Band office with the artificial grass, and we were drinking huge cans of Foster's celebrating, and John accidentally dropped the you-know-what, so we were looking for all of the specks of white powder amongst the artificial turf.
>
> We had such a celebration that day. Here we were in America heading for international glory, and the band was going from strength to strength back home as well, selling out the pubs, the theatres and the sheds as we called them: the Hordern Pavilions and Festival Halls and all of that sort of stuff. They were on fire.

In LA before the band flew on to London, their bookers from the William Morris Agency and a legion of Epic staff were milling around. The agency bookers, ecstatic with the success of the tour and the extra airplay it had generated, were offering Angel City the support spots on the Pat Travis tour which was about to hit the road playing in 5000 to 15,000 seat venues.

> **John:** We were about to fly to London, and Epic and the William Morris agents were saying, 'For fuck's sake, get straight back after that, because it's happening here and we can get you opening sets on some big shows.' By now

we had airplay for 'Marseilles' on over 170 stations, some of it on high rotation, and seriously charting in places like Seattle and Portland and Canada.

But Woodruff insisted we get back to Australia after London for the release of *Dark Room* and play the tour he'd organised to support it. To me it felt like the space shuttle re-entry thing. You've got that window. If you get the window, you're back on Earth. If you miss the window, you bounce off and disappear into the blue yonder.

CHAPTER TWENTY-FIVE
LONDON AND PARIS

The band arrived at Heathrow, got picked up by stately Daimlers and were driven to the decidedly unstately Lily Hotel, around the corner from Earl's Court. The lift was a cupboard, the rooms so small they had to turn sideways to get around the beds, and the phone above the bed-head sounded like a fire alarm when it rang. Doc requested a bigger room with a bigger bed. Staff were unable to make one available, so he checked into an adjacent hotel. Thus the Doc obsession with finding the right bed in the right room began.

A journalist arrived and led a dishevelled John down to the cramped café on the ground floor for a chat with a women's magazine. 'I honestly can't recall some of the places we've played at,' he told her. 'If we weren't working, we were either travelling or trying to get some sleep in the back of a car or some cheap hotel room. It's all a blur.'

And so it continued to be. Next morning they were boarding a plane to Amsterdam and checking into the Hald Centraal, which had been built for the 1928 Olympics. It was surrounded by crowded cafés where you could legally buy a small packet of marijuana, roll a joint and enjoy a cup of fine Dutch coffee – which the entire band did with relish.

'Ah, Amsterdam,' sighed Chris, lighting up, 'this place is so civilised.'

That evening, shortly after midnight, the band mounted a large high stage, set up on the edge of a football stadium – and for the next hour, they battled a cacophony of bells, whistles and firecrackers to an out-of-it throng of thousands who were celebrating some strange local festival and probably had no idea who was playing. All they wanted was a lot of loud noise, which apparently was what the whole thing was about. Out on the perimeter bonfires blazed, and beyond the walls car horns hooted and blared throughout the city.

'What the fuck was that all about?' they moaned coming off, glad it was over.

Next morning was a photo-shoot at various city locations, then back to the airport, board a 707 and into Heathrow by 5 pm. No limos this time, just a train into London and cabs to the Lily Hotel.

> **John:** Our big gig in London was a headliner at the Marquee Club. There were posters all over town and we were doing heaps of interviews. But a few days before the Marquee gig, we were offered the opening spot on a Sunday-night heavy-metal concert at the Lyceum Theatre. We figured it wouldn't hurt as a warm-up for the Marquee, so we took it.

When they walked onstage with their cropped hair and new-wave vibe, it drew deep suspicion, and when the MC introduced them as being 'all the way from Sydney', that did it – the crowd started booing and throwing missiles. They played gamely on until Buzz was hit on the head, whereupon he staggered offstage followed by the rest. 'That's it, you can all get fucked,' Doc yelled, which elicited more catcalls and taunts.

> **Ashley:** That heavy metal gig was a joke. The PA was heavily compressed and several of the mics weren't active. The sound guy didn't give a rat's arse and the majority of the punters were young pimple-faced turds.

The day arrived for the Marquee gig and it was off for a lengthy soundcheck and a jam. Over 500 tickets had been sold and the manager was happy. After the soundcheck they had Peking duck at a nearby restaurant and then returned to find the show was sold out.

The band's Australian journalist friend Ross Stapleton was now Artists and Repertoire manager at Virgin Records. He was there and wrote a review:

> Scarcely believing their good fortune, hundreds of Aussie ex-pats and others in the know easily sold out London's Marquee when The Angels came to town. By any critical and creative divination, The Angels were the equal of any live band in the world, including their one-time Albert label mates AC/DC. Standing next to me, it took only 20 minutes for a rival label MD to scream in my ear. 'Why didn't you tell me about these guys? They're unbelievable.'
>
> And so they were with their big-sounding PA and full-on light show. Blitzing through a slew of anthemic songs as mad professor Doc Neeson and the Brewster brothers stripped the grease from the low hanging ceiling. The Marquee has rarely hosted that level of sustained firepower, let alone an army of punters going totally nuts from the opening salvo. The Angels were hotter than a Marilyn Monroe nude calendar shoot!

After the gig, John and Chris stepped outside the back door to share a joint, only to discover a gang of long-haired punters wearing Status Quo t-shirts wanting to 'talk to them'. The Aussies glanced at each other and tried to calculate how quickly they could wrench open the door and get back inside. Just as they were about to beat a retreat, the punters said they'd been at the Lyceum and had thrown stuff at them and wanted to apologise. They began raving about the gig they'd just seen. There were handshakes all round and promises to come and see them next time they played London – and they'd bring their mates along and hoped they could say hello afterwards.

The next stop was Paris, where they were taken to the CBS office to meet and greet, sign a pile of records and do a photo-shoot. As an album track, 'Marseilles' was getting airplay in Paris and a few regional areas – although in Marseilles itself, it appeared to have garnered little interest – but the promo staff had just received eight boxes of 'Marseilles' singles from America to distribute to radio stations around the country. 'We will present the single to radio in the city of the same name and maybe the situation can be rectified,' their promo manager suggested.

Mildly curious, Rick asked if there was somewhere he could play one and he and John were taken to an office with a turntable. The needle dropped and all sounded good – until it reached the end of Doc's vocal and the song faded out. Astounded, Rick looked at John, who was staring at the record as it slowed to a stop.

Rick couldn't contain himself. 'What happened to the guitar outro?' His solo had vanished, wiped clean. It was still on the album version, so it seemed that John must have mixed this cut-down version with Boylan. 'What the fuck have you done?' he shouted. John fired back that he knew nothing about it – it was the first time he'd heard this version.

Beyond the thin plaster walls, the entire office fell silent as the two brothers went hammer and tongs at each other, Rick grabbing the box of singles and flinging them across the room and out the door.

It turned out that the mix had been recently done and the new version was being distributed to radio stations across the States and Canada. And was about to be distributed to European stations.

With Ray Hearn, Doc and the rest of the band outraged, the French agreed to shelve the singles until something was worked out between band and head office. With that they stormed out and headed back to the hotel, where Hearn and John Brewster had an angry trans-Atlantic conversation with Boylan, who also knew nothing about it and went investigating. But it seemed the culprit had gone to ground and no one was produced to take responsibility.

As with London, their English booking agency had promised a string of gigs, but most had never gone beyond the 'TBA' stage and the band were left with a number of days off, completely blowing their already strained budget.

They played two midweek gigs, one in provincial Clermont-Ferrand and the other in Lyon, where the limited airplay and media coverage managed to tempt small but enthusiastic audiences to come out and see them. Then it was time to prepare for their headline show at Paris's Le Bataclan (which in 2015 would be the scene of a horrific terrorist attack in which ninety people were killed).

It was early June and the heat of the summer day radiated into a long twilight evening. Advance ticket sales hadn't been great, but promoter Frederic Serfatti assured Ray Hearn that interest was high, and that on these balmy summer nights the walk-up was always substantial.

Frederic was right. The band arrived at 5 pm for soundcheck, to discover a good-natured queue forming at the ticket office. When the doors opened two hours later, it snaked back along the Boulevard Voltaire.

> **John:** The Bataclan was the place to play, like the Marquee in London. A shabby but beautiful atmospheric music hall from the 1800s. It was a hot night and it wasn't air-conditioned. We had a sweaty gig and the place absolutely went off. With 'Marseilles' they sang every word. Doc climbed off the stage and went into the audience. They loved it when he sang the French bits and we got two huge encores.

The night before they left France, the record company, ecstatic about the Bataclan performance, took the entourage out to dinner. The entree was at one famous restaurant, main course at another and dessert at a third. At each, copious amounts of expensive alcohol were consumed and by 3 am they were all staggering towards the Eiffel Tower. Doc, skilled at climbing stage scaffolding, decided that here was an opportunity to hone his skills. With Ray Hearn close behind, he started clambering up the tower – to loud encouragement from the rest.

Fortunately, before they got too far, the gendarmes arrived and, in no uncertain manner, demanded they get down 'immédiatement'. Back on the ground, Doc became belligerent, asking what happened to 'liberté, égalité, fraternité', but was told to fuck off or they'd arrest him.

> **John:** We got back to the hotel, packed and went straight on to the airport with no sleep, still intoxicated – flying home to Sydney via London. Air France hit us for excess baggage. It cost a fortune, almost more than the guitars were worth.

Another hit to the budget!

CHAPTER TWENTY-SIX
GOING INTO OVERDRIVE

The whole operation had moved into overdrive while they were away and Angels songs were all over the Australian airwaves.

They were surprised to discover they had a new album in the charts that they didn't know about. On 10 May, Alberts had released a greatest hits compilation, drawn from the various singles they'd recorded while signed to them. As well, 'No Secrets' off the forthcoming album was top ten and introducing the band to a vast new audience.

On the weekend before the release of *Dark Room*, the band performed an album preview at the Stagedoor Tavern. It was their first gig back but promotion was intentionally kept low-key in the hope that it wouldn't be packed out, which would allow room for media invitees and CBS staff. To counter media hacks showing up after the band's performance for the free booze, as had happened previously, complimentary drinks were only available to invitees before the band went on and during their performance. Jocks and journos had to mingle with the fans, instead of having the luxury of reserved seats. For some, that was a first.

On Monday 16 June, CBS threw their considerable resources into distributing *Dark Room* to every major radio station and simultaneously shipping advance orders to record shops coast to coast. Within days it was #8 nationally and on its way to platinum status.

*

The Bexley North Hotel in Sydney's southern suburbs was the first gig of the tour and revealed a new phenomenon. Hordes of girls had joined the ranks of what had previously been a predominantly male audience. The screams were deafening when Rick and John nic-nic'd into the opening chords of 'No Secrets', and then they sang along with Doc: 'Amanda the actress . . .'

The virile young men onstage welcomed their new fans with open arms.

Next night was the Family Inn, in the western suburbs, where the house record was toppled. With the load-out completed at 3 am, crew and truck headed to Melbourne for a big show in the dilapidated Woodfull Hall at the Royal Agricultural Showgrounds. A crew from the *Nightmoves* TV show would film the gig for broadcasting at a future date.

The line-up was a killer, with Melbourne favourites the Models opening, followed by Flowers, whose first single 'Can't Help Myself' was getting serious airplay. But then came the band that rarely played second fiddle to anyone, Midnight Oil. They too would have their performance aired on *Nightmoves*, so it was an opportunity not to be missed.

With 4000 jammed wall to wall and 1500 more outside, the show kicked off late. By the time the Oils took to the stage the condensation was dripping from the high ceilings. Peter Garrett careened about, driving the crowd into a bopping mass. But even Midnight Oil couldn't always overcome the chants that rose and fell: 'Angels, Angels, Angels.'

When they finally appeared, Doc, resplendent in yellow sports jacket, grabbed the mic and screamed 'No!', then stood aside as a muted 'Yes' came back. Another 'No!' got a louder 'Yes!' On the third one, 4000 voices screamed back 'Yes!'

Motionless behind him in black tailored sports jacket and wrap-around Bolles bought in LA, Rick kicked off with trademark nic-nics, and with precision timing the rest thundered in. At their desks out in the heaving audience, Ashley and Ray Hawkins pushed every slide to the limit. With lights blazing and PA cranked to max, the band raged into a blistering 'I Ain't The One' as camera crews focused and moved in.

Late next day, the crew pounded the eight-tonner back to Sydney and set up at an old haunt that would bring back memories for Ashley and Ray – and the rest of the band when they arrived.

Chequers had gradually faded into insignificance since the band had last played there. The old dive hadn't kept pace with the times and, running at a loss, they'd closed the doors. Now a new team had taken over. They'd enlarged, renovated, redecorated, and reopened as 'Rags'. To launch a new era they'd booked who else but The Angels.

One thing that hadn't been replaced was the air-con, installed back in the late fifties when Frank Sinatra had played there. The band took to the stage in front of 1800 punters with the temperature climbing north of 40 degrees. It was a wintry night outside, but in the bowels of Chequers (the new name never stuck), the ceiling dripped with condensation and a throat-gagging smog from cigarettes, sweat and BO swirled round the stage. A sweat-drenched Doc gulped oxygen from an industrial bottle the roadies had stage-side to maintain his athletic momentum, and he never missed a beat.

And so it went. The Angels were back on the road playing one-night stands to fanatical Aussie fans again. As they rolled round the country, *Dark Room* songs gained ever more airplay, and the queues got longer, with more and more being turned away. Extra shows were added but there was rarely enough room to accommodate everyone.

Bombarded with interview requests, their photos and comments were popping up in magazines and newspapers in every town and city around the country. Even the *Australian Women's Weekly* did a spread on them. They were all over *Countdown* and the special on *Nightmoves* went to air. Then they drove back into Sydney for an all-ages concert with support band The Radiators at the 2300-seat Capital Theatre. Next day the *Sydney Morning Herald* reported that fans ripped up seats, smashed a statue and danced in the aisles during a wild Angels concert. The Dark Room tour finished at the Brighton Hotel in Sydney's southern suburbs, with all but two shows of the five-week tour sold out and album sales at well over a hundred thousand copies.

They would now have a few weeks off, their first holiday in over a year. However, the demands of the band kept calling them back – a day here, a day there. As 'No Secrets' came off the boil, CBS released 'Poor Baby' as a single and they made another *Countdown* appearance, followed by a photo-shoot on the streets of St Kilda next day.

When it received only token airplay, 'Face The Day' was released, with a clip that featured Doc crawling along Sydney's George Street in pyjamas. It received huge exposure and the song raced up the charts.

They were then left in peace for two weeks before assembling in Sydney to mount a farewell show at the Hordern Pavilion. With a capacity of 5000, it was the city's biggest indoor venue.

Saturday 16 September arrived and the Hordern was packed. The punters knew it was their last chance to check The Angels out before they headed overseas again. Like AC/DC, they'd probably make it big and it could be years before they returned.

Opening band Outline, fronted by the indomitable Phil Rigger, had 5000 voices gleefully joining him on the chorus of their minor hit 'The Cicada That Ate Five Dock' – 'eee . . . eee . . . eee'. They made it through without the usual chant of 'Angels, Angels, Angels'. The mood gradually changed, though, after Jo Jo Zep and The Falcons came on. Calls of 'Angels' rang through the hall and eventually pissed them off: 'Yeah, we know who you're really here for.' But they won an encore – and then the stage faded to black.

During the change-over the tribal chant rose and fell . . . only to begin again and again.

Then the lights dimmed and the stage slowly washed over with blue light and the chants hit crescendo. The first chords of 'No Exit' crashed out as the lights gradually turned to a dim white that illuminated only the curtains behind the band. Drums pounded in and the chants turned to deafening cheers. Three silhouettes moved through ghostly billowing smoke. Red lights winked from amps. White beams from above momentarily picked out a player, before plunging him back to the gloom. A tall athletic figure hurtled through the gloomy smoke, aiming for the microphone glinting at the intersection of two blue shafts centre-stage. Intense spears of light stabbed down along the back of the stage. Doc raised his hands, his lips touched the mic. The crowd exploded and 5000 voices joined in as he demanded: 'Tell me why, the secrets have disappeared . . .'

CHAPTER TWENTY-SEVEN
ON THE BUS

Los Angeles lay spread out ahead as the long-haul 747 from Australia coasted in. Beneath the orange haze the city was flat as a pancake in the morning sun. Toy palms, a stadium and Matchbox cars on a network of criss-cross lines were enlarging as the plane throttled back and glided towards the runway, then pulling up at the airport gate. Back in economy, five Angels and their five crew stretched and reached for their luggage. Later they boarded a 727 for the flight to Detroit, the final stage of their half-circumnavigation of the world.

In Detroit they checked into the jaded Sagamore Lodge. In zombie state they popped mandies and crashed almost instantly. Next day, a little jaded, Doc and the Brewsters were picked up by James, an Epic rep, and carted around the local media – including a visit by Doc to WRIF to talk about *Dark Room* – and to spruik 'No Secrets'. WRIF, Detroit's leading rock station, was promoting their gig at Bookies 870, the hub of the Motor City's punk and new wave scene, and had been a big supporter of *Face To Face*, playing 'Marseilles' and 'Take A Long Line' since release.

To Doc's surprise, the DJ told him 'No Secrets' was 'soft' and not too different from a lot of other singles constantly presented to the station, whereas 'Marseilles', 'Take A Long Line' and the rest of *Face To Face* had a certain edge: they were tough and more in keeping with the station's hard-rock format. The DJ wasn't too interested in the rest of *Dark Room* either – it was 'too different from what you did before'. Doc made a spirited defence but didn't get far as the guy shifted the conversation, complimenting the band on the high-energy performance he'd witnessed last time they were in town.

In the car with Rick and John, James was curious about why they'd released *Dark Room* so soon after *Face To Face*. 'Everyone loved that album, man, you should have stayed and kept supporting it. "Marseilles" had legs and we were still working it.' He shook his head. 'It coulda been a hit. Now we gotta get behind *Dark Room* and "No Secrets", but the change is too much for the hard-rock stations that were playing "Marseilles". Different formats. We gotta start all over again.'

Back at the Sagamore they found a John Denver lookalike called Joe, the driver of the bus that would be their home while they traversed North America. He pointed it out through the reception-office window and they stared. It was a huge shiny chrome job with dark windows, a replica of an interstate Greyhound. He'd sleep in it that night while they played Bookies and be ready next morning to load their luggage, departure at 7.30 am, destination Cincinnati, Ohio.

> **Ray Hawkins:** Our first gig was at Iggy Pop's former resident club, where he'd refined and defined himself. It was a dimly lit dive with a manager who talked out of a voice box while he continued to smoke with the microphone at his neck. There was an S&M club next door and unemployed car workers on each street corner. The start of a four-month American and European tour. Welcome to the USA!

Next morning, bleary-eyed from partying, they climbed aboard the bus and Joe rolled her out onto Highway 75 and south to Cincinnati, where they were booked to play two shows at Bogarts. Once underway, they checked the interior out, but soon collapsed into the bunks for the rest of the trip. They hadn't been too sure about the bus idea, but now started realising the advantages over the cramped hire cars they'd used last time.

Rick: On each side of the aisle, for the first half of the bus, were bunks behind curtains. They were tiny but comfortable and, once the tour was underway, I was writing songs in mine most nights after the usual distractions were over. There was also a back room with comfy couches and a glass-top table.

It was in the back room where Rick and Mark Pope would stage ridiculous scenarios to break the monotony of the tyre-hum on bitumen highways as the bus rolled along. Mock fights would break out as they leapt about on couches. With red faces inches apart and spittle flying they'd concoct furious 'German' arguments:

'Du bist nach nur FLÜRRRLIGEN SCHNÖRRT!'

'Bach NACH du flunkten dürschtenflört. FAUSTEN SCHLUNKENFEGÜRLICHEN MACHT!'

'Ach! . . . Mach das blästen gelochterferl . . .'

Right at the back, the toilet was all psychedelic wavy mirrors. The lounge room had a TV screen and headphones. They could listen to the radio or to cassettes and there was a good supply of VHS tapes. They watched *The Blues Brothers* and *Caddyshack* – backgammon was big too. Joe was a neat, long-haired dope smoker, happy to have a chat as he drove along. The plan from now on was to have just one hotel room – a 'dayroom' in band parlance – at each stop where they could use the showers and facilities and park the bus outside.

The rock stations in Cincinnati, like Detroit, had given good airplay to 'Marseilles'. It had charted on the alternative 96 Rock station, but had since dropped out. 96 Rock were sponsoring the gig and one of their DJs arrived to tape an interview and record them doing an acoustic rendition of the song.

When John asked if they were playing 'No Secrets' or anything else off *Dark Room*, he shrugged apologetically. 'Sorry, man, nothing there fits our format.'

They turned up for soundcheck at the classy old 400-capacity theatre restaurant with a dance floor in front of a good-sized stage. The manager was crowing about how he'd foreseen the demand for

Angel City and booked them for two shows, an early and a late. The 11 pm one had sold out a few days back and the 7pm early show was three-quarters full.

A couple of hours later, a two-man folky support completed their set and then on stormed Angel City, with Doc glaring like a madman as the band powered into their first number. Taken aback initially, the crowd were out of their seats and down the front by the third song. When the Aussies launched into 'Marseilles' the place erupted, everyone singing along and demanding encores by the end.

Back in the dressing room with everyone still wringing wet, James began ushering in his industry guests for meet and greets. With the late show still to come, an exhausted Doc grabbed Joe and stormed out with Buzz – who looked as though he'd just emerged from a sauna. At the Travelodge they showered and rested up for the second show, swearing they wouldn't do two gigs in a night again.

By 1 am the second show was over, they were back in the bus and gliding through the dark suburbs of Cincinnati. A couple of girls had joined them through to the next gig, bringing a stash of cocaine. Sprawled out on the couches down the back, the band snorted the coke, sipped drinks and discussed the shows that had just gone down. Joe up front turned onto Highway 74 with his wipers flicking off the rain that was steadily falling.

At dawn rain pelted the screen as he cruised past a huge sign announcing 'Madison: 35 miles', and an hour later he was pulling in behind the motel where he switched off the big diesel, and in the silence climbed into his bunk. Check-in at the motel wasn't till noon.

With the night free, arrangements had been made to meet up with Rick Nielsen and head over to Memorial Coliseum, where Malcolm Young had left comp tickets for AC/DC's Back In Black show.

That night they opened with a gigantic bell being lowered onto the Coliseum's stage. To the tolling of 'Hells Bells', new front-man Brian Johnson, hammer in hand, gave it several hard hits to commence the show, and then indeed, all hell did let loose. Out in the audience, Doc and the others glanced around at the roaring crowd. Could they emulate the success AC/DC had achieved since leaving Sydney?

Next night was a headliner at Merlyn's, situated above a record shop on State Street. There was a support but the worksheet didn't give a name or contact details. The university in Madison has a massive 40,000 students and 'Marseilles' had received good airplay on the college radio, while two local album-oriented FM stations had also played a few tracks off *Face To Face*. The latest news from James – still on the road with them – was that local radio WJJO had started playing 'No Secrets'.

They arrived for soundcheck to find a small crowd at the door. Inside the crew were ready and the support band, fronted by a skeletal girl with spiky red hair, was standing by. Ashley mentioned that there was a rumour going round that Angus and Malcolm would be getting up for a blow.

They all laughed: 'Hope they're not too disappointed when all they get is us!'

The venue staff and their friends hung about when The Angels started the soundcheck. Doc wasn't happy with an uninvited audience while they were messing around getting things right and the room was cleared. On the up-side, Delia, the manageress, had organised the chef to cook them all a fine dinner, and by the time they went on, they almost had a full house. Delia had a cunning look on her face, raising suspicions as to who initiated the rumour.

Despite problems with the foldback speakers, the band rose to the occasion and got the place rocking. Doc had gone for a jog just before hitting the stage and was in top form, while the band thundered along behind him. Ray had plenty of lights to play with and trained a follow spot on Doc during 'Shadow Boxer' when he prowled the room and shaped up to startled punters with his flailing fists.

After the show everyone seemed to have an album they wanted signed – with even a few *Dark Rooms* among them. College students hung round Doc and he put on his intellectual Irish-poet vibe and they loved it. Girls said how much they lurved everyone's accents. Two slender black sisters latched onto Chris Bailey, getting him to repeat words so they could hear how he said them. The bus wasn't leaving until next day, so a good time was had by all on an otherwise cold and wet Monday night.

The following morning found a hungover Angel City bidding an affectionate farewell to a handful of new friends and fans. Followed by the truck, they cruised back down the highway to Chicago, where they parked behind the Lakeshore Holiday Inn, the same place their truck had been stolen on the last tour. They had a quiet night on board playing backgammon and talking about the next two shows – opening for the Kinks, who were promoting a live album, *One For The Road.* Their last album, *Low Budget*, released the previous year, had reached #11 on the Billboard charts and the English band was once again a major attraction.

The Kinks concerts were being promoted by Arny Granat, who'd done the Angels show at his Park West club on their last tour. After the two gigs with the Kinks, The Angels were scheduled to rejoin them two weeks later for twelve arena shows spread right across the country. Consequently, for these two gigs they were keen to impress Ray Davies, singer and boss of the Kinks.

The prospective tour would give The Angels a huge leg-up into the American market and Epic had taken out media ads for *Dark Room* in every city the Kinks were playing. For the Aussies, this was a strike at the big time like no other so far – they were all keenly aware of it.

CHAPTER TWENTY-EIGHT
THE KINKS TOUR

The Kinks thrashed through some of their songs at the soundcheck, sounding more heavy metal than they ever had on their classic hits. Eventually Ray Davies looked at the rest of his band, they nodded, and then they strolled off to the waiting limos and were gone, leaving the Aussies and their crew to get on with their set-up and open the show.

As a result, Davies wasn't on hand to see the audience reaction to The Angels' performance.

> **John:** We'd only just got back to our dressing room when Ray pushed the door open. I thought he'd come to congratulate us. He said, 'Is this my dressing room?' I said, 'No, I think yours is next door,' and he turned and walked away. I hadn't seen him while we were on and got the impression he'd just arrived.

It was much the same the following night. Once again Ray appeared to be unaware how well the support act had gone down. As often happened with stars who surrounded themselves with sycophants, he was kept in the dark about anything that would piss him off. Ray Davies had a nasty temper and no one was up for inflaming it.

> **Ashley:** Watching the two bands from the mixing desk was like chalk and cheese. The Angels were full of youthful energy, whereas the Kinks were like a

bunch of retired old men. And there was friction going on between Ray and his brother Dave, and also between Dave and the drummer – it was very obvious. There was a huge argument between them backstage after the gig. To be honest, I don't think they were even aware at that point that we'd blown them offstage. They seemed to be too focused on their own problems.

After The Angels' second show it was the usual mayhem of visitors in their dressing room, handshakes, backslapping, photos, signing stuff. Then they headed over to the Park West to prepare for their headline spot at midnight, where the Kinks had been invited back to party on.

This was where Ray Davies first caught sight of his support act. Rattled, he began making noises about their unsuitability to be the opener. He suggested that a new band be booked for the tour when it resumed in a couple of weeks. Ray was reminded that a deal had been done between his record company and Epic, which he'd endorsed. It was basically a 'pay-to-play' deal where Epic had committed promotional funds to the Kinks tour in return for Angel City clinching the opening spot. This was a common strategy for up-and-comer bands to secure the opening spot on a major tour. This expense was then deducted from future Angel City record royalties earned outside of Australasia.

Contracts had been signed and Ray would have to put up with the young upstarts.

After the Kinks concerts in Chicago, The Angels continued on with their club dates, playing cities whose names had permeated so many of the songs they'd done in earlier times: St Louis, Kansas City, Tulsa, Austin, Dallas, Houston.

Meanwhile, Ray Davies was on a media campaign promoting his tour and new album. For a brief shining moment in the sixties, the Kinks had been in a three-way tussle for supremacy with the Stones and the Beatles at the top of the US charts. Then it all crashed down. They were banned from touring the US by the American Federation of Musicians, a ban that lasted from 1965 to 1969.

Ray Davies: We got banned for a mixture of bad agency, bad management, bad luck and bad behaviour . . . So we deserved everything we got.

The late seventies saw Kinks greatest hits compilations appearing in the USA market, which kicked off a resurgence of interest. Ray signed on with Arista, a new album was issued, and to no one's surprise the Kinks were back in the charts again. Seizing the opportunity for another crack at the American big-time, Ray signed up with a promoter who figured he could justify a stadium tour to cover the fees the singer was demanding.

It was into this situation that the young men of Angel City stepped when they climbed out of their bus in Colorado to join the Kinks at the 11,000-seat Boulder Events Center. Having seen Angel City at the Park West, Davies wasn't about to let this bunch of Australian upstarts mess with his second tilt at America. He'd instructed his crew to turn down the sound system and cut the stage lighting. In future he'd be on hand to see what was going on during their set, so his roadies better fuckin' watch out.

Ray Hawkins: In the last song on that show, the tough sound of Australian rock had worked. I was out front working the lights, or at least the dregs of what the Kinks guy had made available for me. 'Marseilles' was in its final death throes – the crowd, guitars and drums building to an ecstatic climax. From the rear someone threw a frisbee. A great throw curving perfectly on the intended passage to the stage, a majestic arc that visited the entire left side of the massive stadium. John Brewster saw it coming, I saw it coming, the crowd started seeing it coming. I called a follow spot to pick it up, and the guy was good, catching its mid-air flight path.

It couldn't be happening but we knew it was. Everyone knew – rocker, band, security guards. The musical crescendo was almost peaking, five more frenetic bars to go, the whirling satellite veering in towards John, John stepping up to the microphone for his characteristic 'Good night, Boulder.' His hand played down hard on the final chord, then continued to full height and a perfect catch of the frisbee. Rock 'n' roll! Boulder, Colorado went insane.

Next show was a few days later at the Center Arena in Seattle. During the soundcheck Ray kept the Kinks onstage for twice the time they'd been allotted, leaving only a few minutes for The Angels to get things set before the doors opened.

> **John:** This was the gig where a guy got into the roof somehow – wanted to see the show for free. He stepped onto a suspended ceiling tile and fell about twenty metres onto the audience below. He managed to get up and hobble away but four others were injured, one girl with a serious fracture of the spine. Amazingly, no one was killed. It was a complete drama – people freaking and screaming. It was towards the end of their set and they cut the show.

Ray Davies visited the injured in hospital next day with the media in tow. The distraction took his attention away from his support band, until the next night in Vancouver.

One reason Doc was getting such great responses was that he had a radio mic, which allowed him to jump down into the audience, move about and get people involved in the song. Davies attempted to combat that by getting his roadies to stick white tape on the stage each side of Doc's microphone and he was instructed not to go past those lines. Of course, it would take more than white tape and instructions from Ray Davies to stop Doc delivering another high-energy performance.

When that didn't work, the available lights were cut even further, to the point that the promoter's staff had to intervene and demand some commonsense and courtesy. At the next concert the PA was further nobbled, but the redoubtable Angels still had the crowd on their feet.

> **Ashley:** We continued to get fantastic reactions. Doc at that stage was new to most people who came and they were just loving what they were seeing – and the energy from JB and Rick and the whole band was incredible.

Because of the way Ray treated his fellow band members, the Kinks were at breaking point. One night he came offstage screaming at them, saying the support band were better musicians than they were.

There were constant apologies from the Kinks roadies for what was going on. At one gig, Chris Bailey received an apology from the Kinks' bass player for using up the Angels' soundcheck time. A couple of days later he resigned and returned to England and an American bassist was hastily recruited.

While the Kinks flew from city to city, The Angels boarded the bus and truck after their set and drove the hundreds of miles to be at the next gig in time for the show.

> **Rick:** Ray Davies and I once walked towards each other in a long corridor backstage. When he saw it was me he wouldn't meet my eyes, even when I said, 'G'day.' He kept looking at the ground as he passed, without replying.

On a Saturday night, the tour played the San Diego Sports Arena, which had some 10,000 people in attendance. Despite the ongoing restrictions, The Angels once again received a huge response. The tour was to then have a week off before continuing with a run of concerts in big cities on the east side of America where a lot of influential agents and promoters were based – and coming to see the show. The culmination of that leg was a stand at New York's Madison Square Garden where Epic had bought their staff a block of tickets.

However, the morning after the San Diego show, news came through that Ray Davies had given Angel City's management a week's notice that their services were no longer required. They'd been kicked off the tour.

> **Ashley:** Fuck! We were off the tour! All of a sudden all the gigs in the worksheet folder had gone. We had this major tour we'd been kicked off for being too good!

Epic had bought dozens of front-row seats for VIP guests to attend the concerts in the New York State area and acceptances had poured in. Now the invitees were informed that Angel City were no longer appearing, but their free tickets were still valid. Effectively, Epic had bought tickets for their guests to see the Kinks, a band signed to another record company.

The attitude in the upper echelons of the record company was that Angel City had fucked up. They'd been asked to be cool and pull it back. They'd been disrespectful to Ray Davies, who was giving them the opportunity to play to his huge audiences – and Epic had paid out money for that right. It was inconceivable to the execs that these Aussies were unable to accommodate Ray's sensitivities. They'd blown the opportunity to play to an audience of more than 100,000 record buyers. The suits took it as a sign that the band was 'difficult' and probably not right for the international market.

Out in Los Angeles, the Epic publicity staff tried to make the best of it, attempting to turn the disaster around and garner space in music columns and rock magazines: *'Angel City get kicked off Kinks tour for being too good.'*

The band sat round for a week while the William Morris Agency used their considerable muscle to pull together a run of club dates. Then they were back on the road again, doing shows with full lighting and sound and no performance restrictions. They played a string of American clubs, crossed into Canada for three shows and then they were on their way down to New York where they played The Ritz to a sold-out audience, a sign that the band was building a great fan base. Epic organised a meet and greet before the gig, which was hard work for an exhausted band, but the show was amazing. They were playing so many places that John Brewster got confused and had Mark Pope write the name of the city on a large sheet so he didn't make a mistake greeting the audience.

Even if the Epic suits were pissed off, it was clear that the punters loved this cocky Aussie band, and so did their booking agency, taking calls from club managers requesting future dates. And although Epic in New York might have cooled off on Angel City, the LA office still recognised their potential and looked forward to their return.

The band then headed to London and Europe for three weeks where they'd hook up with Cheap Trick again before returning for another bite at the American cherry.

The following year The Angels were on an Ansett flight from Sydney to Melbourne. As Chris Bailey entered the plane, he noticed Ray Davies slouched in first class. After take-off, seated down the back with

John Brewster, the two ordered drinks and had a laugh about the Kinks tour. Chris drank the last of his G&T, smeared the glass with a film of grime from under his seat and gave the lemon an extra twist with his blackened fingers. He took out a sheet of Ansett notepaper and scrawled 'with compliments from Angel City', put the glass on a tray, draped a paper napkin over it and lay the folded note alongside. Hailing a passing hostess, he asked her if she'd be good enough to deliver it to his friend Mr Ray Davies in first class.

CHAPTER TWENTY-NINE
BACK TO EUROPE

London, 1 November. Wives and girlfriends had arrived from Australia and were there to greet them at the airport. After a day of sightseeing they all went out for dinner. Chris Bailey's American girlfriend, Trish, had flown over and joined them too. It had been a decade since the formation of Moonshine and they were reminiscing and laughing about the crazy times back then. They were now road-hardened rock 'n' roll veterans with hit records and platinum albums, and the women shook their heads, knowing how close the guys had come to tossing it in.

The following night they joined Cheap Trick for a run of concerts, with the final one at London's Hammersmith Odeon. The review in *Music Week* stated: 'Cheap Trick laboured under the strain of coming on after a group who were more exciting than they were.' The reviewer was fascinated by Doc, comparing him to Mick Jagger.

On 8 November the entourage arrived in Paris. *Face To Face* had sold 29,000 copies and *Dark Room* almost 10,000, making France their third-biggest market after the USA and Australia.

The Cheap Trick show was at the 3500-capacity Hippodrome de Pantin, a circus big top recently converted for rock concerts, with plenty of standing room in front of the stage. When The Angels came on, to their amazement, the fans down the front knew all the songs.

Doc dived in amongst them during 'Marseilles' for the spoken part. His pronunciation of the French lyrics had them in hysterics but when he climbed back on with a white towel stretched high in a victory salute, they erupted into wild applause. John yelled 'Bonne nuit, Paris,' and the band took a Beatles-style bow. But the French wanted more, chanting 'Angels!' and flicking on lighters until they returned for another song.

In Lyon, a rock 'n' roll city they were told, they had the crowd up out of their seats, while in Nice, they really fired up and convincingly carried the night. The crowd gave Cheap Trick a hard time which freaked them out, so much so that they asked The Angels to go back out with them for the encore. 'It was all for one and one for all,' said John, 'these guys were our friends!' They all took the stage and ripped into AC/DC's 'Highway To Hell' to massive applause.

At a party afterwards the camaraderie was obvious, and they wished each other well for the next legs of their tours. Cheap Trick flew off to Portugal and The Angels drove to Holland for two club gigs.

In Amsterdam, they played the Paradiso, a converted church with large lead-light windows. It was *the* place to play, where people went to, regardless of who was on. After the show some fans led them upstairs to a crowded bar called the Milky Way where counters designed for ice cream and chocolates displayed and sold various grades of hash.

After Amsterdam The Angels played a great gig in Wiesbaden, West Germany, an Army town near Frankfurt. Then, while their wives headed off for an Italian holiday, the band flew back to London, then hit the road for the Top Ten Club in Hamburg, one of the venues where the Beatles had honed their skills. ('Wow, we were standing on the same stage as the Beatles once did,' said John.)

They were staying in a three-star hotel and next morning the band and crew went down for breakfast. They arrived as the cook announced, 'Sorry, it's all closed.' They had an English truck driver, and straight out of Basil Fawlty he yelled, 'Hey listen, mate, who won the fuckin' war? We won the fuckin' war – we want breakfast and you'll fuckin' make it!'

> **John:** We were all in a state of shock. Fuck, do we run for our lives or what? But without a word, the guy gave us a menu, took the order and went into the kitchen and made us breakfast. I was embarrassed and wanted to walk out, but thought it was nicer if I stayed.

They then flew back to London for a show at the Marquee Club. The place was chock-a-block, and their fee was more in keeping with what the band was earning in Australia. 'Next time in London,' advised the agent, 'you should be headlining one of the theatres with a good support band. It'll sell out.'

In the cut-throat business of rock 'n' roll, Rick Nielsen, Robin Zander and the rest of Cheap Trick had generously given them full production and allowed them to shine, sometimes at their expense. The Angels had stepped up to the plate and the groundwork in England, France, Holland and West Germany was done. Beachheads had been established.

On 24 November the band returned to New York for the second leg of the American tour – including dates in Canada.

> **Mark:** We pulled the bus over just before the Canadian border. Jumped out and buried our contraband under rocks here and there and everywhere, and then on the way back stopped and collected it. It was like buried treasure: 'Six paces to the left and four paces to the right and under this rock here. Here it is!'

From there it was back into New York for three shows, then on to Nashville, two shows in Atlanta, a concert with Ian Gillan, then into the bus for more long gruelling drives and gigs in towns they'd never heard of. Eventually they arrived in Chicago for a couple of shows at Arny Granat's Park West again, where numerous lovers from past visits awaited them.

> **Mark:** The groupie thing. It never happened for me, probably because I was the tour manager keeping it all together. Doc didn't fuck round too much. He had Coe by this time, the American girlfriend he had back in Sydney. He'd left Dzintra for her and they were madly in love. What turned Doc on was the mind.

He was a thinker and a dreamer – but you'd never know what he was up to, he was very discreet and private. Chris Bailey had fallen in love with Trish, who he'd met on the tour. He was a ladies man, girl in every port. He dug the ritual of courting. Buzz was absolutely monogamous – besotted by Kay. I'm not too sure about the Brewsters. John had Abigail for a while, but they'd take whatever was flying, the temptations were always there. Then you have a super-fit, red-blooded road-crew.

As the weeks and miles went by, the bus, which had started out as 'Wow, look at this bus, isn't this fantastic' began to feel like a coffin on wheels. And it *was* dangerous. It broke down all the time. There was one night when it groaned to a halt on a bridge flanked by a low safety rail. John woke up, and, disoriented, stepped out the door and nearly went over the side. A cop car pulled up behind to see what was going on. They wanted them off the bridge before the morning traffic.

'We'll push you off,' they suggested, and put a blanket between their bumper and the bus. Their back tyres began spinning, but the bus didn't budge.

Suddenly Joe shouted, 'Hang on, the handbrake isn't off.' He released it and the bus began rolling back, shunting the cop car back with it. The cop kicked the accelerator to the floor but his rear wheels just howled and spewed toxic clouds of molten rubber as the whole kaboosh slid slowly down the incline. Eventually they called a tow truck and were hauled into the next town's garage.

Whenever John Brewster got overly stoned, he'd become paranoid about the bus having an accident – or Joe nodding off – so he'd sit up all night talking to him, making sure to keep him awake. 'Are you okay, Joe? Are you okay?'

On one long stoned journey, John got particularly paranoid.

Mark: We pulled into a truck-stop at 3 am and John said he was really worried. So Rick and the boys donated a packet of coke for Joe to snort. But he was a hippie dope smoker – he'd never done coke before. So, unknown to us, he put the frikkin' lot into his coffee. Within half an hour, he had to pull over. We had to walk him around the bus for two hours because he thought he was about to die.

While that was going on, John woke to find the bus parked at the roadside. Through the window along the dark road he saw the entire entourage walking along, holding Joe between them, trying to reassure their hallucinating driver that everything was fine.

> **John:** I stayed awake with him from then on – he still wasn't right. Every toll-gate he came to, he freaked. 'I can't drive through there, we'll hit the sides!' 'No, Joe, it'll be right, you'll be okay.'

In Florida during a performance, some bad news flashed around backstage. When the band came off Mark told them that John Lennon had been murdered. Everyone was devastated.

> **Mark:** Doc sat down – he was completely shattered. He withdrew and was very quiet. He had tons of empathy; after all, he sang in a band too. John Lennon was probably his biggest hero. Lennon was a poet and an intellectual and a rock 'n' roll icon. I think he was somebody that Doc aspired to – and coming off stage, after a triumphant performance, there was something very personal about it. Maybe a bit too personal.

The tour made its way back to Canada – to Winnipeg, where 'Marseilles' was on high rotation and charting #5 on CITI. It was the number-one station and the highest powered in North America with massive geographic reach. CITI had been playing tracks off *Face To Face* and *Dark Room* since their release and Angel City found that they were big stars. The promoter had booked them into a ritzy hotel while they were in town playing two sold-out shows at the 1200-seat Playhouse Theatre.

After Winnipeg they played the Paramount Theatre in Seattle and its nearby sister theatre, the Paramount in Portland. Affiliated radio stations had 'Marseilles' at the top of their charts and both concerts were promoted at a special ticket price of $1.99. Queues went around the block.

> **Mark:** Right at that point, they were primed, ready to burst right open. They should have stayed on but it was so expensive. A lot of the money they made

in Australia was invested in the cost of touring overseas. Nobody was getting rich. After we finished this excursion into America, Canada and Europe, I was gobsmacked at how big this band was building.

But there were tensions – in that close environment it happens. It got snarky. As tour manager, I'd hear one person's side, and then I'd hear the other person's side. At one stage it got really overt. There was Buzz saying, 'This is fucked, blah blah blah.' Yeah, sure. So backstage one night before they went on, I said, 'Right, just a quick meeting. All of those leaving the band, form a line over here behind Buzz. All those staying with the band, form a line over here behind John. All those not certain, form a line behind me.'

We left for Australia and I went to work for Chisel. I'd had enough. Nicky Campbell the stage tech was over it too – he was an old pro, had crewed for the biggest bands in Australia. But he'd seen too many accidents and ODs and danger and went back to his trade of boat building.

And Buzz, he finally did hand in his notice. That's how much all that touring had got to us.

CHAPTER THIRTY
BRENT ECCLES

February 1981, and AC/DC were returning to Australia with the *Back In Black* tour after four years away conquering the world. They'd left with Bon Scott out front and were about to fly in with new singer Brian Johnson. Bon was now at peace in Fremantle Cemetery after passing away a year earlier in London.

Angus and Malcolm had invited The Angels to do the whole Australian Back In Black tour with them. (Swanee opened the show each night.) Although The Angels had moved way beyond playing support to anyone in the local market, they took it as a compliment from their old friends and accepted.

Buzz was still determined to leave, citing musical differences, but at the heart of it were the constant personality clashes with John and Rick. However, he wanted to go with a bang, so it was agreed that he'd stay on for the AC/DC shows. Following the resignations of Mark Pope, Nicky Campbell and Buzz Bidstrup, Woodruff would make a captain's call on another member of the team – the creative force behind the band's extraordinary light show.

Ray Hawkins: After investing the greater part of my emotional life into The Angels, I got a call from John Woodruff to come to Dirty Pool. I should have known what was coming. John, Rick and I were as close a collaboration as was possible. Management didn't like it, probably as much as I didn't like them.

In any case, Woodruff spoke at length about how he needed to protect the band, safeguard their finances, blah blah blah. Each time he returned from his repeated trips to the toilet, he spoke both with added vehemence and with an itchier nose. I can't remember how he segued from that into sacking me, but he did. Without John and Rick's approval, I was out. Mind you, within three days I was hired by Cold Chisel and then Midnight Oil and went on to do some great gigs. But it wasn't The Angels, it wasn't an expression of my creative yearning – it was just pretty pictures set to brilliant music.

When John and Rick found out, they stormed into Woodruff's office to try to reverse the decision, but discovered that Woodruff had enlisted Doc into supporting him. He'd told Doc that Ray had become an irritant within the band structure and he would no longer tolerate the aggravation. To Woodruff, the highly intelligent Hawkins was a trouble-maker who never held back with criticism of his management style and ethics. Criticisms he might discuss with a member of the band, but not with a roadie on the crew, regardless of how good he was at his job or how close his friendship with band members. Bottom line, Woodruff was no longer prepared to put up with it. In the meantime, as the arguments raged, word had got out about the sacking, and Ray was snapped up by Chisel.

Ray: Sometime in the next few years I was rehired; but like married, then divorced, then remarried couples, the thrill was gone. Also, by that stage the rhythm section line-up changes produced a sound that I just couldn't light. The inner tension integral to The Angels, the energy condensed until it exploded in your face like a landmine, was gone. The band had moved into its guitar-hero, rock-God era and it left me alienated. Our second marriage didn't last long.

Accompanied by new tour manager Tom O'Sullivan, The Angels visited the *Countdown* studios at the end of January 1981 to film a performance for the newly released single, 'Into The Heat', backed with 'Back On You'. They were the last songs recorded with Buzz on drums.

With Doc resplendent in red silk shirt unbuttoned to the waist, two takes in front of the cameras were all they needed. Tom then bundled them into waiting cars and they were on their way to the Myer Music Bowl to soundcheck for the AC/DC show for 40,000 pre-sold ticket holders that night.

> **John:** Something very special happened when we went on that night. We hit our straps like no one's business and the reaction was incredible. AC/DC themselves gave us the thumbs-up as we came off.
>
> The next night, Malcolm kind of shook my hand and said, 'Good on you, you blew us off stage last night.' Which I don't agree with, but we did do an amazing show.

Music journalist Christie Eliezer reported in *Juke* magazine: 'The reaction to the Angels was so phenomenal on some of the shows that observers muttered the tour could well have been billed as a double-header.'

With the AC/DC tour over, the first job was to replace Buzz. A stream of drummers were auditioned in the CBS demo studio in Darlinghurst. One of the things the band noticed was that the tempos the drummers set up were faster than the songs were normally played at. John and Rick wondered if that was because they were picking up on the energy of the music.

Some well-known drummers arrived. They were expected to be brilliant, but many appeared to be casualties of whatever substance they'd been on – or were on – and failed to impress. Others just weren't as good as their reputations suggested, and then there were the egomaniacs, one announcing, 'You'll fucking play great with me on the drums.'

Eventually along came New Zealander Brent Eccles. Most of the others had thought they could get by on their natural ability, but Brent had studied the repertoire. He'd charted the songs, rehearsed them, learnt Buzz's fills – and the band went, 'Yeah!'

> **John:** He was the kind of guy we could relate to – kinda like one of us. He had a similar sense of humour and we were very impressed and that was it: 'Yup, you're in.'

His first gig with the band was in front of 4000 at Melbourne's Festival Hall. It was a fundraiser for community radio 3RRR-FM, where $100,000 was urgently needed to prevent their imminent closure.

Angel-mania had yet to hit New Zealand, and with a Kiwi on drums now seemed like a good time to visit. CBS NZ released an EP called *Into The Heat*. Brent's name was included on the picture sleeve along with the others, but it was Buzz who'd drummed on all tracks. Destined to be a collector's item among fans in Australia where it wasn't released, it also included 'Devil's Gate', 'No Secrets' and 'Face The Day'. It was released on 22 July, the day after the band arrived in New Zealand, and it sold for $3.99.

The first show was at the Windsor Park Hotel in North Auckland, a 'special sneak preview' for only $6.50. It was mainly for media, CBS staff and invitees to experience what was about to be unleashed. Then it was off down to Hamilton for Wednesday and Thursday nights at Macy's, a converted ballroom where, according to the local paper, a small but appreciative audience was treated to a 'fast and furious 90 minutes'. Word spread fast and the following night saw a howling Doc with a white towel round his neck wade through a packed house singing 'Marseilles'.

Then they were back to Auckland to play Mainstreet, the city's premier gig on Friday and Saturday nights. The old ballroom had been overwhelmed with demand for tickets and both shows had sold out.

The first night was full of maniacal punks and new-wavers. A dangerous vibe developed as they pushed and shoved and things gradually escalated into scuffles and punches. There was no jumping into *this* cauldron for Doc and they made a hurried exit after they'd come off from their second encore.

Word flashed round the city next day and all afternoon punters milled about trying to buy tickets. The Angels came on to a deafening

Sydney-style welcome, which never let up. There were constant brawls but this time there were massive Islander bouncers hauling out the miscreants. After an encore of 'Be With You', the band collapsed into the tiny dressing room in a welter of sweat. Next thing, Ashley and Bobby Daniels – the new foldback roadie – rushed in and told them they were leaving *right now*. A violent brawl had broken out between two Maori gangs and they were flailing at each other with knuckle-dusters, chains, barstools and anything else they could get their hands on.

Next day, on a quiet Sunday afternoon, they arrived at a breezy, run-down basketball stadium in Palmerston North. It had industrial louvre windows and a corrugated iron roof. The stage was a wood and scaffold affair, and when they fired up for the soundcheck echoes ricocheted around the empty walls. The promoter had been a big fan when he lived in Sydney and, with unbridled enthusiasm, assumed punters would pour in to see them. He worked at local radio 2XS and organised interviews with the band and played their songs at every opportunity – but all to no avail when only a couple of hundred tickets were pre-sold.

A few more walk-ups bought tickets at the gate, and then the band came on and blazed away as if to a roaring full house. Doc jumped in amongst the mosh pit and got them to sing along. With everyone crowded in front of the stage leaving the rest of the place empty, they chanted for more when it came to an end, until the band walked back on and gave them another two songs. Then Rick flicked his plectrum over the foldback speakers and the tour was over.

Ashley: The promoter of that gig must have dropped a bundle, but for us that first little tour was a great success. We made a lot of friends, impressed a couple of promoters and won over a lot of new Angels fans.

CHAPTER THIRTY-ONE
FASHION, FAME, *NIGHT ATTACK*

It was a wintry Saturday morning on 1 August 1981. Under the watchful eye of veteran tour manager Neil McCabe, The Angels and their roadies mustered at Sydney airport and boarded an Ansett flight for their first concert in Darwin.

Five hours later they disembarked into a sunny 25-degree day, where a fleet of Mini Mokes and a panel van for their instruments awaited them. On the drive in from the airport they passed beneath banners stretched across the highway, '*THE ANGELS – WELCOME TO DARWIN*', and there were more in the city. Girls crowded the lobby, batting eyelids as the guys signed in, and waited for the lifts.

The *Darwin Star* had a photo of an Ansett hostie on the front page wearing an Angels t-shirt. Shop windows displayed posters and Angels songs played from car radios. Next night over 6000 packed the Amphitheatre for the Angels' first show in the Northern Territory and they weren't to be disappointed. After the wrung-out audience called them back a second time, Doc announced that everyone should have an Angels Recovery Holiday next day – including him.

Around midnight they wound up at a club called Fannies, where a couple of them got up and jammed with local band Montaj. Next day they drove the Mokes into the scrub for dirt races, while the Jands semi with the concert equipment headed 3000 kilometres east across the dusty NT and Queensland roads to Cairns. The band flew over a couple of days later and hooked up for a run of open-air concerts down the coast to Brisbane, where they downsized for the pub and club circuit south from there.

Back in Sydney they had a night off at home.

Next night it was all on again at Blacktown's Comb and Cutter hotel. The big room was run by ace promoter Harry Della, who also ran the next three pubs they'd be playing – and recording songs for a new EP, *Never So Live*. With a large mobile studio requiring parking, three-phase power, cables running through windows, and meals for techs and crew, it would be vital to have Harry onboard.

The 12-inch *Never So Live* EP was released in early September and a track in the classic Angels style became the band's next big hit. The powerful 'Fashion And Fame' had started life at John's house on a four-track cassette recorder and a drum machine. He and Rick developed a rhythm track one afternoon in John's music room, then wrote most of the words later that evening. John and Doc then completed the lyrics in a hire car on tour.

Never So Live was a hit, notching up sales of over 80,000, quite an achievement for an EP.

Woodruff had been looking for a suitable producer for the next album and came up with Englishman Ed Thacker, who'd worked on a number of successful albums, among them as engineer on Marianne Faithfull's *Broken English*, which the band greatly admired. Woodruff's co-director Ray Hearn also hired Thacker to produce the debut album for the band he managed, Flowers – they'd imported him on a bulk deal.

Ed arrived in Sydney and they all immediately hit it off. He wanted to see them performing but the tour was over and they were in a demo studio. He grinned. 'That's a shame – I'd really like to see you play live.' Picking up on the undertone, Woodruff called Harry Della and asked if he could organise an Angels gig that night at a special low entry door price. Harry said maybe Blacktown Workers – he'd check to see if the cover band booked to play would be okay about supporting The Angels. The answer came back as 'yes' and it was on.

> **John:** We told Ed we wouldn't have many people because it wasn't advertised. Well, we got there for soundcheck and there was this queue that went for ever. The word was out, and as far as that lot were concerned, the night had started! Long story short, we put on a great show to around a thousand punters that night.

Ed saw the band in action and witnessed the audience reaction.

They moved into EMI's Studio 301, an environment that the band loved, and set to work. The first thing Ed made them do was put new strings on their guitars and new skins on the snare drums. To their intense annoyance, he insisted on new strings and snare skins for every session.

> **John:** It was just ridiculous and cost us a fortune! John Lennon recorded 'Woman' with a guitar that was hanging on the studio wall with rust coming off the strings. He just tuned it up and did the song. And Ed's making us change strings for every session! He was mad.

Despite Ed's idiosyncrasies, or maybe because of them, they became good friends, playing golf and hanging out together. One time in a restaurant, Ed complained about some pain in his hand. John's wife, Robyn, a physiotherapist, offered to have a look. She gently felt it and he fainted.

> **Rick:** He was a nutcase, a bit like us by then.

Spoken in jest. But the truth was that with the relentless work, the adulation, expectations of high-grade creativity and just the hectic life of being in The Angels, something else was taking hold. Away from the public gaze some of the guys were now self-medicating with something more insidious than a joint getting passed around. Snorting lines of coke was now the norm, and in Doc's case a few slugs of scotch on a regular basis would do the trick. They were becoming a little crazy, but the forward motion and inspiration hadn't faltered.

They discovered that Stevie Wonder was in another studio and took the opportunity to chat with him and his entourage now and then. Another afternoon, John stepped out of the studio and bumped into David Bowie. He was recording something in Studio B and congratulated him on The Angels' success since the tour with him three years back.

And so the sessions continued. A song called 'Long Night', hatched by John on the bus in America as it traversed a highway through a moonlit landscape, was recorded.

Thinking they'd be back in France on the next overseas trip, a follow-up to 'Marseilles' was deemed a good idea. Chris Bailey came up with a title, 'Storm The Bastille', and from there Doc, Rick and John got to work. Another song came out of a collaboration with Brent, 'Talk About You' giving him his first song credit as R. Brewster/Neeson/Eccles.

'Small Talk' got them into trouble with Peter Karpin, the highly rated A&R manager at CBS in Sydney. After listening to the demo, not only did he want it on the album, he wanted it released as a single. But Rick and Doc thought it sounded too much like regurgitating earlier songs. There was a raging argument about it: 'Oh, that sounds too Angels!' 'Well I got news for you, you *are* the fucking Angels!'

John: We must have been off with the fairies, because we had this whole thing about not wanting to sound like The Angels, and looking back it was just stupid. We'd developed a successful sound of our own – and now we were disowning it. I can't point the finger and say, 'Oh, it was his fault or Doc's fault.' It was all our faults. And it really pissed off the record company.

Rick: We were trying to get back to the toughness of *Face To Face*. We wanted to toughen up after *Dark Room*. But in a different way, to move on. But really, there was an element of rush with the whole thing. We were coming off that tour and straight into it when we actually needed time for development.

John: After the previous years, I think we were all getting tired of what we'd been doing, Chris especially, complaining that he was getting too old for any of it. At thirty-three! 'Fashion And Fame' came out really well, and it's not like the other songs were bad – it's just that for some reason we were trying to move away from ourselves.

The song 'Night Attack' with lyrics sparked by the Opera House 'riot' had come about through a band collaboration, and as the sessions drew to an end it stood out as a strong title for the album.

Finally, recording was finished and Rick and John flew to Los Angeles with Ed, and mixing commenced at Argent Studios. This was a good time for the brothers. The sessions were harmonious and went well.

Back in Sydney they bumped into John Boylan visiting on business and played him the mixes. He nodded politely but the sting came when he looked up and said it sounded like the band didn't have its creative captain any more.

John Brewster: His view was that if the songs were more like 'City Out Of Control' it would have been a great album. He singled that song out. 'That to me is The Angels – the rest isn't.'

The brothers initially took the 'captain' comment as referring to George Young. But discussing it later, they came to the conclusion he was referring to them, the Brewster brothers, who'd produced *Face To Face* and *No Exit.* The two musicians who George and Harry had passed the baton to and anointed.

They repeated what Boylan had said to Woodruff, but he disagreed.

John: If you think about 'Face The Day', 'Marseilles', 'No Exit', those mid-tempo big riffy numbers, 'City Out Of Control' is a classic Angels song. Whereas 'Nothing To Win' isn't. He [Boylan] might have overstated it, but 'City Out Of Control' was the only song that fitted the bill.

Doc: The 'Night Attack' song interested me but I don't think we expressed what we thought was in that song. It was a song that Rick had begun. For me, it's not one of my favourite albums.

On 30 November 1981, CBS Australia released *Night Attack.* With 'Fashion And Fame' riding high in the charts, the album came to rest at #13 nationally. Despite their misgivings, The Angels had another much-loved album in their canon. Reviewers wrote it up as a welcome return to heavier musical territory. They found the clean precise riffs compelling, loved the frantic-paced songs, the big melodic tracks and Doc's enigmatic vocal delivery. As for the hardcore fans, for many 'Fashion And Fame' would become one of their all-time favourites and *Night Attack* regularly rated fourth among the great Angels albums.

CHAPTER THIRTY-TWO
BACK IN THE USA

Towards the end of January '82 The Angels flew back to New Zealand, this time to play at the annual Sweetwaters Festival in Pukekawa, south of Auckland. The reputation they'd established during the club dates six months earlier had secured a prize spot on the first-night concert, right before UK outfit Ultravox, who'd recently had a huge hit with 'Vienna'.

On Friday the 29th, they mounted the stage after a string of bands, including Men At Work and Mental As Anything. INXS were supposed to open but hadn't shown up. By the time The Angels went on, the audience were ready to party. It was the Sydney Opera House all over again, with yobs heaving their empties stageward. A can bounced harmlessly off Doc's head and a few others landed on the stage, but with Doc holding his towel aloft and screaming, 'This is it, folks, over the top,' the rest kept blazing away behind him.

Ian Moss: We [Cold Chisel], or at least some of us, rocked up on the Friday night. We weren't playing that night, and I guess we had nothing much else to do, so we thought we'd get amongst it and soak up the atmos.

The Angels were on and in mid-flight. I thought I'd get up side stage for a bit and check the boys out. I was in the wings only a few feet from Rick

> Brewster. The guys were playing well and hard. There was a real solid crowd and they were getting into it and were there to party.
>
> The guys came off after their main set. No probs getting a huge encore. Rick came out alone to start the first encore song with an extended guitar piece. He was standing as he did in that sun-glasses-clad, statuesque theatrical pose he'd made his own years before. He was a minute or two into this solo piece when *bang*. Glass shattered across his right cheek bone, eye and forehead. Thank fuck for the sunnies! To Rick's credit, he barely flinched. Maintaining his composure he kept right on playing. In fact he played the whole accidental theatre of it all beautifully. He was cut and as the blood slowly trickled down his face, the guitar playing got angrier and angrier.
>
> Pretty outraged by this, I glared into the audience somehow expecting to instantly spot the culprit, but to a man the whole audience was just as horrified and stared at Rick, mouths agape. The rest of the band came on stage, completely oblivious to what had just happened. Rick always stood stage right and had been hit on the right side of his face, and with it being night-time and the light show still going on, they were never going to see it. Doc, who kept glancing at Rick for a cue as to when to start singing, finally realised something wasn't right and wandered over to discover, to his horror, what had happened. I guess a concerned Doc mouthed something along the lines of 'Are you okay?', but Rick wasn't having a bar of it, almost willing the words, 'Just get the fuck on with it!'

Rick had seen something a split second before it hit him. It hadn't hurt too much and he'd assumed the fluid which filled his shades to be spillage from the missile until Doc came over, wiped his cheek and showed him the blood. He looked down and, for the first time, saw the broken wine glass at his feet. When they came off, Brent called for first aid. After a fifteen-minute wait, an inebriated medic staggered in and dressed the wound with beer and a bandage.

Ultravox came out and did their best, but they'd been comprehensively upstaged. The audience were soon drifting off to their tents for the night.

Woodruff was in the States overseeing arrangements for the next tour to coincide with the American release of *Night Attack* in February.

Back in Sydney, Chris Bailey was having trouble focusing his left eye and took himself off to a specialist to discover he'd developed a serious condition – retinal detachment. It required a delicate eye operation and recuperation in a darkened room with a bandage on his eye to hold it all in place. The bassist was off the road for a month.

With the US tour scheduled to begin in a week, Rick, John and Brent flew to the States to find a fill-in bass player. The first one played with a major band and was available for the period required. They rocked up to his home and entered a large white-washed room dominated by a white grand piano and a pristine double bass. He played a few Angels licks that Rick said 'sounded like shit'. They drove on to the next applicant and located Jim Hilbun in a dingy flat. Like Brent before him, he'd taken the trouble to get hold of an album and become acquainted with the songs. He didn't plug in, just softly played along with the record and floored them. Jim was in.

Starting at the Warnors Theatre in Fresno, California, the first dates were in areas where they'd kicked big goals on the Kinks tour. The support band was Missing Persons, with sensational drummer Terry Bozzio and his stunning wife, Dale, on vocals. An ex-Playboy bunny, she wore a fishnet body-stocking with a mirror on each breast and one down below. The first night the two bands shared a cavernous dressing room designed for an orchestra.

John: Dale began changing and saying, 'Ah yes, we had a nice day – and you?', and we're trying not to look. Because there she was! And she was such a nice natural person. We stood stage-side watching them. Terry, astounding drummer, played for Frank Zappa, Bowie, the greats – and Dale, well . . .

Doc was told by the Warnors Theatre manager, 'Whatever you do, don't stand on that cover over there – it covers a huge pipe organ that rises up from the basement. It's flimsy, it's only there to hide the pipes. Whatever you do, don't tread on that.'

John: So of course Doc has to jump on it during the show. Fortunately it didn't give way – we were like 'for fuck's sake!' The manager's at the side yelling that he'll impale himself on the pipes! But that's what Doc did, climbed PA stacks, scaffolding. And fortunately for him, he mostly got away with it.

From there it was north to San Francisco for a double show at Bill Graham's Old Waldorf club. Production was then up-scaled and required a semi-trailer for transportation to concerts in the Northwest where their performances on the Kinks shows had dramatically boosted record sales and enlarged their fan base.

In this corner of America tracks off *Face To Face* had received high rotation airplay for over a year and 'Marseilles' had been a hit single. The area now represented the band's biggest album sales in the USA. When Ray Davies kicked them off the tour, it was mainstream news in Seattle and Portland and all the way up to Vancouver and beyond.

The Angels had done well in both Portland and Seattle at the end of the last tour – and they'd left behind a huge vibe. The William Morris Agency had no trouble selling a run of theatre shows to the local concert promoters, and major dates had been set up right through to Canada.

First was the Paramount Theatre in Portland. The band played two shows over consecutive nights. The first was a sell-out, the second one nearly. At the second show thirteen people were arrested for disorderly conduct, one for pissing over the balcony during Missing Persons' set.

Having never heard of this Aussie band prior to being invited to audition for them, Jim Hilbun was stunned at what he'd got himself into: truck-loads of gear, roadies, thousands of fans, concerts, the media attention – and lots of female admirers.

Over the two nights in Portland, to the band's astonishment the promoters' merch stand sold thousands of dollars worth of Angels t-shirts and albums, for which the band received a cut.

Billboard listed the shows as grossing $46,873, a result that put Angel City in the same league as Black Sabbath, who were touring the Northwest during the same period.

Seattle followed, with two more shows over two nights at another Paramount Theatre. The underground scene in Seattle was percolating into what would become the grunge movement. Angel City's performances would leave an indelible mark on some of the future players.

Rick's dark lyrics of alienation and angst gouged from the back alleys, shoot-up dens and brothels of Kings Cross shared much of the narrative style of the young Seattle songwriters.

In the years following, Angel City would be mentioned by prominent Seattle musicians as being an early influence. A fourteen-year-old Dave Grohl attended one of the Paramount gigs with his father, and on Pearl Jam's 2009 Australian tour guitarist Mike McCready told journo Kathy McCabe in a *Daily Telegraph* interview, 'I grew up on *No Exit* and *Night Attack* and covering 'No Secrets'. That is the Australian music that meant so much to me and my friends.'

There was a noticeable lack of attention from Epic on this tour *('Oh, are you guys in town?').* Though they were filling concert venues with eager punters wearing Angel City t-shirts and buying the earlier records, the vibe from the American label for *Night Attack* was decidedly cool.

However, no sooner had the band checked in to the Sandman Inn in Vancouver, prior to the next show with Missing Persons, than Dave and Bill, two enthusiastic reps from CBS Canada, showed up. Dave had put together an Angels documentary using their video clips, and had managed to get it played all over Canada.

Big shows followed in Calgary and Edmonton before Missing Persons headed off on their own club tour – they'd score the hit single 'Words' later in the year – and The Angels flew over to Anchorage in Alaska for a double show at Banquet Hall.

That would be Jim Hilbun's last gig. After two successful shows they held a send-off party for him back at the hotel, and then the crew loaded everything onto a long-haul flight to LA and the entourage said goodbye to Canada.

Despite the lack of enthusiasm from Epic for *Night Attack*, spirits were high, with a feeling that they were on the crest of a wave – as in Australia, all they had to do was keep delivering their brand of high-energy performances, and, like their friends AC/DC, they'd ultimately crash through.

*

In LA the band were booked to play a couple of gigs at the Roxy on Sunset Boulevard. Both shows had sold out and celebrities were trying to get their names on the door. Chris Bailey had arrived a few days before and checked into a cheap motel while waiting for the band to arrive, but when they did he was settled and stayed where he was. At the Roxy the crew conducted the soundcheck, so the band didn't assemble until shortly before show-time.

> **John:** We're due on in fifteen minutes and – where's Chris? We don't know where he's staying to phone him up. There's a packed house waiting for us, including Bryan Brown, Mel Gibson, Billy Thorpe and a few others from back home. We try getting on to Jim Hilbun, because he lives nearby, but suddenly there's Chris. 'Where the fuck have you been?'
>
> He says he tried to leave his motel but as he opens his door a voice yells, 'Get back in your room!', and a bullet whizzes past his ear. The cops are having a shootout with some criminal. It's all happening, cops and robbers. Chris is caught in his room until they eventually shoot the guy dead. Chris came up with some good excuses for being late before, but this one topped them all!

That night cigar smoke filled the air as a busload of Epic staff arrived to see the band. They were treated to a red-hot show from the VIP area and afterwards squeezed in backstage for greets and photos. They didn't stick around for long, but said they'd enjoyed the show 'a whole lot'.

Now tension mounted as everyone prepared for the dreaded Midwest run, where the name Angel City meant little or even nothing. But just as they'd cracked the Northwest with grit, determination and killer shows, they knew that the only way they'd crack the Midwest was to get out there and do it all again . . . as AC/DC had done.

One person who didn't enjoy the challenge was Chris Bailey. Still not feeling great after his operation, he constantly complained of being 'too old for this shit' as they checked in and out of crappy motels and played half-empty clubs. Towards the end John took him aside. They'd worked together for over five rags-to-riches years and he knew him well. Chris had always had his downner side but this was different.

> **John:** I said to him, 'Chris, you don't seem happy. Are you genuinely over it with the band? Because if you are, we just want to let you know we got on really well with Jim, and we're pretty sure he'd jump at the chance to take the gig – but only if you want to go. We'd prefer you to stay.' And Chris had this sad look and said, 'Yeah, I think it might be time to move on.'

Chris was a musician – playing was everything to him. He and Buzz had something special musically, and for him that wasn't happening with Brent. After leaving The Angels he went on to play with Buzz in GANGgajang. Over the next twenty years, they'd record some of the finest Australian albums of the era. Chris and Buzz would be considered one of the best rhythm sections in the country.

Back in LA a sense of gloom descended on the entourage. The rush as they mounted another stage – even the 'crappy' ones – to prove their worth to a fresh new audience was behind them. They'd been touring through foreign landscapes for six months, living in each other's pockets, but now the party was over for a while.

CHAPTER THIRTY-THREE
THE SHOW MUST GO ON

Doc's clandestine relationship with Coe Uttinger hadn't come to an end at Sydney airport in April 1980. Once back in Australia the affair had continued. He left Dzintra and moved in with her – not that he spent too much time there. With the *Dark Room* touring commitments in Australia and New Zealand followed by the lengthy second tour overseas, followed by more touring when they got back, life with Doc wasn't conducive to the sort of relationship a spirit as intense as Coe demanded. Eventually the relationship blew up. Doc and Dzintra were reconciled, he went home, and the grand affair was over.

Almost.

Bjarne Ohlin: Sometime in May '82, Coe had returned from a retreat where no one realised she was turning yellow with jaundice. She assumed her weight loss was a result of the diet/fitness regime. I visited her with my partner, Anthea. I was shocked at her condition and promptly had a doctor mate do a house call. He immediately called an ambulance and had her admitted to hospital. Tests quickly revealed cancer in most of her vital organs with no hope of recovery. We saw Doc after an Angels gig and told him she was terminally ill, which appeared to knock him hard.

Doc's life at that point had become very complicated. Not only was Dzintra four months pregnant, but his secret new girlfriend, American Suzy Pointon, a devotee of the Rajneeshee cult – also known as the 'Orange People' – was four months pregnant to him. Despite that, he got in touch with Coe and started visiting her, and continued to do so when she moved into palliative care.

Bjarne: She passed away on the ninth of September '82. After she was cremated we organised a bus with her parents and a group of us who'd cared for her while she was ill, and drove to Kangaroo Valley. Doc was able to attend. We all passed our hands through Coe's ashes as we spread them into a hole we had dug in preparation for planting a tree.

Doc then discreetly licked her ashes off his fingers. He would obliquely refer to the incident at the end of The Angels song 'Underground', which he co-wrote with John and Rick: 'Nails, nails, blood red nails, taste of ashes in my mouth.'

Rick: From Coe's death on, Doc carried a small shrine in his suitcase – a board of photos and mementos – and set it up in his motel rooms with candles, where he drank and howled for hours after gigs. So much so that it sometimes disturbed other guests and brought the manager to his door to see if he was okay.

Mark Pope: I think that she was the one who sent him over the edge. Some years after I'd tour-managed the band, I rang John Woodruff: 'Listen, I've found all Doc's love letters from Coe. Do you think I should give them to him?' John said, 'Are you fucking crazy?'

Doc had that sort of Irish-Catholic black guilt Old Testament, all that sort of . . . I don't know. I really don't know.

The last few months of 1982 were a dark time for John and Rick as well. On Friday morning, 1 October, deep in sleep after a late night at Rhinoceros Studios, John was woken by his wife, Robyn, to take a phone call. A doctor at the other end of the line told him he was sorry to say that his father had just passed away. Shocked, John collected Rick and they flew down to Adelaide to be with their mother.

Later that day, Woodruff was on the phone asking if they wanted to cancel the sold-out show at Maroubra Seals that night: the first of three. They flew back with heavy hearts.

For the next three nights the brothers strode out with the band and blazed their riffs and solos into the super-charged, chanting, sardine-packed audiences. Two of the shows were recorded but the tapes were never used.

On stage, Rick and John knew they'd made the decision their musician father and grandfather would have made in similar circumstances. *The show must go on.*

CHAPTER THIRTY-FOUR
'WATCH-A THE R-RED'

The Angels had taken up residence at Andrew Scott's Rhinoceros studio in Sydney's Surry Hills. It had recently opened and boasted the latest in state-of-the-art equipment. There was a new album to make and the plan for the next few months was to concentrate on blocks of recording, with shows on the weekend. Jim Hilbun had written the basics of a song called 'Stand Up'. It had possibilities as a single and they set about putting down a rhythm track for it.

After the gigs at Maroubra Seals, they returned to the studio, where vocals were completed on 'Stand Up'. Rick and John mixed it down and it was rush-released. By December, The Angels had a new single in the charts.

The sessions continued and, between ferocious table-tennis games out on the back court, more rhythm tracks went down. There was also the cookie saga, in which Brent fronted as spokesman for the band and, after intense negotiations with studio manager Jackie, the kitchen cupboard became regularly stocked with jars of cream cookies, coffee biscuits and various bite-sized goodies.

Maybe it was the influence of the new members – maybe something else – but the sessions were taking on a much more adventurous vibe than anything the band had previously attempted.

John: The best thing about this album was a blow that ran for forty-five minutes – there were some great feels on it.

The blow produced the improvised tracks 'Bow Wow', 'The Zoo', 'Name Dropping' and the drowsy lazy sax-laden 'Stay Away'.

The band flew down to Melbourne to play the 3XY Rocktober concert to 70,000 at the Myer Music Bowl. Doc had broken his arm in a minor car accident and had it in a cast, so he wasn't climbing scaffolds – but that didn't stop him hurtling about and popping up in a balcony beside the stage and coaxing the crowd to sing along on 'Be With You'.

Back at Rhinoceros and Doc had been bringing in a Rajneeshee guy called John. He had MS, he was on crutches and wore flowing orange robes.

John: He sat on a stool in the control room and he was like a cloud of doom. He never said a word, just put out bad vibes. The really scary thing was that we were worried Doc was getting sucked into the Orange cult. He was spending a lot of time at a big old mansion they owned in Centennial Park.

It got to the point where the Brewsters took Doc aside and told him the guy had to go – the rest of the band were finding it difficult to work in that kind of atmosphere. They were paying $2000 a day for the studio and things weren't going as they should. Doc wasn't happy but acquiesced.

Their concern about Doc and the Orange people was well-founded. Away from the band, Doc had become fascinated with the teachings of Bhagwan Shree Rajneeshee. They were unaware of the relationship he had formed with Suzy Pointon, a young American woman living at the mansion. Four months later the band were also unaware that she'd given birth to a baby son, Aiden, arriving into the world twenty-six hours earlier than Daniel, his first son with Dzintra. Unbeknown to both women, the babies were born in the same Sydney hospital.

Many years later Doc's friend Bob Bowes would recall that time:

> **Bob Bowes:** I remember fondly singing outside the railway station in Kings Cross. We were asked by the bikies who had their bikes there to move on. The alpha male in you [Doc], with complete disregard for my wellbeing, told them that we couldn't whilst we were in performance. Eventually we did move. That night we made enough money to buy a couple of bottles of Champagne to christen Daniel, but you and Dzintra could not decide on a name, so we drank the Champagne anyway. Daniel remained 'No Name' for at least a month and several more bottles.

A year or so later Suzy married an Australian man and, with her baby son and husband, returned to the USA where Aiden grew into a fine young lad, tall like his father, with the same matinee-idol good looks and charm. And with his father's surname 'Neeson' on his birth certificate.

Doc had written a caustic tale of a 'calorie attack' while the band was in America and it now morphed into a song called 'Eat City' – and Jim got an opportunity to demonstrate his prowess on the sax.

A French horn player was considered essential by Rick and John to play at the end of a song they'd written with Doc called 'Shoot It Up'. They brought in a guy from the Sydney Symphony Orchestra and explained what they wanted: three rising notes, then hold the last note for sixty-four bars.

'No problem,' he said, 'got the chart?'

The Brewsters looked at him and explained it again, this time adding that it came after the final chorus.

'What's a chorus?'

'Look, we want you in the outro.'

'What's an outro?'

> **Rick:** He was an orchestra player – they can't play without written notes in front of them. So I had to count it out and write in the notes on a sheet of manuscript.

John: And then he did it on take one and it was absolutely perfectly in tune and beautifully played.

Another song that came out of the weirdness that infused most of the sessions was 'Watch The Red'. Two years earlier Rick had been wandering the streets of Manhattan when he came across a wizened old gypsy playing Three-card Mondo. 'Watch-a the r-red, watch-a the r-red. Red-a you win, black you lose,' she called.

Rick stood among the crowd and watched people put down twenty dollars, pick the red correctly, and get forty back. There was a rabbi, a couple of suits, guys in jeans, women with shopping bags. Sometimes they lost, but mostly they won. He moved closer, watched the shuffling carefully and started correctly picking which card was the red queen. Plucking up courage, he reached forward and dropped down a twenty. 'Watch-a the red, watch-a the red. Ah sorry, black, you lose!'

Fuck! How could I have got it wrong?

He watched the rabbi on a winning streak. Rick knew every time he won where it had been, so down went another twenty.

'Black-a you lose!'

Shiiit!

He lost another five times before pulling back and allowing a guy in a tattered jacket to have a go – and he won!

With an awful lurch, he suddenly realised what was going on and started abusing her for ripping him off.

Up she jumped, screaming '*Cops! Cops!*', grabbed her box and raced away. The crowd quickly dispersed and were gone in seconds.

Rick: They were all part of it. The rabbi, he was winning more money than anyone. 'Watch The Red' was written to recover the week's pay I lost playing Three-card Mondo in Manhattan – a classic street-hustle guaranteed to trick a naïve first-timer like me. The voice at the start of the song is from the Walkman I had in my bag. I'd had it on to record the street sounds and it got the little gypsy as she ripped me off, chanting, 'Watch-a the red . . . watch-a the red . . . red you win . . . black-a you lose.'

One night Rick was working at the console when he sensed the door open, and a second later the owner, Andrew, was lifting him bodily from the chair. 'Rick,' he said in a controlled voice, 'we're leaving right now. The building is on fire.'

Rick looked at him – he was serious. He grabbed his Strat and they headed for the office door where manager Jackie was waiting. The studio was on the second floor opposite a pathology lab. They opened the door and acrid smoke poured in. Slamming it back, they took a deep breath and then ran out into pitch-black smoke. Feeling their way along walls they reached the stairwell, scrambled down and fell out to the street. The studio engineer, Al, appeared at a window a minute later and kicked it out. Black smoke billowed through as he hung there until a fire truck arrived and got a ladder up to him. They yelled, 'You okay, Al?', and he yelled back, 'No, sorry, I'm only dying!'

It turned out that someone in the pathology lab had been making illicit substances and had somehow started a fire. He ran from the lab as gas bottles began exploding and didn't raise the alarm. Next day the top of a cylinder was discovered inside the studio where it had ripped through the lab wall, across the corridor and through the ten-inch soundproof door of the studio.

When they were allowed back in next day, they raced upstairs, fearing the almost-completed master tape had been destroyed. The entire studio was covered in chemical dust and soot, including the tape, but as it turned out, it was okay. A few days later, after professional cleaners had gone through the place, the mixing sessions resumed.

CHAPTER THIRTY-FIVE
NARARA

Doc made his way unsteadily to the microphone. He grabbed the stand and swung it side to side, fumbled around, and missed the point where he should have come in. Looking back accusingly at the rest of the band, he made another start. He was off key, although fortunately also off mic. The others watched in trepidation as he staggered about, snarling and groaning the lyrics. The next song in and Doc was leaning over the front row of the crowd, swinging the stand erratically above the heads of those down the front.

'Hey Doc,' John shouted, 'For fuck's sake be careful with that stand!'

Doc tottered over. 'Fuck off, John.'

He gradually got his bearings and somehow they got through the rest of the set, with John and Jim singing and carrying the songs. The show was cut short and they left the stage to polite applause, the audience too stunned to make a fuss.

The band gathered in their tent backstage, fuming, with Doc nowhere in sight. The roadies revealed he'd been drinking all afternoon. This had happened once too often and they started talking about Jim singing at the next gig, the Narara Festival. Doc then appeared and headed straight for John Brewster, screaming at him, 'Don't you ever talk to me like that onstage again!'

When they all turned on him, Doc said, 'Ah, fuck you, I need a piss,' unzipped his fly, turned and blindly urinated on the leg of a female friend who'd come over to give him moral support. With her now yelling at him too, he stormed off, telling them all to fuck off, that he was leaving the band – they should get another singer.

Over the next few days Woodruff shuttled between them, calming everyone down. The dust settled and they eventually agreed that Doc should do Narara. It would be his last show and an announcement would be made soon after. At that point there was some discussion about Jim taking over as front-man after that, but they'd discuss that further after Doc had gone.

Rick: After that last gig I wouldn't have been sorry to see him go. But we never took him seriously. He'd already talked about starting an acting career, and I just couldn't see that happening either.

The Narara Festival was an hour's drive north of Sydney and held over the Australia Day weekend in 1983. It was financed and organised by a group that included John Woodruff and featured an all-Australian line-up headlined by Men At Work, The Angels, Cold Chisel and INXS.

Men At Work, with their mega-platinum *Business As Usual* on top of international charts with over ten million sales worldwide, were headlining Saturday night. Second on the bill: The Angels. The line-up sent ticket sales soaring, topping out at over 50,000.

A couple of days before the show, Doc decided to get his last gig with the band captured on film. He rang Bernie Cannon, producer of the *GTK* series from the 1970s and other rock programs, and asked for a quote. The price was beyond his finances so, on a whim, he rang Rod Muir, owner of 2MMM, who agreed to underwrite the project on the condition he had broadcasting rights. When asked why Doc was leaving, the singer told him that he wanted to concentrate on an acting career.

With two days to get things organised, Bernie went into overdrive and pulled a hotshot crew of ABC news cameramen together, hired four Nagra film cameras, picked up film stock from Kodak minutes before they closed, and on Saturday morning, with Woodruff onside behind the scenes, bussed the team up to ground zero at the festival to start setting up.

John: On the night, INXS were on before us and put on a blinding show. We said, 'Woops, we better play well!', and we just went for it.

Right on cue, a blood-red moon rose into a starry sky as the band fired up to a triumphant roar and a sea of raised fists. The spectacle had begun. '*Angels! Angels! Angels!*' Messianic Doc, guitar-god Brewsters, pounding rhythms – the tribes of berserk believers had come to worship at the altar of Aussie rock 'n' roll with the black-clad high priests of pub-rock.

During 'Marseilles' Doc began climbing the scaffolding of the speakers. The band powered on, watching as their accident-prone frontman steadily ascended, microphone in mouth, until he reached the top.

Doc: I wish I'd organised a camera up there. I asked the fans to light their lighters and suddenly there were all these pinpoints of light across the amphitheatre. It was a starry night and it looked like I was seeing right out to infinity.

He and the band turned in one of the finest performances of their career. The encores were deafening and Bernie Cannon's crew were there to capture it all.

Exhausted but exhilarated, the band staggered off only to be glared at by a cabal of incensed CBS executives, totally pissed off that The Angels had so decisively upstaged Men At Work before they'd even gone on.

John: CBS had the shits because we blew Men At Work offstage – and they were our record company too!

The real problem was the programming. The organisers should have put the laidback Men At Work on before the high-energy Angels.

Saxophonist Greg Ham had said as much to John earlier: 'We're really nervous about following you guys . . .' As it was, half the crowd had drifted away by the time Men At Work got to 'Down Under'.

Over the next few days Woodruff used his influence with Doc and persuaded him to remain with the band.

> **Doc:** It was put to me quite firmly – it was still a choice, but in the end I decided that I preferred music at the time, so I shelved my acting ambitions and went with the band, for better or for worse.

In February, in the wake of the triumphant Narara performance and Doc's decision to remain, came some bad news. Epic International informed The Angels that they wouldn't be picking up their option to release *Watch The Red* and their relationship was now terminated. However, CBS Australia and New Zealand, where *Night Attack* had been a huge success, *had* picked up the option for the new album, despite many in the company believing the band had lost its way. Things had inexplicably become frosty with CBS staff. John Brewster shrugged it off as sour grapes coming from Epic America's direction.

A second single, 'Eat City', was released in March after they'd performed it on the Countdown Awards, and in May *Watch The Red* finally made it into the stores – and saw The Angels return once again to their rightful place in the top ten of the album charts.

The soundtrack for the Narara film was mixed down by John Brewster but there was a problem with Doc's vocals. With all the leaping about and scaffold climbing he'd done, much of his singing was off mic and he had to come in and overdub the vocals while doing his best to lip-sync with the film running on a screen.

Then it was back on the road with two of the loudest outfits in the country, Rose Tattoo and The Choir Boys. With equipment loaded into two semi-trailers they rolled away to play the biggest indoor venues in the land, selling out shows wherever they went.

To coincide with the June tour, CBS released a third single, 'Live Lady Live', with Doc at his screaming best. A 12-inch collectors' edition of the single was released in early July with a picture cover, and finally, when this single failed to chart, a fourth song, 'Is That You', was released in late August.

In September *The Angels – Live At Narara* was shown on the Nine Network and simulcast over the Triple M FM radio network. It went to air on a Wednesday night and many rock venues decided not to open, fearing the punters would stay home to watch TV – which they did. It was the highest rating simulcast up to that time and the video of the concert was released for sale soon after.

Now with all possible singles released from *Watch The Red* and sales easing off, CBS Australia (and New Zealand) officially informed the band that they wouldn't be re-signing them – which came as a surprise after the commercial success of their latest album.

Many years later a story came to light that could explain some of the negativity coming from the CBS Australian head office during this time. When The Angels had first signed to them, Woodruff had given a stern warning: 'Don't dip your pen in the company ink!' Asked what that meant, he came back with a more direct instruction: 'Don't go fucking any of the CBS girls – it'll only lead to tears.'

The instruction had been ignored by a number of the band and they'd got away with it.

But while they were performing in Perth a month or so before Narara, Doc had struck up a conversation with a very sweet lady who worked in the CBS Sydney office. She happened to be on Christmas holidays in Perth with a friend and rocked up to a gig one night. Later she went backstage to say hello and fell under the spell of the tall, blue-eyed Irishman, spending the next few days and nights at his side. What the Irishman didn't know was that she was the discreet girlfriend of one of the top CBS executives.

On arrival back at Sydney airport she was pleasantly surprised to find her much older lover waiting in a limo with an expensive bunch of flowers. But it soon turned nasty when he revealed that word had filtered back about her recent fling. Jealous and humiliated, he swore that Doc and the band would pay for it. Over the following weeks she watched him assiduously spread fact, fiction and rumour about their cocaine and alcohol abuse. He compared The Angels to Dragon, who'd been with CBS for a number of drug and booze-fuelled years, finally calling it a day in 1979 with their drummer dead from a heroin OD and most of the others regularly off their faces.

When Epic in the USA dropped The Angels, it just supported the executive's assertions that they had no future in the local company either. At meetings he argued that the band had lost its way and CBS should be putting their resources into Men At Work and recent signing Midnight Oil.

CHAPTER THIRTY-SIX
TWO MINUTE WARNING IN LA

For a top band to have been dropped by two record companies within a year would have crushed most managers – but John Woodruff was not like *most* managers. He saw it as an opportunity and headed straight for America looking for a new deal.

He schmoozed and networked his way through every contact he had and by early 1984 he'd got MCA – run by Eagles manager Irving Azoff – hooked. After a buying spree of smaller record companies, MCA had nearly gone bankrupt during the last year or so. They'd recently brought in Azoff who'd consolidated the artist roster; dumping non-performers and signing up new opportunities.

The MCA executives who signed them up knew about Angel City's strength in the Northwest, and figured that with the right album they could build on that and break the band into the mainstream. They weren't interested in *Watch The Red* but loved the earlier albums. If the band could give them demos of songs like the earlier ones, they'd sign them.

John: We'd been spending a lot of time in Sydney's EMI's Studio C, which was a little cupboard one floor down from the main studios and didn't cost a lot. It was Rick, Brent and me. We'd sit in there and write songs. At night we'd go upstairs and record demos of those songs free of charge with young engineers getting experience.

The demo of 'Small Price', which is actually better than the final recording, basically clinched the deal with MCA for us. Woodruff got me to fly over to meet Steve, MCA's A&R manager, a really nice guy. We talked about what kind of album we'd make and then I flew back.

EMI's studio manager Martin Benge had already pitched a deal to Brewster for The Angels to record their album at EMI's 301 if or when the time came. It was a $56,000 flat fee for Studio A, and $4000 to use Studio C to do the writing. It was open-ended, regardless of how long it took to record.

John: The demos we'd done were really good so it wouldn't have been hard to go upstairs and do them for real and end up with an album. But Woodruff said we should record in Los Angeles. He'd done the deal with MCA and he wanted us to be on their doorstep. He wanted their active involvement. I said, 'EMI's Studio A is an amazing studio. It was good enough for Bowie and Duran Duran and Stevie Wonder.' But Woodruff insisted he could get a top studio just as cheap in LA and convinced us to go.

A $200,000 advance had been negotiated, of which Woodruff took out his management commission, leaving approximately $160,000, with another whack out of it to cover legal costs. That left around $130,000 for recording and living expenses while the band were in LA. The advance, as was normal with such deals, would be deducted from the band's future record royalties.

On 1 May, The Angels flew out of Sydney bound for Los Angeles. With the band was Luke Richmond, aka Spartacus, their protector and fixer. No one fucked with Spartacus.

The plan was to record at the famed Record Plant Studios. Producer Ashley Howe, chosen for his stellar work with guitar-oriented hard-rock bands, had been contracted at fifty grand against percentages to produce the killer album that would break them internationally.

They checked into the Oakwood Apartments opposite Universal Studios in Toluca Lake and a new episode in their journey began. While the rest of the band went to the supermarket, John went out and returned at the wheel of a white 1964 Cadillac De Ville bought for $450. Everyone gathered round in admiration and christened it *Caddy White.*

After a meeting with Howe, specially flown in from his home base in London with his wife and staying five star at the band's expense, they moved into a pre-production studio for two weeks.

Steve, the A&R manager, arrived with two colleagues. It was the first time anyone from MCA had seen the band and it felt like an audition. They hung with Ashley and watched, creating an air of unease.

Next day Rick and John were driving in *Caddy White* with Ashley when he cleared his throat and said, 'We've got a problem. The record company wants you to sack your drummer.'

'Oh yeah,' said Rick, 'why's that?'

'He doesn't swing.'

According to Ashley, drummers were a dime a dozen in LA and they could easily get a session player.

John looked at Rick and back to Ashley. 'Well, tell the record company there's no way we'd do that. We're a band and he's our drummer.'

Brent had played well on *Watch The Red* and he'd played well on the demos they'd done at EMI.

After two weeks they moved out of the rehearsal studio and into the Record Plant. On the first day, Gary the engineer messed around for hours mic-ing the drums, while his assistant slowly drifted off to sleep. By 6 pm an exasperated Ashley made a phone call and Lee DeCarlo arrived. Lee had engineered Lennon's *Double Fantasy* and was with him earlier on the night he was shot.

Lee removed the carpets and mic-ed the drums in the incomprehensible DeCarlo method, muttering to himself: 'Shotgun twelve feet into the air, parabolic dishes focused on the drum stool, swinger bass D12 drum mic, high overheads and the close mics.' No one knew what he was on about. He then chirped at another mic: 'Hello there, this is Lee speaking and you're fucked and you know it – bye bye,' and he was ready.

Brent eased in behind his kit and to those listening in the control room it sounded amazing.

> **John:** It was fantastic, but it didn't go down on tape. We paid for him to get the sound and he got it. But then he disassembled it at the end of the session. He said, 'That's my drum sound. If you want to get it back, you'll have to hire me.' We didn't realise that.

So Gary disappeared and Lee was in and the biggest lines of coke the band had ever seen were chopped out and consumed.

> **John:** Now we've got Lee DeCarlo – at huge extra expense and more days spent on the drums. We're well past the sixty-grand mark by the time we have the drums sorted. Then the guitars, all this multi-track stuff – stuff that Rick and I wouldn't normally do. Ashley would sing a part, then we'd copy what he was singing. It didn't make sense really, but he's the man hired to produce a great record. There was more time messing round with the bass, and it was all taking forever! I was adding everything up in my head: airfares, accommodation, studio time running over, all these people. Oh my God!

Welcome to the music industry boom-years of the eighties – USA style.

A new assistant was brought in, and they started recording rhythm tracks. Ashley *was* inspiring and DeCarlo was *happening*. Doc was up in a loft and singing his heart out. On a day he wasn't needed, he too came back with a Cadillac: a '67 De Ville, gold with a black roof and a 6.2 litre V8. It was dubbed *Doc's Caddy.*

They attempted 'Run For The Shelter'. 'It's great,' said Ashley, 'just a couple of small changes needed.' A new drum track was then worked out and they got a take.

Jim came up with a half-time tempo idea for the verse. After each 'keeper' rhythm track, Doc broke out the champagne.

Ashley came up with a great solo idea for 'Razor's Edge' and it was whacked down. Celebration, inebriation and a few lines of cocaine.

Lee DeCarlo had to leave to produce another band.

> **John:** From then on we had to try and reach for that drum sound but we never really achieved it.

Their time at the Record Plant was running out. Another band was scheduled in, so a studio at A&M was booked for seventeen days and the whole caboodle moved over there.

The vibe of the place was something else. Once owned by Charlie Chaplin, where he made most of his movies, it had a 1920s feel with a high roof and deco-style wood panelling.

Jim did an excellent bass track for 'Underground' on which the tape was sped up. Rick and John started their guitar parts.

> **John:** Ashley had a theory about recording the guitars. You play your guitar, then you play it again – and again and again. So you do four tracks of exactly the same part to get this big guitar sound. It actually does produce a big guitar sound. But you know how to get a big guitar sound? One fucking amp, a lead and a guitar. That's how you get it. We tried all sorts of things. Once we hooked up twelve double-stack Marshalls to try and get a really big rhythm guitar sound. You know what? It sounded small.

Eventually they completed the rhythm tracks on 'Run For The Shelter'. Later that evening over a couple of margaritas, John and Brent came up with an album title after watching an NFL football game on TV. The two-minute warning is given when two minutes remain on the clock in each half of a game. They were both excited. Rick was in agreement, Doc and Jim not sure.

Eccles drove downtown at 2 am and was blown away by the size and shape of the buildings – *maybe this is Angel City*? He drove back and drew an album cover inspired by his observations.

The guitar parts on 'Small Price' were recorded and sounded tough and clean. Back in his apartment that night, John came up with an explosion idea for the back cover.

Rick pranged *Caddy White* – there were no injuries but it destroyed a little Jap car. *Caddy White* was slightly damaged but undrivable. Spartacus was sent to sort things out.

Doc spent a day on the vocals for 'Between The Eyes' and Rick did a solo on 'Gonna Leave You'. Though they often worked through to 7 am, everything was taking twice as long as expected. But what they were doing sounded great – so why push it?

John bought a blue 1970 Eldorado Caddy with black interior. It had an 8.2 litre V8 and was very cool. He was now a two-car fleet owner.

Ian Moss arrived and slept on Brent and Jim's couch for two nights. Brent seized the opportunity to demonstrate his culinary skills and cooked a magnificent dinner for everyone.

Time ran out at A&M, so the band moved into MCA Whitney studios and Brent put down percussion on 'Sticky Little Bitch' while Doc did more vocal patch-ups. A new take on 'Small Price' was chosen, one that sat better. The rhythm guitars on 'Front Page News' were stunning.

It seemed that Ashley's greatest attribute as a producer was to bring out the best in individual players while retaining the overall band style and sound. He had amazing stamina. No matter how late in the night, he was always very particular about what went down on tape.

One thing he couldn't get was Doc's vocals. Ashley rang John's apartment one night, saying, 'Help!'

'What's wrong?'

'I have no idea how to record Doc. Have you ever recorded him?'

John and Rick drove to the studio and recorded him the way they always had. He was brilliant onstage. In the studio he was brilliant too, but there were tricks to getting it.

Ashley had been coaching Doc. 'No, Doc, that's a bit sharp,' he'd said. 'Keep in your head that first note you sang, "Dah dah dah". No, no, it's a bit higher than that.' Eventually he'd thrown his hands in the air.

John: That was all part of the process that you just had to go through with Doc to get something that was really good. There were times he'd end up with a completely different melody, but it really worked. Some songs it was easy, some were hard, and the process could take a long time.

Time. Time slipped away as Ashley and John recorded more vocal patch-ups on 'Underground' and 'Between The Eyes'.

With three days to go, all backing vocals went down – who sang on what or where no one knew for sure. Two days left and there were still twenty-six guitar parts to be done, plus lots of bits and pieces.

John and Spartacus found time to sneak off and watch *Spinal Tap*, which had recently come out. As it unfolded John groaned and sank deeper into his seat.

On the final day, in one of those special touches that make good albums great, Brent recorded an electrifying typewriter part on 'Look The Other Way'. (Yes, there was an actual message tapped out.)

As everything was getting wound up, John lent his friend Molly his blue Eldorado until his return for the next tour. Displaying his Irish 'gift of the gab', Doc sold his beautiful Caddy to a carpetbagger who hung out at the studio, Rick Rock (*'I play for Aerosmith')*, who came through with the cash only hours before they left.

Everybody made a last-minute dash to stores for cool clothes. Then they packed up and jumped onto the Qantas flight back home.

Back in LA, Ashley Howe remained on the project for another two weeks, mixing the tracks down to the finished album. The precious tapes arrived in Sydney. John and Rick drove in to EMI Studios to have a listen – where they sat in mounting apprehension as each track rolled by.

John: We just went, 'Oh fuck! We can't release this! This is fucking terrible.' The forty-four barrel sounding snare drum, no high hats, stiff kick drum snare. The whole thing stiff and clinical . . . it was just fucking awful.

They called in EMI's affable chief engineer Jim Taig, and had another agonised listen.

With the original demos recorded in Sydney, they'd produced something great. MCA had heard them and wanted an album like that, in the classic Angels style.

After discussions with Taig, time slots were booked for the mixing studio, where a beautiful Neve desk held pride of place. This time there was no flat-fee deal as they despondently set about remixing the whole album – except 'Small Price'.

John: The original demo of 'Small Price' was wonderful. MCA had heard 'Small Price' and said, 'Oh, so that's The Angels. Oh, yeah.' I know because I went over with it. We wanted the album to sound like that. Rick and I knew how to do that. It ended up nothing like it. We loved Ashley, but why would our management and MCA want to break up the chemistry Rick and I had that actually worked – and bring in a producer we'd never met before? We did all that multi-guitar stuff but it wasn't us! It wasn't The Angels.

All up, going to Los Angeles to make the album, and then remixing it in Sydney, cost an astounding $450,000.

John: I can talk about this in retrospect when it's easy to see where you've gone wrong. I guess Woodruff's motives were fair enough, but, for fuck's sake, he said he could get the studios just as cheap in L.A. Are you kidding? Not to mention that we had to actually live there for nearly three months. Well, you've got to live somewhere, but you've still got family back home and a mortgage to pay. There were all those airfares. We had Spartacus on wages taking care of things. And all those overpaid Yanks. And then we had to pay for EMI's mixing studio when we got back.

We had a massive debt and had to play from here to Woop Woop to repay the bank. And Woodruff still commissioned management fees on the gigs while we did it. As Americans say: go figure.

CHAPTER THIRTY-SEVEN
KALEIDOSCOPE OF MADNESS

On 12 December 1983, Cold Chisel had played their final show at the Sydney Entertainment Centre. Apart from bringing Chisel's working career to a close, it also signalled the end of Dirty Pool. Chisel manager and Dirty Pool director Rod Willis went into semi-retirement, while the other two partners – Woodruff and Ray Hearn, manager of Icehouse – formed a new management company, Gentleman's Agreement Pty Ltd, and continued on. However, with the disbandment of Dirty Pool, Richard McDonald, Dirty Pool's agent, became co-manager (with Mark Pope) of Jimmy Barnes and went out on his own.

Consequently, Woodruff and Hearn made the decision to return to the powerful Premier/Harbour Agency, the outfit they'd dumped in 1978 when they'd formed Dirty Pool.

The Angels hit the road in August '84 with the usual kaleidoscope of madness. Pubs, clubs, concerts, film clips, and Doc getting booked for speeding – to *and* from a gig. 'Between The Eyes', the first single of the yet-to-be-completed *Two Minute Warning* (*TMW*), was released, followed by a *Countdown* performance. There were sellouts in Melbourne and Adelaide, then back to Sydney, where John finished mixing *TMW* and sent the tapes to MCA.

> **Tony Grace (a young agent at the Harbour agency):** They were playing all over the country, anywhere, everywhere, and pioneering lots of different areas. They were going out for anywhere from eight to ten grand versus percentages [a guarantee of between $8000 and $10,000 fee against a percentage of the ticket sales, whichever was greater], and for the big venues they were getting twelve to fifteen grand versus percentages. They took around fifty grand on a typical week. They were definitely one of the hardest working bands of that period. I used to call Doc 'The Prince of Pub Rock'. He owned that space!

Of those figures, 10 per cent went to the agency, 20 per cent to management. Out of the rest came the crew wages, production costs, promotion costs and accommodation. There was a lot of money swirling around, but after all the slicing and dicing and the chunks of money transferred to pay down the debt from the LA indulgence, none of the band were getting rich.

A contract was signed on Rick's kitchen table with Michael Gudinski of Mushroom Records for distribution of *TMW* in Australia and New Zealand. It came with a $75,000 advance. After Woodruff deducted his management commission, the rest was put towards paying off the LA recording debt.

> **Michael Gudinski:** It was an important signing for Mushroom. I'd always thought that The Angels were one of the greatest hard-rock bands Australia had ever seen. They'd made good records but CBS had never taken it as far as it could've gone and I knew that we could.

On 28 November '84 Mushroom proudly released The Angels' seventh studio album. A few days later the Triple M network put an Angels special to air and played *TMW* from start to finish. The following week it entered the ARIA charts and by Christmas it was #2 nationally. But without a single getting airplay, it soon slipped back down the rankings.

Steve from MCA had called to say he loved the mixes, and *Two Minute Warning* was released Stateside on 12 December. It got picked up by ten stations and was mentioned on the front page of USA record-business magazine *American Tip Sheet*. By the following week another twenty stations were airing tracks as a re-recorded version of 'Be With You' was released as a single.

As the new year approached, life was a relentless treadmill of band-related work. However, Rick broke out of the bubble and returned to domestic life on 25 December, when Bitsy gave birth to a special Christmas gift in the shape of a tiny girl. Fortunately, Christmas Day was a holiday for the band – otherwise it would have been difficult . . .

Next day Rick was picked up and back inside the hurricane, heading for another town, another sweat-drenched pub, another coke-fuelled gig as a rock-star guitarist.

CHAPTER THIRTY-EIGHT
TRIUMPH AND DISASTER

3 March 1985. John Brewster removed his shades and stared vacantly out the 747 window as the Pacific Ocean met the California coast and the pilot swung towards the LAX runways. After flying in and out of this city so many times during the past five years, the thrill of arriving in America had long gone. This time there was a sense of unease.

Since the American release of *TMW* three months ago it had received little attention and 'Be With You' had gone nowhere. He was wracked with angst; he knew the album hadn't captured the magic of their earlier work and he suspected MCA weren't working it.

The MCA guys had told him early in the piece that although Angel City had made inroads in North America, it could still take another two albums to break through and they were prepared to go the distance. 'Just be The Angels. We know the level of success you've had in Australia – we believe we can achieve that here.' But *Two Minute Warning* wasn't good enough, and John knew it.

He glanced over at Rick and Doc nearby and recalled the band meeting three months back when Woodruff announced plans for the next American and Canadian tour.

> **John:** I said, 'Look, we've been talking about it. We don't want you sending us back to America unless there's a really good reason to go. Otherwise we'll come back broke again.'

Woodruff phoned John later to say how offended he was at the suggestion he wasn't looking after their best interests. 'Do you really think I'd send you to America if it wasn't going to be a really good tour?'

> **John:** I went, 'Well, all I know is that we finished up with a lot of debt from recording this album over there and we don't want to put more good money after bad. We've finally paid it off. We don't want to go into debt again.' And I said, 'That's not me that's saying that. That's the band.'

At the next meeting Woodruff explained how they'd be keeping costs down by supporting Triumph, a major MCA band, on a tour playing arenas. MCA would supply a dedicated promotional manager to travel with them, and all touring expenses and wages would be covered against future album royalties – not their bank accounts. He'd also engaged a new booking agency who'd do a better job than William Morris at setting up a great run of top club gigs. He soothed their concerns and by the end of the meeting had talked them into going.

Ashley Howe met them at LA airport – a nice surprise but no sign of anyone from MCA. He gave them the latest gossip. There'd been a staff purge at MCA and most of the old brigade had gone, with a new team being installed. Irving Azoff had instigated another 'roster rationalisation' in his drive to get MCA back into profit.

It was unsettling news but Steve from MCA would be at the first gig and that was cool.

The following morning Doc was on location shooting segments for Australian TV while the roadies picked up hire cars and a small equipment truck. By day three they were heading to their first gig, the Golden Bear at Huntington Beach, accompanied by the TV crew and various LA friends. ('You have how many on your guest list?')

It was a small club and the show went well. A couple of hundred fans turned up as did Steve with some colleagues, all of them new to MCA. Steve said little and it was clear the others knew nothing about the band or earlier conversations and promises made by previously employed executives during the signing process. After the show they politely shook hands, said goodnight and left. Another guy introduced himself: Rob Kahane. He was from Triad, the new booking agency Woody had engaged. He came across as a smooth LA corporate type: besuited, tanned and manicured.

Next day they drove up to San Francisco for the first gig with Triumph. With them was Tom, an enthusiastic promo guy from MCA. Until Woodruff had mentioned them, the Aussies had never heard of Triumph, but Tom assured them they had a rock 'n' roll following who'd love Angel City.

The show was at the 10,000-seat Cow Palace. Just before they went on, someone on the Triumph crew thought it amusing to play a Michael Jackson song through the PA. The booing and catcalls were still in the air when Angel City was announced. A very pissed-off band strode out and plugged in, intending to do a killer show. Instead, the audience attempted to kill them. Or at least a vocal minority down the front did, pelting them with coins and toilet paper. Rick had a lens of his shades broken but played on. Despite a rousing call for an encore from some of the audience, they didn't go back.

> **Rick:** Triumph came on, a three-piece metal band, and they were absolutely pathetic!

Needless to say, no one was too keen to do more dates with Triumph, but with five concerts remaining, it would leave a hole in their finances they couldn't afford if they'd cancelled. Tom was quite sure that this show had been an aberration: 'Wait and see how the next few go.'

The band fronted Triumph's tour manager and told him that if the next show was like that, they'd walk off. To his credit he said he'd talk to his crew about the Michael Jackson tape and instruct security to evict coin throwers.

The Angels returned to LA and ran into more trouble – the truck got stolen from outside their hotel while they slept. In a rerun of the last time their truck had been nicked, the police were no help. Unbeknown to the band, a shoe-shop owner nearby had noticed a Ryder truck parked behind his shop with a smashed driver's window. Peering in, he could see band equipment chained up inside and reported it to the police. The police didn't connect the guy's report with the band's stolen truck and failed to investigate for twenty-four hours. By then everything was gone, only the roadcases left behind. Spartacus spoke to the shop owner, who said there was 'a bit of police activity around the truck last night', but refused to elaborate. Although everything was insured, it was a gloomy day as the musicians digested the loss of their prized instruments as well as the hired equipment.

Nine days after they'd arrived in the US, Angel City were booked to appear on the 'Rockers Convention' in an old theatre in a rundown part of LA. Run by a radio network, it was a showcase concert with a big line-up. Radio programmers were flying in from all over to check out various record companies' new signings. With Aussie grit the crew talked the headliner, King Kobra, into letting them use their stage gear, and with borrowed instruments the band opened the show and immediately impressed the 2000 audience. They were supposed to do three songs but powered into five to a general freak-out from stage managers on each side. *'Sorry, we're Australians, thought that's what you wanted . . .'*

Next up were The Blasters, a country-style band who were pretty good but got a subdued reception. Back in the dressing room Angel City were introduced to radio people but came out in time to catch King Kobra.

> **John Brewster:** Oh gawd, they were all blond Greek gods playing heavy metal crap. It was Carmine Appice's band and they'd rehearsed for a year but they were rank. We were totally unsuited for the line-up but we were told it was a radio-promoted show and it was going live to air and we should do it. It probably did us more damage than good.

In Seattle with a day off they bought new instruments and amps and prepared for the next show with Triumph, which no one was looking forward to.

> **John:** It was ridiculous. Angel City, who'd headlined to 6000 people in Seattle over two full Paramount Theatre shows. Why the fuck were we supporting this dinosaur heavy-metal rock band?

That night they were welcomed with cheers and encored with 'Comin' Down'. Angel City fans had come out to see them.

Backstage, Tom brought in Beau Phillips, program manager from KISW, the number-one rock station in the Northwest. Beau was a huge Angels fan, had put 'Marseilles' on high rotation a few years back and told them the station was still playing the Epic albums. It seemed he wasn't playing anything off *TMW* but was 'considering it'. As Triumph walked past their room in their spandex and buffed hair he turned to Doc: 'Jeez, this reminds me of Spinal Tap.'

Next morning, Rick, Jim and Doc flew down to Portland with Tom for a big record-store promotion. Everyone else drove to the gig at the Portland Coliseum for the soundcheck.

> **Rick:** We were signing records and all these people were asking, 'Why are you opening for Triumph tonight?'

Again the Angels fans were there in droves and sang along to 'Marseilles'.

Tom knocked on their door after they came off, asking if he could bring in two special ladies. They were from KGON, whose boss, Inessa, had been a fan for years. She told them the station had played the imported *Watch The Red* album the previous year and it had reached #5 on their 'listeners' playlist'.

John called Woodruff, demanding to know why they were supporting this completely inappropriate band instead of headlining their own concerts. Woodruff explained it was about reducing financial risk while playing to substantially bigger audiences.

After Vancouver and Edmonton, Calgary was the last gig with Triumph. Knowing they wouldn't have to deal with Angel City's whingeing any longer, the Triumph crew cut the PA volume and gave them half-a-dozen lights and there was nothing the Aussies could do about it. To add insult, there was a rerun of the first Triumph show when a bunch of bozos down the front started throwing coins at close range. However, with so many Angels fans in the audience, the band soldiered on. Then a firecracker exploded near Doc's face. Bobby Daniels on foldback saw who threw it, and leapt down and punched him in the mouth as the band ground to a halt.

John yanked the lead from his guitar and yelled, 'See you later, arseholes.' Doc had staggered back but then raced to the front. 'Thanks, cunts, see you later,' he said, and stormed off with the others to pandemonium from the audience.

> **John:** We had no idea about Triumph when that tour was set up. We were thrown to the wolves, completely sacrificed. After our first gig we never saw anyone from MCA again, apart from the promo guy they put with us. MCA had no intention of re-signing us so they sacrificed us to save Triumph, who some idiot had paid money to sign up.

Their next gig was headlining their own show back at the Playhouse Theatre in Winnipeg, where they'd sold out two shows previously. Here the number-one station CITI had consistently played all their records for the past five years. Doc had done a number of interviews with them since they'd arrived in America and been told there was a lot of excitement around town for their show. With its large French ancestry, Winnipeg had sent 'Marseilles' into the top ten back in the day.

To get there they took the train – a sightseeing spectacular across the Rocky Mountains. With the drudgery of the Triumph tour behind them, their spirits and camaraderie returned.

They arrived to news that the show had sold out and a second one had been put on sale. That night they played their first theatre headline since arriving in the States and the next night they did another. The venue's PA was brand new and their lighting guy did a great job. Doc, now free of the constraints he'd been under on the Triumph shows, was brilliant, the band rocked out and by the end the audience called them back again and again.

They headed south, working small clubs on a journey that finished up at a 'shitty little gig' in Milwaukee. They then sat idle in the hotel with their crew, hired vehicles and equipment for five days waiting for promised worksheet itineraries from their booking agency – not knowing where or when the next gig was.

It cost them all the money they'd made in Winnipeg and then some. A booking finally came through for Detroit, followed by another the following day for a dive in Toledo where fifty bemused punters turned up after hearing some ads on the radio. A few days later they were directed to a club in Cincinnati, a last-minute booking. Local radio WEBN had been playing tracks off *Face To Face* and *Dark Room* for years – the program director was a big fan and the station promoted the show with a big push. Despite the fact that it was announced at the last minute, nearly 500 tickets were sold. The station was playing *TMW* and 'Be With You' had entered their charts. As a mark of appreciation, Tom took Doc and some of the radio jocks out to dinner before the show.

After that night, the flow of gigs dried up again with shows getting cancelled at the last minute. In Texas they played a hastily organised radio-promoted club gig with a one-dollar ticket and pulled a halfway decent crowd.

John: Then, after a few more days sitting around blowing our budget, we drove to Austin and it's some fucking joke of a gig with no promotion and hardly anyone there. That's how gigs were coming in from our wonderful new agency. After band and crew sat in a motel for five days waiting for the next one, and supposed run of gigs after that, I'd had enough and rang Woodruff in LA: 'You've got to come down and talk to your band. We're going fucking broke!'

He flew down and we had this terse meeting in a disused room with old furniture stacked up and I let him have it. 'You told me you wouldn't send us to America if it wasn't a good tour. Well, it's a fucking disaster, which has probably destroyed our career here, and we're going back to Sydney right now.' He said he'd changed agencies and they were setting up a new tour – but it was too late for that. We'd blown another huge bundle that we'd have to slog round Australia to make back. I was over the whole fucking thing.

Back in LA they had four days to wait before seats were available for the return flight to Sydney. More money down the drain. While the rest took it easy, John, having sussed that a lot of money appeared to be missing from their bank account, went through the income and expenditures with Woodruff and an accountant. Shocked, they discovered numerous instances where substantial funds had been syphoned off during currency transfers, and a $10,000 payment in tour support from MCA had gone missing.

The band were in even more debt than they'd realised.

Leaving the problem of recovering the money with Woodruff, they made their way to the airport, climbed aboard a plane and gratefully watched America disappear into the LA smog.

What the band didn't understand at the time was the real reason for Woodruff taking them out of the powerful William Morris Agency and placing them with the much smaller Triad Artists. Woodruff had an arrangement with John Marx, one of the directors at Triad, to bring to Australasia a number of the major artists Triad represented. The first was The Stranglers, followed by Paul Young, who'd had a string of big hits internationally.

Dirty Pool had been reborn as a promotion company and Woodruff had ambitions to become a major player in the Australasian concert touring market. To cement the relationship with John Marx, Woodruff had taken The Angels out of the mighty William Morris Agency and placed them with Marx's agency, Triad. When the tour fell apart, Woodruff was forced to pull The Angels out of Triad, and now, unwelcome at William Morris, he'd engaged the DMA agency to take on the band. In doing so, he'd deeply offended John Marx and put at serious risk the lucrative down-under tours of The Stranglers and Paul Young.

DMA hurriedly pulled together a club tour to commence on 20 April, unaware The Angels had abruptly returned to Australia. Woodruff had expected his band to sit round for three weeks until the DMA tour started, just to keep MCA onside, who were anticipating them continuing touring to support sales of *TMW*.

However, with The Angels back in Australia, DMA had to cancel the tour and Woodruff was left scrambling to deal with the fall-out.

Following a blistering meeting with MCA executives demanding reasons for the disorganised tour and the band going home early, he'd written an apologetic letter to Irving Azoff, promising that they'd return in July to pick up touring where they'd left off.

As for his tours with Paul Young and The Stranglers, after a series of apologetic faxes, calls and meetings with John Marx, his agreement with Triad remained firm. Dirty Pool was able to bring both acts to Australia during the next few months for what proved to be two immensely successful concert tours.

Another fact held back from The Angels was that Azoff himself actually managed Triumph, which explained why they had supported them – Azoff knew Angel City's album sales had been strong in the Northwest. He also knew they'd played huge Kinks concerts and headlined their own shows in the area – from his perspective, it made sense that they support his band to strengthen the bill. Unfortunately, the whole fiasco heralded the end of The Angels' attempts to 'conquer America'. John Brewster's earlier comments comparing their American career to the space shuttle re-entry would be prescient: 'If you get the window, you're back on Earth. If you miss the window, you bounce off and disappear into the blue yonder.'

Footnote: The missing tour money was never recovered.

CHAPTER THIRTY-NINE
COMIN' DOWN ON ME

It was hometown Adelaide where the homecoming tour kicked off. The first gig was a three-night stand at the Bridgeway Hotel. With posters all over the city and ads on the radio, there was a big Angels vibe in the air. Tickets for all three nights had sold out and they were looking forward to getting up before a wild Australian audience again.

Doc and Jim had done an interview with Phil Bartsch in the Adelaide *Advertiser*, discussing the album and the band's recent activities. 'We never seem to know until the last two minutes what we're doing,' said Jim. 'After this tour we're supposed to go back to America but that could change at any minute.' Bartsch observed that such was life with the international success of the *Two Minute Warning* album.

John Brewster read it and smiled wryly. He'd seen another article suggesting the album proved that 'The Angels were still the number one candidate for breaking throughout America from Down Under'. In another, Doc said that the band would be back touring the States in July. John shook his head. *Bullshit!*

Three singles had now been released in Australia and all had failed to chart. However, the album continued selling steadily. There'd been some good reviews, one by music journalist David Sly in the *Advertiser*: 'For my money this is the most exciting offering from the quintet, and definitively as important as the landmark Angels album of '78, *Face To Face*.' Pity radio didn't agree.

Steve from MCA sent them some encouraging magazine reviews and a small list of stations who were playing tracks – but never mentioned any who'd stopped playing tracks. And tellingly, there was never a mention of 'Be With You'. Brent, scanning the articles, started suggesting that maybe Woodruff was correct in insisting the band go back in July for another crack at the prize.

John, at the wheel of the car as the tour rolled towards Melbourne, became increasingly irritated at Brent's rising enthusiasm to return. It broke into open warfare when the drummer accused John of talking the band into leaving America prematurely.

> **John:** Everyone had wanted to come back to Australia! If we'd stayed we would have ended up with so much debt that we would never have been able to repay it and would have probably broken up.

The bickering rarely let up. With Rick remaining silent, or appearing to side with Brent, John became more despondent as the days ticked by. Doc sat quietly in the front passenger seat reading the paper or turning the pages of a book. He was covertly drinking more than ever and Rick and Brent's cocaine usage was now a series of rituals throughout the day. Jim – the 'hired hand' as he sometimes called himself – rolled another joint and stared out the window. John had given up smoking dope a few years before and coke had never appealed, so now he was an outsider.

The constant bickering began affecting the band's performances, which set John complaining about falling standards. Since the Austin meeting his relationship with Woodruff had deteriorated too. Woody was still bristling about 'John pulling the band out of America'. He was holding fast to his belief that in lieu of obtaining a hit record, the best strategy to crack America was to conquer it city by city – as AC/DC had done.

No one was aware of their manager's behind-the-scenes business dealings and how close they'd come to derailing his nascent touring company's plans. When The Stranglers and Paul Young toured Australia, The Angels were also unaware that it was their manager bringing them through, even though the touring crew he assembled was manned by ex-Angels roadies, including Ray Hawkins on lights.

> **Doc:** John just got jack of it. He'd lost faith that we could actually make it in the States. There'd been so many setbacks and he was just sick of it. It was understandable.

Doc could well have been talking about his own feelings. He too was sick of playing the game in America and had no ambition to go back to the grind of playing small clubs and having to put on the charm for the endless meet and greets. But he stayed clear of the parry and thrust of arguments between John and Brent. It was easier to let them sort it out. He had his own dreams and aspirations but he kept them to himself for the time being.

It all became academic when MCA advised that they wouldn't provide financial support for another tour until the next album. That put an end to discussing American tours, but intensified the argument about whether the band should have soldiered on when the support was still available.

On 12 July they arrived at the Sydney Entertainment Centre and made their way to the Green Room. They'd been invited to perform four songs on the 'Live Aid Oz For Africa' concert, part of the worldwide fund-raisers organised by Bob Geldof.

Two of their songs would be telecast to a massive audience in the States, so the band was being billed as Angel City. They went out before the 12,000 Entertainment Centre audience and performed 'Small Price', 'Eat City', 'Underground' and 'Take A Long Line'. ('Marseilles', the band's most played song in America, inexplicably wasn't performed.)

On a bill that included Men At Work, Australian Crawl, INXS, Mental As Anything, Mondo Rock and many others, the four-hour telethon was broadcast in Australia on Channels 7 and 9 and on MTV in America. All up, over ten million Australian dollars were raised and passed on to the International Disaster Emergency Committee.

Back on the road, positive feedback from MTV's broadcast just fed into more discussion about returning to America.

> **John:** I just didn't want to go back. If we had, it would have been on our own cash! There was no way we'd break anywhere in the States with that album – obviously MCA had lost the vibe for us and fuck the dodgy agents. We couldn't go back anyway, we were still paying off the debts we'd clocked up. We were playing small country towns that we wouldn't have normally gone near, just to stay out of the cities where we were now overexposed.

He'd lost his passion for the band to such an extent that he hadn't bothered showing up for the filming of a promo clip. On tour he went off on his own playing golf when he should have been at soundchecks.

> **John:** The band was playing like shit. It was no longer the band I'd started out with – it wasn't The Angels for me any longer. Rick and Brent were thick as thieves doing copious amounts of cocaine and forming a new power bloc. Doc was drinking heavily and Jim was just being everyone's hippie friend and going along with it.

Whenever John and Woodruff were in close proximity the animosity between them quickly boiled over – but Woodruff had other business interests he was focused on and wasn't around too often. As John became ever more jaded he retreated from his leadership role and a vacuum developed. Brent, intelligent and ambitious, gradually moved into the space left vacant.

Doc had long ago eased out of the day-to-day affairs of The Angels. He largely kept to himself, a tall solitary figure, eerily beyond reach. Backstage the crew built his curtained-off area, 'Doc's World', where he remained isolated before a gig – and after a show, once recovered from his performance, he disappeared.

John: I'd been band leader for fifteen years, but no question I'd lost interest. If you're a band and you're all pulling together, writing and recording great songs, doing great shows, then it's like a football team and there's real camaraderie. You want to take it all the way and be the best there is – top dog. Now the camaraderie was gone and I felt like an outsider. During the Alberts period, we had the greatest rhythm section, we had the greatest producers and we had the key to the best rock studio in Australia. I looked back and realised how much the band had lost since then.

The mentoring by George Young couldn't be underestimated. His quality control and high standards. The suggestions he made that fundamentally changed the band. His suggestion that Doc become singer and helping him find his feet had been only one of his many influences. His seemingly casual comments: 'Have you guys ever thought of cutting your hair short? You'd be the first band in the country with short hair. Maybe worth considering.'

How could a value be put on that? It had led to the band taking off in a new direction: the leather jackets, black t-shirts, tight jeans, sunglasses. Rick statuesque – his idea, but sparked by the revolution George had begun. It had all led to the new tough stage show. Doc's search for an 'image' and exploring German expressionism, inspired by Wal Cherry's drama lectures – which led to designing a light show and bringing in Ray Hawkins, who took it so much further with his brilliant techniques. Each change had led to another. Doc taking his stage persona deeper and weirder – until it had probably now taken him over.

John: You could see how the slide began after we left Alberts. *Night Attack* wasn't a bad record, but it's not as good as any of the previous ones. *Watch The Red* was fun to make but we knew it wasn't up to the standard of earlier albums. We took management advice and left Alberts – big mistake – and then we took management advice to go to America to make *TMW* – it cost a fortune and when it was finished it wasn't good enough! You have a good look and you realise the band is in a long decline and everyone's pretending it's not. Buzz's departure had nothing to do with leaving Alberts or management, but his leaving precipitated the resignation of Chris and so went our crack rhythm section. And the band, musically, was never quite the same again.

One day in September John went home and remained with Robyn while she delivered a healthy baby boy, his second. While there, he composed a letter addressed to all the band members. He told them that The Angels had lost its way and needed to find itself again. He suggested they approach Alberts and try to get back to where they'd started. Fifa was still there, as were George and Harry. They had the studios where they could make some decent records again. George and Harry were high-quality advisers. If you took a song to them and it wasn't good enough, they'd say, 'Nah, not good enough, boys,' whereas the band among themselves would go, 'Ah yeah, that's alright,' and it was just getting weaker and weaker.

He was now seriously concerned for his brother and his cocaine habit. Their relationship was in tatters and Rick's personal life seemed to be sliding out of control. It was the same with Doc's drinking. Maybe George was the only one who'd make the two of them sit up and take notice.

But it wasn't to be. They'd signed a deal with Mushroom, and the charismatic Michael Gudinski with his belief in the band loomed large, and changing record companies again had little appeal to the rest of the band. Brent and Jim weren't around back in those halcyon years, so they didn't understand the significance. Doc, who'd once been so much a part of the triumvirate, now showed little interest in what was going on. His long-term aspirations lay beyond The Angels. If or when he discussed future plans it usually revolved around his dreams of a career in theatre or film.

However, most days he slept late, and when awake, read books, sipped scotch, and only truly came alive at showtime – sometimes with flashes of brilliance, sometimes just a parody of his old self. He moved among friends who were mostly outside the music business. They stroked his ego and that can play with a person's sense of themselves and their place in the scheme of things.

Rick's interests too had gone beyond the confines of the band, with his attention now focused on major upheavals in his personal life.

> **Rick:** My affairs were not unlike the one I had with cocaine – full on. I'd fallen for a girl in America a year before and that had come close to causing my marriage to split. My wife and I gave it a good go at reconciling . . . for a while, at least. But an intense affair in Sydney was too close to home. Playing in a touring band took a heavy toll and many relationships suffered.

With the band no longer signed to them, CBS Australia released *The Angels Greatest Hits Vol. 2* in November 1985, with highlights of the albums the band had recorded during their time with them. It immediately charted and, with the might of CBS behind it, sold well.

It was almost a year since *Two Minute Warning* had been released and there was some talk about the possibility of doing another album. After the expensive failure of *TMW* and with limited funds to finance studio time, it was decided to put out a live album. It was agreed that, despite the internal tensions, John was the one to mix and produce it. He was offered a small fee to do the job, and, happy to have a productive role to get his teeth into, got straight to work.

It was during one of the mixing sessions that John's loyalty to The Angels was questioned by Brent again. In a heated exchange late one night, the drummer claimed that John had put his family ahead of the band in 'taking us out of America', adding that the real reason he wanted to return was for his son's birth.

The accusation incensed John – the band had actually returned five months before his son was born. 'We could have toured America with that album forever,' he shouted, 'and we'd still never have cracked it, because that album *wasn't good enough*!' He stamped out.

Once again John found himself desperately seeking solutions to the many problems within the band – as he saw it.

But suddenly the situation was resolved for him.

> **Rick:** A meeting was called to tell John he was out, and that was it. He was to be out of the band from that day. It was horrible, especially the period leading

up to it where we all knew, we'd all considered it and talked about it behind his back and worked out that this is what we were going to do and how to adopt that strategy. We just thought, 'Well, John's making a prick of himself . . .'

For me it was huge, emotionally. I'd just left my wife, and within a week we kicked John out and it all happened at Cammeray where I rented a flat. I had no furniture and we were sitting around on the floor, overlooking the Harbour. What made it worse was that when Doc began the conversation, he just sort of picked a topic and asked John about it, and started in a roundabout way of getting to what I knew we were all there for, to kick him out.

I listened for a few minutes with John answering and not knowing, and because I knew him so well, I was just internally screaming 'Tell him!', so I just cut across and said, 'John, we want you to leave the band.' He saw very quickly that it was definite and he got up and walked out. Oh, it was awful – telling the family, John's wife, everyone around me. It was like divorcing your wife. In some ways worse.

I don't know how John felt, but it must have been devastating for him. Well, I know it was.

CHAPTER FORTY
GOTTA GET OUT OF THIS PLACE

It wasn't that simple for John to be 'kicked out of the band'. For a start, no replacement had been arranged and there were still some more gigs to do before the end of the November tour. After months of relentless gigging, the debts had been cleared and the exhausted band would then be off the road until the end of January.

At the time of John's sacking, he'd made a good start on sorting through old concert recordings, so he was invited to continue the job.

It was decided that two gigs at the end of January would be his last. One was a big farewell concert at the Myer Music Bowl for Australian Crawl, who were calling it a day, and that night there was an Angels concert planned for The Palace nightclub in St Kilda, which would be the band's farewell to John. There was also the small matter of negotiating a separation fee that would include the income tax owed from his band earnings.

After watching Jimmy Barnes go multi-platinum with his second solo album, *For The Working Class Man*, Doc was again muttering about starting a solo career. In December he flew off to LA for a month to write songs with Chas Sandford, who'd co-written 'I'd Die To Be With You Tonight' with Barnes.

*

The life of former Skyhooks guitarist Bob Spencer was about to take an unexpected turn. It was New Year's Day 1986, and he'd decided to give his mate Rick Brewster a call, wish him well for the year and hustle up a bit of business. Bob was working at Paradise B, a small-time studio in Oxford Street, Darlinghurst as a studio engineer and thought The Angels might be interested in doing some recording with him.

> **Bob Spencer:** I'd known Rick for years. We were both guitar geeks – I used to visit his place. We came from completely different musical backgrounds. I'd never listened to anything he had, and he'd never listened to anything I had, but we got along really well. I rang him one day and said, 'Hey, man, I'm working at Paradise B. If you want to do any demos, let me know. I can get the studio at a good rate and I'd really like to record you. He said, 'Okay, thanks.' I said, 'So how are you guys doing?' and he said, 'Oh, John left,' and I said, 'Well, if you need a guitar player give me a call.' That was it really.

The end of January rolled around and Doc was back from LA. His time with Chas Sandford had been unproductive, but a number of writing sessions with Jeff Lieb had resulted in three strong contenders for the solo album he had in mind.

He found the band in rehearsals and the roadies loading equipment for the drive down to Melbourne. John was preparing to get up with The Angels at the Myer Music Bowl for his second-last show with them.

In front of a huge audience the onstage vibe was lacklustre and they put in what John considered to be a poor performance. He stomped off and said so to a nearby journalist within earshot of Brent, which resulted in an angry confrontation between them in the dressing room.

In contrast, that night at The Palace, in front of their own fans, the band fired – as they often did when tempers had flared. Woody was side of stage next to John, urging him on to a higher plane like a football coach with his star player. Also in the wings was John's wife, Robyn, and the man from Mushroom himself, Michael Gudinski.

After a high-energy performance The Angels were called back for more, and Doc gave a short but gracious speech of farewell to his band-mate. John took a final bow, flicked his guitar pick over the foldback monitors and walked off, emotionally wasted.

During the next few days, John, Robyn and their kids were guests of the Gudinski family at their grand mansion. John played golf and dejectedly discussed his future with his host. After settling with the ATO, there would be little left of his separation payment and no foreseeable income. Jaded and exhausted, he briefly contemplated getting into the administration side of the music business, where his band accountancy skills would be valued.

Instead, he was recruited to be a Party Boy.

> **John:** Out of the blue, I got a call from Paul Christie with an offer to join his very successful all-star band. He'd read I was out of The Angels. Back in Sydney I started rehearsing with the band and that's where I met Alan Lancaster from Status Quo and we started writing together. Alan was playing bass, Kevin Borich was lead guitarist and Angry Anderson did vocals. They were packing out every venue they played.

John Brewster was back where he belonged: with a hard-rocking band, great company and a good income. A few months later he was chuffed to be offered a place in Jimmy Barnes' band but turned it down. He was happy where he was and soon he and Lancaster were producing a new album for the Party Boys, with Barnes' brother Swanee on vocals. The album produced the #1 hit 'He's Gonna Step On You' and a great chapter in John's life ensued.

Mushroom had been vacillating about an advance for a new Angels album due to the disappointing sales of *TMW*. But following a meeting with Woodruff, they were requesting demos of newly penned material to see what the band had in the saddlebags.

Doc had a folder of songs from his time in LA. His solo album didn't look like coming to fruition any time soon, so he played his band-mates a tape of one he'd written with Jeff Lieb called 'Nature Of The Beast'. After jamming around on it, they saw some potential and recorded a demo. Mushroom liked it and booked them into Rhinoceros with British producer Steve Brown, who'd worked with artists ranging from Elton John to the Sex Pistols, Dire Straits to Boomtown Rats and Freddie Mercury.

The demo was recorded without JB and sent to Mushroom, but they were non-committal when asked about investing in a new album.

The Harbour Agency had been working on a run of dates beginning mid-February, under the banner 'Tour de Force', and a temporary rhythm guitarist was needed to fill in for John. Rick thought back to the conversation he'd had with Bob Spencer. He was a cracker of a player who Rick knew well. He'd started out in a young band called Finch that scored a deal with CBS in the mid-seventies and had a modicum of success. His big break came in 1977 when he was headhunted to replace Red Symons in Skyhooks.

> **Rick:** I invited Bob to join us for the tour. We wanted to see how he'd fit in. Almost straight away he and I started writing together. He had some great riffs. One really memorable one eventually went into 'Don't Waste My Time'. It was a good collaboration. I'd write the lyrics but we both tended to write the music and he'd come up with the riffs.

Spencer brought a new energy to the band, and a new lease of life. As far as the members were concerned, he was in, although Doc had reservations.

> **Bob:** The band advised me that they'd be deciding, whilst on the road, whether I'd be asked to join permanently or not. That did happen, though not before Doc had to be convinced. Not due to my fitting in musically or personally, but because he felt that my being bald made him look old! Bloody hilarious! Makes no logical sense, of course, but that's Doc for ya!

Bob was a talent – and a showman. Bald at twenty-nine, he was a slight, gentle, softly spoken soul, but under the lights a firecracker brimming with confidence. On stage he was either planted with legs wide apart and flailing away, or striding about, athletically leaping on and off his Marshalls. Among the fans there was dark talk initially that 'he's trying to upstage Doc!'. It was true that Doc didn't have the same enthusiasm he'd had in earlier days, but with competition from Spencer he quickly upped his game again.

Word came through in April that Mushroom would pony up for a new album and 'Nature Of The Beast' would be released in early June.

As a consequence, the arrangement they had with John to mix the live album was abruptly terminated and the project put on hold. Instead, blocks of studio time at Rhinoceros were booked throughout May and into June, and work began on song ideas.

> **Rick:** We got Steve Brown back as producer – a great guy. We roped in Eddie Rayner, the keyboardist from Split Enz who we all loved. That was a big coup for us. He added a new dimension to that whole album.

With 'Nature Of The Beast' picking up airplay and edging into the charts, a crew was brought into a gig to film the song. As the cameras moved in and out and panned across the audience, they captured the band's wives and girlfriends dancing down the front beneath Doc in a Bowie-style tailored suit. While the band went full tilt the cameras zoomed in on their gorgeous girls, including Mandi, Rick's new obsession, with her shaggy blonde hair and skimpy white top. Onstage he watched her through dark shades as his fingers leapt up the fretboard, peeling off solos that spiralled into the ether.

Back in the studio, someone suggested they record a cover of 'We Gotta Get Out Of This Place'.

> **Rick:** The Animals had done a great version and I felt that we recorded another great version with that whole keyboard/brass intro. We changed the riff and put it down an octave.

Doc had written a second song with Jeff Lieb, 'All Night For You', which the band considered worthy of recording. However, a third one he'd brought back, 'Look In The Mirror', didn't fare so well. The band worked on it one night when Doc wasn't in the studio with the intention of getting him to put down the vocal when he next came in. But in the early hours of the morning, after trying out various arrangements, they abandoned it.

> **Rick:** Some months later Doc said to me, 'I'll never record another album with you, Rick.' I said, 'Why's that?' He said, 'Because the band didn't record "Look In The Mirror" and I know it was your fault.' I said, 'Hey, Doc, we did record it but everyone rejected it, not just me!' But that was it for him. I don't know what changed his mind, but we did record another three albums after that.

Following the break-up of his marriage, Rick had been doing some introspective writing. He'd written such songs before, but usually hid his true feelings behind shrouds of obscurity. When the band first ran through 'Man There' in the studio, the words raised some eyebrows.

> **Rick:** That was a pretty personal song. It was my story of meeting Mandi and leaving Bitsy, and the lyric was: 'Out past midnight every night, keeping secrets out of sight, making love till morning light, she's got a man there.'
>
> I was the man, yeah. It was just a way of telling my story. Probably the most personal song that I've ever written.

With recording completed on budget and schedule, Steve Brown recommended it be mixed by Bill Price in London. Bill was the chief engineer/manager at Wessex Studios, where the Clash and the Sex Pistols recorded much of their work.

The Pistols? The Clash? The Angels needed no more convincing. Rick was nominated to go over with the tapes, and flights and hotel were booked.

London. The last time he'd been there was five years ago, playing at a sold-out Marquee. From his hotel window on the third floor he looked down on a phone box, or where a phone box used to be, now ringed with yellow police tape. It had been the scene of a bombing – reportedly by the IRA – which had happened the week before.

Wessex Studios was a few minutes away and Rick spent much of his time there with Bill Price in the control room, watching him efficiently go about his work, unable to fault anything he did. This would be an album to be proud of.

Back in his hotel room he learned to master the email system on the Tandy computer John had bought in LA a year back.

> **Rick:** Putting on the suction cups that had to go on the big black British phone, and sending and receiving emails with the office in Australia was very handy. I discovered a default word program in the computer that spat out lines that were like Shakespearean phrases. Random words and lines like 'the babbling brook runneth mightily'. I used to spend a lot of time playing with that and grabbing lines that sounded really good, and just writing random stuff into a notebook to draw on later for songs.

The craft markets nearby fascinated him and in the mornings before going to the studio he'd make his way among the stalls and watch the artisans make leather belts and handbags. He bought all their stuff: leather bits and pieces, rivets and tools.

Back in Sydney he began making leather straps and belts. Dave Leslie of the Baby Animals proudly wore a Rick Brewster-studded guitar strap for many years.

While he'd been away, Jim and his girlfriend, Chrystine Carroll, both accomplished photographers and designers, had completed the album cover artwork.

A media statement was issued from Woodruff's office heralding the imminent release of the album and also announcing Bob Spencer's induction into the band. Erasing the name of founding member John Brewster from the history of The Angels was also underway.

Howling was released on 25 November 1986 with the fiery new single, 'We Gotta Get Out Of This Place', going straight into the charts and running up to the #3 spot nationally. Reviewers and punters embraced the change of tack the band had taken. They welcomed the keyboards, horns, female backing vocals and additional percussion – but all acknowledged that it was still the dual guitars and Rick's spine-tingling solos that distinguished the band. By the time the album had run its course, 'Nature Of The Beast' and the dreamy 'Don't Waste My Time', written by Rick and Bob, had also both gone top forty. *Howling* had come to rest at #6 on the ARIA charts.

After two uneven records, The Angels had once again dominated the nation's airwaves and sent new tribes of young punters flocking to gigs – checking out what their older siblings had been raving about for years.

The following March Jands rang. They'd had a last-minute cancellation for their mobile studio and were now offering it at a cut-price rate – were The Angels interested?

Howling was still high in the charts and the band were criss-crossing the country on tour, but with the plan to release a live album still in mind, they grabbed the opportunity. Everyone was happy with the song selection that John Brewster had been working on, but with Bob Spencer now firmly ensconced as a fully-fledged member, the rest wanted him featured on rhythm guitar, not John.

On 19 March 1987, Jands parked their mobile studio out the back of the huge Bankstown RSL and ran their cables into the auditorium. That night, as the band rocked out to 800 punters, their old friend Andrew Scott from Rhinoceros recorded the show. The tapes were then put in storage and the band resumed their Howling Across Australia tour schedule.

CHAPTER FORTY-ONE
HOWLING ACROSS AUSTRALIA

It was the hottest must-see homegrown show ever to hit Perth.

The Howling Across Australia tour arrived at the Perth Entertainment Centre on 12 June 1987. Young support band Noiseworks with their new single 'Take Me Back' was all over the radio, as was 'We Gotta Get Out Of This Place'. The 8200-seat venue had been sold out for a month. Demand for tickets was so strong that an extra gig was justified, but the Entertainment Centre was unavailable so a show was booked into a big pub two nights later.

It was here, before a chock-a-block audience that Doc did what Doc often did at the end of a wild Angels show; he stood balanced on the monitors and stage-dived into the audience. Unfortunately, not enough hands were ready for him and he crashed through, knocking a punter to the floor and landing heavily on top of him. Shaken but unhurt, Doc scrambled back onto the stage, but not before the very-pissed-off punter grabbed his leg and tried to pull him back.

> **Bob Spencer:** One of the punters was still holding his leg and Doc, being the stubborn nonsensical type, proceeded to jerk his leg from him with the result that he tore his knee ligaments.

The tour manager called an ambulance and Doc was raced off to hospital for a temporary fix and painkillers. Then it was on to the flight back to Sydney, where two shows were cancelled while he consulted Dr Merv Cross, the go-to doctor for fixing footballers' knees.

It appeared that the tour was over but Doc wasn't prepared to throw in the towel that easily. He told Woodruff not to announce a cancellation until he could ascertain his mobility. After all, he could still sing. Within a couple of days he was hobbling around and figured he could do the show in an armchair carried out by the roadies. Someone then suggested that a dentist's chair might be more fitting. Next thing a 1930s chrome-plated barber's chair was located and the show was back on the road again.

Over the next two months the band toured the East Coast, Tasmania and NZ to standing-room-only shows. Every night the roadies ceremoniously wheeled Doc out in the barber's chair to an ecstatic roar and placed him onto a riser at the mic. Dressed for the part and with a dead parrot beside him, he sang like a bird. It was 'Mr Damage' incarnate and the fans adored him for it.

Rick: Doc sang the best he'd sung for years while he was in that chair. Instead of running around and out of breath, he concentrated on singing into the microphone and it was fantastic. He looked great and thousands of people who saw him never forgot those shows.

Eddie Rayner had played keyboards on many of the *Howling* sessions but had other commitments and couldn't join them on the road. Someone suggested an Australian/Lebanese guy called Michael Caruana.

Rick: We called him Habib Habib. He dressed as an Arab sheikh onstage and played keyboards with what you'd call a 'key-tar' that hung from his neck like a guitar. In Perth we stayed in a giant hotel that Alan Bond had built called Observation City. Habib walked into this huge lobby in full Arab regalia with Jim's Steinberger bass on his shoulder and talking in an exaggerated Lebanese/Arab accent. The Steinberger had no headstock [the top of the guitar where the tuning pegs normally are] and in its black soft case looked like a machine-gun.

Jim Hilbun was in a blue polyester suit and platform heels acting as Habib's interpreter. While Habib flicked his eyes suspiciously round the lobby,

> Jim was explaining to the receptionist that Habib wanted a room with a bath. Suddenly from every corner of the lobby pairs of security guys strode over and bustled the protesting Habib off to a back room.

The band had turned their hand to making their own video clips, editing together footage shot on camcorders – and Habib's arrest became another scene.

Another running gag was Jim borrowing Doc's crutches and then, in front of a crowd, Habib would kick one of them away so Jim would fall over . . .

Back in Sydney Jimmy Barnes was recording his next album, *Freight Train Heart*, at Rhinoceros and Rick and Jim got a call to help out. Rick played slide guitar on a Dylan composition, 'Seven Days', while Jim played and sang backing vocals on a couple of other songs. The album went #1 for a month and sold mega platinum.

> **Rick:** That was the first time I'd seen Jimmy work in the studio and he was a monster. Every take, he was out there at the microphone screaming his guts out. I've had a huge respect for him ever since then because he worked so hard. I wasn't used to that. There were so many times I'd wished Doc was there when we put down the rhythm tracks, but it rarely happened. He'd come in and do the vocals later.

The Angels juggernaut crunched across the country playing every conceivable venue: pubs, clubs, town halls, open airs. It didn't matter where it was, the queues would begin forming in the morning and the doors closed by the time the support band began.

On the production side there was a semi-trailer full of equipment, including Doc's wardrobe-case full of stage clothes, aka the Tardis. Plus the scaffolding and blacks (black curtains) needed to build 'Doc's World'.

By now there was no requirement for the band to do soundchecks. The roadies who played instruments would do it. They even had a band name for themselves: Fat Albert and the Genitals was one that lasted a while.

> **Rick:** Sometimes I'd go in during set-up to check that my gear was working, so I could at least get that part of the nerves out of the way before going on. And I'd take photos of the poor bastards sweating their guts out. It was a shifting family, lots of different faces. You'd hear them playing during a soundcheck. Occasionally you'd get someone who could really play and you'd be 'Wow!'.

Doc had his own pre-gig ritual, as agent Tony Grace discovered.

> **Tony Grace:** At Parramatta Leagues Club I dropped into the bandroom to say hi to the guys, just popping in before going to another gig. I said, 'Where's Doc?' Brent pointed towards the stage. So I went to one of the stage roadies, 'Where's Doc?' He pointed to the other side. I walked across the stage which was in darkness, and found another roadie: 'Where's Doc?' He pointed to the back of the stage. I'm thinking, 'What the fuck's going on here?'
>
> I walked to the back of the stage and saw this sign pinned to a black curtain: 'Doc's World'. I pulled it back a bit and there's Doc in his chair. He had an oxygen mask plugged into a tank and all ready, candles burning, bottle of wine and some book he was reading. He was getting in the zone. As I opened the curtain he saw me and I saw him. We both gave each other the biggest fright. I just said, 'Mate, you get back to what you were doing and have a great show – I'm outa here.'
>
> I didn't know about Doc's World until then. I wouldn't call it a secret – it was just one of those things that people just accepted as being part of Doc's behaviour.

The Howling tour ran through to the end of 1987 and took The Angels on a sixteen-month jaunt around Australia and New Zealand, playing to over 320,000 people. *Howling* attained double platinum sales and produced three big singles. There were a couple of breaks, but on the road takings were around a quarter of a million dollars a month. However, after agency and management commissions and the enormous costs of crew, transport, accommodation, airfares and band wages were deducted, profit retention sometimes went as low as a tenth of the total take.

CHAPTER FORTY-TWO
LIVELINE

Mushroom released the long-awaited double album, *Liveline*, in February 1988. It was the fan's ultimate dream come true: track after track – some with John Brewster playing, some with Bob Spencer – of The Angels in their raging glory, performed to hordes of manic pub-rock punters. It was all there: Doc's quirky raves and the call/response 'No way get fucked' chant, the scorching guitars and pounding drums. These were the songs that defined the perfect night out for any red-blooded suburban Aussie kid during the previous ten years. The soundtrack of their youth.

It came with a booklet of candid photos offering glimpses beyond the cloak of privacy that covered the band's individual lives. To a fan, *Liveline* would be a personal memento every bit as important as photos of their cars, lovers, mates, pets and everything else that defined who and what they were in their youthful single years.

The cover shot of Rick's sunglasses reflecting Doc in the distance and a huge crowd beyond had been taken by Bitsy Brewster. Twenty-four tracks spanning a tumultuous era of The Angels, it would go on to become one of the biggest sellers of their career. It prompted radio to respond to thousands of listeners requesting the live versions of old favourites.

Within weeks *Liveline* came to rest at the #2 spot.

*

After a lengthy break to recover from the Howling tour, The Angels commenced preparations to mount another national tour in June and July. It would be their most ambitious to date: Liveline: This Is It Folks – Over The Top (Then Now And Everything In Between).

In late May '88, band and crew gathered for rehearsals and stage design at the Enmore Theatre in Sydney. There was much to do. Each of the three planned performances during the show would be unique. The first would be as the Keystone Angels line-up, with Doc on bass guitar. On a minimalist stage, they'd present songs off their first album. The plan was to then take an intermission, while the roadies arranged a bigger stage set-up. The next bracket would kick off with everyone playing acoustic guitars, including Jim taking a solo spot on 'Madman's Paradise', an early song that had never been performed.

For the final bracket, intricate scaffolds would be swung into position to launch a blitzkrieg of the band's greatest and most loved songs. Every member of the crew had to know precisely what his role would be for this spectacular. But the show also needed to be flexible enough for downsizing from theatres to fit into the big pubs and clubs they'd be playing along the way.

In a reprise of a highlight executed during the original Pooled Resources tour, Rick would be stationed on the scaffold catwalk above Brent's drum kit playing the outro to 'Take A Long Line'. As the guitar wailed into the final notes, Doc would stride towards 'Rick', now replaced by the cut-out they'd used years before, and with a karate-chop send 'him' toppling over the back of the scaffold.

The extravaganza hit the road and into four provincial cities at big clubs chosen for their large stages and auditorium capacities. The morning of the eighth of June saw the semi pull back into the laneway behind the Enmore Theatre, where every seat for the next three nights had been pre-sold.

The first show was unfolding perfectly until the start of the second set.

John Brewster: I was in Doc's specially set-up dressing room wishing him well for the show when we heard the intro to 'Outcast' begin. He made for the stage door and I headed off. Next thing I hear him frantically bashing on the stage door because it's locked! The irony of the situation hit me. I said, 'Hey Doc, they're playing "Outcast" and you're it! You're the outcast!' He was frantic and didn't see the humour . . . I raced down a corridor and alerted a roadie.

The door opened and Doc sprinted for the microphone to the roar of the crowd.

The reviews raved, extra shows were added. There was a berserk night at the Shellharbour Workers and then the semi headed down the Hume to St Kilda Town Hall where the Chantoozies were opening for them, earning an encore from an audience wired for a raucous night out.

The Angels won accolades for their first two sets but the third wouldn't end well for Bob Spencer.

Bob: At the end of 'Show Me The Money', Doc and I would engage in a 'fight' which ended with me dragging a Marshall quad box from the side, climbing onto it, and, now taller than Doc, proceeding to push and kick him. That night, Doc kicked the top edge of the box, it toppled and I went with it, breaking the headstock off my guitar, smashing my teeth through my lip and snapping my right wrist.

The band came to a crashing stop. As Bob was carried off writhing and groaning, a chastened Doc bid the stunned audience goodnight and vanished stage right with the rest. It would be the only show of the tour without an encore.

While Bob spent the night in hospital, the rest sat about their hotel rooms in shock. With two sold-out shows scheduled for the weekend at Melbourne's Palais Theatre and another six weeks of the tour to go, things looked grim. Someone suggested calling Platinum Studios – they knew all the young hotshots in Melbourne who might be familiar with The Angels' repertoire and style.

Jimi Hocking: Eccles called me up. It seemed like a prank call, but it was too matter of fact. He said, 'I really don't have time to bullshit around. You need to tell me if you have the chops to do a gig with The Angels tomorrow night – or not.'

I may have been a cocky twenty-four-year-old but I was also a realist. I was a strong improviser and had a good ear, so I told him it was doable. He asked me to come straight over to the hotel.

Jimi was greeted by a very sombre mood. Bob's arm was in plaster and the possibility of the tour being cancelled was heavy in the air as the band sized him up.

He pulled out the guitar he'd just bought on HP and Rick and Bob fired requests: 'Play the riff from "Long Line" . . . play "No Secrets".' Everyone began to relax. The kid was good – maybe it was possible. They had a tape of the previous night's show. They switched it on and left him with it.

Jimi: After I had a few listens and made some notes, Eccles returned and walked me to the elevator. In an effort to impart the gravity of the situation, he looked me in the eye and said, 'You'd better be shit hot.' I looked him straight back and said, 'I am.'

The band went into a rehearsal room the next day and ran through every song of the show with the young guitarist. Then it was straight onto the soundcheck.

Jimi had been a fan of the band, had their early records and knew those songs. The new material was on the radio so that was also okay – it was just some stuff in the middle set that he wasn't familiar with. He walked onto the stage that night in front of 3000 highly expectant fans and bravely strapped on his guitar.

Jimi: 'Watch The Red' was my personal disaster. I had some cheat sheets stuck to the floor, but in the second set I was asked to stand at the top of this scaffolding they had. I couldn't see the cheat sheet for the song I knew least! I fumbled through it. Not only that, but they forgot to mention that I was to play bass in 'Eat City', while Jim Hilbun played sax. Jim handed me the bass: 'Here, play this.' I watched Eccles and played along with the kick drum.

The band's intention was to get through the Palais shows and then take stock of the situation, but after that first gig there was a brief meeting backstage and then Rick turned to Jimi: 'So what are you doing for the next few weeks?' Overnight the twenty-four-year-old found himself on a major rock tour.

The tour was a storming success – at every venue the sold-out sign went up. The manager at the 2000-capacity Newcastle Workers Club told them they'd sold more booze during their gig than with any other band. In Perth they sold out three Entertainment Centres: 24,600 seats in all. It was a record that no other Australian band had come close to. Supporting them for the three shows was a highly talented Perth band called Johnny Diesel and the Injectors. Brent thought so much of them that he did a deal to bring them to Sydney and manage them.

While Bob Spencer was temporarily out of The Angels, he took over front-of-house mixing and remained on tour.

> **Bob:** I had battles with our sound engineers – they were addicted to having the bass drum 428 times louder than the entire band, and I refused to do that. I wanted a mix that sounded like a record. Yak, the drummer from The Injectors, said [about my mix] it was the first time he'd heard Eccles' cymbals and also heard the whole band clearly. It made me very concerned about what the previous sound engineers had been doing to us.

Eventually the semi and the rest of the convoy made their way up the Snowy Mountains and parked behind the Lake Jindabyne Hotel. Icy winds numbed the crew as they loaded in and prepared for four shows over five nights. After a national tour of lugging tonnes of equipment in and out of one-night stands, this would be a holiday, hopefully with female company.

The tone for a decadent few days was set when the band and some of the crew decided to engage in some pharmaceutical indulgence on their first night off.

> **Rick:** We all took an x [ecstasy] before we walked over the road to the restaurant that evening. We ordered meals but while we waited the x came on with a rush.

A covert meeting suddenly seemed to be required, convened under the table, followed by really important speeches standing on chairs. There was deep love professed to people they'd never met. Bob had an intense conversation with a waitress on a couch and Rick went around meeting patrons who were there for a quiet dinner.

> **Jimi:** I'll probably never have that much fun again! We all went out to a restaurant and sat at the same table, but by the end of the night someone from our group was holding court on every other table in the place. During the course of a tour like that, you find out a lot about each other and a genuine affection emerges.

With the bonus he got, Jimi was able to pay off his new guitar and bought an old Les Paul Junior as well. Soon afterwards he landed a record deal and had some chart success before joining the Screaming Jets in 1993.

CHAPTER FORTY-THREE
YOUSE GUYS

During the Liveline tour a punter cornered Jim Hilbun after a show. Bursting with compliments for what he'd just seen, he pumped the bass player's hand and uttered these immortal words: 'Last time I seen youse guys, youse were shithouse. This time youse really carved it.'

There'd been numerous dressing-room jams during the tour, usually riffing around on radio songs. One time Rick did a piss-take of Talking Heads' 'Psycho Killer'. That led to someone else doing a send-up of 'Achy Breaky Heart' and suddenly it was on, a race to the bottom to see who could come up with the funniest rendition of a popular song.

When Jim regaled the rest about the punter's praise, it set some tacky ideas in motion. During their break, after the Liveline tour ended, The Angels morphed into a cringeworthy cover band called Youse Guys. They scored a month of Thursday nights at a pub near Brent's place, where young bands catered to North Shore yuppies.

Brent talked the pub into it on condition their real identity was never advertised. He negotiated a $1000 fee and away they went. At the start of the first night the fifty or sixty people in the room blinked when they saw who had come on to the stage. Despite their sixties safari suits, garish sports coats and wide salesman ties, there was no mistaking the identity of the tall handsome singer with the Irish accent. In minutes there were queues at the two available phones in the foyer and within an hour the place was jammed.

> **Rick:** The whole idea was as if Monty Python had formed a band. It was completely out there. The promo shot was mannequins in a shop window, dressed in old suits, all smiling and shaking hands. That was our image. That's how we dressed. We went to op shops and bought suits. Ill-fitting suits, along the lines of Basil Fawlty. Safari suits. Anything that looked awful.

They had a repertoire of cover songs and everyone sang on at least one, even Eccles, who couldn't sing in tune. He took on the most difficult song of all, 'You're The Voice', re-named 'Youse The Voice'. The whole band did the backing vocals but no-one sang in tune. They were rarely able to finish it due to hysterical laughter from band and audience.

> **Bob:** Rick sang 'Psycho Killer' and did a fantastic job, he was very funny. I wore a second-hand suit – it was just a hoot, a lot of fun. We played at a few bars and somehow got booked for a harbour cruise. People really got it.

> **Rick:** Yeah, they got it. You couldn't not get it. It was so bad, but still it was the band playing, so the playing was good and the feel was good. We all played it for laughs but Doc was a bit more serious, that was his nature. He sang things like 'Come Together', which was good fun to play. My first song in the show was from the thirties, called 'You Can Be Sure Of Me', retitled 'Youse Can Be Sure Of Me'. There was a dramatic pause in the song while I fished a handkerchief out of my top pocket and dried my eyes, and then we launched into 'Psycho Killer'. Another one I did was the Sex Pistols' 'Pretty Vacant'. That was a riot.

T-shirts were printed and a couple of hundred were sold by Mandi, the merch bitch.

For a band who had taken their career so seriously for the fifteen years since the madcap days of the jug band, it was a time to let their alter-egos take over and discard the rules. Especially after touring with tonnes of equipment in a semi-trailer and running a nine-man road crew.

Angels fan Marty McFadyen was there from the start.

Marty McFadyen: I heard about the upcoming gigs from my roommate. He was working at North Sydney police station and they'd been notified The Angels would be playing at the Crows Nest Hotel under a different name while recording a new album. This would be every Thursday night for five weeks.

I'd seen The Angels many times but for five weeks I had the opportunity to see my favourite band play their favourite songs. Beatles, Stones and heaps of seventies classics, often working from sheet music, making it more like a rockin' jam session. One night one of the members couldn't make it, so they called up a couple of punters from the crowd who could play guitar to stand in with the band. Even asking the crowd to yell out requests.

It's been many years but their slogan's stuck with me: 'Last time I saw youse guys, youse were shithouse . . . but this time youse really carved it!' Hundreds of thousands have memories of seeing this legendary Australian band, but only a rare few can say they've been to a Youse Guys gig. I'm glad I'm one of the few.

CHAPTER FORTY-FOUR
BEYOND SALVATION

During his many trips to LA, John Woodruff had become acquainted with maverick band manager Alan Niven. New Zealand-born Niven was a huge admirer of Rose Tattoo, who had greatly influenced the imagery and style of the band he managed, Guns N' Roses. Niven was also a massive fan of The Angels and songs from both bands had been in the Gunners' repertoire for years.

After the success of The Angels' last two albums in Australia and three years of huge tours, Woodruff and the band were again keen to have one more shot at breaking into the American market. Woody had introduced Niven to The Angels while both were in New Zealand the previous year and they'd hit it off; Doc to such an extent that he and Niven had done a bit of carousing in Doc's hotel room after a gig, ending up in a bear-hugging wrestling match, crashing around and breaking the furniture. With the band's blessing, Woodruff had come to an arrangement with Niven to co-manage The Angels outside of Australia and NZ.

Using Niven's impeccable connections, the pair presented a batch of songs to Chrysalis Records and landed a worldwide deal (except for Australasia where they remained with Mushroom). It came with a substantial advance which would allow the band to record in the USA with producer Terry Manning who'd worked with ZZ Top, Led Zeppelin and a great many others.

In early June The Angels flew out of Sydney bound for their next American adventure, with wives, girlfriends, soundman Ian Taylor and road manager Bicci Henderson. They were met at the airport by Niven and that night joined up with the Gunners for a few drinks. Angry Anderson, who was in LA, arrived and some serious partying got underway.

During the evening Niven mentioned his displeasure with Woodruff – who wasn't there – for commissioning 20 per cent of half the advance from Chrysalis.

> **Rick:** They could've both commissioned it, but Niven's story was that Woody took his, but Niven didn't. He thought it was wrong of Woody to take a commission because that money should have stayed to help pay for the recording. I guess Niven was a millionaire and didn't need the money, but Woody wasn't doing too badly either.

Whisky a Go Go, Los Angeles, 6 June 1989. The band had been onstage for well over an hour, stripping the paint off the wall. The place was packed and Chrysalis had turned out in force with a specially invited group of industry guests. The set crashed to an end but with chants for an encore ringing in their ears, they staggered back on again. Doc looked up at the balcony VIP area and invited a few 'friends' down to join them. He stood back as roadies brought on extra amps and plugged in more mics, and then Angry hopped up in a black t-shirt with cut-down sleeves, followed by Axl, Slash and Izzy Stradlin, all three from one of the biggest bands in the world at that point in time, Guns N' Roses.

To pandemonium from a seen-it-all-before audience, the assembled super-group proceeded to rip into several Angels classics, including Guns N' Roses' own favourite, 'Marseilles'. The Angels and their exalted fan club then spent the rest of the night partying on the balcony, swapping yarns, drinks and drugs with a bevy of admirers and Aussie expatriates.

Suddenly, cracking America didn't seem to be the struggle it once had been.

*

A few days later LA music magazine *BAM* reported: 'The Angels are one of the truly great rock bands that pioneered that driving rock sound from Down Under.'

The LA *Rock Review* had also been at The Whisky: 'When Doc invited most of Guns N' Roses down off the balcony to jam on 'Marseilles' for the encore, it was no surprise to see that Axl knew all the words, the song had been in his repertoire for years. The audience hadn't expected this, and a sold-out Whisky freaked out bigtime.'

Next day Niven invited Rick and Bob to New Orleans to see another band he managed, Great White, play at the Basketball Arena. At the gig, the pair were invited onstage to join them on 'Face The Day', which Great White had recorded on their first album.

From there the two guitarists flew on to Memphis and met up with the rest of The Angels and entourage, all busy setting up the apartments that would be home for the next few weeks. That night Terry and some friends took them all out to a restaurant. As the dinner progressed and the drinks kept coming, things got a little wild and noisy. But amongst all the hilarity, one thing disturbed Bob: 'That night I witnessed how badly white Americans in the south treated African Americans and it shocked me. Nothing had prepared me for the overt racism I saw.'

They were booked into Ardent studios – home to Manning for twenty years. Hopes were high that The Angels would soon have an award-winning album on Ardent's walls along with all the other famous names displayed there.

Four songs had already been worked on at Rhino and they'd be completed and mixed at Ardent. After that, Chrysalis had insisted that a number of older songs be rerecorded and placed on the American edition of the album and available for a Christmas 1989 release. However, the band had held out for the Australian album to feature all-new material. The plan was to get songs for the American release recorded first, and then get to work on songs for the Australian album, which would be released at a later date.

So, once again, the Australian album would be different to the international album of the same name. It wasn't a situation they were happy with, but to get the deal over the line that was what they'd signed up for.

Terry had a strict work ethic. The band were expected at the studio every day by 10 am. There'd be lunch, tea, coffee and soft drinks provided in-house, and work would end every night at six. He also wouldn't tolerate drugs or alcohol during work hours, which made for some covert activity among the band on a regular basis.

It left plenty of time for the Aussies to get out at night and do some bar crawling along Beale Street. Every place had a world-class band playing with no door charge. One night Bob struck up conversation with an all-black blues band, was invited up and acquitted himself well.

Bob: From then on I spent many nights going out and blowing/jamming with local musicians and striking up friendships. The natives were very friendly with the odd-looking little white bloke with the funny ponytail.

Memphis was Elvis' hometown and they made the obligatory tour of Graceland, where Rick was 'blown away seeing where Elvis lived, and seeing his plane over the road that he never flew in'. Bob got dirty looks for laughing and making jokes about the tawdriness of it all.

Terry Manning was an Elvis freak – he knew all the songs. When Brent suggested they become an Elvis band and do a few gigs, Terry jumped at it.

Handy Park was in the middle of town and on weekends it filled up with bands jamming in every nook and cranny.

Rick: Terry rented an electrical power socket at the park supervisor's office to supply power for the guitar amps and microphones. That was the deal to busk in Handy Park. It was free if you wanted to do it acoustic, but we wanted amps, so we plugged in. With no rehearsal, we played a set and all these people came round. Terry sang Elvis, Doc sang a few of ours and a few of Chuck Berry's. We were halfway through a song and this huge black woman came dancing up and said, 'Hey, what's the name of your band?' Off the top of my head I said 'Dancing Dick and the Richards', and that stuck for a week.

Two days later Terry marched in with a box of t-shirts emblazoned with a dynamite stick with a lit fuse and 'Dancing Dick and the Richards' written in big letters. Within days a new name had been democratically agreed on: The Cow Demons. Next thing, in comes Terry with new t-shirts displaying bulls and steers with horns. With friends all over Memphis, he then pulled a series of party gigs, and, incredibly, got the Cow Demons onto the big annual Fourth of July Independence Day Concert.

> **Rick:** There's this island in the Mississippi and every year on Independence Day the whole city comes down to the banks and all the entertainment is set up opposite on Mud Island. Terry used his contacts to get us on the bill. He had a friend, Jimi Jamison, who used to sing for Survivor. Jimi and his band were the headliners so Terry brazenly rang him and said, 'Hey, we've got this Aussie band and I'm singin' and how about we open for you?'

With an estimated 80,000 audience, the Cow Demons strapped on their instruments while Terry draped a banner across the stage front: '*G'Day mates, from the Australian Cow Demons*'.

They then went full steam into a couple of Elvis songs, followed by a couple of Angels songs with Doc out front.

> **Rick:** We finished with 'Am I Ever Gonna See Your Face' and all these pockets of Australians jumped up and started screaming 'No way, get fucked.' By the end the entire crowd was into it, it spread that fast. It was like you could visibly see what happened in Australia, the bush telegraph in one rendition of the song to a huge crowd – it happened that fast.

In between the frivolity, work on the still-unnamed album steadily progressed, although things ground to a halt for a couple of days at one stage. Jim needed to go in and record the bass lines on two songs. Rick rang in the afternoon to see if he'd finished.

'No, man,' Jim's Californian drawl came down the line, 'I'm still searching.'

Next day came the same stoned response, 'Still searching, man.'

Bob: I first heard that one during *Howling*. Oh how I hated that. How long does it take to find an A on an E string?

Eventually Rick and Bob lost patience. Rick played bass on 'Let The Night Roll On' and Bob played bass on 'Dogs Are Talking'. As for Jim, he didn't seem perturbed by the tensions he'd caused and continued to drift along.

Rick: Doc couldn't be found when it was time to do the vocals – he was missing in action for a couple of days. We sent Bicci, our road manager, out to find him. After asking around, he discovered him in a jelly house. It wasn't jelly wrestling, it was jelly floating. Some sort of treatment. He's the only guy I've ever known who's floated in jelly. I saw him do a few things; he got into crystals and he almost got into the Orange people. I don't know how many hundreds of books he read on self-improvement and I guess the jelly was part of that.

Some of the songs still didn't have lyrics. When Doc explained how creative he felt after a jelly float, he was given the task of completing lyrics for a song of Rick's.

Doc: 'Dogs Are Talking' is a sexual rites of passage song in the vein of many Chuck Berry songs about cars, such as 'No Particular Place To Go'. I guess sex for many of us growing up happened in the back seat of a car. The 'dogs' are those disapproving gossips who probably missed out and can only bitch among themselves because they never made it to the car!

The four songs were completed but not before there'd been another delay in the studio created by Jim's 'still searching' antics. Frustrated, Terry had to call Bob back in to play bass on 'Jump City' and 'Rhythm Rude Girl'.

The band was well into re-recording the batch of older songs to go on the American edition when Alan Niven, dressed in trademark black on black and wraparound shades, flew in to see how things were going. At the conclusion of a play-back session, he loudly declared that he hated what he'd heard and made it clear that he had no time for

Terry or his talents as a producer. Strangely, he then stretched, glanced round and suggested a game of cricket.

> **Rick:** It was burning hot and we played out on the asphalt car park. While he was fielding, Niven took his shoes off, and by the time we'd finished his feet had blistered out of control. He was really disgruntled with the band, the producer, his feet, everything. He demanded to remix the four songs we'd done. He was a control freak – if things weren't done his way he didn't like it. We said 'no way'.

Without a word, Niven got up and went back to his hotel where he discovered he'd been robbed and all his flashy diamond-studded rings were gone. It was the last straw. He checked out and flew back to LA without calling the band. The following day he sent a terse message: 'That's it, I've resigned.'

> **Bob:** In LA I'd overheard Alan on the phone with one of the Gunners, explaining how to use his Amex card to buy a guitar, like a dad might patiently instruct his son. Alan seemed to represent some sort of father figure to at least some of the members. I feel that this was the crux of our doomed relationship with him. He was used to giving orders to 'his band' and we never saw ourselves as anybody's band. A manager is an employee, after all, and we were quite independent in our thinking and didn't need a father figure. On a better note, Alan did find the graphic for the *Beyond Salvation* album cover, which was terrific!

The graphic of the fallen angel in her Wonderbra all-in-one corset came with a biblical-flavoured name, *Beyond Salvation*, which they also adopted for the album title. The angel and her title went on to inspire the lyrics for a new song co-written by Rick, Bob, Doc and Brent. Jim was invited to participate but didn't show up.

Finally, the American version was completed and ready to be pressed and marketed in time for the USA Christmas release. The problem was, it had taken longer to record than planned, and Terry was now booked to produce another album. Recording for the Australian

Beyond Salvation would have to wait. The band decided to head back to Sydney for a couple of months and return for another block of studio time when Terry was available again.

Before leaving, there was one more chore to complete.

Bob: Jim was going back to Sydney via San Francisco where he was from. We all had the shits with him. He was smoking dope all day every day and most of the time he was in a dream. We had a band meeting and I just said, 'Look, Jim, it's pretty obvious you're not really into what we're doing, and we think it's best that you leave and pursue whatever it is that you would like to do, because it's not working for the direction that we're going in.'

CHAPTER FORTY-FIVE
MEMPHIS, TAKE TWO

Back in Sydney they took time off from being in The Angels.

Mushroom had released the recently completed 'Let The Night Roll On' as the second single, with ads announcing a new album was on the way. This was the first single ever released by Mushroom on the new CD technology that was revolutionising the recorded-music industry.

There were return dates at the Crows Nest Hotel, scene of the sell-out season of the Youse Guys gigs the previous year. This time, however, it was under the guise of the Cow Demons. Again, word quickly spread about the real identity of the band, leading to more nights of madness.

Meanwhile, despite a casual look around for a new bassist, no appointment had been made. Rick and Bob were more than capable of playing bass in the studio when they got back to Ardent.

Over in Perth, twenty-one-year-old James Morley was bassist in a cover-band specialising in AC/DC and The Angels.

> James Morley: Brent and Bob had jammed with us a couple of times in a club called Rockwells. I sort of knew Bob and if The Angels were in town I'd ring him and ask if he'd put a couple of names on the door. I found out that Jim had left, so I got Brent's number and told him I wanted the gig. I flew over and auditioned, but they didn't want me to play Angels songs – they said anyone could do that. They just jammed and I played along with them. I slotted in perfectly and got

the gig. So I stayed in Sydney for three days while my passport was rushed through from Canberra, and then flew to Memphis.

This time Terry had organised a share house for Brent, wife Helen, and Rick and Mandi – the rest had small apartments nearby. While the days were spent in the studio, the nights were back cruising Beale Street and hanging out at the cluttered Rum Boogie Café, a favourite from both sides of the mic. They were known by name there and the strawberry daiquiris arrived at a special price for the Aussie boys whenever they got up for a blow.

Beale Street had been the centre of black music in the twenties and thirties and it remained the cultural hub of Memphis. Blues, rock and R&B musos gathered there, some as scheduled, others looking for like-minded souls to swap a few licks. Night and day, live music poured from every door. Bob Spencer was a good spruiker and managed to wangle the Cow Demons onto a stage or two.

'Have we met?' he'd open. 'No? Okay, well, we're an Aussie band over here making a record – mind if we have a play with you?' It was risky, but most times they *carved it.*

Doc: We'd crash any gig, anytime. Even busk on the sidewalk. It was very easy for me being in Memphis – our knowledge of those old blues and jug-band songs they played in those places. It felt like Beale Street had been waiting there for us to complete things.

Despite writing profusely, Doc seemed less than enthusiastic about presenting his work to the band.

Bob: We had lunch together and he came up with a line, 'too hot to handle, too cold to hold', which he dramatically wrote on a napkin. In all the time we spent in Memphis, that was the only time we spent one on one. He never hung round the studio while we worked on stuff, never popped in to say 'hi' or ask how it was going. Rick was there with him whenever he put down vocals. Rick also worked with Terry to compile the final vocals from the takes for each song. It was Rick and Terry who did that work.

Since they'd signed with Chrysalis a year back, there'd been a corporate shake-up and a 'roster rationalisation' – shades of MCA. The last time the band had seen anyone from the company was at the Whisky gig five months before, although they were too focused on recording and just living in Memphis to think about it too much.

Chrysalis released the American version of *Beyond Salvation* in November. There was no official launch involving the band and no fanfare. Without Niven to shake the tree, and with Woodruff back in Australia, it all slipped quietly by. Once again, The Angels were the victims of a record company shake-up and *Beyond Salvation* in America very quickly became just that: *beyond salvation.*

With time running out, the final sessions for the Australian version of the album wound down and everyone but Rick and Bob went home. The two guitarists had some overdubs to do and loose ends to sort, so they stayed on for a week; then Terry was left to complete the mix-downs.

The last thing the band had done together was the promo clips for 'Dogs Are Talking' and 'Let The Night Roll On'. They'd driven out to an abandoned meat works with director John Jopson, a lovely good-hearted man. Those two clips had captured a rock vibe and given them an identifiable 'look' again, after some wobbly representations over the previous few years.

Living together in Memphis had helped them refine and define who 'The Angels' were these days. Away from Australia, away from families, little contact with management, none with record companies or agents. Just the musicians and Terry.

> **Bob:** I think these are some of the reasons why the album turned out so well. Camaraderie. In Memphis I came into my own and found a solid place in the band. Terry was extremely supportive of my playing and writing and I learned a lot by watching him in the studio.

Bob and Rick flew back to Sydney thinking they were on the verge of something big with what they'd just done. And there were some recorded songs left over – maybe they could be put on the next album.

As the hours slipped by they talked over the good times they'd had in Memphis. *'Do you remember going to that Memphis gospel church service? Amazing! And the trip to New Orleans with the incredible a cappella group singing "Return To Sender" and "Wimoweh"?'*

A few days before leaving the States they'd heard that back home Sony had released *The Angels Collection*, a boxed set of the first six albums released by the band, and that it was selling gangbusters.

As the plane glided in over the suburbs of Sydney on Christmas Eve 1989, they knew they had something special to carry them into the 1990s.

CHAPTER FORTY-SIX
THE DOGS ARE TALKING

Brent had been co-hosting a night show on Triple M called 'Homegrown' that played demos by unsigned bands and artists. With the radio show in mind, he'd come up with an idea for the new single 'Dogs Are Talking'.

The concept was to put three songs by three unsigned bands on the B-side of the new single. It could then be promoted via the Homegrown show, and from there it would hopefully help the A-side leapfrog into Triple M's playlist. The concept also included taking the unsigned bands on the road for the upcoming Dogs Are Talking tour. The bands chosen were the Hurricanes, the Desert Cats and the Woodruff-managed Baby Animals.

By May the plan had worked and 'Dogs Are Talking' was high in the charts. Triple M were also playing the B-side tracks and a tour of the same name was about to go out on the road. Woodruff and Eccles had negotiated a live-to-air broadcast with the Triple M national network: The Angels would play all the tracks from *Beyond Salvation* from a rehearsal studio they'd be moving into a week before the broadcast.

The support bands were offered the studio to practise in and become acquainted for the last couple of days. During the final afternoon members of The Angels arrived and mixed with the young musicians, shaking hands, chatting and checking their own equipment.

Doc had the flu and sat it out as the band ran through the songs for the broadcast. The four months off since the last tour had been good for the singer. He'd been on a fitness kick, eased up on his drinking and, despite the illness, looked healthy and youthful.

They took a break fifteen minutes before they were due on air, topping up drinks, getting into position and waiting for the word to come through from the station. Rick slipped on his shades and checked his tuning, while Doc went through a series of grunts, screams and howls, warming up his flu-croaky voice.

The ten-second countdown began and then they burst into action. In a split second Doc's demeanor changed as he grabbed the mic, leant forward and became a demented madman. Even in this rehearsal studio with only the young musos looking on, this was to be a full-blown performance. Out in radio-land an eager public was treated to The Angels' first new studio album in four years.

The Dogs Are Talking tour kicked off in Adelaide on 29 May and by Saturday 8 June the semi was parked hard against the loading dock behind Selina's, the rock venue purpose-built onto race bookie Terry Page's Coogee Bay Hotel. Inside, a broad stage fronted a vast room with a long bar running the length of the back wall. Steel steps climbed to a VIP platform overlooking the whole scene, with a bar and a manager's office tucked into a corner. The place legally held about 2000, but regularly hosted closer to 3000. This was big-time pub rock 'n' roll and Terry Page had the budget to present major local and international acts on most weekends.

By midnight the support bands were backstage, elated, laughing, joking, downing drinks. They'd survived the chants of '*ANGELS, ANGELS*' and been applauded at the end of their sets. Then The Angels came on to a rapturous response, returning for wave after wave of encores. However, it was the three opening bands that had set up the magic for the night.

From the start of the tour, Rick and Brent in particular had made it their duty to offer advice and criticism, and tonight, in front of this hardcore Angels audience, these bands had shone. At four in the morning Rick was still listening and making suggestions.

> **Rob Tognoni of the Desert Cats:** It's weird talking to Rick Brewster about guitars and he's talking to you on the same level. You've got to snap your fingers and remember who it is. They're just normal guys.

It was 5 am when Rick and Mandi stumbled out to his BMW to find a beer barrel in the backseat after some idiot had heaved it through the rear window. So much for the accolades – welcome back to the real world.

A week later the video for the new single, 'Backstreet Pickup', was filmed during a day off. The band had just been told that *Beyond Salvation* had hit #1 nationally, a first for The Angels.

The tour wound up at the Alexandria Headlands Hotel on the Sunshine Coast north of Brisbane. Final night and things got a bit crazy, with Brent heaving powder bombs at the Desert Cats from the wings. There wasn't much they could do other than dodge, but war had been declared!

While The Angels blasted into their set, the Cats snuck behind Brent's drum riser and gave the carpet an almighty heave. Instead of pulling him off the riser, a footlight was thrown against a curtain. In seconds smoke billowed up followed by flames. Consternation and roadies ruled while Brent drummed gamely on with sidelong glances and plans for revenge later on.

The tour flew on to New Zealand where the 'Dogs Are Talking' single had been released with songs from the two support acts chosen for the concerts there: Nine Livez' 'Live It Up' and Shihad's 'Down Dance', both first releases for these bands. Shihad would go on to become New Zealand's most successful domestically based band ever, with five #1 albums and twenty-five charting singles at last count.

CHAPTER FORTY-SEVEN
BEYOND SALVATION TOUR

The staging for the Beyond Salvation concerts was conceived by Rick and developed over dinners at his place with tour manager Bicci Henderson and lighting whiz Tim Bradsmith. Models of the stage lay-out were mocked up. Bicci and Tim worked out how to make it capable of surviving being trucked the length and breadth of Australia, and then shipped to New Zealand for six concerts. There were hundreds of lights and specialised projectors, dozens of dry-ice machines to send waves of fog across the stage. There'd be a gargantuan sound system requiring two huge sound desks to manage it – as well as scaffolding, backlit screens and an acre of curtaining.

Over forty people were involved in bringing the concept to fruition: designers, tradesmen and specialised crew covering the full spectrum of stagecraft. This would be the biggest and most expensive locally produced tour ever to hit the road in Australia and NZ. The Hordern Pavilion was hired for five days to assemble and test it, do rehearsals, and then pack it away. It would take two semi-trailers to haul it from venue to venue and a total of fifteen crew to operate it. Ten casual luggers were required at each show to help with the load in and load out.

The upfront costs were horrendous, so enter Michael Gudinski's Frontier Touring Company. Frontier agreed to finance the set-up costs in return for promoting the tour for a slice of the profits. As Gudinski also owned Mushroom Records, it was a win/win for him to be promoting the album at the same time.

The band needed to consolidate its position in the Australian and New Zealand market. Fresh-faced young bands were emerging, new heroes were climbing the charts and radio was adapting to the next generation. The Angels' older fans were moving on, buying homes, starting families, moving into different phases of their lives – and not going out to pubs to see rock bands as much as they used to. The band had to reach out to a new market or go the way of so many before them; into oblivion.

Cheap Trick were embarking on a world tour promoting a new album and were keen to get back down under. It was years since they'd been in the Australian charts and a tour on their own wasn't financially viable – but combined with old friends The Angels, it stacked up. In a testament to Gudinski's negotiating skill, he'd been able to talk Trick's management into opening the show. It would be marketed as a double header, with tickets priced to reflect the value of the show.

The tour commenced on 22 August 1990 at Brisbane's Festival Hall and it quickly became obvious that things weren't panning out the way it was planned. For a start, many of the punters were the targeted audience: new Angels fans who'd bought *Beyond Salvation*. They weren't familiar with Cheap Trick or their repertoire. And the older fans got impatient. Despite the American band turning in a fine performance and singing old classics 'Surrender' and 'Dream Police', it wasn't long before chanting for The Angels began.

During the changeover the area in front of the stage became a crush and tension rose to fever pitch. The band came on and delivered such a high-powered spectacle that one reviewer could only compare them to bands such as Guns N' Roses and Mötley Crüe and their extravagant performances. And certainly The Angels, resplendent in studded leather jackets and jeans and chains wrapped around waists and boots, had the metal image down pat.

To the hardcore older fans, though, all the showbiz glitz was a sell-out of what the band had once been: a no bullshit pub-rock band. To watch Bob Spencer windmill his arm Pete Townshend style just looked like derivative crap to those who knew them in former times. Songs from the 'classic Angels' albums were played too fast and where the lyrics of those early numbers spoke to them with substance and mystery, the new songs sounded trite. By the time it was over, with too many of the gems left out, including 'Marseilles', a divide had been drawn. For the younger punters the band was sensational, but most of the long-termers shrugged and walked away. This wasn't the band they'd fallen in love with back in the day.

Two nights later at the first of two full houses at Sydney's Hordern, James Morley stepped up to his mic during the encore and started singing Rose Tattoo's 'Rock 'n' Roll Outlaw'. A strange song to be doing in an Angels concert until Tattoo's Pete Wells walked out and joined them. His tall, lean, tattoo-covered frame oozed pure rock 'n' roll as he launched into his trademark slide guitar to a crescendo of applause.

The old guard loved Pete Wells – he was the real deal – but this was an Angels show and there were so many earlier songs they wanted to hear that had been dropped.

The members of Cheap Trick were also not happy – by the audience response, but also backstage. When John Brewster visited them after the show, Rick Nielsen grabbed him. 'John, what's happened to this band since you left? The production gets cut for our set and we're being treated like assholes by the management!'

The tour rolled on round the country and then band and crew boarded the ship across Bass Strait to Launceston's Silverdome in Tasmania.

> **Ian Taylor:** We were setting up the equipment and the Christians were outside with big placards – pissed off with this evil rock band coming to town and playing to thousands of kids with a concert called Beyond Salvation. I went out with my camera wearing a tour t-shirt and they were incensed! One of them hit me with his placard. I tried to explain we were just a band playing some music but that got them even more aggressive.

After the show that night Rick and Mandi went cruising the local casino and came across Tom Peterson, Cheap Trick's bassist, at a blackjack table.

Rick: Tom had lost his money. He was down to his last few bucks. We'd heard he was a mad gambler and always after loans from his band-mates. He saw me and started begging for money. I said, 'For Christ's sake go to bed,' but, convinced his luck had turned, he took off his expensive long leather coat and tried to sell it to me for $200 – it would have cost him ten grand in New York! Rick Nielsen was the smart one. When Trick hit it big internationally he bought a suburban shopping centre and he's never looked back.

On 10 September the show was transported to New Zealand, while Cheap Trick flew on to Japan.

Beyond Salvation's chart longevity was given another marketing push in October with the release of the next single, 'Rhythm Rude Girl'. The 'private dancer' sequences in the promo clip were performed by a naked Mandi, backlit and projecting her erotic moves onto a screen behind the band as they played onstage during a concert. The entranced lyrics Doc sang were all Rick's: 'Show me that rhythm / show me body talk / got no inhibitions / no reserve at all . . .'

Mandi: I danced on a huge riser behind a curtain to 'Rhythm Rude Girl', which was written about me as I was an exotic dancer at the time. I'm in the live clip. The roadies used to set up this extremely high riser and fight over who would direct the spotlight on me to create this giant shadow behind the band for that song.

Being on the road with The Angels was never boring. Flying from WA after dropping acid with Rick was the funniest flight ever. We couldn't stop laughing all the way.

Rick married his rhythm rude girl on 6 October, surrounded by band and friends, with Brent as his best man. The happy couple then flew off for a honeymoon in the Maldives.

After a two-month break, the band went back on the road on 25 November. This time it was a good old-fashioned pub tour to put some cash in the bank. The Beyond Salvation tour had grossed nearly a million dollars, but after Frontier's profit, Woodruff's management commissions and the massive production costs, the band members walked away with wages only. What profits it did make went towards paying off the debts still outstanding for their time in Memphis.

In the aftermath of the tour Rick would take stock of feedback many of their old fans had offered about the new songs. While *Beyond Salvation* had introduced hordes of younger fans to the band, he acknowledged what the older ones were saying; that the new songs didn't stand up to the glory of the 'classics' on their former albums.

CHAPTER FORTY-EIGHT
MANAGEMENT

With a new run planned for March, a tour EP was suggested. Two songs were lifted from *Howling*, one from *Beyond Salvation* and a new one that Rick and Mandi had written together, 'Blood On The Moon'.

> **Ian Taylor:** Rick and I recorded and mixed that song late into the night. We were listening to the mix on the way home in Rick's BMW and decided to turn around and go back and mix it again. To this day I'm sure the mix that was released was not the mix we'd chosen. There were five mixes on the tape that went for pressing and I think the wrong one was pressed, but who knows?

Rick's personal life was changing. He and Mandi were talking about having a family and buying a house and he was having a hard look at his financial situation after all these years. He'd been a major creative force behind one of the country's most successful bands – and yet there wasn't an awful lot to show for it. His band was still carrying debts from the Memphis sojourn. The American version of *Beyond Salvation* had died and disappeared – and any royalties from it would go to Chrysalis to pay off the advance they'd paid to the band.

When he and Bitsy were divorced, Rick had given her his share of the house they'd bought back in '79. The band had generated millions since then, but apart from wages and Australasian royalties, not much in the way of profits had come his way.

The Angels operated through an entity called Tutankhamun Nominees. The director/owners were originally John, Rick and Doc. Soon after Brent joined he was invited to become a partner. When John was sacked, he resigned from the partnership as part of his settlement, leaving Rick, Doc and Brent as owners of The Angels. At the end of a tour the profits were split between those three.

The Beyond Salvation tours had pushed sales of the album through the roof, which had generated substantial royalty cheques for the songwriters. But after he'd received little more than wages from the multi-million dollar tours, what had really got up Rick's nose was that Woodruff had not only made a fortune in management commissions, he'd also received 20 per cent of the guitarist's songwriting royalties.

When the management agreement had been thrashed out back in the seventies, it was explicitly agreed that songwriting royalties were sacrosanct to the writers, and wouldn't be part of Woody's commission. (Actually, the band had never signed Woodruff's management agreement – it had remained a verbal contract.) However, during the shuffle from Alberts to CBS, Woodruff had negotiated his way into receiving 20 per cent of *all* the band's gross income, and for the past ten years, 20 per cent of publishing (songwriting) royalties had been paid to him. With *Beyond Salvation* now at double platinum, and previous albums being snapped up by the waves of new fans, Woodruff was about to receive another hefty slice of Rick's royalty income.

Rick: I began stirring Bob up about this because we were the main songwriters now – Doc no longer contributed. So at the end of the tour, off we went to see Woody at his house overlooking the ocean at Coogee, to tell him that we didn't want to pay publishing commissions anymore. Woody was clearly not happy but eventually said, 'Okay, if that's the way you feel, so be it.'

Doc: They had a falling out and John said that he didn't feel that he could work with the band anymore with the relationship between he and Rick.

Soon after, Woodruff sent the band a curt two-sentence letter of resignation and put out a press statement. It said that he was parting company with The Angels to devote himself full-time to his record label Imago, and to managing The Baby Animals, who he'd recently signed to Imago.

Brent immediately offered to manage the band for a 10 per cent commission. It was a smart move which won everyone over and would leave an extra $5000 a week in the band's coffers when they were on tour and generating income.

> **Doc:** Brent took over as manager, which was a situation I enjoyed because he would be at the shows that he'd organised, so to speak. Woodruff had a different relationship with the band. He came to lots of shows but he wasn't there every night as Brent was.

> **Tony Grace:** When Woodruff and The Angels went their separate ways and Eccles took over, I already had a good agent relationship with him from him managing Diesel. He was extremely thorough on making sure that every time the band went on the road there was a really interesting new message.
>
> From my perspective, Eccles was an excellent manager.

Beyond Doc's life within the Angels, he and Dzintra had also gone their separate ways and he'd been living the bachelor life for some time. That changed one night when he met air hostess Kym Moore at Benny's, a Kings Cross nightclub that catered to the denizens of the music industry and their friends. Kym was a party girl and had Doc laughing and thoroughly enjoying himself after a period of doom and gloom. He began seeing her regularly and soon enough they were an item.

After his divorce came through from Dzintra, he booked an old biplane to tow a huge banner behind it with a message for Kym. He rented a vintage car and drove her down to the harbour to a lookout where they'd enjoyed watching the yachts out racing. The plane flew slowly by with the banner: '*Kym I love you, will you marry me? BPN.*' She laughed, fell into his arms and said, 'Yes!'

CHAPTER FORTY-NINE
RED BACK FEVER

After the failure of the American version of *Beyond Salvation*, Chrysalis advised that they wouldn't be providing an advance for a new album. A polite way of saying the band had been dropped.

So one of Eccles' first management tasks was to open discussions with Mushroom about providing the finance for the next album. After the success of *Salvation* in Australia and New Zealand, they were receptive, but with a deepening economic recession now affecting recorded music sales, Mushroom could only offer a modest budget.

Rick and Brent had met English producer Steve James the previous year. Steve had relocated to Australia and had recently produced the successful first Screaming Jets album. Rick and Brent liked his work, and, with Doc, enjoyed his company. In May Brent negotiated a deal with him to produce their next album.

Steve had worked with a string of top English bands and, curiously, he'd also produced the soundtrack to one of the band's favourite films, *Life Of Brian*.

Rick: *Red Back Fever* had to be a low-budget recording. We were still suffering from the huge costs of living for five months in Memphis and there was little money in the bank. But we needed to do a new album. We found a small 24-track studio called Trackdown in Camperdown. Between pub tours, we started working with Steve on some new songs we'd written since the Memphis sojourn.

Almost immediately tensions between the band's old guard members and the new began coming into play. After the rock-star experience of Memphis and Terry Manning, the plans to record in a modest suburban studio like Trackdown were a shock to Bob and James. Rick and Brent argued that they could make a great album in Sydney with Steve at a fraction of the price of *Salvation*.

Bob: This crazy thing happened. *Salvation* was the only #1 album the band ever had. But instead of wanting to capitalise on that success, these guys wanted to retreat. They wanted to save a thousand here, five thousand there.

Rick: Bob and James were hired musos who hadn't had to share in the cost of recording *Salvation*. The travel, accommodation, studio, producer fees, management etc. They were probably unaware of the true reality of the band's situation. We'd blown a fortune recording *Two Minute Warning*, and we'd done it all over again on *Salvation*, and we just couldn't do it a third time. We'd recorded *Howling* in Sydney and it was a great album – there'd been no logical reason to go to Memphis to record *Beyond Salvation*.

Doc: At the record-company level in America, we just never got the kind of long-term support you really need. It was very frustrating and at times we came close to breaking up because we were so disheartened by it all.

Bob and James found it difficult to understand why the band had no money. Since returning from Memphis eighteen months back, The Angels had scored what other bands could only dream of: a #1 album, with 'Dogs Are Talking' reaching #11 and 'Let The Night Roll On' hitting #17. They'd stomped back and forth across the country with four sold-out pub tours and one massive concert tour. They'd done much the same in New Zealand.

But that wasn't the only gripe. Serious music differences were also apparent.

> **Bob:** My vision for the band was to have funky riffs and grooves like Aerosmith. What I had in my head was moving forwards in the way that Aerosmith had done. They were my yardstick. I looked at us and went, 'Some of these guys want to go backwards,' and I'm not a backwards sort of guy.

To Rick, who'd carried the flame from the birth of The Angels, Bob's vision was anathema. To him the 'moving forward' had watered down the original vision; a style and repertoire which still stood up twelve years later. That was the band that got worldwide attention. Having begun with the notion that The Angels would be unique and, if anything, others would copy *them*, they'd become unexceptional. Lessons from AC/DC, who'd stuck to their original vision with unprecedented discipline, had been ignored. Not only had Angels songs become pedestrian, but Alan Niven's insistence on 'changing the image for America . . . you need more ATTITOOD, boys', which Brent had picked up on, had them in leather, studs and chains. To Rick, who'd refused to don the 'new' image, the band now looked like they'd been churned out by the same PR factory that produced all the American metal bands they'd once ridiculed.

Bob saw it differently.

> **Bob:** Terry would have fashioned our ideas into something coherent and world class. But they wanted to revert to the way the band had sounded before *Salvation* – which I didn't get. And neither did James. They were also saying, 'Ah we don't want to go to America again, we don't want to tour America again.'

Doc was acutely aware of the reality. After all the years of giving his heart and soul in sweat-drenched performances to massive crowds, he had so few assets to show for his life's work that it sent him reeling into a series of depressions, days in bed and bouts of binge drinking.

> **Doc:** That's what broke the back of The Angels – the attempts to crack the States.

For various reasons, the recording of *Red Back Fever* wound up being rushed. Bob and Rick had written some good songs in the past, but with the unrest this time, the collaboration suffered and the results were mediocre. When the time came to move into the studio, there were a few songs that had been previously recorded in Memphis. Rick had written one, but there weren't enough for a whole album. Consequently two covers were recorded, one of which, Ian Hunter's 'Once Bitten Twice Shy', had gone over well during the Youse Guys gigs.

> **Doc:** Everyone had been involved in the writing except myself. I'd found it really hard going. We'd been touring for ten months so I just went bush.

Doc going bush included a saga of camping out for a few weeks in the 900-acre Lane Cove National Park, which was within the metropolitan Sydney area. He also spent time in the nearby Blue Mountains, walking bush paths to the lookouts, and down into the blue-haze valleys.

Meanwhile, back at the studio, the rest of the band got on with it.

> **Bob:** I don't want to disparage Steve – he did the best he could with what he had – but the band was in disarray, the songs were not very well thought out, lyrically it was pretty terrible, and we should have spent more time writing. I played bass on one track because James was being such a petulant little shit.
>
> We chose to take a step back and play it safe instead of exploiting the situation we had with *Beyond Salvation*, which I think stands up as a great album.

> **Rick:** *Beyond Salvation* was an okay album. Great production let down by some B-grade songs and some shit lyrics. I really missed my brother's input. He and I had always been able to sort the wheat from the chaff until a song started to glow – nothing less would do.

Despite the hassles and lack of enthusiasm, Steve enjoyed recording Bob and Rick. He'd worked with some of the world's finest guitarists and rated the two of them right up there with the best. But he had problems recording Brent's drumming and spent days coaxing the feels he required from him.

As for Doc, Steve was surprised to find the image and reputation of the high-energy singer hid a lonely and jaded man. Doc confided to Steve that, other than Rick, the band was no longer the outfit he'd started off with, and that he felt disconnected from the new members.

Steve: Doc wasn't in a good headspace. He was depressed and cynical about the whole business – everything. He announced he was leaving the band and obviously that was a major problem. Brent managed to get him back now and then and we eventually got some wonderful vocals down. I just got him to enjoy himself. I tried to get some feel out of it and use that wonderful depth he's got.

At the end of the sessions Steve and his wife invited Doc and Kym over for dinner. Doc was very taken with a series of pictures on the wall of English comedian Sid James. When Steve told him that Sid was his father, Doc stared, totally dumbfounded.

Steve: Tears started rolling down his face and he became visibly emotional. He told me that as a kid growing up with his dad in the British Army, one of his weekly highlights was listening to *Hancock's Half Hour* [which featured Sid] on the BBC. Whether it was in Malaya, Germany, Ireland, he and his brothers always tuned in and they still remembered the jokes. He'd seen Sid in the Carry On films and loved them. He came over and gave me the most affectionate hug and just held onto me. It was like he was hugging something deep and very meaningful from his youth. That my father held such an abiding memory for Doc was extremely moving for me.

After they'd finished recording *Red Back Fever*, the band did a gig under a made-up name (Angels spelt backwards) at Springfields, at Kings Cross.

Ian Taylor: Just for fun, Steve James did sound. The night was insane! It was a secret show but you don't do a secret show and not tell anyone! It was packed. If anything had gone wrong . . .

> We had the oxygen bottle next to the stage and Doc was sucking it every chance. He absolutely needed it that night. Woody was there and we staggered out and took a deep breath and the cold air nearly knocked me out! We looked like we'd just got out of a pool.

That was in front of their peers and friends. A review they got in the *Canberra Times* a week later was a better indication of what was happening during this period: 'This is very painful for me,' said the entertainment reporter, 'something I thought I'd never do. But simply, The Angels did not play a good concert at Raiders on August 24.' The review said that Doc had tried to ignite the audience, unlike the rest of the band. They'd managed to get an encore, but the mic was moved to Rick and he sang it. 'I couldn't tell you what the song was,' wrote the reporter, 'the sound having disintegrated into mush.'

> **Ian Taylor:** We had some unbelievable nights and some real stinkers. The band was crazy loud on stage as well. Some rooms would cope with the level – others wouldn't.

The first single, 'Some Of That Love', was released in October '91. An impressive clip was filmed at a naval airbase with the guitarists performing by the tarmac as F18s roared past. After banging on for years about how he'd like to fly to gigs in a chopper, Doc got to go up in one in full naval flying gear, grinning ear to ear. A second clip was filmed that day for 'Once Bitten Twice Shy', which would be released early the following year.

Despite a tour where the first half of the 'show' was a 'listening party' with *Red Back Fever* played loudly through the PA, followed by the band onstage for the second half performing older material, 'Some Of That Love' failed to get any airplay.

Mushroom suspected that this album would be a disappointment after the excitement of *Beyond Salvation*, but gallantly launched it and gave it everything they could. As feared, it was not greeted by the critics with the same adulation as the previous one. Reactions were mixed – some enjoyed it, but mostly it was disparaged.

However, the fans weren't interested in reviews, they bought it regardless, and in time *Red Back Fever* reached #14 on the ARIA charts and achieved gold album status.

The music industry was rapidly moving to CDs. Recognising that this would be the last Angels twelve-inch album before the CD format took over, Mushroom pressed it in red vinyl to mark the occasion. As a promo gimmick, a unique package of the album was also issued. This came in the form of a small wooden crate, the lid stamped with the *Red Back Fever* album cover. The crate came with a metal jemmy bar to open it. Once opened it revealed a CD of the album nestled in a web of cotton wool and a plastic red-back spider.

In early January '92 the second single, the cover of 'Once Bitten Twice Shy', was released, but it too failed to make the charts.

CHAPTER FIFTY
TEAR ME APART

In November 1991 Steve Gilpin, singer of the disbanded Mi-Sex, was severely injured in a car accident and lapsed into a coma. He died in Southport Hospital, on the Gold Coast, on 6 January 1992, aged forty-two.

As Mi-Sex's manager during their heyday, I decided to gather the band's old members up, and with the help of some friends, organise a benefit concert for Steve's wife and young family. The first call I made was to The Angels, who immediately came on board. Within a couple of weeks we had an all-star line-up, including Jimmy Barnes, Peter Garrett and John Farnham. I called the Hordern Pavilion, explained the situation and got the venue gratis for Sunday 16 February.

During the organisational madness of the final days before the show, Doc rang to say that he'd be in a health retreat on the day of the concert and could I arrange a helicopter to collect him so he could be backstage on time.

A helicopter? 'Er, sorry, Doc, but I can put The Angels on a bit later if that'll help.' He said he'd call back but never did.

John Brewster: I was playing with the Party Boys on Steve Gilpin's benefit. Backstage was crazy. Hundreds of musos, roadies and industry people in party mode, with Richard Wilkins from MTV moving around interviewing people with

> a camera crew. One of the Mi-Sex guys wanted me to get up with The Angels but Brent and Doc nixed it! They were promoting a new single and wanted to perform it as the existing band.

I was in the wings, watching the roadies complete the Angels set-up. It was twelve years since I'd been around them – the last time was LA in 1980 when Mi-Sex and The Angels had arrived on the same day to begin their first USA tours and we'd hung out together. Two cocky antipodean bands on the same record label aiming for the same dreams. I'd moved on from the music biz but seen them from the audience many times since in packed-out pubs. Now there were only two I knew, Rick and Doc. Buzz, Chris and JB were gone. But there was Rick backstage, wafer thin, shades in place, fingers practising up and down his guitar frets. He looked over and flashed a grin. Doc was still the tall, blue-eyed handsome devil with the Irish lilt in his voice. He'd given me a hug when he arrived and congratulations for the success of the show.

Richard Wilkins was MC and he was suddenly out there yelling into the mic, '*Would you please welcome . . . The Angels!*', and the band walked on and fired up. I glanced round the stage – *where's Doc?* – and then he came barging past, face set and in the zone, shoving stage-side guests aside, striding out to his mic, blue eyes sweeping across the audience, fists raised to acknowledge their roaring welcome.

Nothing had changed there.

Three days later they were back on the road for the Dog's Hind Leg tour. Being a leap year, it carried them through to 29 February.

A Government initiative with a three-million-dollar budget, the National Drug Offensive Campaign was being set up to combat drug and alcohol abuse among the young. With a manager's nose for a lucrative business arrangement, Eccles clinched a deal with the organisers, who agreed to pay the band a fee and to pick up the tab for the expenses of a national tour. The Angels would spearhead a twelve-month campaign highlighting alcohol-related violence and a third single off *Red Back Fever*, 'Tear Me Apart', would be released as the campaign's theme song.

The announcement brought more than a few chuckles from around the industry. Like most of the major bands of the time, The Angels and their crew lived the rock 'n' roll life to the hilt; alcohol, cocaine and marijuana were part of the accoutrements of their touring life.

Eccles followed the announcement with a comment in a newspaper article: 'We're not telling people not to drink – we can't do that for no more reason than credibility. I mean, we've made a living over the years from playing in pubs. We drink, we're not wowsers. It's all about alcohol-related violence, which I think everyone finds abhorrent.'

The Government connection also opened doors for Brent to hustle The Angels onto the Wizards Of Oz concerts to be staged at The Palace in Los Angeles during April. This was an Australian Government-sponsored showcase of rock bands and contemporary musicians. For The Angels it was a huge coup to be included.

Within the industry, though, there were grumbles. The showcase was ostensibly for young unsigned bands and musicians without international record deals. It was designed to give them the opportunity to perform in front of the influential LA music industry, and hopefully get signed by a major label.

> **Brent:** There seemed to be a bit of confusion about whether we were eligible for this. The fact is that we filled the criteria in that we had no international deal to get our records around the world. Neither *Watch The Red, Howling, Liveline* or *Red Back Fever* had seen the light of day outside Australasia.

They nearly didn't go. Brent was one of Rick's closest friends but they almost came to blows two days before they left during a rehearsal of the songs they'd perform.

> **Rick:** We were screaming at each other. His drumming was too fast – I couldn't stand the speed we were doing the songs at. We were slaughtering them. Songs that should have been mid-tempo were like punk songs. I kept yelling to slow the fuck down. He just screamed back, 'This is how it should be.' Bob loved playing fast, so he wasn't giving me any support. I was wishing John was there, because the two of us had always made a formidable team when it came to tempo and feel.

Eventually an uneasy compromise was reached and they did get to LA. After a major PR campaign, the Los Angeles music industry were there in droves. Unfortunately The Angels didn't get a deal, but for Bob and James this was more like it. They were back in America.

Bob told a reporter, 'One of the things about this band is that you can't guess where opportunities are going to come from. Where will we be in six months' time?'

The *Hollywood Reporter*'s Mark Pollack posted a review: 'Angel City were the most original on the bill with a vocalist who can sing and a band that can play! Angel City have the best chance of breaking into the US market.'

That was backed up by another from Jim Filiault in *Kerrang!* magazine: 'The Angels are undoubtedly my favourite band ever to emerge from Oz. I love their bare bones, no-frills bar rock. This band should be as huge in the States as they are back home . . .'

While in LA the band met up with Terry Manning, who remixed the as-yet-unreleased 'Tear Me Apart'.

Bob: Remixed it? Terry turned the bloody thing upside down. Fantastic!

Back in Australia the song was speedily pressed in time for the launch of the wordy 'National Drug Offensive Alcohol and Violence Campaign'. The attention and airplay it garnered would see it get good airplay and briefly sneak into the national top 40 charts.

While they were in LA, Terry Manning had introduced The Angels to a hot young band called Rhino Bucket he was producing for Reprise Records. The Alcohol and Violence Campaign wanted a tour that would make an impact on big audiences of young pub drinkers, and with the money being thrown around, a big and successful tour was what Eccles would deliver. What better way than to introduce Rhino Bucket – *'The Next Big Thing'* from America. That meant he'd require a third band as an opener for the shows. The Poor Boys were a young metal band with a great singer who'd supported The Angels in Darwin and were in negotiations to sign to Sony, so they were added to the bill.

*

Brent was constantly coming up with promotional ideas and met with Mushroom to discuss a strategy to promote the ailing sales of *Red Back Fever.* He had a concept: *Left Hand Drive*, a CD of obscure B-sides, remixes and previously unreleased versions of songs.

> **Rick:** We'd been digging through the vaults and what we found surprised even us. For this tour Mushroom repackaged *Red Back Fever* and *Left Hand Drive* as two CDs for the price of one.

According to the hype that the Mushroom PR machine churned out, it would be a 'pretty frightening double package'. Actually it added little value. B-sides and previously rejected songs had been left behind for a reason – they weren't that interesting. And neither was *Left Hand Drive.*

Still, it had been worth a try.

> **Tony Grace:** Brent was extremely thorough in making sure that every time the band went out, there was an interesting message. He and his wife, Helen, the unsung hero of that period, were always coming up with new marketing ideas. Their contribution through this time period was very important.

On 22 July the 'Tear Me Apart' Drug/Alcohol Offensive tour hit the road in provincial Tasmania as a warm-up. First the Warehouse in Devonport, then on to Launceston, before setting up at the Tasmania University Great Hall for two sold-out all-ages shows. From there it was back to the mainland for nine weeks playing pubs and all-age concerts from one end of the country to the other.

Along the way Doc dutifully parroted the campaign's message in interview after interview: 'We've been on the receiving end of alcohol-related violence many times.' He'd recall being knocked out by a projectile at the New Year's Eve concert on the Opera House steps and the time Rick was slashed within an inch of his eye by a glass at the Sweetwaters Festival in New Zealand. 'It goes on all the time – whenever we go out on stage we wonder what will happen. We just want people to enjoy themselves with a drink, but not get harmful to themselves or others.'

During the tour a Drug Offensive TV commercial was aired, graphically depicting alcohol violence with 'Tear Me Apart' running as the soundtrack, and ended with lists of tour dates.

Alberts had picked up on the high-profile tour and on 19 August issued a compilation CD, *Their Finest Hour And Then Some*, with liner notes by John Brewster. All the tracks had been remastered and the package featured four bonus songs, including 'Open That Door', written way back in the seventies at John Forest's place – when the milkman knocked on the door and joined in for a sing-along. Recorded twenty-five years earlier, it had lain in the vaults awaiting its time.

Their Finest Hour And Then Some immediately began outselling *Red Back Fever* and the interest pushed many radio stations into putting some of the old songs onto high rotation. Once again The Angels were back on the airwaves.

At the end of the ten-week tour, James Morley, with eyes set on a career in Los Angeles, handed in his resignation.

Soon after, Bob Spencer called a meeting with Rick and Brent. 'Guys,' he said, 'I have to leave – I've gotta do other stuff.'

Brent said, 'Why don't you stay and do other stuff as well?'

But ever since the recording of *Red Back Fever*, Bob had been unhappy. Although he would come to regret not taking up Brent's suggestion, he was impetuous: 'No, no, I really have to leave.'

He gave them a list of guitarists he thought would be great replacements and they asked him to continue playing with Youse Guys. In the gravity of the moment, that added some humour, and that was important. They'd spent six intense years making hit singles, platinum albums, constantly touring and playing to sold-out venues.

Bob: When I left, everything was really good. Within any band there are always cliques fighting, but with this there was no acrimony. I liked Doc's funny sense of humour in particular. I thought he was well meaning. Sometimes misguided as we all are. He did some stupid things as we all do – he was his own worst enemy. We had some tragically terrible arguments, but I really liked him.

CHAPTER FIFTY-ONE
MOONSHINE REUNION

In a throwback to the early seventies, Rick and John had recently met up with some of the old members of the Moonshine Jug and String Band and they began discussing doing some reformation shows. This eventually happened when a block of time became available after the Drug Offensive tour. Two shows in Adelaide were booked and Rick, John and Doc met up with Spencer Tregloan and Pete Thorpe and put in a couple of days' rehearsing. To their surprise the old songs effortlessly sprang back to life with all their former panache and charm.

On Monday 14 September they did a well-publicised lunchtime busk in Rundle Mall in the heart of the CBD. Camaraderie ran high as crowds gathered to watch the hometown rockers display entertainment skills that few of their peers could ever aspire to.

It was the first time Doc, Rick and John had played together since 1985. All the angst and anger slipped away. There was lots of marijuana, wine and laughter and the vibe slipped back to their good ol' days again.

John: It was obvious how much Doc loved being in the jug band. The pressure was off him to go into character as The Angels' front-man. In Moonshine he wasn't the main singer – we all took turns at it. So he just relaxed and played guitar, did harmonies, and when he did sing he was really melodic and a natural entertainer with a huge grin on his face.

A few days later they played one of their former haunts, The Old Lion Hotel in North Adelaide.

> **Pete Thorpe:** I was glad I hadn't chucked my washtub bass away – it was a weird feeling to dust it off and string it up again. It was funny to see the faces of what used to be our old regulars, but with twenty years' worth of wrinkles added on. They were still singing along in the choruses – what a flashback that night at The Lion was with the fans wearing old Moonshine t-shirts. The Big Ticket bar was next night, lots of fun and a good time had by all. It gave me warm fuzzies to be playing the stuff I cut my teeth on – with the guys I musically grew up with.

It was so much fun that the group decided to do something that was never done back in the day: they'd get together again and record a CD from the jug-band repertoire. John rang Alberts and booked two days of studio time and they each agreed to chip in to cover recording and manufacturing costs.

And so it was that all five members of Moonshine gathered at Alberts' Neutral Bay studio in mid-January 1993 to record their album, *Rent Party*.

> **John:** It was fantastic. Apart from being a really lovely experience to get together with Pete Thorpe and Spencer Tregloan, it was also great to play music with Doc again, recapturing something of what we had from the very beginnings. We set up in a circle, everyone had a vocal mic, and we just went through the repertoire and recorded that album live. All the old songs, including 'Blues My Naughty Sweetie Sang To Me', which Doc sang. We just went bang bang bang, one after the other, warts and all. It wasn't polished – and we captured it.

Spencer and Pete went back to Adelaide and John and Rick set about making an album of it. However, when they pulled up the tracks for mixing, it was obvious Doc's guitar was not usable. Having rarely picked it up over the years, he was playing the wrong chords and the timing was out. Rick and John set up two mics and, with Doc's guitar track muted, they recorded their guitars right through the whole set of songs. It produced a nice stereo sound. Their recording engineer Simon Sheridon then added his magic touch. They listened back and knew they had nailed it.

CHAPTER FIFTY-TWO
'CAN I CALL HIM?'

The Angels hadn't officially broken up but the chances of them playing again were looking slim. After the band had finally worked its way out of debt, Doc told Brent and Rick that he wouldn't be available for Angels gigs for the foreseeable future. He was going to study for a psychology degree by correspondence and also pursue an acting career.

However, following a phone conversation with the band's agent, he realised he could still earn some handy pocket money without too much interference with his new agenda.

Tony Grace: Sometimes the dance clubs would have guest DJs – I booked Doc into a lot of those where he played rock dance tracks. He lost his licence for DUI and somehow I got the responsibility of driving him to a gig. I pulled up outside this old mansion in Bellevue Hill, which he shared with some friends, and beeped the horn. No Doc. There was an inclinator lift on a rail running up the hill to the front door so I jump on and but it stops halfway up. In the dark I step off into flower gardens and bushes – I find some old steps and climb up ninety-seven of them. At the entrance I bang on the door. Doc comes out wondering what the fuss is about. He's forgotten the gig. I get him into the car and he's talking his own language – lots of philosophy and different things. At the gigs they loved him. The Prince of the Pubs.

Doc was doing a bit of voiceover work for ads too, which led to a suggestion that he had a great voice for radio, so he decided he'd have a crack at being a radio DJ. Brent showed him the studio rudimentaries and somehow he managed to score a midnight-to-dawn shift on Triple M when someone called in sick. Doc was never good with anything mechanical or technical, so when he hit the wrong button trying to take a call, he was unable to find the one called 'station goes back on air' and caused Triple M to go dead until someone arrived and sorted it out. Unfortunately he wasn't given another chance.

Brent was always busy with his various business interests, among them managing The Poor, who had released their first single 'Love Shot'. He also continued his lucrative radio program on 2MMM's *Homegrown* with co-host Trevor Jackson.

Rick got busy with his hobbies of wood turning, leather work and photography. It was the first extended quiet period of his life since the start of Moonshine over twenty years back, and he now had time to spend with his wife and their two little kids. He had a small home-studio set-up and to bring in some extra cash he ran an ad in a rock magazine.

Rick was introduced to Ross Wilson and a friendship sprang up, culminating in the two meeting regularly for writing sessions during Ross's visits to Sydney. A number of songs came from the association, including the wistful 'Let It Go', which Jimmy Barnes recorded with Deborah Conway on his CD *Flesh And Wood.* On release it went to #2 on the ARIA album charts.

The success of the writing sessions with Ross reignited Rick's creative juices and he and Brent came to an arrangement with Cadillac Rehearsal Studios to rent one of their rooms for two days a week. Situated in a hub of band-related businesses out back of the Jands factory in Mascot, they jammed on ideas each week for months. Sometimes Doc joined them and a few songs came out of it.

Cadillac also made road cases and Rick got them to build him a work desk with a soundproof box beneath it, capable of housing a guitar amplifier. It meant he could then record loud guitars in his suburban home.

*

On his drive to the studio one morning Brent's mobile rang – it was the New Zealand chapter of the Hells Angels. Would The Angels be interested in coming to New Zealand to play their annual City of Cycles Ball?

'Maybe,' said Brent, 'what's the offer?' It was good enough for him to say he'd get back within a couple of days.

To Rick and Brent's surprise Doc said 'Sure, I'll be in it', but the thought of hiring new members and teaching them enough songs for a set was less than appealing.

After the Moonshine gigs, Doc had mentioned to Brent how well he and John Brewster had got on. Now Brent suggested they get JB back for the Hells Angels gig: 'We wouldn't have to teach him the songs.' Doc said, 'Fine by me.'

Rick was so stunned he could only stare at the two of them.

> **Rick:** It was something I never expected to happen. I would never have mentioned John, because I knew how Brent felt about him. When they'd suggested to invite him back, even just for this one show, it was, 'Oh yes, can I call him?' And it was the greatest call I've ever made. The Angels had ground to a halt. We'd been trying to come up with an album, trying to come up with songs, and not very successfully, and not doing any live work. In my enthusiasm, I think I told John we wanted him permanently!

John had formed a band called The Bombers with his close friend Alan Lancaster after they'd moved on from the Party Boys. They'd signed a deal with A&M Records in the USA and received the largest advance ever paid to an Australian-based band. The band had recorded an album that received five-star reviews in the UK music press, but just as things were beginning to happen for them, A&M was sold to Polygram. In a corporate 'rationalisation' that followed, thirty acts were dropped from A&M's roster. Unfortunately, The Bombers were one of them. Back in Australia, having come so close to international success, they'd decided to keep striving, but the going was tough.

> **John:** When Rick called me there was never any suggestion that I'd be rejoining the band to do one gig. I played my last show with Alan Lancaster

> and The Bombers in September 1993 and resigned – a very difficult and heart-wrenching decision. I didn't know what was in Brent's mind. All I knew was that I was rejoining the band that I'd started with Rick and Doc in 1974. I was excited to be reuniting with my brother – we'd exorcised our demons a few years before – and a bit apprehensive about Doc and Brent, to be honest.

They decided to give Jim Hilbun a call. It made sense, but he was much more cautious – he'd never been one to make quick decisions. His split from the band four years back hadn't been pleasant. He said he'd like to come over and talk about it.

> **Jim:** When I walked in I found them working on all these new songs. I just fell back into it again – it was easy.

> **Doc:** The great thing for me was that these guys were still Angels – they knew what The Angels should be. We didn't have to go through a long introduction process with Jim and John. We went over to New Zealand for three days and did the show. I really enjoyed it and we thought, 'Well, this is working. We all like it, so let's keep going and see what happens.'

The whole music scene had changed since the eighties. The great pub-rock era The Angels had helped kick-start was over. There'd been carnage in the rock scene during the past three years. Many venues, faced with new fire regulations and noise limits governing music venues, had switched from bands to poker machines; others had converted to dance clubs to ride the changing fashions in public taste. The economy had crashed into the worst recession since the Great Depression. By 1993 the country was staggering out of what Federal Treasurer Paul Keating had famously called 'the recession we had to have'. Unemployment was over 11 per cent and much higher among the young, who'd become careful about how they spent their money.

But Brent instinctively knew that the old Angels line-up would bring out the loyal fans in droves.

He put on his management hat and, with wife and assistant Helen, met up with Tony Grace and hatched a marketing strategy. From this, the Terror Australis Incognito tour came to be: two weeks on the road accompanied by two hard rock outfits, Judge Mercy and The Poor.

Selina's at Coogee Bay, 5 November 1993, and Sydney's biggest pub venue was sold out and jam-packed. Backstage, The Angels and Tony Grace were shaking hands in congratulations – they could barely believe it. The door take was astronomical and The Angels' share would probably be the best they'd ever received.

For this one the reformed Rose Tattoo had been added to the line-up. Wrecking Crew had replaced The Poor and, right from their opening set, the vibe beyond the stage was electric.

The tour, promoted as the 'original' line-up, had been a triumph. Every show a sell-out and with no new album to push, they played songs from earlier times such as 'No Exit' and 'No Secrets'. John and Rick clicked in and played as powerfully as they had when the band first hit the bigtime in '78. The return of JB brought back the heavy blues style of their earlier days and it came through tighter and stronger than it had in years. Also, to the relief of old-time punters, the chains and studs had been discarded.

Doc risked life and limb climbing up the speaker stacks and along the outside of the balcony rail. He stretched out over the crowd, one hand gripping the mic, the other the railing, a spotlight holding him in a white-shaft circle.

The night ended with 3000 voices roaring along to 'We Gotta Get Out Of This Place' and then the roadies were packing up and the semi and crew bus were back on the road heading north.

At the sprawling Mansfield Tavern in Brisbane, 4MMM brought in an outside broadcast van and did a simulcast as part of *Aus Music Month*, which was broadcast nationally throughout their network.

The Angels had regained their momentum. They were the biggest and most exciting touring band in the country once more. And radio was drenching the airwaves with their songs again.

CHAPTER FIFTY-THREE
ONE OF THE HAPPIEST TIMES

After a three-month break, the Terror Australis Incognito tour regrouped in March '94 and flew over to Western Australia for six shows. Then it was across the continent to Cairns, and from there down Queensland's coastal cities to finish up in the unlikely city of Maryborough – Brisbane having been played early in the tour.

It was a happy tour despite John and Jim's irritation with Brent's refusal to give them a share of the merchandise profits, given that the t-shirts were selling like hotcakes with their names boldly emblazoned across them.

Darren Carey was a big fan and saw the show at the Metropolis Hotel, Mackay on 11 March:

> **Darren Carey:** Crazy night. It was sold out, and they'd jammed way too many into the top floor of this old Queensland pub. It was about 45 degrees, the floor was bouncing, we thought the place was gonna collapse. Girls passing out had to be hoisted over the crowd. As soon as it finished there was a big crush at the doors to get out to fresh air which turned into a huge street party. Then it turned into a fight club with a mixture of cowboys and bikers, never a good mix. I travelled 200 kilometres with some young kids I worked with in the country, it was their first gig. They didn't know The Angels, didn't know anything, they shit

themselves when we walked into that place, instant fans. Didn't stop talking about it for weeks.

In April, with the band now off the road, Doc, Rick and John met up with Moonshine's Spencer and Pete in Sydney for a mini jug band tour to promote the *Rent Party* CD and have some fun. The highlight was a spot on the top-rating *Denton* show on Channel 7, where the band excelled.

For the first few gigs Doc performed well, but then he arrived late at a gig so drunk he could barely stand up. At the Three Weeds pub in Rozelle, their old friends from the Captain Matchbox Whoopee Band, Mic and Jim Conway, joined them onstage and again Doc was drunk. After the show he was politely asked not to bother showing up for the final dates.

Rick: We had to tell him we couldn't work with him. He'd let Moonshine down, which is the one band he shouldn't have let down, because he was really good in Moonshine. But he couldn't play his guitar and it just didn't work. He got too drunk.

None too happy at being sacked by his Moonshine mates, Doc took it one further and announced he wouldn't be available for Angels gigs while he investigated opportunities in the theatre world. The rest just shrugged – 'here we go again' – and got on with it. There was enough in the kitty for each member to draw a small wage until Doc signalled a 'return' and another tour could be set up.

As it was, the other four were keen to write and rehearse new songs. Someone knew someone, who gave them permission to use the recently abandoned Sydney ABC-TV studios at Gore Hill, while the site awaited its fate with the developers. Having obtained the keys, what they discovered was a rabbit warren of offices with discarded furniture along corridors leading to a vast television studio. And they had the whole place to themselves.

They took over the old control room and set it up as a rehearsal studio with a four-track cassette recorder.

> **John:** It was one of the happiest times for the band. I wouldn't be surprised if the other three said the same thing. Doc wasn't there, so we were all pissed off about that. But it didn't stop us – we wrote songs and had a lot of fun. We took push bikes in there. We had time trials over an incredibly dangerous circuit in this huge studio. Some of the circuit was along building ramps six foot up, then down along trestle tables. Flat-out time trials! It was amazing no one got hurt!

They set up a badminton court and belted a shuttlecock back and forth across a net, and in the spirit of competitive excellence they ran a point score which tipped one side or the other depending on what drugs were being consumed and by whom. While not a lot of songs were produced, lost cohesion was regained and a strong studio band was built.

Eventually the fun at Gore Hill came to an end. It was back to Cadillac where they set up some recording equipment, then buckled down and completed demos for eight new songs.

Mushroom were now being distributed by Sony and Gudinski had wrangled a deal with both them and Alberts to release a collection of hits that would span the entire recorded history of the band. As it would be evidence to a younger generation of The Angels' stellar history, *Evidence* became the name of the set.

While the Gore Hill and Cadillac sessions were taking place, Doc had attended auditions for various stage productions. Among them was the lead role for a rock play booked for a Sydney season that had debuted in Melbourne in 1989 with a young unknown actor called Russell Crowe in the lead. The play was *Bad Boy Johnny and the Prophets of Doom.* Doc got the role of Johnny and it would open in Sydney.

With co-star Chris Bailey from The Saints (not the former Angels bass player), the production went into rehearsals and opened on 14 September for a ten-week season at the Enmore Theatre. However, despite the high profile of the co-stars, it soon became apparent it wasn't grabbing the attention of Sydney theatre goers. The reviewers panned the show and it limped along for two weeks until the plug was pulled on 1 October.

It had been produced by a plumber from Melbourne without the permission of playwright, Daniel Abineri, who lived in London, and that too had created problems. In early October a demoralised Doc returned to the bosom of The Angels.

A Screaming Jets tour for which dates had been pencilled in for November was converted into the Barbed Wire Ball tour, with The Angels co-headlining with 'special guests' The Screaming Jets. Brent's management clients The Poor were booked to open the shows.

While Doc was rehearsing for *Bad Boy Johnny*, he'd agreed to record vocals with The Angels for two new songs – 'Don't Need Mercy' and 'Turn It On', which would go onto *Evidence.* These were recorded at EMI's Studio 301 and produced by Englishman Paul Northfield.

With Mushroom aware of the upcoming tour, they rush-released 'Don't Need Mercy' as a single and rescheduled *Evidence* for a November release to coincide with the first dates.

Having coasted through the past eight months with an absent singer who had been off chasing an acting career, they now commenced rehearsals for another onslaught of sweat-drenched pub-rock mayhem.

Eccles' behind-the-scenes scheming with the Jets to 'co-headline' (but really supporting as they were on before) had succeeded in putting The Angels on top billing for another tour extravaganza. The big pubs and clubs on the 'circuit' prepared themselves for the sort of excitement they hadn't seen since . . . well, since the last time The Angels had come to their neck of the woods.

With the glossy dance magazines sneeringly asking, 'How many dinosaur bands and rock fans can you fit into one beer barn?', the loyal punters answered by queuing for tickets which sold out in hours. The concerts introduced yet another wave of young first-timers to the power of an Angels show – and swelled the enormous ranks of Angels 'true believers'.

Tony Grace: It was a massive tour. It played all the big rooms: two nights at Selina's, then 2000 punters at the rebuilt Newcastle Workers next night. If a room held less than 1500 it didn't qualify. It set box office records for a pub tour and it was bringing The Angels and The Screaming Jets together in a celebration of the greatest of Aussie rock 'n' roll.

Dave Gleeson: We'd done some earlier gigs with The Angels and that relationship grew into us doing the Barbed Wire Ball tour. We'd had a few hits which had elevated us to a different level by that stage. The Angels headlined, but we were also a bit of a drawing factor. That was probably the first time we felt like we were in their peer group. Not that we were on the same level pulling crowds and stuff, but on the level of hanging out with the boys and macking on and having a few laughs.

The tour ended up at the Hobart City Hall. By then, *Evidence,* The Angels' sixteenth album, had gone gold.

CHAPTER FIFTY-FOUR
PARTING WITH MUSHROOM

Following the Barbed Wire Ball tour of the previous year, Mushroom released one of the newly minted tracks from the *Evidence* CD as a single – the acoustic 'Turn It On', written by Rick, Doc, Brent and Bob Spencer. The song fitted perfectly with the 'unplugged' phenomenon that had swept the music world.

Desperate to get a new song on the radio and into the charts, Brent had come up with a very different strategy to present it to the right people: a ten-date national tour playing half-hour acoustic sets at some weird and wonderful venues. Instead of playing the beer barns and 'sheds' – Hordern and Festival Halls – they'd play to radio staff in their boardrooms, or in their studios on-air. They'd play shopping malls opposite record shops, do TV shows, grace the backyards of people who'd won a gig on a radio show.

The Never Before and Never Again tour commenced on 15 February and ran through to 25 February. Confusingly, it was also called the 'Turn It On' tour on some of the promo.

Doc: For as long as I can remember we'd played acoustic songs in our set. Things like 'Be With You', 'Love Takes Care', 'Out Of The Blue' and so on. They were a great contrast to the harder stuff, they gave the audience a breather. But this would be the first time we'd played a stand-alone acoustic set.

It was a good idea when they'd sat round discussing it, but in practice it was seen as a huge come-down for a band that had strutted their rock 'n' roll credentials on the massive Barbed Wire tour only a couple of months before – and it failed to get their new single any prolonged airplay.

Only slightly perturbed, Brent met with Tony Grace on his return and work commenced on a full-blown electric tour – five weeks of it. Brent cajoled a noticeably cooling Mushroom, unimpressed with sliding sales of Angels CDs, into having another go at kicking a hit up the charts. With the *Evidence* album still ticking along, he'd come up with a new tour name: The Hard Evidence tour. With an EP of the same name containing 'Don't Need Mercy', 'Turn It On', 'Spinning My Wheels' and 'Blue Light', he was determined to have another shot at cracking the charts.

The tour began in country NSW, worked its way over to Adelaide and on to Perth, where they were the first band since INXS in 1983 to fill two nights at the huge Metropolis Concert Club. Then it was back to Sydney, up to Queensland, down to Melbourne and back to the harbour city, finishing with a two-night stand at the Metro Theatre, where the performances were recorded for a possible future live release. Despite drawing capacity audiences everywhere and doing dozens of interviews with the radio stations that promoted most of the gigs, the EP rarely got an airing.

The band met with Mushroom executives to discuss a new album, but received a cool reception. They'd been with the company ten years, the first few extremely fruitful, but *Red Back Fever*, released three years ago, had basically flopped and there'd been a lack of interest from radio for their new offerings ever since. The 'greatest hits' *Evidence* had done reasonably well and the new format golden-oldies stations constantly played tracks off it. Mushroom was well aware of the drawing power The Angels still commanded, but that power no longer converted into CD sales for their new music.

Relationships with Michael Gudinski and the staff at Mushroom had always been good, but the label now considered that The Angels had run their course. Mushroom was moving on too, developing new markets. The parting was sad but amicable and The Angels were once again without a record company.

CHAPTER FIFTY-FIVE
A VERY SPECIAL VISITOR

Being a member of The Angels was a relentless twenty-four-hour activity cycle. While there was a lot of fun and laughter, there were band meetings, rehearsals, writing sessions, recording, interviews and constant phone calls. Life on the road meant being squeezed inside of cars together, fast-food, motels, bickering. And, yes, on occasion succumbing to the enticements offered by warm nubile admirers. There were audience expectations, the build-up, the nerves, self-medicating with alcohol, cocaine, pills, marijuana. The times onstage and the highs that came with it were what they were there for – but those times were all too short before they again strapped into the back of a car or bus for endless hours on the road between the last show and the next one.

This had been the all-encompassing lifestyle of being a member of The Angels – and it often came at the expense of family relationships. John and wife Robyn were still together but the last few years had been financially tough ones with a young family to provide for. Rick and Mandi were doing okay with their young family – he was still besotted with his rhythm rude girl – but there were stresslines there too. Once she had travelled everywhere with Rick and the band as their 'rock merch chick', but now, with young children, she was home-bound and constantly fretted over what he might be up to. Rick's sideline business of producing demos at his house for amateurs continued to bring in additional funds to augment the wage that Brent doled out, as he did his best to retain funds to finance the band's plans while they were off the road.

Doc and Kym's marriage of five years was on the rocks. He'd reneged on his promise to start a family and that was a deal-breaker for her. Brent himself had a family life that was in need of TLC, but he also had other business interests to attend to. Jim was easy: with no family commitments, he went along with whatever was happening.

And so it was that The Angels largely dropped out of public sight for a while.

In June the band convened at the Darling Harbour Rehearsal Studios. They were situated on the third floor of an old warehouse leased by a demolisher where Ike Brunt, the demolisher's business partner, had built a number of soundproofed rehearsal rooms with salvaged office partitions. An old industrial goods-lift, big enough to drive a car into, clanked up and down all day with musicians, roadies and their equipment. The studios were cheap and convenient and accommodated a floating community of Midnight Oil, Jimmy Barnes' band, and other musos who came and went. There was a funky vibe to the place, conducive to catching up, hanging out, making music.

The band's aim was to start working on the new album they'd been talking about since John and Jim had rejoined two years before. Calls were made to Doc: was he in or out? Was he up for recording a new album? Was he prepared to tour again?

During February Doc had begun meeting with Harry Miller and members of his staff to develop and refine his motivational speech skills. Harry had been one of Australasia's most successful concert promoters in his day but had now built up a lucrative 'star' speaker circuit and had a gold-plated list of corporate clients on his books. His speakers' fees were in the thousands and he had big plans for Doc Neeson. Harry was meticulous in preparing the new recruits he signed up and Doc was no exception. There was staging involved: a video collage, PA, lights.

And a technician and personal assistant would accompany him to all appointments.

Interviewed by Liz Armitage of the *Canberra Times* he'd talked about going out on the speaker circuit, giving motivational speeches. He said that using his experience with The Angels as his inspiration, he'd be advising business leaders how to be more successful in their endeavours. 'There are a few common principles in any business,' he said. In The Angels' case, success had come from the ability to turn adversity into triumph. 'It's how you turn a negativity around into something positive. That's been my story, and that's what's made The Angels.'

In the same interview he said he'd also be devoting more time to acting, following his recent lead role in *Bad Boy Johnny*. He mentioned a solo album he planned to release. 'It'll be passionate music with different instruments and textures.'

Doc had his first speaking gig with a large Brisbane-based company. Unfortunately he arrived drunk, made a hash of his speech, and as a result Miller decided not to take Doc Neeson's motivational speaker's career any further.

Since then he'd read scripts, and auditioned for roles in a film and another play, but nothing had come of it. He'd also tossed around song ideas for his solo album, one called 'Millionaire Middleman', another about his now ex-wife called 'Airline Girl', and another called 'So Much For Love'. By June he still hadn't come up with lyrics to complete any of them. He'd hit a low point and the offer to rejoin his band-mates was timely.

They set themselves up in the 'Tour Room' at the Darling Harbour studio – their biggest one – and songs written during the ABC period were rehearsed and refined. A twenty-four-track analogue tape machine was brought in and hooked up to the studio's mixing desk. While the band played along, Brent laid down thirteen new drum tracks. These were then transferred to Rick's home studio, where a newly purchased multi-track digital recorder had been installed. The first song to be recorded was one written in a car as they'd toured country Victoria the previous year, 'Call That Living'.

With the band self-financing this one, there was no budget for a professional producer. Wearing his manager hat, Brent nominated Rick as producer and Doc agreed. Rick wanted John as co-producer but was outvoted.

> **John:** Brent seemed hell-bent on keeping me and Rick apart, which was just stupid in my opinion, because if you look at our track record, it's pretty impressive. We know how to work together, Rick and me, and we did it anyway on that album. But officially I wasn't there. Just a lot of fucking bullshit. I don't care whether Rick got paid for it, that's fine. I don't give a fuck about any of that, but I do give a fuck that he was trying to keep us separated.

Having taken control of the band's management, Brent was wary of giving John too much sway – even banning him from interviews in case he said something negative about the band.

After recording the guitar tracks and then going through the usual difficulties in getting Doc's vocals down, 'Call That Living' was completed.

On a whim Brent offered it to 2MMM who were relaunching themselves back into the blue-collar hard-rock market in Sydney, tradies and the like, a big spending sector they'd drifted away from. The Triple M execs loved it and incorporated it into their new promotion campaign. Triple M in Adelaide, Melbourne and Brisbane also picked it up, and all of a sudden The Angels were back on the airwaves with a new song. The fact that the song wasn't available for purchase suited Triple M fine. If people wanted to hear it, they'd have to tune in. Listeners loved the working-class lyric and the driving rock vibe and they turned up the volume whenever it came on.

Not one to miss exploiting a new song on the radio and the interest it generated in live performances, Brent called a band meeting. Everyone agreed to go back on the road and Harbour began booking a national run as the Mr Damage tour. Among the merchandise for sale would be a CD single of 'Call That Living'. With no record company distribution, gigs would be the only place it could be bought.

*

Time spent at Darling Studios now turned to rehearsing the songs they'd perform on the upcoming tour.

Doc arrived ahead of the band one morning and told studio manager Ike Brunt that he had a special visitor arriving that day. Could Ike make sure he got safely up to the office?

> **Ike:** I said, 'Sure, happy to do that, I'll send one of the boys down,' but he said, 'No, could you go down and get him yourself?' It was a special request, you know, so I said, 'Yeah, sure.' He muttered something and said, 'Yeah, I've never met him before, so, anyway, come and get me when he's here. Don't tell the band, just come and get me, and I'll come out.'

Around 2 pm the bell rang and Ike heard a young voice on the intercom saying he was there to see Doc Neeson. He went down and found a tall slender boy in his mid-teens.

> **Ike:** We just said 'hello' and went back up to the office. I looked into the studio and signalled to Doc and out he came. Very nervous, he followed me to the office and looked at this young guy – and the young guy stared back at him. It was very intense, and then they gave each other a hug. They didn't say much. I said, 'Okay, I'll leave you to it then,' and started closing the door, but Doc grabbed me and said, 'Oh, er, Ike, this is my son, Aidan. Take care of him for me, will you? After the next set we'll be taking a break and I'm taking him out for lunch.'

And so Doc met his fourteen-year-old son Aidan, who'd flown over from America with his mother and dropped into Sydney en route to their new home in New Zealand.

It was around this time that I rang Brent to ask if The Angels would consider headlining a fundraiser I was organising for the MS Society at The Basement nightclub in Sydney. This was an annual event I ran with Jim Conway, blues harp player extraordinaire and MS sufferer. Brent rang back a few days later to say there'd been a unanimous 'yes' from the guys.

With the mighty Angels on the bill and Michael Chugg as MC and auctioneer, the 450 tickets quickly sold out. Slim Dusty's daughter Anne Kirkpatrick and her band were opening the show and it occurred to me to ask if she'd do a duet with Doc. She was up for it but there was an anxious pause when I rang Doc. 'Er, Bob,' he said, 'I'm actually not that good a singer and I've never sung with anyone before. I don't think it would work.' By the time we'd hung up I'd convinced him that whatever he thought of his singing ability, there were hundreds of thousands who loved it – and it would be something very special if he'd do it.

Anne Kirkpatrick: I turned up to rehearse the song with Doc and the band at a studio somewhere in town. Doc was very welcoming and rehearsal was all very straight ahead. However, when I stepped on stage at the Basement, the lovely easy-going Doc I'd rehearsed with suddenly came alive as this wide-eyed leaping ball of energy that totally took by surprise this rather static laid-back country performer. I laughed and enjoyed the experience!

CHAPTER FIFTY-SIX
TOURING DRY

In late August the band assembled at Sydney Airport with crew and Suzi Dhnaram, their merch seller, for the flight to Alice Springs for the western leg of the tour. Doc had recently come out of rehab and, as a show of support, the whole band had committed to the tour being 'dry'. No alcohol on the dressing-room rider, and no drinking – period.

The equipment truck had already made its way to Alice Springs and the stage was set up at the basketball stadium and ready for the first show, a full house. It wasn't often a band of the pedigree of The Angels played the Alice.

After the show the truck was loaded and immediately left for Broome 2735 kilometres away. As for band and crew, they took a plane and arrived that afternoon. The Broome show was not for another three days until the truck arrived and the equipment was set up at the big outdoor venue at the back of the Roebuck Inn. Meanwhile, the band checked into the salubrious Cable Beach Resort, while crew and Suzi moved into a 'shit-tip', as they called it, further up the road.

John: We'd decided there'd be no alcohol whatsoever on the whole tour. So Doc didn't drink. And he was fantastic. It was like rediscovering the old Doc Neeson – the guy we did the jug band with and formed The Angels with, who was essentially a lovely guy. We went surfing – I almost pinched myself, I could hardly believe it was happening.

Later on I went to his room with an acoustic guitar. I had this idea for a song inspired by the camels that trekked along the beach, and we came up with the lyrics for 'Invisible Man'. Jim contributed to the song later on. It was like the old days – the band rehearsed it at soundcheck and within days we had it in the set.

That evening, with the red sun dropping into the sea, John rang Robyn back in Sydney.

John: I told her, 'You should see this beach, it's unbelievable. It's 32 degrees – I've just come out of the water.' She said, 'That's great. The kids are trying to kill themselves at the moment, I'm trying to cook and it's like a blizzard here.' Click. Hang up. I thought, 'That's a phone call I shouldn't have made.'

He and Robyn, with three young sons, were only just keeping their heads above water. More often than not, they found themselves clashing about finances. Despite the success of the tours and the good money he was paid while on the road, the long periods off the road were tight times for John. Whenever Doc had left the band, the singer could still make extra income from voice-overs and DJ work. As a result of The Angels having given him the opportunity to become a celebrity, he could earn extra cash while the rest of them paid the price of his absence.

From Broome they drove over to Derby for a show and then turned south and headed along the Great Northern Highway to Port Hedland 800 kilometres south. There was something about the country they travelled through that began to infect them, the endless highway spearing into the shimmering distance. They pulled into the lone Sandfire Roadhouse with its caravan park behind, filled up tanks and spare cans, had a feed and pushed on to Port Hedland for their next show. Punters poured into town from far and wide, awestruck that The Angels were doing a show in their neck of the woods.

After Port Hedland they turned inland and drove on to Newman for the next one and it was in his hotel room after the show that Rick wrote the riff for 'Northwest Highway'. He played it to John next day as they drove through the Hammersley Gorge en route to their next concert at the Spinifex Hotel at Mount Tom Price. That evening 'Northwest Highway' was further developed during a soundcheck jam. Lyrics were added a couple of days later by all the band at Karratha's Walkabout Hotel after the show, which was staged in an old drive-in theatre where over 2000 turned up. The crowds around Suzi's merch stand were so boisterous, with hands reaching between bodies, filching CDs and t-shirts and mauling at her, that she packed up and moved next to the stage for protection by the crew. Merch sales went through the roof that night with XXL t-shirts and CDs being the biggest sellers.

John: That trip was special. It reeked of the frontier spirit and it fired up our creativity. 'Northwest Highway' is about our experiences on that tour. We'd pull off the road into these gorges where you could walk down a track and find these magnificent pools. We'd all strip off and go swimming in crystal-clear water. We'd never written songs before about Australia.

The tour finally rolled into Kalgoorlie for the last gig before flying on to the Perth shows. Next day the plane was delayed. They'd seen a big sign announcing 'Best coffee in West Australia' and decided to pass the time there. Inside they discovered a huge Italian espresso machine with an American eagle mounted on top of it.

John: So we ordered coffees and this girl turns on the steamer and froths up the milk. Then she puts a spoon of instant coffee into each cup. They've got this giant machine and all they used it for was to froth the milk! We just fell about laughing.

Rick: I asked for a cappuccino at a roadhouse and the guy disappeared and came back and said, 'Sorry, mate, we're all out of tuna.'

From Perth they flew on to Adelaide, while the truck was loaded onto the train for the run across the Nullarbor.

CHAPTER FIFTY-SEVEN
SKIN AND BONE

With more than enough drum tracks recorded, it was anticipated that guitars and vocal tracks would go down over the next two or three months and they'd have a new album to present to record companies. But it dragged on and on, until it was necessary to break off and do some gigs to keep finances in the black.

After his marriage ended, Doc had moved into the spare room of a North Shore house owned by a friend of Kym's, Annie Souter, and the situation had gradually morphed into a relationship. After the break-up with Kym, and his return from the last tour, his abstinence from alcohol had come to an end and he was back on the booze again.

Rick would make arrangements with him to come over to his place to sing his vocals, but Annie would then call to say he'd got the flu or the trots, or just that he was sick. Then he'd turn up, but when he did very little was useable.

When Annie moved to the Blue Mountains 80 kilometres west of Sydney, Doc went with her. When he did manage to come to Sydney, he'd catch the train from there to Normanhurst station, which was a short walk to Rick's place and also happened to be opposite the bottle shop.

> John: We recorded heaps of takes of his vocals, then painstakingly went through each one to get a master. We had to cut and paste almost every word

of those songs. Doc had a great sounding voice – it was just really hard to record it. Once we had a master vocal we'd record backing vocals, with Jim and me mostly, sometimes Rick too.

Rick would spend hours and days tapping the edit buttons on the multitrack recorder: cutting, pasting, moving phrases, sometimes just syllables of Doc's voice. It was the same with the drum fills. The sound of Rick's endless tapping earned him the title from Jim of 'Mr Tappit', and an appropriate sign got stuck up on the wall above his head.

It was during this period that John, Jim, Brent and Rick decided to go to an Al-Anon meeting for advice on how to deal with Doc's drinking.

Rick: It had become so bad that on the rare days that he actually turned up to record, he used to hide his hip flask in an old greatcoat he wore and regularly slip into the toilet. He'd take long lunch breaks and walk down to the corner store, which was next to a bottle shop, then come back well cabbaged and try to sing.

The meeting was held in an old church in Wahroonga, or at least they thought it was. The four of them sat in pews, and heard one speaker after another either talk about their desperate lives, or how they'd turned their lives around. They lasted half an hour before someone told them they were actually in the AA meeting: Al-Anon, which was for families and friends of alcoholics, was in the hall next door.

It was a very different vibe there, as advice was given on how to deal with alcoholics and help guide them out of their addiction. Rick and the rest didn't speak but afterwards the guy running it advised them, 'Tell Doc to put it out on the table and drink in front of you. Tell him to stop hiding it.'

Rick: So next time he came to record, I tried that approach. Of course he furiously denied he was drinking and continued with his long visits to the toilet and the bottle shop.

*

By February it was obvious that the album wouldn't be finished for months – if ever. Brent, with an eye on the band's financial position, needed another tour. The trouble was that the last one had taken them to every major venue in the country, and with 'Call That Living' having done its run, he needed a new angle to excite media and punters.

> **Tony Grace:** The Angels have always done interesting things and I give Eccles a lot of the credit for this. He came up with this concept and John Brewster came up with the name: The Lounge Lizards. It was a semi-acoustic kind of vibe and they had guests: Ross Wilson and Angry Anderson.

It was the first tour in years for both Ross and Angry, two of the 'old school' heavyweights of Aussie rock. As soon as the word got out – *Angry and Ross Wilson with The Angels* – it was confirmed a masterstroke. Demand from venues for gigs was overwhelming, and with very little nudging the publicity snowballed into a life of its own and an extensive national tour was set up.

At the heart of it, the concept was to perform the show in the 'unplugged' style using acoustic guitars, with Jim discarding his electric bass for an acoustic twelve string. Brent would keep his drum-kit, but he'd use wire brushes instead of solid sticks.

> **Angry:** By the time we'd finished rehearsals, we'd evolved into the loudest acoustic band in the world!

The convoy of semi-trailer and two Taragos set off around the country playing classics from the singers' various bands and closed doors at every venue they played.

Brent had come up with a promotional gimmick for each show involving local radio stations: a listener competition for the best couch for the show, free tickets for the winners.

> **John:** Everywhere we went, someone would bring along a couch that went up on the stage. We had a microphone at each end so whichever singers weren't singing, they'd sit on the couch with a mic and do backing vocals.

Despite the massive sound the band generated – reviewers compared them to the Billy Thorpe shows of a bygone era – it was the acoustic 'look' as well as the style that made these shows different to anything else these rockers had done. The guitars were plugged directly into the PA eliminating the usual stacks of Marshalls, and the stage set-up included plants, palm trees, a clothes rack and a park bench – plus some brilliant theatrical lighting.

Following the success of their tour through the northwest of WA the previous year, Harbour had booked an encore tour through the region for the Lounge Lizards.

Once again, it was the section they enjoyed the most.

> **John:** We were driving down to Port Hedland after playing Broome. We saw a little speck on the horizon and it gradually came into focus and it's Cliff Young! Shuffling along followed by a car pulling a caravan. We did a U-turn, went back and said g'day and he invited us into the caravan for a cup of tea while he had a breather.
>
> There were these two gorgeous young girls of about nineteen or twenty. Angry said, 'So how's it going?', and he said, 'Ah well, with these two young girls here, no problem.' We laughed and spent half an hour with him. He was seventy-five and running round Australia for charity. Eventually he said, 'I gotta go now,' and exited the caravan. We tossed a few dollars into the tin, said goodbye to the girls, stepped out into the heat and by then Cliff was a speck in the haze. That's the Pilbara for you. You come across Cliff Young running along 600 kilometres of lonely highway.

The morning after playing Newman someone told them about a backroad to Karratha that would cut the 650k drive via the highway to under 500. The truck had left after the show and the band and some of the crew were driving there in the two Taragos.

They set off and 200k's later they drove through Wittenoon and swung onto the backroad with another 260k to go. John, driving the second Tarago with Rick, Brent, Angry and tour manager Bicci onboard, dropped back to keep clear of the lead vehicle's dust.

Angry was admiring the hills rising out of the flat country ahead and suggested they pull over for a piss stop and to enjoy the view.

> **John:** We're standing there and I noticed steam coming up from under the Tarago and remembered how we'd kissed the centre mound in the road further back. We'd cracked the sump and the oil had all come out – the car was undrivable. We checked for phone reception – zero. Fortunately we had a few bottles of water and we carried these little portable eskies with ice packs and sandwiches for lunch.

They figured the Tarago ahead had about three hours before they reached Karratha, and it would take another couple of hours before they started back to look for them – then another three hours before they arrived. And then they'd have to wait for a rescue truck. Unless someone else came along, they were going to be there a long time.

> **Rick:** There was a tree nearby, one single beautiful little tree with a few leaves in this red dirt from Mars desert. We sat under it and shared the food and water and talked about how long we could be there for, because we were seriously in the middle of nowhere.

During the afternoon, knowing how cold the desert could get on a winter night, they walked around gathering pieces of wood to light a fire later on.

> **John:** Angry said, 'Hey Jack' – he always called me Jack – 'get the harmonica and give us a play.' We didn't have any guitars but as I was playing and Angry was singing a blues song, a little speck of dust appeared on the horizon and this Land Cruiser comes along with two geologists in it. We're all out on the road waving our arms. 'Stop! Stop!'

The geologists were on their way to Newman so Bicci said he'd go with them and organise a tow truck.

As evening came they lit the fire and then, with darkness falling, a sudden burst of birdsong came from the sparse foliage above them.

John: Incredibly, there was a flock of birds up there. It was really musical and beautiful.

It got colder and everyone – Rick, John, Brent and Angry – moved closer to the fire. They lay back, eyes adjusting, and found the Hale-Bopp comet with its long bright tail voyaging through the sparkling galaxy, silently skimming its way past Earth.

Suddenly swarms of huge grasshoppers winged out of the dark and dive-bombed into the fire, exploding like firecrackers. Strange lights appeared and zigzagged above the southern horizon. 'What the fuck was that?' Rick had a theory: it was very weird. There definitely were aliens out there. Spaceships for certain.

The geologists got back around midnight with Bicci. The truck was about two hours behind. He'd rung Doc and explained the situation.

John: We talked for a while and then the conversation died away and we just gazed into the crackling fire, it was magic. Just the kamikaze grasshoppers going 'poof, poof'. About 2 am or so, bearing in mind that the first time Angry asked me to play the harmonica the geologists turned up, he said, 'Play that harmonica again, Jack.' And as I played and he sang, the truck lights appeared as pinpricks jn the distance. The harmonica had beamed our rescuers in again.

The driver was a rough-looking character in a flat-top truck. An Angels fan, he'd arrived with several slabs of beer for the boys which they immediately got stuck into. In no time the Tarago was winched onto the back and they were off. John was in the cabin to keep the guy awake and slow down his beer intake, while the rest were in the Tarago with three of the slabs. The road quickly degenerated into ruts and pot-holes but that didn't slow down the truckie. Meanwhile the Tarago was leaping around on its springs like a mechanical bull, while John on his bench with no seatbelt was gripping the dash.

John: The guys in the back were having a party. When they wanted a piss they'd flash the lights and get out legless drunk, because of the beer and being bounced around on top of the truck. We finally got to the motel at five in the morning and all the rest were still up waiting and the cops were hanging out with them and a celebration was underway.

At Karratha they played the same drive-in cinema as they had on their previous tour, but with Ross and Angry they pulled an even bigger crowd. Angry had become a national television star in recent years, best known for his reports and charity 'challenges' on *A Current Affair.* Out in the bush, he was the biggest star of the tour.

Rick: He couldn't go anywhere without being recognised and getting accosted, people wanting autographs, and it drove him insane. He waited till after dark to cross the motel courtyard to do his washing. In the supermarket, I hid him under a coat, but when we got to the checkout, he couldn't hide any longer and the checkout chick recognised him immediately. The whole place stopped totally. Every other checkout, everyone in the supermarket, just descended on him.

The tour continued on to South Australia, up to Darwin, over to Queensland and down the eastern coast to Sydney, finishing up at Selina's before one of the biggest audiences of the thirty-one date tour.

It had been a success financially but there'd been dramas and frustrations between musicians and sound engineers when intolerable feedback squeals had brought performances to a halt – a constant nightmare when acoustic guitars were turned right up. But those problems apart, every show was filled to capacity and by the end of each gig they'd knocked their audiences out.

John: There we all were on acoustic guitars and Brent just playing brushes and it really swung. It was great what he was doing and we had a really good time with Ross and Angry.

Back in Sydney and work on the album continued, but Mandi was sick of having her house being used as a studio and putting up with the constant interruptions to family life. It all came to a head one day and Rick packed all the equipment up, loaded it into a van and moved back to Darling Harbour studios. Doc had eased up on his drinking during the Lizard tour and over the next two weeks all the lead and backing vocals were cut, with Doc producing some of the best vocals he'd done in ages.

Mushroom had just issued three Angels videos, *Live At Narara*, *Beyond Salvation Live* and *From All Angels*. With all of them clocking up respectable sales, Brent suggested to old acquaintance Mark Opitz, currently putting in a stint as Mushroom's A&R manager, that he should have a listen to a few of the band's newly completed songs.

> **John:** We played him tracks and as he listened, I looked down at everyone's feet – and no one was tapping their toes. We'd learned from George Young that if you weren't tapping your toes – then it wasn't happening. Mark was unimpressed and went back to Mushroom, and Mushroom passed.

Undaunted, Brent sought out David Williams and Andrew McGee at Shock Records, Australia's largest independent CD distributor, and discovered two major fans of the band. In August 1997 a deal was done. A new single, 'Caught In The Night', was released in October and received nationwide airplay and some chart success.

Rattled by Opitz's reaction, John and Rick began to seriously examine the drum tracks on the rest of the songs. It wasn't that the drums were that bad, but the new digital technology made it possible to do things that could never have been done with tape. Because they could make it better, they did.

> **Rick:** When one section felt better than another I copied it and pasted it in. Other parts were moved, sometimes just a millisecond made the difference – until it all felt good. Guitars and bass then had to be replayed to the corrected drum tracks. Compiling and messing with Doc's vocals was even more tedious, but we achieved results that would never have been possible in the old days of recording to tape.

The last process involved the final mixdown. Shock flew in a maverick technician they'd worked with in New York, Kevin 'Cave Man' Shirley, who magically achieved this at Studio 301.

> **Rick:** There were anxious moments as the 'studio-in-a-box' spat its parts back on to analogue tape to recapture the warmth of tape. This was groundbreaking technology; probably no one had ever done it before. It worked, it was done. After five years, the fucking thing was done!

CHAPTER FIFTY-EIGHT
MICK COCKS

In November The Angels were back on the road with a full-on traditional rock 'n' roll show – this time for a second Barbed Wire Ball tour with the hard-rocking Screaming Jets and opening band Horsehead. The Jets were now well-established headliners with big hits on the board, and Horsehead, with two albums under their belt, were being hailed as the next big thing.

The tour was a success and wound up in Brisbane playing a well-attended gig at the RNA Showground, where a reviewer commented that Doc had put in a 'flat performance'. For most of the tour John and Jim found themselves having to sing along on every song to cover Doc's vocals, which had to be turned down due to him either singing out of tune or forgetting words. Despite that, few in the audience seemed to notice.

Dave Gleeson: The Angels were the band that gave the Jets their work ethic. We'd get out there and play and play and play and put on shows that made people just go, 'I can't believe it!' That came from The Angels and our love of The Angels. Their songs from the late seventies and early eighties, they're more ingrained in me than even Jets songs, because they've been with me since I was twelve or thirteen years old.

And *play play play*, The Angels continued to do. With that tour behind them and recording now over, Brent scheduled three weeks off. But it was only to allow time to write liner notes for the album, create the cover artwork and agree on a title.

While they'd been touring down the Great Northern Highway, the band had pulled over for a piss-stop. Jim had come across the dehydrated corpse of a dingo lying on the red earth and taken a photo of it. He'd always had a keen interest in the cover art of Angels albums and he now put the photo up as a suggestion, along with a title to go with it: *Skin And Bone*. The others nodded approval, but Rick barely glanced at it.

> **Rick:** I was absolutely sick to death of it. It took so much out of me. I didn't want to know about the cover. Didn't give a fuck – I was just, 'Yeah, whatever.'

The Barbed Wire tour had been an unqualified success as far as filling rooms and grossing big money was concerned. But once again, a big slab of the take had been eaten up by the production costs. Consequently, a 'money for the band' tour was already in the advanced stages of preparation when the Barbed Wire Ball ended.

On 30 December, The Coast Trip tour kicked off at the Crown Hotel in Victor Harbor, south of Adelaide. This tour would hit all the coastal towns full of holiday-makers and deliver a healthy profit to be split up at the end of it.

Unfortunately it didn't quite work out that way.

> **John:** It soon became apparent that all these coastal towns were full of families with young kids and they weren't the sort of people who were going to pay to see a loud Angels rock show. We were lucky to break even on some shows, and we lost on others. At one gig we had forty people!

It eventually came to a finish at Yamba on the NSW north coast and they returned home with little to show for their effort.

*

The *Skin And Bone* album was released on 2 March 1998 on the Shock label and Brent had a unique tour ready to head out and promote it. Initially it was to be promoted as The Angels playing their new album *Skin And Bone*, but then he changed his mind. Instead of going out as The Angels, he decided to call the band Skin And Bone and booked them into small venues for intimate performances.

> **John:** In one way it was a good tour because we stripped back and we didn't have all the crew we usually had. We looked after ourselves, including Doc. He was good on that tour. We played that album live all round the country and we played it great. But there were fuck-all people because they'd never heard of the band. I have to say that it was fun to do, but it was a flop as far as getting decent-sized audiences.

Despite the band's indifference to *Skin And Bone*, and sales being only moderate, the album received glowing reviews and was nominated for an ARIA award as one of the year's best Australian recordings. However, it would be fifteen years before Rick Brewster would sit down and listen to it again.

For now, once again, the band needed to get back out and do what they did best, tour a full-blown rock 'n' roll show to promote the album, to put some money in the bank and to have some fun. And who better than the reformed Rose Tattoo to help them do it.

The highlight of the tour was undoubtedly Mick Cocks Day. The redoubtable Mick Cocks was playing rhythm guitar with the Tatts and fancied himself as a bit of a Keith Richards – a sweet guy who took his rock 'n' roll image very seriously. Unfortunately for Mick, Rick and Brent also took their on-road prankings very seriously and went to great lengths to bring them to fruition.

> **Rick:** Brent and I decided we should have a Mick Cocks Day, so we went out and bought stuff to make black wigs and black vinyl material to make caps like the leather one he wore. We sat up all night turning out caps and black long-haired wigs. We made enough for both bands and had them delivered to all the rooms with instructions.

Next morning the guys in both the bands started turning up for breakfast as Mick Cocks. And then Mick Cocks arrived.

> **John:** We're all saying, 'Good morning, Mick,' 'Hi Mick,' and straight-faced introducing each other to him, 'Er, Mick, I'd like you to meet Mick Cocks – nice to meet you, Mick.' Everyone looked reasonably like him. There was Angry in his black wig and black cap leaning back with a coffee, and all the rest of us just acting normal. Mick's image was so cool – he couldn't smile but he was like, 'Ah yeah, I know what's going on.'

The one guy who they were sure would consider all this was beneath him was lanky, slow-talkin' Pete Wells, one of the most laconic and reserved men in Australian rock 'n' roll. When he turned up as Mick Cocks, the mirth round the table could barely be contained.

It continued all day, all of them remaining as Mick Cocks.

> **John:** That night there was karaoke in the bar – the place was full-on partying and all these different Mick Cockses got up and sang karaoke songs – Angry, Doc, Pete Wells, Ian Rilen, all the rest of us. I don't think Mick ever got over it.

CHAPTER FIFTY-NINE
ARIA HALL OF FAME

On Tuesday 20 October 1998, The Angels were inducted into the ARIA Hall of Fame at Sydney's lavish State Theatre before an audience of 2500 – plus another million or so watching via the Channel 10 live broadcast.

Looking splendid in embroidered waistcoat and bow tie, Angry Anderson walked out to the microphone and did the presentation on behalf of the ARIA committee. It was all quite formal and correct and in stark contrast to the roaring sweat-drenched suburban beer barns where The Angels had earned their fame – and still reigned supreme.

Angry, who'd just toured with the Tatts and The Angels, spoke well as he ran through the band's achievements. He then called them up and presented the award. In formal attire, Doc delivered what *Rolling Stone* would later report as a speech worthy of an award for the longest of the night. Which was unkind. Unlike the younger artists receiving awards, most of whom had only been around for a few years, The Angels had almost three decades of acknowledgements to deal with.

David Williams from Shock Records had made the nomination. The Angels' one-time tour manager Mark Pope was now on the ARIA board, and with his deep knowledge of the band and their long and glorious history, he'd successfully championed their nomination to the rest of the board.

On being advised of the decision, Brent then told the band that only the current line-up would be allowed to go onstage and receive the award and inductions.

> **John:** I didn't think that was right, because the Hall of Fame was for achievement over the lifetime of the band. I said, 'You can't leave out Buzz and Chris, or Bob Spencer.' Brent said, 'The board of ARIA won't allow anyone but current membership.' I said, 'Well, if those guys aren't inducted along with us, I'm not going.' That probably forced the issue a bit. Then Rick said the same thing. Brent came back and said, 'Alright, well, they can come up for the awards, but they can't go to the press conference afterwards.'
>
> Everyone that was in the band played a part, and I respect them for that. That original line-up, everyone gave it their all. We had lots of arguments in those days, but a lot were creative ones.

So Bob Spencer, Buzz Bidstrup and Chris Bailey joined them and were also inducted. Doc gave a particularly extended acceptance speech. Writing it had been a joint effort. In the process, they'd found it a profound experience looking back over the highlights of their long career, and the toll of blood, sweat and tears in getting to where they now were.

The band were then escorted to a hospitality room to chat with some of the gathered music press, while Chris, Buzz and Bob returned to their seats in the theatre.

> **John:** A journalist asked a very reasonable question: 'You started out in Adelaide, so tell us a bit about growing up there.' Doc, who I think was a bit inebriated, said, 'It was a great place to leave.'

There was dead silence as everyone gaped. Doc realised what a derogatory remark he'd inadvertently made, and began a stuttering explanation of what he meant to say, but John and Rick jumped in.

> **Rick:** We said it was a *great* place to grow up. The music scene was unbelievable. That's why so many successful bands came out of Adelaide – because there was music in the streets. You could walk around on a Saturday

> night and it was club after club, little basement joints with fantastic bands playing. A great place to leave? It was a fucking amazing town. It still is.

A few years later Rick rang Mark Pope to discuss something, and as they wound up he said, 'You were on the ARIA board. Why weren't we allowed to have the original members?' He said, 'What do you mean? The board has nothing to do with that – it's totally up to the band who they have.'

There was one more major event for The Angels before the year was out. That was Mushroom's modestly entitled Concert Of The Century, which Michael Gudinski had organised at the Melbourne Cricket Ground for Saturday 14 November. It had taken a year to prepare and celebrated twenty-five years since he'd founded the company. Just about every act that had ever been signed was on the bill, but not Skyhooks or Split Enz – neither would agree to a reformation, not even for the persuasive godfather of Australian rock 'n' roll.

On a warm evening in front of 70,000 punters, The Angels took to the stage and pulled off one of the finest sets they'd performed in a while.

> **John:** That was a pretty amazing concert for us. They had a revolving stage, so that, as one band was performing, the next was setting up out of sight behind them, then it spun around and, bang, you were on. The band played really well that day and Doc was great.

But it was the end of an era for the homegrown Mushroom Records. Shortly after the concert, Gudinski announced the sale of 50 per cent of the company to News Ltd (who'd bought the other 50 per cent six years previously) for a total reputedly in excess of $70 million.

Mushroom Records would now be run by James Murdoch and his executives.

However, even though The Angels were no longer signed to Mushroom, there would still be an association. By year's end Mushroom was planning an Angels two-CD compilation album, *Greatest Hits – The Mushroom Years*, to celebrate their induction into the ARIA Hall of Fame.

CHAPTER SIXTY
HOTDOG

The strange tale of Hotdog began back in 1996 in Adelaide.

Two original members of Moonshine, Peter Thorpe and Spencer Tregloan, got together and had begun writing songs specifically for kids with the idea of forming a band. They'd both enjoyed their Moonshine Jug and String band years and thought that the jug band style was appropriately musical, up tempo and good fun. In mid-1998, aware that things had become increasingly fractured on the Angels front, they ran the idea past John and Rick.

> Spencer: They liked it but Doc's relationship with them was not ideal due to various factors. So we decided on a quartet format and threw a variety of ideas around with regard to characters within the band. Because none of us were getting any younger and we were well known in other roles, we moved towards the idea of the dogs who would be ageless and completely new identities.

> John: One other factor that contributed to forming this kids' band was that we had such fond memories of Moonshine, always enjoyed the company of Spencer and Pete, and were sick to death of Doc and his addictions and demands.

And so Hotdog came to be – a jug band for kids, a hybrid of Moonshine. They all developed more songs with lyrics for children and had dog heads made. Like Sesame Street, the idea was that Hotdog would appeal to both kids and adults.

Initially Peter Vaughton, who'd been briefly a member of Moonshine and gone on to produce children's TV shows in Germany, worked with the band. Banjo, Rufus, Digger and Rusty were created.

> **Spencer:** Rick had his own studio and was very good with his digital recording equipment, and we recorded an album and later made a DVD. Rick and John still had Angels commitments, so we weren't able to work on Hotdog every day. For Pete and me that was a bit of a frustration, because we'd put our lives on hold back in Adelaide for the project. Pete picked up some clown work and I did some relief teaching.

Through 1999 and 2000 it was complete madness, with Hotdog, by now with costumes, masks, CDs, t-shirts and posters, performing fantastic shows at clubs, schools and on TV programs with a great deal of success.

> **John:** Hotdog in an air-conditioned club with a proper stage and 200 to 300 kids and mums was one thing – fantastic and great fun! But Hotdog outdoors in summer at racecourses or Darling Harbour or wherever was another thing – exhausting. It was the masks. They were brilliant, quite realistic, but hot. An apt name for the band!

In 2000 Peter Vaughton left, to be replaced by John Spence, who'd managed The Wiggles. John did a great job but his involvement waned when the ABC didn't take them on. The head of children's entertainment at ABC-TV decided – without even seeing them – that kids wouldn't go for men in dog masks, that they'd be scared of them. Spence did, however, convince her to bring a contingent of ABC people to a Hotdog show at the Burwood RSL Club in Sydney. It was a full house and the ABC crew witnessed a great show, followed by the signing of CDs and t-shirts and kids hugging their legs, not the least bit scared of them.

John: She told John Spence afterwards, 'I think I may have been wrong'. But the damage was done. Even though she moved on to ABC Country, she'd put a negative vibe through the kids department. The ABC would have been perfect for us.

One of their best performances was at Carols By Candlelight at Bonython Park, by the Torrens River in Adelaide. There were 40,000 people, and it was a warm magical night in their hometown with thousands holding candles in the darkness. Hotdog performed their songs and then sang a couple of carols backed by the Adelaide Symphony Orchestra. In what would become the highlight of the evening, Rusty (Rick) ran over to conductor Bruce Raymond, ripped the baton from his hand and began conducting the orchestra. Raymond was taken aback but quickly realised that Rusty knew what he was doing. Wearing a big grin, he stood aside and let it happen. Beneath the mask Rick swelled with pride. This was the orchestra that in a distant time his grandfather had formed and conducted and in which his father had played first cello.

Spencer: Hotdog continued to get some good gigs but the impetus was difficult to maintain without constant media exposure. It eventually finished and Pete and I went back to our 'normal' lives.

CHAPTER SIXTY-ONE
LIVELINE99

Doc was living with Annie in her house on the edge of the Blue Mountains National Park at Faulconbridge. He was able to move about without being constantly hassled by fans and well-wishers.

He was now fifty-two. During two decades of high-energy performances he'd broken bones, ripped muscles, fallen through and off stages, been hit with flying objects, and now his body almost creaked. And then there was his prodigious alcohol intake. Although he still cut a handsome figure, he'd put on weight and the heavy drinking sapped his energy and left him sleeping much of the day.

With voiceover fees, including a lucrative one for Audi, he drifted comfortably through much of 1999 reading books, the daily papers and scoping *Phantom* comics – an obsession he'd had for years.

The Angels had last toured in August the previous year and had only done a handful of gigs since. Rick was working from his home studio with local artists and joining up with his Hotdog pals for kids' shows around the suburbs, but the next Angels tour couldn't come soon enough for him.

The band was asked to play a one-off show at the conclusion of the Adelaide 500 Grand Prix on Sunday 11 April. It was a welcome chance for them all to perform in front of a huge audience. It went over well and provided a welcome injection of funds.

The next gig was right up Doc's alley and drew him from his mountain lair like a block of steel to a magnet. Celebrated film director Jane Campion – among her films was the Academy-Award-winning *The Piano* – had been an Angels fan since her younger days. She wanted them to be, yes, The Angels, for her new film *Holy Smoke*, starring Kate Winslet and Harvey Keitel.

Rick: They set up a dance in an old pub and Kate Winslet appeared in the crowd when we played 'Am I Ever Gonna See Your Face Again'. During a break in the shoot she was sitting on a step on her own. I took the opportunity to go over and introduce myself. 'Hi,' I said, 'I'm Rick Brewster.' She went, 'Ahhhgg grrresh,' or something. She looked at me like I was a piece of shit, then got up and walked away.

John: On the other hand Harvey Keitel was just fabulous. At the end-of-filming wreck party Rick and I sat at the bar with him, having a few drinks, and had a fantastic conversation.

Brent had been taking a hard look at the future of The Angels and now decided it was time for him to move on, to sell up and return home to Auckland. Looking for new business opportunities, he'd spotted a niche in the New Zealand entertainment industry for a top-line touring company. With his close connections to The Harbour/Premier Agency, his long association with Gudinski (who ran the successful Frontier Touring Company), and his experience in organising national Angels tours, the time appeared right to become New Zealand's next big-time entertainment impresario.

He had a number of projects keeping him busy for the time being, but the imminent arrival of a new century seemed like a good time to begin quietly planning the next phase of his career.

In May Mushroom released the two-CD set, *Angels Greatest Hits – The Mushroom Years*. It came in classy packaging and with a must-have repertoire. As most of the Angels albums hadn't yet been released in CD format, it sold well as fans replaced their vinyl collections.

John had been reminding everyone that 1999 marked twenty-five years since Moonshine had morphed into the rock band that became The Angels, and they should be doing something special for it. There was no budget to record a new album, but one idea put forward gelled with everyone: remaster and repackage 1988's *Liveline* album.

Rick: The main reason for re-releasing *Liveline* was to digitalise and remaster it for compact disc, and, while we were doing it, change the 1988 live recordings to earlier live versions that would represent the current line-up with John in the band again.

They slotted in tracks recorded at four Sydney pubs at the end of a tour in 1980, then added another fourteen bonus tracks.

Brent: We hadn't planned to do much around the re-release, but I was walking in the park and thought, 'It would be nice to do a show like we did back in '88, with the band performing three sets.' Then I thought, 'Why not do a whole tour using that format?'

Before he aired that idea, Brent needed to lay out his own personal plans and dropped in to see each member of the band. John was helping country singer Keili Mead hone and refine some of her songs at the compact Rondor Publishing studio in North Sydney. Brent arrived, took John aside and told him he and his family were moving back to Auckland at the end of the year. He was quite confident he could continue managing the band from there. It was only a three-hour flight over to Sydney, so he could also still carry on as drummer. But if the band wanted to find a new drummer, he said, he was fine with that.

John: I told him I had no problem with him managing the band from Auckland, but said I didn't think it would work having him remain as drummer. The rest of the band lived in Sydney and we needed the flexibility of being able to rehearse at will – it just seemed too inflexible if he wasn't close by. He seemed okay

> about that and it wasn't taken any further. He then took the opportunity to mention doing a tour based on the remastered *Liveline* CD, which was a great idea and had my support.

The rest loved it too, and so the planning began. There'd be three sets complete with clothing changes and no support act. Rehearsals commenced at the Darling Harbour studios, starting with a Keystone Angels era set-up with Doc in denim jackets and flared jeans. Next set was as they were in the late seventies: shades, leather jackets and Doc out front in casual jacket, and the last bracket he'd be in formal suit and Ascot tie. Stage production would step up for the final scenario too: drum riser with Brent perched above the rest, scaffolding, follow spots, the works.

> **John:** I was complaining to Brent about the way we were playing. I said, 'You don't get it. For me, it's all about the music – if the music's not played right, I'm not happy.' I was just being honest. And he said, 'Jim thinks it's you.' My playing? Good on him. My runs are on the board. I can play like a motherfucker with a good rhythm section. I suggested that he and Jim – the rhythm section – go back and listen to the old records for the right tempos and the grooves. And in fairness to them, they did do that and they nailed it.

It would be a total night of The Angels. Songs they wouldn't be performing would be played through the PA between the sets and before and after the show. Such was their repertoire now that they could do that with more than enough 'classics' to choose from.

On the third day of rehearsals, Doc arrived late in a neck-brace and told them how a truck had run into the back of his car on the way home to Faulconbridge the night before. He'd decided to have a check-up by his doctor, who detected some stiffness in his neck and suggested he wear a neck-brace for a couple of weeks. But the doctor assured him it would be okay to remove it when he was onstage and said there was no need for it while he slept at night.

Curious about the extent of the damage, Rick, John and Jim went down to the car park during a break to inspect Doc's Corolla. Expecting a crumpled-in boot and broken tail-lights, they were happy to see it was just a small punched-in dent above the number plate.

Fashion and fame was washing back over them. They were featured in a major film, they had a song on the massively selling *Mushroom 25 Live* CD and hot young band Grinspoon had recorded a cover of 'Take A Long Line'. Their Narara set of fifteen years ago had been given a new lease of life with the *Live At Narara* video on the shelves and selling well. And then there was the internet – the past few years had witnessed an explosion of home computer owners plugging into the worldwide web.

> **Brent:** The internet really opened our eyes. We were getting hundreds of hits a day, 25 per cent from overseas, and what it showed us was that there's a really strong feeling out there, around the world, for The Angels. There's something quite cultish about the band, even in Australia. We've never really been part of the mainstream – we've always stood off to one side. A lot of people say, 'Oh, that's just pub rock. Pub rock has gone.' That's shit. Pub rock is very much alive – just get out and have a look!

And with that, they hit the road to celebrate their eminent status with another all-encompassing tour to relive some of their highlights, and to prove that age had not wearied them and they could still get up and blow the roof off any beer barn in the country.

Meanwhile, John and Robyn's marriage had completely unravelled after twenty-five years together.

> **John:** Robbie and I found ourselves clashing a bit about finances, and maybe realistically we'd been together a long, long time. I feel sorry for women who marry musicians, because a lot of the time you're apart, and then you have young kids growing up. I thought the world of her but it culminated – I knew I had to go.

After the tour made its way back to Sydney there were a few days off. It was John's birthday and some golfing friends threw an impromptu party for him at the 'Moth's house. The 'Moth' was a golfing buddy and when John arrived at his house for what he thought would be a quiet evening, to his surprise he found sixty more friends awaiting him.

> **John:** They knew I was going through a tough time. It was a Tuesday but it went right through the night – it was after four in the morning when the last left and I crashed out in the spare room. I hung around all next day and then asked Mothy if I could stay another night. 'Of course,' he said, 'it'd be a pleasure.' I liked the room I was in, so the next day I said, 'Mothy, do you mind if I move in?' He said that would be fantastic, so in I moved.

But by the end of the week John was back on the road with the band, winding up at the annual Hells Angels Broadford Concert, held on their property in the hills 70 kilometres north of Melbourne on Saturday 4 December.

> **John:** Doc was sober and in great form on that tour, and the band played the best that line-up ever played. It was a great tour – I'd rate it as one of the best ever.

CHAPTER SIXTY-TWO
DOC DOES DILI

About the time the band commenced rehearsing for the Liveline99 tour, the Australian Army had led an international peace-keeping force into East Timor to protect the population from a retreating Indonesian army, ordered out of the country after the East Timorese had voted for independence. During the withdrawal there were violent clashes between soldiers and Timorese and hundreds were killed and townships destroyed. It sparked a humanitarian and security crisis, but with the arrival of the Australian-led forces, the situation was brought under control.

In the rehearsal studio during breaks, Doc had avidly read about the events in the papers. It brought back memories of his time as a 'nasho' serving in New Guinea. Over the following days, more details hit the news as units from twenty-two countries joined the Australian force. There were fighter planes at Dili airport, warships in Dili harbour, gunboats patrolling the coast, amphibious beach landings and jungle clashes with Indonesian-backed militia.

For Bernard Patrick Neeson, raised as an Army brat in foreign countries with a sergeant-major father, it was stirring stuff, and he wanted to be part of it. He thought back to the famous concerts for the troops during the Vietnam War – Johnny O'Keefe, Col Joye,

Little Pattie – and he started to wonder if he could do something similar for the troops stationed in East Timor.

He'd checked his tour itinerary – the last Liveline99 gig was 5 December, and then there were four weeks off until a New Year's Eve concert in Darwin.

He began talking to other artists. This was a project he wanted to do independently of The Angels. John Farnham and his manager, Glenn Wheatley, were walking the Great Wall of China at the time, but on their return, someone told them about Doc's idea. Wheatley gave him a call: 'John and I would like to do something as well, so let's join forces.'

While Doc continued rehearsals with the band, Glenn made contact with General Peter Cosgrove, who was in charge of the Army in East Timor, and set things up, then worked on getting corporate support and contacting other artists. Dili Stadium on 21 December was locked in.

One morning Doc read that Kylie Minogue was spending Christmas in Australia with her family and invited her to join them. The date fell on her grandmother's birthday party, but her gran graciously agreed to move the date and Kylie was in! Then the concert was announced: Kylie Minogue, John Farnham, Doc Neeson, Gina Jeffries, The Dili Allstars, and the Australian Army band's Rachel Starkey would sing 'Silent Night'. Doc had also managed to snare the hottest band in the country, The Living End, with their debut album having just been certified quadruple platinum and their current single the biggest seller of the nineties.

With the Dili concert taking on a life of its own and Glenn Wheatley firmly in charge of operations, Doc joined The Angels for the Liveline99 tour. But once on the road, he remained in constant phone contact with Wheatley, helping pull the loose ends together. He stayed off the booze and kept a clear head: he had a lot going on. Channel 9 and Channel 7 put aside their differences and agreed to join forces to televise the show around Australia. Comedians Roy Slaven and H. G. Nelson came onboard as MCs and the RAAF agreed to fly in the concert equipment, stage crew, artists and entourage.

Three days after the Liveline99 tour ended, Doc headed into Darling Harbour Rehearsal Studios to meet up with Kylie and John Farnham and his band, finessing their performances.

> **Doc:** Everybody did a really top job. We went over [to Dili] the day before the main concert. Kylie and I went out in Blackhawk helicopters to these little outposts where the troops were holding back the rebels and did shows on the back of flatbed trucks with minimal PA.
>
> At the concert there were 5000 troops – men and women. John Farnham was there, Kylie Minogue, The Living End, James Blundell, Gina Jeffreys and the Dili Allstars. We closed the show with an all-in 'Am I Ever Gonna See Your Face Again' and had all these soldiers shouting, 'No way – get fucked – fuck off!' and John Farnham just had this flash and said to the crowd, 'Okay, we'll turn it around – you sing the song and we'll answer it.' And as they sang and we answered, I looked across the stage and there was Kylie looking like a petite princess enthusiastically singing, 'No way – get fucked – fuck off!'

Most of the Australian troops came from the Army base in Townsville where a huge screen was set up with a satellite dish. The concert was beamed onto the screen and a camera crew in the base was able to beam back and forth with the Dili concert and their big screen. Conversations between families were broadcast and babies held up for fathers to see for the first time.

With Channel 7 and Channel 9 jointly broadcasting, it rated as the largest viewing audience of the year. Two hours after the show, the musicians were all flown back to Darwin and the great adventure was over.

'It was the concert of a lifetime,' Doc would write in the *Daily Telegraph*. 'We were both honoured and humbled to be there . . . We achieved what we wanted to achieve.'

CHAPTER SIXTY-THREE
DARWIN MILLENNIUM CONCERT

The Angels arrived at Darwin Airport at 9.05 pm on 30 December 1999.

Doc had stayed off the booze during the Liveline99 tour while he helped organise the Dili show, but if the band had hopes his sobriety would continue for the Darwin 'Millennium Concert', they were dashed when he staggered off the plane. Despite having his two young sons with him, he and Annie had been in party mode all the way from Sydney. Doc had landed but he was still flying high.

Next afternoon the band gathered at the gated-off area behind the casino where a particularly large stage had been erected. In the oppressive heat they waited as the crew completed setting up for soundcheck. Brent's wife, Helen, took the opportunity to hand out t-shirts emblazoned with the logo 'The Angels – 2000 and Beyond', including small ones for Doc's boys. Rick had his family with him and there were tees for his kids too.

As the sun set and the humidity and mosquitoes became even more intense, Mark Lizotte and his band took to the stage with around 1500 punters spread out on the grass in front of them. The 6000 expected hadn't materialised. When Daryl Braithwaite came on an hour later, there were a few more but still plenty of space in front of the stage for dancing.

As announced earlier in the day on radio ads, prior to The Angels coming on the MC threw envelopes containing $20 and $50 notes into the crowd. That brought a rush to the front where the hardcore fans were already pressed against the protective barriers. The Angels came out at 10.30, but by then Doc was drunk and the band, having hung around backstage getting hot and irritable, had lost their edge and put in a lacklustre performance. As midnight approached, Doc led the crowd into the countdown to the stroke of midnight and then, with drumrolls and a burst of guitars, rockets and fireworks shot into the sky. The crowd roared and cheered and the world clicked into the twenty-first century.

> **John:** Brent came to my room after the gig. He knew I wasn't happy about the show – I said the band played like crap and Doc was no good. I told him I didn't have a problem with him managing the band from New Zealand. 'But to be frank,' I said, 'I think we should try and get the original rhythm section back. Get Chris and Buzz, because that's the one – no offence.' But of course offence was taken. I just said how I felt, but Brent never got it with me. The thing is, if you stand onstage and it's not played right, if the songs are played too fast and they're lumpy and stuff, it's not much fun. It might have ended my renewed friendship with him, I dunno, but I just said the truth.

Next morning Brent called a band meeting and explained details of the tour he was working on for mid-2000 and handed out the itinerary. Called the Liveline Encore Tour, it would commence in May and run through to July, opening with two shows at the State Theatre in Sydney. He was in negotiations with Channel 9 and the Triple M network to promote the entire tour and broadcast various shows. One thing he wanted was for the band to write some new songs to record: 'If we can get a new song on the radio, it'll kick this tour through the roof.'

Rick said he had some ideas he'd been working on and Doc nodded enthusiastically: 'So do I. Let's get together when we get back and get something down.'

With that, Brent wished everyone all the best for the year ahead, then he and Helen caught a plane to Brisbane – and from there on to Auckland.

CHAPTER SIXTY-FOUR
GETTING ON WITH LIFE AND MUSIC

John flew down to Adelaide and stayed with his sister and her family for a week. He brought Tom, his middle son, over from Sydney. He showed him where Moonshine had started, took him to the harbour and visited his mother.

> **John:** I wanted to spend time with him, I hadn't seen much of him since the split with Robyn. We flew back a few days later to keep a promise I'd made to the Moth I'd be home for a party. And that's where Sue walked in. I wasn't looking for a relationship, but the moment I saw her I flipped. There were sparks flying! We spent the whole evening talking. After she left, a friend gave me her number. I wanted to call next day but held off until Monday: 'I was wondering if you'd like to go out to dinner.' She said, 'I can't tonight,' but agreed to the next night and that was it.

During dinner Sue said she didn't really know The Angels. John assured her that that was okay, they'd be playing the State Theatre in May and then going on tour. She could come and see them then.

Meanwhile, Rick's marriage had come to an end.

> **Rick:** Mandi left me under similar circumstances to me leaving Bitsy years before. Some sort of karma, I guess.

Rick sought solace in writing music. In Darwin, Doc had told him he had some lyrics that needed music put to them. He said he'd like to get down to Rick's, work them up and do some demos. Following up on that conversation, Rick called him in mid-January. Doc rarely answered his phone and Rick landed on his machine for the first few attempts, before Annie picked up. Doc was in bed with neck and back problems – he'd been getting treatment but was still in a lot of pain. Rick passed on his sympathy and said he'd post him a tape of the music he'd been working on.

At the end of January Rick's fax machine began clicking and a two-page typed letter dictated to Annie popped out. It was accompanied by two sheets of lyrics titled 'Whiplash' in Doc's scrawl. He apologised for being so difficult to get onto but said he was suffering horribly from pinched nerves in the neck and a partially dislocated shoulder – a result of the car accident before Christmas. He'd had MRIs, CAT-scans, x-rays and steroid injections, and his osteopath was now considering an operation. He'd been in traction and was 'living in a haze of painkillers which have kept me groggy for days on end'.

Rick glanced at the lyrics, then put them aside until Doc could come down and pick a tune that would suit the feel he wanted.

By March John had moved into Sue's inner-city terrace where she lived with her young daughter, Georgia. It was here in May he received a call from Brent. He'd flown over from New Zealand, hired a car and driven up to Faulconbridge.

'I just had a meeting with Doc,' said Brent. 'Do you mind if I drop in and see you in an hour?'

'Sure,' said John and called Rick to come over and join them.

John: Brent arrived ropable. Doc had told him he couldn't do the tour. He had back issues and needed to take a year off. Brent had suggested he perform in a barber's chair – people still talked about how good that tour was. But Doc had flatly refused. Since the accident that had left barely a scratch on his car, he'd done the Liveline concerts with no mention of back pains at the time. He'd actually been really good. He'd done the Timor concert and the Darwin concert with no indications of injuries. It just felt like more of the Doc bullshit we'd had to put up with going back to Narrara. Brent had put a huge effort into this tour and he was totally pissed off – as were the rest of us.

In August there was a flurry of emails from Brent's Auckland office. Doc had agreed to do one show, at New Year's Eve. Brent wanted the rest of the band to keep the date open while he worked on locking something in.

However, the four Hotdogs were now working regularly across the major cities and had signed a contract to perform a string of gigs at Darling Harbour over the New Year period. They'd be finished at 8.30 pm on New Year's Eve, so they could do a late Angels gig if it was in Sydney – otherwise they'd have to pass.

Jim Hilbun was visiting family in America, but sent back an email saying he was getting on with life and thought that putting New Year's Eve on hold for an Angels gig not yet booked was a 'bit silly', considering the confirmed work he'd been offered. He added how disappointed he was to be in a band that hadn't toured since the previous millennium – as no doubt Rick, John and Brent were too.

By October things had changed again. Doc advised he was no longer available on New Year's Eve. That suited his colleagues, busy with their own pre-arranged gigs that night. But frustrated that the band he'd started with Rick and Doc was sliding into oblivion – it was ten months since their last performance – John rang Chris and Buzz to see if they'd like to have a blow and see how it felt – and got an enthusiastic response. Next he called Jim, who'd sung their hit 'Stand Up' and often taken the mic at gigs, to see if he'd be interested in being their singer. He got a tentative yes. On 26 October they began rehearsals at Rick's place and discovered the magic was still there. Brent came over from NZ for a meeting in Tony Grace's office where management and touring and fees were discussed. However, it was soon apparent there were too many individual projects in the pipeline and it was too problematic to put the band on the road for the time being.

CHAPTER SIXTY-FIVE
A BAND OF ANGELS

In February 2001 Ted Mulry revealed he was suffering from brain cancer, with little chance of recovery. TMG had been with Alberts when The Angels were there. During The Angels' lean years they'd often supported Ted's band, and during that time they'd become backstage friends. When John was asked if The Angels could do a set at a benefit to raise money for Ted's treatment and care, he thought it appropriate to have the original line-up that had known Ted. Chris and Buzz were into it, but when Rick called Doc, knowing he'd performed Angels songs at the Tour of Duty Encore! concert at the Australian War Memorial in Canberra the previous week, the singer refused, saying it would be disloyal to Brent and Jim if he were to play with Chris and Buzz.

> **Rick:** No amount of persuasion would move him so we asked Jim to sing – and he accepted with no sense of disloyalty to anyone.

The band arrived for the sold-out Ted Mulry benefit at Fox Studios, Sydney, on 9 March. They'd agreed to back their friend Ross Wilson on a few of his songs, which went over well. Then, following fifteen months of silence, The Angels were announced, and with Jim Hilbun out front they fired up and *carved* it. After twenty years' absence, the

Bailey-Bidstrup powerhouse delivered the groove that was such an essential part of the magic during their blazing early years. Backstage afterwards, surrounded by backslapping guests, an elated John and Rick exchanged glances – maybe, somehow, there was a way forward.

John's divorce came through in April. A week later, over Easter, he took Sue up to the stately Carrington Hotel in the Blue Mountains and, during a romantic dinner, asked her to marry him. She accepted.

Driving home, they decided to drop in to Doc's place and see how he was going. They found him and Annie hosting lunch with friends, including Dzintra and her husband.

> **John:** He greeted us in a very friendly manner, inviting us to join them, and poured us glasses of wine. Later on we went into a room on our own and I asked him about the possibility of him joining us again. He started feigning injury and told me his body wouldn't allow it. It all seemed a bit silly – he'd been walking around quite normally and in a really good mood.

It was soon after this that Rick got a call from Alan Niven. Rick hadn't heard from him since '91 when he was still managing Guns N' Roses – and had briefly co-managed The Angels. Now Niven was inviting him over to his ranch in Arizona to write the music for an album that he'd written lyrics for.

> **Rick:** He then emailed me some verses and I said, 'Yeah! Great lyrics. I'll go but you'll have to pay me, because I have to earn some money every week.' He said, 'Sure, no problem.'

Rick jetted over for two weeks and flew home to Sydney, satisfied with the music he'd left behind. But Alan wanted him back to record a professional demo of the songs that he could present to record companies.

> **Rick:** I'd told him, 'I want to bring Chrissy Thomas with me. She's an incredible singer and we should get her to record the songs for this demo.' He agreed and Chrissy and I went over in June and spent a month recording it in his home studio.

Back in Sydney, the 'Band Of Angels', as they'd called themselves at the Mulry benefit, had been getting together when they could, and rehearsing.

In his Auckland office, Brent was continually fielding enquiries for Angels gigs. After feedback about the benefit, and hearing they were rehearsing, he flew over to Sydney for an update on his management client. Present were Jim, Buzz, Chris and the Brewsters.

> **John:** Buzz was unimpressed with Brent and he boiled over when Brent left his sunglasses on as we sat round the table: 'Take your shades off, will you? It's rude, man.'

Despite the undercurrents, they continued rehearsals three days later, and with Jim on vocals recorded two new songs, 'Let Me Feel Your Hands On Me' and 'Woman Who Will'.

In July, the latest edition of *New Idea* hit the newsstands. Inside lay an interview with Doc Neeson entitled 'An Angel No More'. In it Doc announced that he'd been forced to quit as lead singer of The Angels. He told of his traumatic recovery from a 1999 car accident that had left him on the brink of suicide. The injuries had included a broken collarbone, dislocated shoulder and severe damage to his neck and lower back. He added that in some ways he'd been set free from having to do the same things he'd been doing for twenty-five years and maybe it was now time to move on.

For the band, it confirmed that Doc no longer planned to rejoin them. While it wasn't a surprise, they were pissed off at finding out in this manner. What was a surprise was that he'd never mentioned the broken collarbone, the dislocated shoulder or the neck and back injuries during the final tour he'd done with them after the car accident, or at the Darwin show.

In November John and Sue were married, with Rick the best man. There were also developments for the brothers on the musical front, when former Angels tour manager Bicci Henderson, now working as entertainment manager at Sydney's Star Casino, got in touch; 'Mate, I was wondering if you and Rick would be interested in doing an acoustic duo thing in the Volcano Room,' he said. 'You can do Angels songs – or anything you want.'

> **John:** He said I can pay you so much, and I said, 'Yeah, great.' We'd have taken anything because we had no band anymore. It was just this bar where you're part of the ambience. But it was kind of good because I'd call chord changes to Rick, or vice versa, and we just played what the hell we wanted to play. It wasn't like you had an audience that was captivated. But we were grateful because it kept our heads just above water.

And so the Brewster Brothers were born. They started out with some acoustic renditions of Angels songs, then drew from a range of Dylan and other old favourites.

From there, work started picking up. A small agency got involved and placed them into a string of suburban venues – mainly bars where the TV screen above them ran the trots and the dogs. They were mostly what they referred to as 'shitholes' paying a few hundred bucks – definitely a long way from the top. It was a dispiriting time but they were brothers who were both with women they loved. John had Sue and Rick had recently met Michelle.

In late August there was another meeting with Brent and the Band Of Angels at Tony Grace's office. During the meeting Buzz attacked Brent for 'confiscating my royalties'. Brent said, 'So sue me.'

> **John:** That incident probably caused Brent to pass on managing the band and probably the reason Jim left soon after as well. And with them, the resurrection of the band too.

Two days later Ted Mulry died. The funeral was at St Andrew's Cathedral in Sydney. Doc followed the coffin out into the sun where he spotted the Channel 10 TV crew. He strolled over and talked about his friendship with Ted and the gigs they'd done together and the nights watching him make records at Alberts.

On 16 December John picked up Spencer Tregloan to take him to the Hotdog performance at Bonython Park for Adelaide's Carols By Candlelight. It would be their final show.

Hotdog had continued performing throughout the year but Spencer had come down with a severe case of interstitial cystitis and he'd had to get by with heavy painkilling medication.

John: Every step for him was incredibly painful. He took fifteen minutes to get to the car, a distance of no more than thirty feet. I offered to help but he waved me away. It was awful.

CHAPTER SIXTY-SIX
AN ALBUM OF NEW SONGS

The income Rick was making from working with artists at his home studio and playing with the Brewster Brothers wasn't enough for him and his family to get by on, so with great enterprise he started 'Rick's Clean Cut Handyman Services'. He advertised in the local papers and soon found himself paving, gardening, house painting, fixing kitchen cupboards. One of his jobs was installing toilet roll and paper towel dispensers at two big hospitals.

They paid him at $5 a dispenser, so it was all about speed. Armed with his cordless drill and a trolley full of dispensers, he devised fast routines and tore through hundreds of wards. But one disastrous day his average was destroyed by two events beyond his control. With one of his batteries flat, he'd plugged it with the charger into a power point in an empty ward and kept on going with his second fully charged one. When the second went flat, he raced back for the first one, only to discover the ward was closed while a woman gave birth. Unable to keep up his schedule, Rick was left in the corridor watching the clock and asking the nurses, 'Er, how much longer do you think she'll be?'

Later the same day, now running way behind, he left a battery recharging in a vacant casualty ward and kept working with the charged one. When that one gave up he shot back for the first and got a taste of the black humour that helped keep the nurses detached from the tragedies they witnessed every day. 'Sorry,' he was told, 'you'll have to wait until the old man in there dies. We tried plugging him into your recharger but it didn't work. His family is with him and the priest is on his way.' An hour and a half later the family left, the body was wheeled out and Rick got back to work.

They were playing to a handful of drunks in a backstreet pub one night when a young, t-shirted punter introduced himself during a break. His name was Darrel Baird, a go-getter on the make in the music business, representing a young blues duo called the Brown Brothers. Darrel immediately saw the potential of The Angels guitarist brothers and offered to arrange gigs for them on commission.

His first effort was to put together a show at The Basement, with the Brown Brothers supported by Brewster Brothers. Billed as 'The Brotherhood', he promoted it heavily and pulled just over 200 on a Thursday night. The Brewsters won over a lot of new fans and it opened doors to some long-lasting relationships. Darrel next took the Brotherhood concept to Adelaide's Governor Hindmarsh with similar success.

> **Darrel:** I told them how I'd put together twenty-two shows in twenty-six days up the coast of NSW and into Queensland for the Brown Brothers and could do the same for them if they wanted to go that way. And that was how our business relationship got going.

By mid-year, John and Rick decided to invest their creative energy into developing the Brewster Brothers further. They'd added a couple of original compositions to their sets, but were still relying on Dylan songs, acoustic renditions of Angels numbers and a few others to fill out their repertoire.

> **John:** Rick and I started talking about writing an album of new songs. We made a start but maybe because we didn't live it the way we did in the early days when we'd write in hotels, the studio, each other's houses or in the car

travelling to gigs, it was harder to focus on lyric writing. It was much easier to come up with musical ideas.

Then Rick suggested getting Alan Niven involved.

Rick: The lyrics he'd written for the album I'd done in Arizona were fantastic. So I called him: 'Would you be interested?' He jumped on it: 'I'd fucking love to.'

For the next year or so, the three exchanged emails and long phone calls. John would talk about his life and Alan would take notes. Some of the late-night calls became very intense as Niven probed into their lives. In the following days he'd come back with emails full of insightful lyrics reflecting their responses. One night he asked, 'John, you've obviously had your highs and lows. Would you do it again?' John said, 'That's a good question and I'd have to say yes, because I'm really happy with what's going on with my life. If I didn't do it again, it'd be different, wouldn't it?' A few days later Alan emailed lyrics that eloquently traced John's rollercoaster life and it became one of the Brewster Brothers' most defining songs.

Rick: It was an interesting way of creating a song and we really enjoyed it. But we'd get it wrong sometimes. We'd listen through and go, 'You know what, the music is good but it's not right for the lyric.' So we'd go back and rewrite it. 'Would You Do It Again' is a great example, because we absolutely had it wrong at first. People were loving it – they'd get up and start dancing around the floor – but the music was wrong for the lyric.

Rick went back to the drawing board. He tried different keys, tempos, then went round to John's and said, 'I've rewritten the music to "Do It Again".' John said, 'That's funny, so have I. What key?' Rick said it was in G. John had done something in C. 'Let's hear what you've done,' John said.

It was in the same groove and tempo as John's. 'You know what, Rick, if you put yours to mine, it will all work!'

So the first verse was rewritten in G, after that it changed to C, and a work of art was completed.

John: It was one of those weird things that happens between brothers. The end result was fantastic, because if you do the whole song in C, it would be one thing, or the whole song in G it would be another, and it would be alright. But when it changes to the other key, and the groove remains exactly the same, it's amazing. One of those things that just happened.

It was a painstaking process and it took time. The collaboration with Niven ran off the rails after John once referred to his lyrics as 'poetry' while talking with him on the phone. It was some months after that comment that John mentioned to Rick that he'd been leaving messages on Niven's voicemail, but hadn't heard back from him in quite a while. Rick said, 'Oh, er, yes. I've should have shown you something,' and produced an email from him.

Rick: It wasn't just 'Hey, tell your brother it's not poetry, it's lyrics.' It was 'How dare he! You will instruct your brother to never refer to my lyrics as poetry again!' The thing with Niven is that he was, in his own words, clinically depressed. It could last for months.

John sent his apologies, Niven's anger evaporated, and an extraordinary canon of work came into existence. The songs were tested at gigs and demos eventually recorded at Rick and John's homes. They were then ready for the next stage.

Harry Vanda had remained a friend since the Alberts days. While George Young had moved to the UK, Harry was in the process of completing a new studio in Sydney called Flashpoint.

John: I rang and said, 'We'd like to play you some new songs we've written,' and Harry said, 'Yeah, great, but I don't want to just listen to them – come in with your instruments and play them to me.' So we set up as if we were playing in a pub – sound system, lights, the whole rig – and then put a chair in front of us for him. Right there in his big recording studio.

As Harry quietly sat with one leg crossed over the other drinking long-neck beers, they performed to their audience of one. At the end he clapped: 'Great stuff, boys, come on in.'

Harry offered unlimited studio time as long as it didn't interfere with paying jobs the studio took on. It was similar to the old Alberts arrangement: they'd be working the graveyard periods, which was fine with them. The trade-off was signing a publishing deal with Harry's company on the songs that went onto the album.

They had their studio, now they had to make a record.

CHAPTER SIXTY-SEVEN
THE ORIGINAL ANGELS BAND

The year started with a $3000 fee Darrel landed for the Brewster Brothers for New Year's Eve, a substantial one for them. However, the hotel management thought they were getting a variation of The Angels and promoted the night as a party rage. When the two brothers stepped onto the stage, they found themselves faced with a roomful of drunks screaming, 'Where's Doc?'

A lot of venue managers convinced themselves they were getting a cut-down version of The Angels and promoted the shows as such – it caused problems when they realised that wasn't the case. John's way of handling it was to smoke a few joints until it was over, while Rick would lie back in his car during breaks with the air-con running and Beethoven on the player.

Darrel Baird started vetting the various agents and venue bookers and gradually worked the duo into more appropriate gigs on the pub and club circuit. He even pulled the occasional festival. He was a hard worker and made a difference, but finding suitable venues prepared to pay up for The Angels' ex-guitarists was always a hard sell.

John: It demonstrated to us the value in an established brand name. Brewster Brothers was an unfamiliar name to most – we even had people thinking we were a Blues Brothers tribute act!

Supporting Vika and Linda Bull at a house-full leagues club one night was a classy highlight Darrel pulled off, but those were few and far between. Mostly, they were paying their dues all over again.

When their residency at the casino ended, it was replaced by a regular Thursday at a suburban RSL where they won over some new fans. While there was a lot of drudgery, they were writing and recording new material, they were in love with two wonderful women, and they believed they still had a viable future as musicians.

Darrel set up a run of shows in Western Australia for March and they flew over for a one-week tour with Angry as their guest. With their eskies filled with food for the distances they had to drive, and Angry talking non-stop, they'd pull over for a rest and picnic. Those memories, like the earlier ones on the Lounge Lizards tour, would remain.

During July Darrel landed them a nine-date season at the piano bar at the Alpine Hotel in Thredbo. John's sons accompanied them and they spent their days on the slopes. It was rare for John that his work provided the opportunity for a holiday with his young sons.

By mid-2003 Doc had recovered from his 'life-threatening injuries' and was getting restless. Out and about visiting some of his old haunts around the city, one night he dropped into the Civic Hotel, now owned and refurbished by eastern suburbs entrepreneur Rodney Adler. Onstage was a band called the Rockets, whose guitarist was David Lowy, a friend of Adler's and scion of the billionaire family that co-founded and controlled the Westfield shopping-mall empire. David spotted the six-foot-four Doc in the crowd and invited him up to do some Angels songs. After the show they talked for hours and a friendship developed between the pony-tailed businessman and the rock 'n' roll singer.

> **Doc:** David's big interests were flying and rock music. As he was growing up one of the bands he was really into was The Angels, and in particular Rick's guitar playing.

The following day Lowy rang Doc and asked if he'd be interested in working with him on some musical projects. With his curiosity piqued, he accepted. The relationship eventually led to Lowy financially backing Doc in putting together a group of hired musicians with a view to touring and making records. Word about the plan got back to the Brewsters when overtures were made to Rick to be part of Doc's band. But unless John was involved, Rick wasn't interested. At one point a rabid Angels fan on the sidelines became aware of this. He took it upon himself to track down Rick's home number, calling him late at night and threatening him with harm if he didn't join and co-operate with Doc.

John woke one morning and thought about all this; about Doc's recovery from the injuries that had 'destroyed his life' and about this new band he was forming to do the Angels repertoire. It had rankled reading Doc state in the *New Idea* article that 'the band called and asked me to step down as lead singer of The Angels', when quite the opposite had been the case.

He rang Rick.

> **John:** I said, 'You know, I'm over all this. Just because people don't want to be in The Angels with us anymore doesn't mean The Angels has to be over for us. We're The Angels. Whatever people may think, we wrote the songs – we should be playing our repertoire as the band we started.'

They called up Buzz and Chris. 'Look, are you guys interested in joining us to go out and do some shows as the original Angels band?'

The answer was an unqualified 'yes'.

The next call, to Jim, wasn't so positive. He said he'd have to think about it, and after further prodding over the next few days, he declined the offer, with no reason forthcoming. Disappointed but undeterred, John opted to be singer, with the rest supplying harmony support, and they'd go out as a four piece.

> **Tony Grace:** From an agency perspective, I'd often find myself sitting in the middle as bands came and went and I'd just deal with what was in front of me.

> Rick and John had been doing their own Brewster Brothers thing but we still kept in touch. Then suddenly one day I'm dealing with Doc Neeson in the office, no Brewster brothers, talking about 'Doc Neeson's Angels'.

When John and Rick walked into Harbour to discuss their Angels band's possible touring potential, Tony threw up his hands and told both sides to get together and sort themselves out.

> **John:** We met with Doc, David Lowy and lawyers on 12th November to discuss the various names that each band might use other than 'The Angels'. We eventually reached an agreement that never felt right. It seemed to us that no matter which way we turned we were blocked by people who no longer wanted to be part of The Angels. Doc now had a substantial source of financial clout provided by money people, we had our shit gigs for shit money . . . and our self-respect!

The year came to an end with the Brewsters starting work on a new project. For over two decades Alberts had wanted to release a video of The Angels' brilliant performance at La Trobe Uni in Melbourne back in 1979. However, there'd been obstacles. There was the huge job of working through the hours of footage taken by three camera crews, compounded by Brent's constant objections because he didn't believe the finished film would represent the band that he was then drumming with.

In 2003 the idea was resurrected by Alberts and this time Rick and John got involved. They entered Alberts on 1 December and made a start on what would be an on-and-off labour of love over the next few years. It would culminate in the release of The Angels' defining DVD *This Is It Folks – Over The Top* in 2008.

CHAPTER SIXTY-EIGHT
THINGS FALL DARREL'S WAY

The Bridge Hotel in Sydney's Rozelle is a glorious remnant from rock's golden era: gig posters line the entrance, shoes stick to the carpet and the odour of stale beer hangs in the air. In the dim backroom, spotlights clamped to blacked-out ceilings focus on a dilapidated stage spanning the far end. While the roadies set up during quiet afternoons, they sense the ghostly presence of the old rockers who haunt the place. This is where the pure stuff still happens.

The Original Angels Band (TOAB) did their first gigs there on the weekend of 5 March, and crowd-wise they stiffed. Tony Grace was caught off-guard as he watched them: a high-powered unit performing The Angels' repertoire note perfect as no others could. But instead of welcoming them into the agency, he dithered due to conflicting loyalties with Doc and said he'd think about it.

> **Tony Grace:** To be honest, I should have moved immediately. I didn't and I regretted that afterwards.

The truth was that he believed an Angels without Doc would never draw a viable audience. However, the Doc Neeson's Angels weren't setting the world on fire either. Tony didn't want to encourage TOAB to continue when what the fans wanted was The Angels, not two half Angels, and he didn't see the two-band situation lasting for long.

> **John:** I love Tony for the way he says it like it is. He came back after the show: 'I know you guys can play, but you have to turn it into pulling crowds.' He represented The Angels, and he didn't see us as The Angels. Nor did I in truth. He was also close to Doc as well as us. Anyway, he worked on a bigger level representing acts who were up there and we weren't up there. I got it – no complaints.

The man who also got it was Darrel Baird, who at this point only represented the Brewster Brothers duo. When Tony passed on TOAB, it fell Darrel's way and he grabbed it.

> **Darrel:** I took on all the weight of booking, marketing and promotion, built the website, organised production and crews across Australia, streamlined the touring costs and then tour managed over 400 shows. Chris Bailey jumped in with his experience and in particular helped with logistics and taught me a hell of a lot, but the workload was stifling. I was also handling the Brewster Brothers.

On hearing that John and Rick had got their Angels band up and running, a disconcerted Brent Eccles called a meeting at John's place during his next visit to Sydney. This, like the previous one, was not pleasant. He made it clear that the name 'The Angels' belonged to Tutankhamun Pty Ltd, the company that owned the registered name 'The Angels', and he was a third shareholder, along with co-owners Rick and Doc. He also reminded John that he was still The Angels' manager. John pointed out that The Original Angels Band was not being promoted as The Angels and they had every right to play any Angels songs they wanted to, as many cover bands did most nights of the week.

As Brent got up to leave he eye-balled John. 'I can do The Angels with Rick and Doc,' he said. 'I don't need you!'

To which Rick shot back, 'Well, I won't be playing in any band that John's not in.'

*

In May the band flew off to WA for a ten-gig tour. The crowds were substantial and Rick and John were back in a favourite part of the country at the right time of year.

Darrel: On the plane home Rick was leaning into the aisle of the plane at a weird angle. I leant over and asked him, 'What's wrong, Rick?' He said, 'I can't sit straight – there's too much cash in my back pocket.'

John: I'd been happy singing in the Brewster Brothers, and happy singing in Moonshine, but I never felt that I was a really ballsy rock singer. But I did alright in the Angels band. The vocals were good, the band swung, and Chris was there with his great voice – and we had a wonderful rhythm section. We had to put up with Buzz and his whingeing and carrying on, but it didn't matter. It was worth doing.

Behind the scenes, Rick and John were pressing on with recording their album at Harry Vanda's studio Flashpoint, and it was becoming apparent that something special was emerging.

On a Thursday night in November The Original Angels Band mounted the stage at Sydney's prestigious Basement nightclub. Darrel had done a good job promoting the gig and an enthusiastic audience cheered and clapped as they plugged in. The Basement had an excellent recording and filming set-up and the band took the opportunity to record the show for release as a DVD.

The year came to a close with a masterstroke that Darrel had pulled off for his charges – a $15,000 New Year's Eve show at Tumbalong Park, Darling Harbour.

CHAPTER SIXTY-NINE
REKINDLING A FRIENDSHIP

Mem Brewster-Jones, John and Rick's mother, died on 29 March, aged eighty-seven. She'd been their biggest fan since the beginning, standing on tables and rocking out to the band as her sons raged away onstage to manic hordes. At eighty she was doing the Charleston at Moonshine reunions.

Rick and John were in Harry Vanda's Flashpoint studio that evening when they got the call.

> John: We'd flown Chris Wilson to Sydney to play some harmonica. He wouldn't accept a fee – he was just proud to be on it. While he was setting up I had to keep leaving to use the phone. I thought he'd be offended seeing me walking in and out so I told him what had happened. He started packing up: 'I'm so sorry about your mum, but you don't need me here right now.' I said, 'You're wrong, we do need you with us.' He stayed and it was a magical evening.

A week later the family held the funeral at the tiny church behind the Encounter Bay home his grandparents and parents had owned. The brothers played as Spencer sang one of Mem's favourite Moonshine songs: the WW2 era classic, 'Don't Ever Walk In The Shadows'. Mem loved the Moonshine Jug and String Band.

*

In May The Original Angels Band did a big concert at the Darwin Casino then flew to Cairns for a run down the Queensland coast: nine successful shows. There was a problem looming, though, as the band's well-connected publicist, Jodie Davies, couldn't continue for personal reasons. With the imminent release of the TOAB's *Live At The Basement* CD and DVD, recorded earlier in the year, the band needed another hot publicist in a hurry. Jodie suggested Cat Swinton and a meeting was arranged.

> **Cat:** That's when I started with them. With the band's new CD coming out, my first job was to publicise it and it basically went from there. Then Darrel invited me to a Brewster Brothers show at a hotel in Surry Hills and I fell in love with that. It was all encompassing from then on – Angels Band and the Brewster Brothers.

Angry invited the band to perform at a benefit for Pete Wells with whom The Angels had toured so many times. Pete was in terminal decline with prostate cancer and a huge line-up gathered for the concert on 7 September at the Enmore Theatre. Doc was invited but didn't make it.

Meanwhile, Cat was searching for publicity opportunities that would get her clients into media outside the usual channels. One thing different about these guys, she discovered, was snakes. Darrel kept two and Rick had a yard full of them.

> **Cat:** I said, 'Well, let's try *Totally Wild*,' and the show's producers loved the idea. We got the TV crew and went up to Rick's place on the northern edge of Sydney. He had all these beautiful glass cages for his snakes. He also had turtles out in the backyard. It was like a mini menagerie of reptiles. Fantastic, actually.
>
> I'd never held a snake and I have to thank Rick for getting me over my phobia of them. One wrapped itself up my arm. I was going, 'Ahh . . .' They're beautiful creatures and I discovered why he loved them so much. He's quirky and he likes quirky things. *Totally Wild* loved it. It got a huge response when it went to air.

*

Work on the album was now inching towards completion. But it hadn't been without drama and high farce. The madness of Alan Niven had been visited upon the Brewsters since mid-2003 when he arrived to check on the progress of the album. Rick had paid for his visit so he could see for himself how the Brewsters were performing the songs for which he'd written the lyrics. While in Sydney, Alan moved into Rick and Michelle's home. However, Michelle didn't like him and he frightened the kids.

He was back in Australia a year later, this time with petite new wife Heather. He'd talked his new father-in-law into paying for their return airfares. He accompanied the Brewsters to the studio most days and gave them a constant stream of his 'high-handed opinions', as an infuriated Rick would relate to his friends.

> **John:** They stayed with Sue and me for a while in the little cottage annexed to our house and came in to the studio most days with me. Whilst there were good moments, the bad won over. He now called himself The Reverend Ether Graham. Reverend? Give me a break!

> **Rick:** While he was here we had a four-date season in Thredbo. It was during this time that the final nail went into the coffin of our relationship with that scheming low-life. He demanded that he manage, produce and control the Brewster Brothers and we refused him flat.

On John's return from Thredbo, the Nivens, who'd been staying with friends, arrived back in a cab to collect their things. As Alan stowed his bags in the cab's boot, John, standing at the gate, noticed he was loading a guitar.

> **Rick:** He caught Alan attempting to put my Strat in the boot and took it off him, thank Christ! Although he did manage to take off with my brand new digital camera I'd loaned to Heather.

The Brewster Brothers were billed to play a small theatre restaurant in the Blue Mountains about half an hour from my bush retreat. I hadn't seen the guys for a few years so my lady Christine and I were keen to go and see what they were up to.

I had no idea what to expect, certainly not the intriguing mix of moody Pink Floydian music and Dylanesque lyrics. After the show they told me about their lives, and about their hopes for the Brewster Brothers and their new album being readied for release the following year. They also mentioned the Angels band and working with Chris and Buzz again.

I had just begun organising my rural community's annual ball in our local hall. In an inspired moment, as they climbed wearily into their van, I asked if the band would play for us. 'For you,' they said, 'special price. Two and a half grand plus accommodation.'

Saturday 4 February 2006, the night the Angels Band played to a jam-packed Megalong Valley Ball, would become a topic of local conversation for years. Nothing had ever shaken up the little bush hall like that – especially when old fans chanted back at the band, 'No way, get fucked, fuck off!', to the consternation of those not in the know.

It was the rekindling of a friendship between me and the brothers that would last to this day.

CHAPTER SEVENTY
MEDIATION

Hankering for the stimulation of creative spirits, I began attending Brewster Brother gigs in Sydney and got involved with editing the liner notes in their CD centrefold – now titled *Shadows Fall* after one of the songs. They were booked into the popular Vanguard in Newtown for their album launch and I suggested they get Jim Conway, one of the finest harmonica players in the country, as a guest sideman. Jim was a star in his own right and would help attract a wider audience. Jim then introduced stand-up bass player Paul Robert Burton and he was signed up. We invited fiddle player Claire O'Mara to make a surprise appearance. On the night, as the band began the haunting intro to the CD's title song, the strains of her violin came from the back of the room. Waif-like and gypsy-scarfed, she gracefully eased between the tables as the guitars pulled back and John set into the opening lyrics. Everyone was mesmerised. The show ended with the entire audience on their feet calling for encores – a well-earned triumph, resulting in Jim Conway and Paul Burton becoming regular Brewster Brothers' sidemen.

When the CD arrived from the manufacturer I'd found my name on the back cover as 'manager', a surprise. John cheekily explained: 'Ah well, why not, you run our weekly group meetings, commissioned our brilliant backdrop, come to all the gigs, you almost are!' We had a laugh. If I was, it was only honorary.

Meantime, TOAB continued their solid touring regime, the Brewster Brothers being slotted in wherever there were free dates – among them, some plum festival spots Darrel landed them.

> **Cat:** The Angels band were the hardest working guys I've ever worked with. They were continually on the road. Darrel Baird coordinated gigs with the booking agencies, but he also booked a lot of shows direct – he was a real go-getter. Some things didn't work out. There was a bikie gig in Canberra that the boys didn't get paid for, but he'd usually manage to get round things.

While Rick and John had been busy with their projects, in 2005 Doc, with David Lowy's backing, had assembled a new band with Lowy on rhythm guitar. As Red Phoenix, they toured around the country and then, feeling they were ready to create an album, the band and their ladies boarded a plane for the Bahamas. For the next few months they worked with producer Terry Manning at his elite recording facility, Compass Point Studios. This studio had serious pedigree. AC/DC had recorded their seminal *Back In Black* album there and giants such as the Stones and U2 had graced the place with their illustrious presence.

After spending what was rumoured to be the highest figure ever lavished on an Australian album, Red Phoenix released *Red Phoenix* in November 2005, and it unceremoniously stiffed.

Doc would valiantly explain to anyone who'd listen that David Lowy had come to the view that without the right record company support, they were wasting a good album, so he pulled it. According to Doc, it would be released again at a later date when a better deal could be arranged. Whatever the story was, Doc relapsed into a series of health problems after the album was withdrawn and Red Phoenix found themselves having to cancel an extensive tour and disband.

However, the time he'd spent with Lowy and the rest of the band had been a creative period, and it had put him back in the limelight, a place he always enjoyed. Although he'd done numerous interviews insisting he didn't want to be 'Doc the Angel for the rest of my days', as he got back on his feet a few months later, he decided to give it one more go. He got a group of musicians together, formed 'Doc Neeson's Angels' and began playing in a few low-key suburban pubs.

Things picked up again in 2007, when Doc recorded an unplugged-style 'solo' album of Angels songs. It was released in September on Liberation's 'Acoustic Sessions' series of Australian lead singers reinterpreting their classic band songs. It garnered reviews from one extreme to the other: 'brilliant' through to 'dreadful'.

Around this time Doc was invited to tour the country as part of the 'Countdown Spectacular 2' revival shows where his band was billed as 'Doc Neeson and The Angels'. Seven or eight minutes was allotted to each act to do whatever they wanted. Doc performed a medley of greatest hits and the ecstatic reactions at every show were a constant reminder of the legacy The Angels had built up over the decades.

By now the legal argy-bargy simmering between Doc's side and TOAB regarding the use of The Angels name was ramping up. A new legal opinion from TOAB's lawyer was suggesting that Tutankhamun's ownership of the trading name 'The Angels' was unlikely to be upheld in court. He reasoned that there were thousands of entities in the world using 'Angels' in their name. He advised it could be argued that as a band name, if anyone owned it, it was probably the original musicians who first used it in 1976 when they signed to Alberts.

> John: We had this lovely old barrister, Malcolm. Basically, he said, 'You need to be seen using the name, otherwise you'll lose it,' so we started calling our band The Angels. That pushed the envelope!

Much aggrieved, Doc's side sought an injunction in the NSW Supreme Court and gained an interim order forcing TOAB 'not to identify themselves as currently being members of The Angels, perform as The Angels, market or release any recordings as The Angels'.

The presiding judge prevailed on both sides to try to settle their differences in private arbitration, as opposed to their lawyers going toe-to-toe in what could be costly litigation. As a result, a mediator was hired and a meeting set up. On one side of the table sat the members of TOAB, plus Malcolm, their elderly barrister. Facing them were Doc and his partner Annie, Doc's personal manager David Edwards (appointed by David Lowy), plus the lawyers Lowy had arranged.

> **John:** At one stage Doc and some of the others left the room and then David Edwards came back and said, 'Doc wants to talk to two of you.' Rick pointed at me and Chris, so we followed Edwards into this room where Doc and Annie were. He said, 'Well, I grew up with The Angels,' and goes, 'You guys should just think about playing together again.' Doc looked at me, but with a smile on his face, and said, 'Well, I'd have to think about it,' and I said, 'Yeah, well, I'd have to think about it, too,' and we both laughed, and Chris laughed. Suddenly the whole vibe got nice.

The meeting was adjourned with an 'Alright, we'll get back to you.'

Edwards was manager of Spitfire Productions, the company David Lowy used for his music enterprises. It was in this capacity that part of his responsibility was to be Doc's personal manager. Edwards reported back to Lowy, 'They might be playing together again,' and at that point a meeting was set up in Lowy's office, on the top floor of the Westfield headquarters building in Sydney.

> **John:** Rick and I went in there and met with Edwards and David Lowy. That's when they said, 'Well, Doc is happy to do it again.'

Both bands still had contracted gigs and tours in the pipeline and a few days later Doc Neeson's Angels flew out with other Australian entertainers on the Tour de Force bill, playing thirteen shows to troops in Afghanistan, Iraq and Kuwait. For his connection with the military going back to his national service days and in gratitude for his East Timor concert, Doc was awarded the Australian Services Medal, personally presented by Lieutenant General Peter Cosgrove.

In the final settlement of their differences, Brent's share of Tutankhamun was bought out and all remaining hurdles were removed to clear the way for a long-overdue reunion.

> **Tony Grace:** I'd had a conversation with Dave Edwards before that meeting when they all got together for the first time: 'Mate, this is bullshit, we need to get these guys back together again.' Dave agreed to reach out to the Brewster brothers – and all of a sudden they were meeting and working out an agreement on how they would work together, which was followed up with a legal deed that their lawyers drew up and they all signed.

In the early days of 2007, John and Sue left Sydney to live in 'Yelki', the old house by the sea, which had been in the family since 1894 at Victor Harbor, south of Adelaide. It was where he'd stayed during surfing weekends with Pete Thorpe during their teenage years. Soon after, Rick and Michelle bought a rural property outside Hobart and also farewelled Sydney.

CHAPTER SEVENTY-ONE
REUNITED

Part of the deal the TOAB camp accepted was that Dave Edwards, while continuing to work for David Lowy's Spitfire Productions, would also manage the reunited Angels. John Brewster, as the nominal leader of TOAB, wanted to bring Darrel and Cat into the new regime, but accepted that Lowy and Edwards would have last say. John extolled Darrel and Cat's virtues and interviews were set up.

> **Darrel:** David Lowy called me into his office and told me that I had done what no one in the industry thought could happen, and that was to make The Angels band a success without Doc. It was the ultimate compliment.

But Dave Edwards would have the final say.

> **Cat:** Darrel and I had to go and see whether we could keep our jobs, basically. I did but for Darrel, up for the tour manager gig, it didn't go the way he wanted. After all the hard work he'd put in, he was shattered. It was very sad, but that's the industry.

Tony Grace, never one to give another agent a compliment, rang him to commiserate and to congratulate him on the job he'd done in making the band a success against all the odds.

Darrel: John and I had clashed a lot but we'd achieved a hell of a lot together and we stuck with each other for seven years and ran a strong business. As for Rick, he was always just fun to be around, very left of field and a genius on his tools of trade. At the end of the day, what goes on tour stays on tour and as soon as the music started on stage, all the hardships of touring and business washed away.

David Lowy had been closely involved with Doc for some years, and now wanted to get to know John and Rick. He'd become an Angels fan at a young age, and was a great admirer of their guitar prowess, in particular Rick's unique style.

David appeared to live parallel lifestyles, effortlessly moving from corporate executive to champion daredevil pilot to rock musician. The Brewsters would meet him at his office in the Westfield building and sometimes at Bill and Tony's, a back-street café close by. Rick and John liked him, he was down to earth, said it like it was and talked about his fondness for Doc. But as John came in from a game of golf one afternoon, he received a call from an emotional Lowy.

John: He told me how Doc had just let him down – again. He'd missed a string of important meetings and David was personally hurt and offended at how Doc had been so constantly unreliable and uncontactable.

Despite his frustrations, Lowy remained friends with Doc throughout.

Dave Edwards' team was now finalising logistics for the tour – and ready to confirm the rumours, he instructed Cat to dispatch a press release: 'The quintessential Angels line-up will be touring for the first time since 1981: Brewster, Neeson, Brewster, Bailey and Bidstrup.'

Cat: The response was massive. People were aware of the two bands and the legal stuff, so for them to come together was a big news story.

The Brewster Brothers had a special show booked at The Basement in May. With advance sales suggesting a good roll-up, it seemed like an opportunity to invite Doc to join them for a couple of Angels songs. It had been eight years since they'd played together, but despite that, after only a quick run-through backstage, the sparks flew when he took to the mic.

Cat: Wow, that was pretty special! I got that goosebumps thing where you go, 'Whoa, this is gonna be a ride!' I'd heard about Doc being such a scary person, but when nobody had introduced me, I thought, 'Well, I'll go and introduce myself.' So I walked over and said, 'Hello, my name is Catherine Swinton, I'm your new publicist.' He looked me straight in the eye and said, 'Finally, a publicist I see eye to eye with,' meaning I was tall. I said, 'Well, let's see how long that lasts,' which as it turned out, was quite poignant.

To acknowledge thirty years since the release of their breakthrough album, Alberts were releasing a remastered and expanded edition of *Face To Face*. And finally, the long-awaited release of *This Is It Folks*, the DVD of the 1979 concert at La Trobe University – considered by privileged insiders to have caught The Angels at the pinnacle of their youthful power.

Over at Harbour Tony Grace's team had booked eighteen of the biggest rooms across the nation. Some had needed cajoling into moving other acts they had on nights Tony wanted. Some had baulked at the deals, and drawn-out negotiations were required. The big orange carrot had been: 'This is the *original* line-up – It will be stupendous!'

Tony: I got a call from John. 'What are your thoughts if Buzz wasn't in the band?' I said, 'For fuck's sake, we've announced it as the reunited original line-up! We can't do this to the fans.' I said, 'Just let it go – let's everyone try to work together. We can revisit it at the end of the tour.'

Music Max had discussed doing a tour documentary, but the deal had fallen through. However, Mikael Borglund, who once worked as The Angels' accountant and remained close friends with Rick, John and

Doc, was now CEO of TV production company Beyond Productions. John gave him a call.

> **Mikael:** We had dinner a week or so before rehearsals and came to an agreement for us to start shooting – and that I would sell the film to ABC or SBS, both of whom were very realistic about the value of this kind of project.

With only days to go before rehearsals began, Mikael instructed producer Ben Ulm to put together two camera crews and prepare to go on tour with The Angels. By 3 June, Ben's team was packed and ready for action.

> **Mikael:** We managed to film Doc leaving home for the first rehearsal with the band – he was late, of course. There was some great material captured that day and we could see that this could be a very interesting film. I showed the footage to SBS and they agreed to buy it.

There was just one stipulation: Borglund wasn't to show it to the band when it was completed.

> **Rick:** He gave us the opportunity and we said, 'No, don't do it, we'll just want to sanitise it.'

> **John:** It would just open a can of worms. It would never see the light of day because we'd all go, 'Oh, you can't have that bit in there.'

So Borglund's brief to Ben Ulm was: just follow them round and be a fly on the wall.

Cat got the band a prime spot on TV for the nationally broadcast NRL *Footy Show*. It was their first public performance, and it went without a hitch. It was followed by a chat and a list of the tour dates to their 500,000 viewers. It was all grins and backslaps in the Green Room afterwards.

On a blustery afternoon two days later Cat was onboard for the ninety-minute drive out of Sydney for a warm-up gig at the backwater

Davistown RSL. She would be learning the ropes for her job as on-road publicist and den mother, once the tour got underway the following week.

It was the first time she'd encountered the way Doc prepared himself.

Cat: He asked me to help with his make-up and make sure his tie was right and his suit was on properly. He was warming up his voice, getting into character. I saw him go from Bernard Neeson to Doc Neeson. To me he'd become this really gorgeous person but he morphed as the make-up went on, as he fixed his hair, put on his clothes. I could see that it was a bit of a ritual: donning the cape to become the king type thing.

My job was to also 'nicely' clear the band's dressing room before the show to give them space to get into the mood. And that show was just brilliant! I mean, just amazing musicians – the chemistry between the originals was very special.

A couple of days later they did an honorary performance at the closing of the Golden Staves, the entertainment industry's annual dinner that raised funds for children's charities. Held at the Hordern Pavilion, there were over a thousand music biz luminaries at a sit-down lunch where $700,000 was raised.

Mark Pope was there, and while The Angels were onstage his thoughts drifted back to the time he was their tour manager twenty-five years back.

Mark: I felt so sad for Doc seeing him doing the signature thing with the towel for 'Take A Long Line'. When you're a handsome young athlete bounding like you're on a pogo stick, it's fricken awesome. But when you're seeing an overweight guy going, 'Un, un, un,' it's sort of sad. I was truly shocked to see how much weight he'd put on, how bloated he looked.

I caught up with him and the rest afterwards. He was still charming but it was like the light had gone out. I think it probably went out in the mid-nineties. I don't know what happened. I don't know the dynamics of what went on within the band.

The tour got underway in earnest the following week with a run of seventeen shows. Tony Grace was more than just their long-serving agent. He was a fan and truly loved the band:

> **Tony Grace:** Everywhere, sold out, sold out. You couldn't get a ticket for love or money. It just brought everyone back together again. And it set the new pathway for the last chapter.

Meanwhile the documentary crew kept filming . . . and filming. They could see they were recording something historic. Borglund was shocked at times with what was captured – but he knew it represented the truth.

> **John:** I thought it was very honest. A lot of these reunion documentaries are like, 'Oh, we all love each other,' but this didn't come across like that at all. We were all very true to our feelings. There's one thing there, where Buzz was saying to David Edwards, 'I'm not a fucking idiot, David.' We almost all chimed in, going, 'Oh yeah?' You put five people together in pretty intense pressure-cooker situations and you're bound to get conflict.

> **Mikael:** I certainly did not want the film to embarrass anyone – I was a huge fan and personal friends with John, Rick and Doc. The film only shows what went down. We didn't 'produce' or encourage any actions or events.

The tour was a huge success and proved beyond doubt that the total was far greater than the parts. But having completed it, the band then waited months for the profit share to arrive in their accounts. They were told that the accountancy company was still finalising tour expenses, but for musicians who'd been doing this sort of thing all their lives the delays were unacceptable.

> **John:** That was the first indication of how things were to be under Edwards' management system. The warning bells were sounding and there were many more to follow over the next few years.

While the band took a ten-week break, John and Rick got to work on a new project. The previous year Rick had written a song based loosely on their experience with Alan Niven, aka The Reverend Ether Graham. Called 'Wounded Healer', it had kicked off a burst of writing activity and they now had a parcel of new songs for the next Brewster Brothers album. Jimmy Barnes had built a studio on his property in the NSW Southern Highlands, which he'd recently sold. Rick, John and Paul Burton took up residence there for two weeks and buckled down to creating what would become their third Brewster Brothers' album.

While they were there, David Edwards emailed a suggested run of dates for the next Angels tour. John and Rick checked them out and emailed back: 'Yep, sounds good.' Doc got back, 'Yep, fine with me,' which was followed by an affirmative from Chris.

Rick: Then we got an email from Buzz demanding to see a detailed budget for the tour. Like two to three months out, 'I need to see a budget first, and by the way I'm not available for this date, and this one, and this one.'

John: Of course, the answer was how can we tell you what we're going to earn when we don't know how many tickets we're going to sell? We're on door deals. That's the way it works on this level – always has.

Buzz came up with the concept that he'd pick the gigs he wanted to play and then he'd choose a drummer to fill in on the ones he wasn't available for. But he wanted to be paid in full and then he'd pay the stand-in out of his share.

Chris was unimpressed and demanded a 'no show, no dough' rule – which resulted in Buzz's lawyer writing to David Edwards and to each band member repeating Buzz's instructions about being paid for all performances, but for some gigs supplying a stand-in.

Rick: He would use lawyers like they were some big threat: 'You've got to pay Mr Bidstrup his full share even if he's not there.' I don't think we even responded to it. We just said to Buzz, 'There's just no fucking way.'

John: On the last day of recording Doc rang me: 'Look, anyone who doesn't want to play in the band shouldn't be in the band.'

The documentary screened on the SBS network on Saturday night, 11 October 2008, and was a ratings success. The title was, *The Angels: No Way Get F*#ked F*#k Off!*, which would have raised the eyebrows of many of SBS's regular viewers.

Mikael: Most of the reactions from the general public were very positive – as were the reviews. From the band there were only positive comments. Michael Gudinski, head of Liberation Records, thought it was a disgrace that we let it go out in the form it was. He was wrong in my view – and he's never mentioned it to me again after that day.

Rick: I didn't want to see it, and I would never have seen it. Michelle put on the DVD six months later and called me in: 'Wow, I think you should have a look at this. It's pretty raw and in your face!'

In September, John Brewster, Doc Neeson and Rick Brewster were the 2008 inductees into the Australian Songwriters Hall of Fame. In its fifth year, the award was to 'honour the lifetime achievements of Australia's greatest songwriters'. Held at the Canterbury Leagues Club in Sydney, it was a gala dinner attended by those in the publishing and recording industry and presented by Glenn A. Baker. On accepting the awards, Rick, John and Doc, accompanied by Paul Burton on stand-up bass, then performed acoustic renditions of a few Angels classics. Doc went over the top and leapt into the audience, which wasn't quite what was expected. But it was an honour to find themselves joining an august list which included the men who'd so profoundly influenced them, Vanda and Young.

CHAPTER SEVENTY-TWO
HEART ATTACK TOUR

The Angels were halfway through the Night Attack tour. They'd played seventeen shows through NSW and Victoria, and after a few days off in Sydney, they were booked to play the huge Revesby Workers Club and then head north. Suddenly, the sound engineer, who hadn't been well, became unable to continue and handed in his notice. Someone capable was urgently required to step in and mix the sound at the Revesby gig that very night.

Blicka was a sound engineer John and Rick had known for years, but the friendship had deepened after they'd invited him to help mix their *Shadows Fall* album in 2006. Working in the loft in John's house, the brothers had come to admire Blicka's professionalism and patience.

He was always in demand, but John rang and asked if he could jump in and do their sound that night – and the ever-accommodating Blicka obliged. He'd never mixed The Angels, but he'd been a fan for years. He knew what was required and how to go about getting it. Thrown in at the deep end, he excelled and accepted their invitation to mix for the rest of the tour.

From Sydney, the band flew north for four shows in Southern Queensland. Friday night was the big one: the Mansfield Tavern – sold out. Brisbane in November is hot, the Mansfield Tavern loaded up with 2000 excited Angels fans is boiling point.

Barricaded into his work-station among the audience crouched Blicka, operating the big sound console, sweat dripping off his chin.

> **Blicka:** A barrier had been erected a metre out from the stage front, leaving room for security staff to patrol and deal with troublemakers down the front, or rescue fainting punters. At one stage Doc was leaning across and high-fiving the hands reaching out to him. I was watching and the next thing he wasn't there. I saw tour manager Ben Turner racing across and then I heard the microphone bumping around. Next thing I heard was, 'Where's the mic? Where's the mic?'

Ben helped Doc back onstage and he did the rest of the gig. After the show Blicka saw him in the band room:

> **Blicka:** His buttock was purple and he could hardly stand up. But he just kept performing night after night. Weeks later I asked him, 'How's your bum?' And he showed me, and the bruise was still there. You wouldn't know it on stage. Even within minutes of having that fall, he was straight back into it, because the audience, the audience, the audience. That was his thing.

John had been experiencing some chest pains since a game of golf in Sydney a couple of days before.

> **John:** It was 48 degrees on stage. We came off and everyone looked like they'd had heart attacks. Doc had nearly expired because it was so fucking hot. The thing is that I was actually feeling alright, but still with these pains I'd had since leaving Sydney. The next day, we went down to the Gold Coast for a gig. I was driving. We had a black Statesman, a good rock 'n' roll car. Just Rick and me – we had our car, and the others had theirs. As the *Get F*#ked* doco showed, me being in the same car as Buzz for any length of time created explosive situations.

They played Seagulls that night, a modern air-conditioned club, and once again it sold out. The show went well, but for John the uncomfortable pains in the chest persisted.

After being prompted by several people, Ben Turner called John next morning. 'Mate, you keep talking about these chest pains,' he said.

'I've booked you a three o'clock medical centre appointment. You can go there before you drive to Toowoomba for tonight's show.'

John was having breakfast: 'Oh, okay then.'

That afternoon, feeling fine, he was in the process of dialling the centre to cancel when he had second thoughts. 'Jeez, Ben's taken the trouble to make that appointment. I should keep it.'

He turned up and the doctor took one look at him. 'You're in the wrong place,' he said. 'You get straight to the Mater Hospital. And don't drive there either.'

John drove back to the hotel and met Ben, who took him to the hospital.

> **John:** They put me onto this gurney thing, then wired me up and gave me something pink to drink. I immediately felt fantastic and called Ben. 'Come and pick me up. I feel great – it's obviously just a digestion problem.'

That's when the doctor, an American, walked in. 'Hey you, you ain't going nowhere. You're having a heart attack.'

'This is a heart attack? But I feel fantastic.'

'You're having a heart attack right now, buddy. Your enzymes are all over the place.'

John was still on the phone. 'Ben, I'm having a heart attack. Get Rick.'

Rick arrived soon after to find his worried-looking brother propped against pillows and hooked up to monitoring equipment. 'Get a pen and paper,' he grunted, 'I want to write my will.' Rick wrote down what he wanted, John signed his name, then was wheeled off to surgery.

Needless to say, the sold-out Toowoomba gig at Rumours Night Club had to be cancelled.

> **Sam Brewster:** Tom, Harry and I [John's sons] flew up to Brisbane to visit him in ICU post-surgery. I got the job of waking him up. After several attempts I called out, 'Hey, Dad, you're due onstage!', and he immediately woke up and looked like he was prepared to go on. It was quite hilarious and indicative of how much the band is his life.

Once Rick was over the shock at the turn of events and knew that his brother was out of the woods, he began tuning in to what was now uppermost in everyone's mind – there was a ten-tonne truck full of hired equipment and a lot of people waiting for leadership back at the hotel. The news was out and venues and punters were ringing, inquiring about the fate of the last seven shows of the tour: were they on . . . or off? To cancel would disappoint thousands of fans and also create a financial black hole for the band. A replacement had to be found, the truck put back on the road, and the tour set in motion again.

The show must go on.

Rick had jammed with John's sons and was always impressed with their prowess – Sam had been around the Angels' music since birth and he was now at uni studying music.

> **Sam:** I was asked if I could replace Dad for the next lot of shows. I only had a couple of days to learn the set, which was quite a challenge. Although I knew a lot of the guitar parts well, I wasn't very well rehearsed on the arrangements.

In the middle of this, David Lowy called Rick, offering to play. Not knowing how long John would be unavailable, Rick welcomed having a second player who knew the songs. It was just a question of logistics.

> **Rick:** David was only available for the last three shows, so we arranged for him to do those, and Sam to do the four earlier ones. David was understandably keen to rehearse with the band, so I sent him some live recordings and arranged two rehearsals with him back in Sydney.

Sam was thrown in at the deep end: a big pub show at Mildura, followed by a concert with Rose Tattoo at the Thebarton Theatre in Adelaide. Then The Angels drove 335 kilometres southeast down the Princes Highway to headline the Robe Craft Beer Festival. That was followed by a 500-kilometre drive to Melbourne for a raging sold-out beer-barn gig out in the suburbs.

Sam: It was a surreal experience playing in large packed venues with huge sound and lighting production. I hadn't been involved in live performance on that scale before. It was an experience I'll never forget. I think I pulled it off, but in hindsight I was naive about how those guitar parts really need to be played live, and about the role that John plays in the band.

It's the kind of thing you can only appreciate when you play in the band with him. Most people wouldn't realise how integral those parts, and the man playing them, are to The Angels sound. I've heard other great guitar players play them, and it just doesn't sound like The Angels.

Blicka knew young Sam, knew he'd cut it, but David Lowy? He'd heard he played guitar but Lowy wasn't a career musician and in amongst The Angels who he considered 'ultra-good', he was concerned about how he'd go and how he'd sound in the mix.

But Rick and the band were now relaxed.

Rick: David was a hard worker. He'd done his homework and came to rehearsals knowing the repertoire and that had put both him and us at ease. He was a good guy to work with and very respectful of the band.

On 5 December David nervously walked onto the stage at the Pier Hotel in Frankston in Melbourne's southeast, and fronted a sold-out Angels audience.

Blicka: He knew all the songs, inside out. He even played a harmony in one of the solos in 'No Secrets'. I didn't realise until I heard it coming through the desk. I went, 'Wow, this guy knows every little detail of these songs,' and he was a great backing vocalist. It was an exercise in proving that roadies shouldn't be too pre-judgemental!

The Angels' music relies on leaning on the beat. It's all about quavers and downbeats and he didn't rob that pulsing energy in any way by not being experienced. He just gave it that same push. Now John Brewster is a unique, one-of-a-kind musician, and David Lowy is no John Brewster, but considering who he is and what he does in his daily life, he did an excellent job of covering the bases while John was hospitalised.

2008 wound up with TOAB playing the Christmas party for Henry Davis York, the lawyers who'd gone in to bat for them in their legal battle with the Doc/Eccles forces during the previous few years. In return, the law firm deducted one third of the band's horrendously large account with them.

> **Rick:** It was a seven-piece band! We set up two drum kits and both Buzz and John's son Tom played. John's other sons, Sam and Harry, played guitar and Sam's friend Nick Norton fronted the band and did an amazing job. Some time later we got an email from the lawyers to say they were prepared to wipe the slate clean. it was a very generous offer which we gratefully accepted.

CHAPTER SEVENTY-THREE
CHRIS BAILEY FRIDAY

The Angels' first gig of 2009 was for the St Kilda Street Festival in front of tens of thousands on Sunday 8 February. It was a 'Max Sessions' promotion and after watching the *No Way Get F**cked* doco, they made sure they had a cameraman in the car that was carrying Doc. If they were hoping for hostilities – well, that wasn't going to happen with mild-mannered Chris Bailey beside him. What they filmed was two frustrated old rockers calling directions from their phone's GPS and going round in circles. Instead of the seven-kilometre drive from the city to St Kilda taking fifteen minutes, it took an hour.

Bushfires had swept the state the previous day, resulting in 173 dead and over two thousand homes lost. The papers were calling it Black Saturday. Under dark smoke clouds they came out to a roaring welcome. They kicked off by blasting into 'After The Rain', written by John in the Car-O-Tel across the road.

Doc had lost a bit of weight and the puffiness evident during the last tour had receded.

> **Blicka:** Standing at the front-of-house desk doing thousands of shows over the years, I'd got a pretty good grasp of the difference between a good singer and a great entertainer. And I don't think people in the band sometimes noticed how

good Doc was because they were concentrating on their instruments, but he'd be working an audience and he could read an audience. He knew when he had to project or when to pull back and let the song and the guitarists do the work. He was older by the time I worked for them, but he still put in a big amount of energy.

Two weeks later they flew into Adelaide for a Day On The Green show at the prestigious Annie's Lane vineyards in the Clare Valley, two hours north of the city. After arriving at the airport, the band were signing for their two cars while the crew loaded the stage gear into a Tarago. As Blicka was getting into the driver's seat, Doc strolled over and asked if there was room for him.

Blicka: He sometimes took to hanging out with us to get away from the day-to-day band norm. We got into some great conversations on that drive about the early days with the jug band when they were all sharing houses in Adelaide and cooking bacon and eggs together. He nearly electrocuted Rick when he was using a drill on the roof. He enjoyed talking about those days.

On Anzac Day, there was an afternoon show at the Enmore Theatre, featuring Rose Tattoo and The Screaming Jets and headlined by The Angels. Billed as The Australian Monsters Of Rock it was a sell-out and possibly the loudest concert ever held there.

Rick watched the Jets from the wings. They'd supported The Angels many times across the years, but at this show he was particularly impressed with Dave Gleeson's maturity as a singer and performer. He'd come a long way from the young crazy he'd been fifteen years back.

The internet was exploding and a social network called Facebook was rapidly catching on, but with the drama The Angels had put themselves through, they hadn't kept pace with the times. With an eye on building their fan-base email listings, Dave Edwards came up with a tour concept and Cat had another presser to send:

> The Angels By Request Tour gives fans the unique experience of being able to choose the songs The Angels perform. By logging onto www.theangelsbyrequest.com fans get to choose their favourite fifteen songs from the Angels catalogue. Their votes along with thousands of others from around Australia will be tallied up and the top songs chosen will comprise The Ultimate Angels Set List. A fan that chooses the correct set list will win the Ultimate Angels Fan Pack.

The concept worked. With the email list greatly expanded and the song list settled, the tour got underway in July. Once again, Blicka was hired to operate the front-of-house desk. But Blicka was more than a hired soundman. He'd been friends with John, Rick and their families for years. He was a trusted mate and they loved having him along on these tours.

> **Blicka:** If everyone's really professional and knows their craft, you can have a fun day at work, and it's what I like about this industry – it's outcome based. As long as you're doing your job properly and you're not offending people, you can laugh, and even be a little arrogant.

One night he and Ben Turner were talking about Chris – how he came along to soundchecks and quietly did his thing while the others bickered and bitched around him as they adjusted amps, microphones and foldback speakers. He'd taken a buffeting recently so they resolved to personally look after him the next night, a Friday.

> **Blicka:** He arrived and we went, 'Let me carry your bass in, Chris – we'll put your leads on stage.' Then we got his drinks and he's, 'Oh, thanks, guys.' You know, he's a gentleman and very polite.

But then the prank streak kicked in. The crew decided that next Friday he'd get the royal treatment again, but through the week they'd be offhand with him and let him sort things out himself. They could see a slightly bewildered look on his face as they fussed around with the others, and did only the basics in his area.

Next Friday arrived and it was 'Oh hi, Chris, how are you going? Can we grab your bass?' and they got him a drink. Chris had been around road crews long enough to suddenly sense that something was up. He got wary, expecting something to happen, but when it didn't he gradually relaxed, shrugged and got on with his preparations.

Rick heard about the ruse and the following Friday sent him a text: 'Good morning, Chris, how are you today? Everything alright?'

Chris texted back: 'Why are you asking? You've never asked if I'm okay before.'

> **Blicka:** It became known secretly as 'Chris Bailey Friday'. It came from the heart. He really deserved being treated like royalty because he never asked for much . . .

The tour finally arrived at the sprawling Doncaster Hotel in suburban Melbourne for the last performance. While the band was onstage a party was hurriedly set up. Girlfriends and crew converted the dressing-room into a Chris Bailey temple, with specially printed posters based on *Thank God It's Friday* movie posters. There were streamers, blow-up guitars and a cake emblazoned 'Chris Bailey Friday' and a big card signed by the whole entourage.

After the encore the wrung-out troubadours staggered in and a stunned Chris Bailey looked around and spluttered, 'What's going on?'

> **Blicka:** That's when he realised it was Fridays. He was a man not to make a big deal of himself. But to his credit, he came to the floor and made a speech and thanked everyone for doing it. And it was a whole lot of fun. It's part of taking away the boredom of being on the road, because it can be pretty mundane some days. And I couldn't think of a musician more deserving of having his own day of the week.

CHAPTER SEVENTY-FOUR
PART OF THE CULTURAL HISTORY

The Angels took a break but there was no let-up for the Brewster Brothers, who went straight out on their own tour of small venues, travelling light around the country as a trio with Paul Burton, their biggest piece of luggage being Paul's full-size orchestral bass guitar.

Their tour finished up on 8 November with a special concert at a well-attended Basement show in Sydney. It was John's sixtieth birthday and a couple of the Moonshine members flew in from Adelaide. With Burton on bass and Doc joining in, they opened the show with a set of Moonshine favourites. Whatever enmity there may have been between Doc and the brothers, there was no sign of it that night as Doc looked approvingly on during the Brewster Brothers' set.

When the audience called them back for an encore, they walked out with John's sons Sam and Harry on guitars and third son Tom slipped behind the drums. They then called up a grinning Doc and ripped straight into a clutch of Angels songs that had the entire place up and dancing the night away.

The Angels hit the road again in November and December. The differences and disagreements between some members had never been fully resolved and Blicka found himself caught up in constant undercurrents.

Blicka: I'd known Buzz for quite some time, but I was also close to the Brewsters, and I'd known Cat for years and I got on well with Chris and Doc. So I'd get to hear everyone's opinion from different points of view about who owned The Angels' name and so on. At one stage Buzz tried talking to me about it and I told him I didn't want to know. He'd gone past trying to get me onside – he just wanted someone to talk to about it.

The ever-patient Blicka rolled a joint and told Buzz how he believed the band was bigger than the individuals and the music was larger than the band. He was convinced that a timeline could be drawn: the depression, the war, the fifties, baby boomers. The pub music scene in the sixties, seventies and eighties was an era in the country's social and cultural history, and he saw The Angels as very much a part of it.

Blicka: We had these conversations and I'm not saying he was the only one – others got into my ear and I told them not to, but they did anyway. They'd explain why this stuff in the band was happening, and I'd tell them I didn't want to know. I found myself coming up with this expression that basically they were like a five-way divorce trying to remarry.

I'd say it's a testament to them all that they could supersede that and still go on stage, because it's hard enough for two people to get divorced and become remarried. I think it showed their strength and fortitude as people and their belief in wanting to play their music again. Audiences loved it but those guys went through the fire and ice of their situation to get up and do their performances.

One source of tension was Doc's travelling requirements. The singer decided that if the drive between country gigs was longer than an hour and a half, he wanted either a commercial flight or a small plane, because he claimed to be having trouble with his back sitting in the Tarago.

John: A small plane? They're like a little cigar and you're all cramped up and we're like, 'But Doc, you're in a Tarago with all this leg room.' 'Yes, but it's the bumps. They upset my back.' 'What about the turbulence?' But no, you couldn't use a logical argument. One time, we had some country gigs and Doc, Buzz and Chris were picked up in a small plane and flown to the next town. We beat them in the car by an hour.

Rick: It cost a fortune, and of course we're all having to wear that, so the whole thing was getting sillier and sillier.

With The Angels tour completed and band off the road until June, apart from a special show in April, Rick and John locked in an extensive string of Brewster Brothers dates, culminating in several appearances during the three-day Port Fairy Folk Festival in Victoria over Easter.

Cat: When they played there in '07, it was to a few hundred. This time they started off in a small marquee, and by the last day their show had been transferred to the largest marquee where they played to over 3000. They were the livewire of the festival. Everybody was like, 'Have you seen the Brewster Brothers? Have you seen them?' It was awesome.

Then it came time to focus their sights and creative spirits on what promised to be one of the highpoints of their career, where their music shook hands with those of their immediate ancestors.

CHAPTER SEVENTY-FIVE
SYMPHONY OF ANGELS

On 17 April The Angels were scheduled to perform the 'Symphony Of Angels' at the Adelaide Festival Theatre with a forty-piece orchestra. Conducted by Rob John, it would be one of the highlight performances of the band's career. The press release put out by the event's coordinator Rob Pippan was the first indication to Angels fans of what was afoot. This was highbrow stuff for the long-term champions of Aussie pub rock and to many it might have been an incomprehensible concept. But for John and Rick, it marked a full circle back to where it had all begun.

> Rick: We grew up surrounded by classical music. Our father and both his parents were classical musicians – performing, composing, teaching, conducting. Those early influences had remained with John and me right throughout our careers.

Rehearsals were to be held with the orchestra the day before the concert. The music scores had been written by Rob John – and a few by his associate for the project, Jamie Messenger. Orchestral demos of songs were constantly shuffled back and forth to Rick and John to make suggestions for arrangement and melody. In rehearsals the biggest hurdle was to make sure the band played to the same arrangements they'd signed off on for the orchestra. There was no room for error as they played exactly to the charts they were given.

That night the band was officially greeted by Adelaide Lord Mayor Michael Harbison at a jam-packed civic reception welcoming them back to Adelaide. The last time an Adelaide mayor had given such a reception for a band was for The Beatles in '64.

> **Cat:** I'd been talking to Doc about ideas to publicise the concert and he mentioned the keys to the city, which The Beatles received when they went to Adelaide. He said he'd always wanted the same for The Angels so I wrote to the lord mayor's office and it went from there.

A minor earthquake shuddered the floor and rattled the windows during the proceedings. Few noticed, but those who did joked that it was a harbinger for what was about to happen next night when the show began.

> **Cat:** It was roll out the red carpet and it was the mayor with all his regalia. When The Beatles did it, the whole city had stopped, madness. It wasn't quite the same for The Angels, but it was an absolute honour because they'd never done it for another band since then.

Next afternoon the dress rehearsal got underway.

> **John:** No matter who you are, you rehearse with the orchestra the day before, and then you have a dress rehearsal just before the show. The band has to work in with the orchestra, who have their charts, and the conductor takes control and conducts the whole thing. Orchestral musicians don't come up with ideas, or change anything – they play precisely to the scored arrangements. But now Buzz and Doc complained that we should have had more rehearsals with the orchestra. What we actually needed was more band rehearsals and that hadn't happened.

But the audience weren't concerned about that. The tickets were a hot item in Adelaide and the show quickly sold out. By 8 pm on Saturday night, 1900 highly expectant fans were seated and ready.

The orchestra opened with the 'Symphony Of Angels Overture', a piece taken from the Symphony 'Australia Felix' written nearly 100 years previously by conductor/composer Hooper Brewster-Jones, grandfather of John and Rick. The band then walked on to a standing ovation to perform a set-list from rock heaven. They were all dressed for the occasion, including Rick in a formal-style leather suit and tails.

As the band kicked in with the orchestra on 'After The Rain', a thought flashed through John's mind: *This one's for Dad, Gran and grandfather 'Bopo'*.

With songs like 'Straightjacket', 'Fashion And Fame', 'Skid Row', 'After Dark', 'Face The Day', 'Take A Long Line' and 'Marseilles', they unleashed the second earthquake in Adelaide that weekend and finished the first half with one of Rick's finest compositions, the dark 'Outcast', now transformed into a classical masterpiece.

The second half began with 'Love Takes Care' and 'Be With You', with John on acoustic, Doc on National steel resonator guitar and Rick at the grand piano. Then Rick moved to a beautiful old Hammond B3 organ for the haunting 'Dawn Is Breaking', with the orchestra billowing up beneath.

> **John:** Rick and I had such a rich heritage of classical music that when we came up with chord progressions and solos for songs like 'Take A Long Line', I always heard a classical element in there. It was almost like Rick was playing the melodies on a violin. When we recorded 'Mr Damage', we'd hum orchestral parts to the song.

The audience, many of whom had flown in from interstate for the occasion, loved it. But what was evident to Rick, John and the rest of the band was Doc forgetting words and singing out of tune. The show was recorded on full multitrack in the expectation of having a truly remarkable album, *A Symphony Of Angels*, but Doc's vocals rendered it unusable. A tragedy, as it would have been the final album with Doc singing for The Angels and a brilliant bookend to his legacy.

CHAPTER SEVENTY-SIX
REBUILDING

A band meeting was called at David Edwards' office in early September. The situation among the members was becoming ever more problematic and things needed to be thrashed out.

It was at this meeting Doc made the announcement that he would no longer be available for Angels gigs after October, ' . . . unless special gigs come up, which I will consider on an individual basis'.

A shocked Edwards pointed out that Harbour had already started working on the Dark Room tour for November. Doc said he'd want to see the dates before confirming he'd do them. 'And I'm not interested in recording any more Angels albums. I'm going to do a solo album, and I'm going to be touring the world. I'll be playing in China, Japan, England, Europe and America.'

> **John:** Rick and I glanced at each other: 'Who's he kidding?' We knew how hard it had been to establish the Brewster Brothers. I think Alan Niven may have been talking to him – he'd given us exactly the same spiel a few years before when he was writing lyrics for *Shadows Fall*.

Chris Bailey listened to all this with rising consternation. 'What about us guys?'

'What about you?'

'Well, how am I going to feed my little boy?'

'I don't care.'

The room went still for a minute until Chris tried another one. 'Why can't you have a solo career and do The Angels as well – like Buzz and I do with GANGgajang and John and Rick with the Brewster Brothers?'

'Because I can't be seen to be singing in The Angels if I'm doing a solo career.'

John: I thought, 'Is this a joke?' To do a solo career you've got to come up with something new. New songs, new album. That's what we did with the Brewster Brothers. Look at Jimmy Barnes, Mark Seymour, James Reyne. But for Doc it was a 'Don't you know who I am?' kinda thing. His response to Chris – 'I don't care' – was really offensive because a band is like a team – you look after each other, even if you have clashes. And the funny thing is we weren't having clashes with Doc.

What was going on with him was his own problem. He wanted to do this thing, I think he was put up to it by people around him: 'You don't need a band.' Pointing at people like Jimmy. 'You can hire the musicians, make most of the money.' I know people had said that to him. 'You don't need the rest of the guys in the band – *you* are The Angels.'

A few weeks later Doc flatly refused to do a contracted concert for the Queensland Performing Arts Centre (QPAC) at their 1800-capacity Concert Hall in Brisbane. When a fuming Edwards demanded an explanation, Doc told him that it clashed with a solo gig an agent had booked for him. The QPAC concert was to have been a repeat of Adelaide's 'Symphony Of Angels', but this time with the Queensland Symphony Orchestra. After much argument and embarrassment, it was cancelled until another date could be arranged.

However, shortly after, an agent claiming to represent Doc wrote to QPAC offering Doc Neeson, presumably with a band of hired musicians, to do the show. QPAC's management copied the email from Doc's agent to Tony Grace. Exasperated, Tony sent it on to Edwards and the band. The following week a letter arrived from QPAC advising that what Doc and his agent had attempted to do was unethical, they didn't operate that way, and wouldn't be doing business with Mr Neeson in the future.

While Doc vehemently denied any knowledge of his agent's activities, a trail of emails soon emerged revealing otherwise, culminating in a retraction and apology from Doc. However, similar situations began to surface elsewhere and tensions escalated between Doc and Edwards, still working under the umbrella of David Lowy's Spitfire Productions.

> **Rick:** The QPAC drama was when the shit really hit the fan. Now Doc was undermining The Angels' operations and we began to seriously think about replacing him with someone else. Doc's agent trying to steal the QPAC gig was a despicable and ultimately stupid act. They didn't have any orchestral scores. Doc's agent made their offer to QPAC as if the Symphony Of Angels was their concept and that they'd organised the Adelaide concert.

Things then quietened down enough for Doc to confirm that he'd honour four contracted dates in Melbourne at the end of November, but he rejected a fifth one that had been offered to the band – to headline the huge Queenscliff Festival in Victoria – because he had a solo gig that night at Lizotte's Restaurant in Gosford. Buzz was too busy to do any of them.

On 8 January 2011, Doc fronted with The Angels for the last time at the Summernats, a big muscle-car event in Canberra. Again, Buzz was busy so John's son Tom played drums. After that, Doc sent an email to David Edwards announcing that he wouldn't be available for any more Angels dates 'for at least six months and up to three years' while he concentrated on his solo career.

> **Tony Grace:** Rick and John came to see me. They said Doc had left with no promise of return. He didn't want to record with The Angels anymore – and they couldn't work with Buzz. It was a mess. John was upset and Rick doesn't get rattled, but let me tell you, he was rattled. They had mortgages like everyone and Rick had a young family. Chris wasn't there but he had a three-year-old son.

All they wanted to do was work – a very Australian thing. They didn't want a sugar-daddy, they didn't want handouts. They wanted to work for a living and what they knew best was to play guitar. I wanted to show some leadership, give them confidence.

I said, 'Guys, it's all about the guitars. We'll put it together. Listen to your songs, listen to the music you created. Timeless. We'll rebuild this.' And they go, 'Do you think so?' I said, 'Absolutely.' From there we threw a few names [for a singer] around and Rick mentioned Dave. I didn't want to crush him, but I thought there was no chance that's going to happen.

Greatly buoyed, the Brewsters met with Marcus Ahern, their legal adviser. He looked at the deed the five had signed to see what they'd agreed to do. He pointed out that it didn't even discuss the name 'The Angels' – it was more about how they should work together and the distribution of royalties. He listed a number of ways in which Doc and Buzz had repudiated the deed, centred around their refusals to come to work. The thrust was that each signatory had committed to continue the business of The Angels, and they had both continually failed to honour that commitment.

Marcus sent Doc and Buzz letters explaining that the deed made it clear that their responsibilities were to continue the business of The Angels. If they continued to refuse to work with the band, the remaining members had the right to replace them. It launched a torrent of legal letters back and forth.

Rick: All of them read like Buzz had dictated them. They went through five lawyers, one after the next, and I don't think Doc ever knew much of what was really going on.

Meanwhile offers for gigs kept coming in.

John: Around late February, after Doc had knocked back more future shows with the band, and after further discussions with Marcus, I called Doc and said, 'Look, I'm not going to debate with you what you're doing. We're not married. You're free to leave the band if that's what you want.'

I said something about how Rick and I knew what it was like to go building a career outside The Angels. It's not easy. I said, 'I guess you must have written some new songs,' and he said, 'No, but I'm going to be.' I said, 'Okay, that's your business, but our business is the band. We're not going to leave it in limbo. We need to continue, so we've had legal advice and that advice is that we can replace you. I'm just letting you know that we're going to replace you if you don't want to work with us.' Doc said, 'Oh, well, you can't do that.' I said, 'I'm not going to argue with you, Doc. Somebody else will take up the argument. We'll have our lawyer write to you or to your lawyer and then you can discuss it with our lawyer, but that's what we're going to do.' He said, 'Okay, fair enough,' and then we hung up.

In May Dave Gleeson heard the Brewster Brothers were playing a restaurant/acoustic venue in the Adelaide Hills not far from him.

Dave: I went along and talked with the boys between sets and John said, 'What Angels songs do you know?' I said, 'All of them,' because I was a mad Angels fan, always was, probably up to *Howling*. So I accepted their offer to get up and I did four or five songs with them.

With Dave out front, the energy leapt. The response was immediate, with the audience and staff on their feet and dancing. John looked over at a grinning Rick and they just nodded.

A few days later John called Dave and told him that Doc was no longer in the band. They had some demos they wanted to do: would he like to sing on them?

Dave: I was a bit hesitant because of my reverence for Doc, but at that time it wasn't about The Angels, it was just about some new songs they'd been writing. I was off the road with the Jets so, yeah, I said I'd have a crack at it.

It wasn't how John saw it. Excitement got the better of him and he called Rick. 'We've got a singer!' Then he called Chris Bailey. He didn't call Buzz because Buzz had announced that if Doc wasn't in the band, nor was he. *That's fine*, John thought, *see you later, Buzz. No problem.*

John didn't initially let management know. That would be dealt with later, after he'd seen how the sessions with Dave went. He called Philip Mortlock at Alberts and explained the situation. The Angels wanted some studio time to record four tracks. Philip said come on in.

Multi-instrumentalist Nick Norton had been working as a drummer/sideman for the Brewster Brothers at their dinner shows, fitting right in and obviously enjoying himself. One night John discreetly mentioned that there might be a new version of The Angels. He sounded him out and got an enthusiastic response.

> **Nick:** Sure enough, the call came a couple of months later and in May we were in the studio putting a few things down with Dave Gleeson singing.

By the time Gleeson showed up, the rest had made a start on recording the tracks. Listening to the play-back, he could barely contain his enthusiasm and immediately got to work getting a feel for the lyrics and the music. During the next two days his vocals were laid down in an atmosphere he would later describe in interviews as: 'Just a bunch of blokes doing stuff in the studio and I got to know them during that time'.

> **John:** We recorded 'Waiting For The Sun' as the lead track and it was amazing right off the bat. There was an undeniable chemistry, that magic that either happens or not, despite how good the players are. It was great to see how excited Chris Bailey was. He was always wanting us to write and record new material.

Tony Grace liked to keep a finger on the pulse of his top bands and dropped in. He'd heard a rumour that the Screaming Jets singer was holed up in Alberts with the Brewsters, Bailey and Nick Norton.

> **Tony Grace:** I saw with my own eyes and there was Dave Gleeson. You couldn't write a better script. That was the beginning of a whole new cycle. Now I held

> in high regard what Doc did in his generation – he was amongst the last of the Mohicans. But Dave Gleeson, he was the best of the best in the current crop. He is what rock 'n' roll and Australian pub rock stands for.

John and Rick took the next step and formally asked Dave to join the band. There was no hesitation: 'Mate, it would be an honour!'

David Edwards was informed that he had a band again. Still unsure of their legal right to call themselves 'The Angels', they released the EP, now titled *Waiting For The Sun*, under the name 'Rick Brewster's Angels'. The Triple M network gave 'Waiting For The Sun' an airing, and although not enough to give it chart action it did give the band's diehards a clear message that, for better or worse, The Angels were now moving into a new era.

CHAPTER SEVENTY-SEVEN
THE DEED

Tony Grace now jumped in and things began to hum. Two warm-up gigs were arranged, one on 30 June at the rough and tumble Annandale in Sydney and next night in Adelaide at the Norwood.

Rick: Edwards said, 'You can't have Nick Norton play Adelaide. You'll have to get another drummer, we're not flying Norton to Adelaide.' That's when the bells really started ringing. Fucking hell, he wants to tell us who we can and can't have in the band. We hit the roof. Needless to say we played with Nick on the drums.

John: Both places were packed, the punters loved it, we loved it. 'Oh fuck, let's go!' And we went, 'You know what? We've got an EP, everyone's buying it, but we have to do an album straight away.' We didn't want Dave to be seen as purely taking over as the singer. We wanted our own validity with the new line-up.

Within three months of doing the EP, the band were in Japan playing at Mate Fest. An Australian owned a resort and the gig was originally for his fiftieth birthday, but after the tsunami that devastated Fukushima, he turned it into a benefit to help the locals. Sparing no expense, he booked his favourite Aussie heroes, Barnesy, Angels and Kevin 'Bloody' Wilson.

Dave: We went over and did this outdoor festival at a place called Hakuba – an amazing experience. It was summer in this beautiful, mountainous country. That was my first real foray with The Angels – going to Japan. Rock on!

John, Rick and Chris had been gung-ho to record a new album since the 'original' band had reformed. They had songs and now they had two new members who were as keen as they were. At the end of October the five of them walked into Alberts studios and began the creative process that would produce the first Angels album featuring Dave Gleeson. Their last album with Doc, *Skin And Bone*, had taken five years to do. This one, *Take It To The Streets*, would take three weeks.

Dave: John and Rick were so grateful just to be back in the studio creating and doing stuff. Nick had some great songs and I gave Rick some words that he was inspired by and wrote songs around them, and that was a process that I had never been involved in before.

In November the band flew to Perth for four big pub gigs, then on to Adelaide, back to New South Wales, then down to Victoria, finishing up on the Gold Coast in Queensland prior to Christmas. Cat pumped out the publicity and much was written in the press, much was said on air and the punters knew there was a changing of the guard. Dave was a star in his own right as front-man for the Screaming Jets, so he pulled Jets punters to check him out at his new workplace, and The Angels had their loyal fans – but not everyone was happy. There were people at the Governor Hindmarsh in Adelaide discussing the upcoming show with one of the roadies: 'This is fucked, Doc's not in the fucking band, I'm not going to like this Dave Gleeson.' Then, by the end of the night, they were raving.

John: In Melbourne there was this couple determined to put shit on us. They stood in front of me and Chris, going, 'Fuck you!', and they're pointing at Dave – 'Fuck him!' – and pointing thumbs down. As the show went on, this couple, a bit feral, started pointing less at Dave and being less angry and started singing the songs. Then they disappeared and I went into Chris's ear,

> 'Thank the fuck they've gone.' All of a sudden they're back in front of us again, they'd put a Jim Beam and Coke can in front of me, one in front of Chris, and pointed at Dave, and then went 'YEAH!'

But the band loved him right from the start. They loved his whole approach – the mixture of dramatic actor mixed with that of a clown. And the guy could belt it out, sing in tune, he was never breathless, remembered the words, was high energy – and offstage he was easy-going and affable. What was there not to like?

A venue manager came backstage and handed John a DVD of their performance one night. Concentrating on his guitar parts and facing the audience singing backing vocals gave him little time to take in what Dave was doing, although he could see the reactions of the audience. But when he watched Dave projected onto a large TV screen later, he muttered 'Wow!' to himself.

The other new recruit to the band was also shining. Not only was Nick winning high praise from his rhythm-section partner Chris Bailey, but he had a particularly fine voice which enriched the harmonies.

> Nick: When they gave me the drumming gig, I think they liked the idea of a younger musician with no ego, no set way of doing things, who was a songwriter and approached the music like a guitarist/vocalist. They knew it wouldn't take me long to learn to be a real rock drummer. That's exactly what I had to do. I thought I would stroll on in, having played so many types of music before. But authentic rock drumming is a different discipline, and it has to be learnt, and sweated into the DNA.

But while the band was busy re-establishing themselves on stage and in the studio, relations with their manager were deteriorating. Edwards was well versed in the art of divide and rule.

> John: Rather than having a go at Chris personally, he'd say 'You tell that Bailey . . .' or 'I want you to write to Dave's wife, Katie, and tell her . . .' – that sort of stuff. He was always trying to get one person to attack another.

Edwards refused to allow them to book their own air fares, or to let them cast around and hire their own production outfits. He would hire a production company to do an entire tour, instead of using the many excellent state-based companies, which was now the industry norm. It resulted in huge fuel bills and crew accommodation expenses – often single rooms for each roadie, sometimes seven nights a week.

> **John:** The days of punters coming out to pub and club shows during the week are over. We're mainly working weekends. And we're paying for it, not Edwards. And there were so many other things – it was outrageous.

Things got worse. Edwards relocated to Singapore, leaving the band in the hands of a young kid who was hopelessly out of his depth.

One morning Edwards called from Singapore, saying, 'I hear you've gone behind my back and spoken to Lowy.'

> **John:** Right. We always had an open and friendly relationship with David Lowy; in fact, we were often encouraged to call him by none other than David Edwards. So now Edwards comes back and says, 'You do anything like that again, you'll find yourself in court.' It was extremely aggressive and threatening. That was it for us. We called David Lowy again and he said, 'You need to take control of your own business.'

Rick, John and Chris composed an email advising Edwards his services were terminated forthwith, and clicked 'send'. There was a scramble to change the password for the band's website with its precious email list, but they were too slow to secure their Facebook site and, to their chagrin, Edwards took control of it.

> **Rick:** He never called us after we sacked him. He never communicated with us again.

It was 30 April 2012. For the first time since John had rung Woodruff in Adelaide in 1978, suggesting he get back to Sydney because his band was taking off and they could afford to pay him, John and Rick were back in control of the band they'd founded in 1970.

While Rick and John had spent the previous nine months rebuilding the band from the ground up – new singer, drummer, album and intensive touring – Doc was working the pub circuit in his new guise as Doc Neeson, but with a backing band. His repertoire was mostly Angels songs sprinkled with a few covers such as John Lennon's 'Working Class Hero'. The solo album he'd talked about recording hadn't eventuated and his ambitions for a new career appeared to have stagnated.

> **Rick:** Despite the fact that Edwards had constantly made loud and disparaging remarks about Doc from the time he'd stopped working in The Angels, he now joined up with Doc and Buzz and formed an opposition band with Bob Spencer, James Morley and Jim Hilbun, calling it The Angels 100%. This with Doc who'd said in interviews that he didn't want to be known as 'Doc the Angel'.

It was clear that a vengeful Edwards was planning to use the Angels 100% band to attack them and create as much mischief as possible, but as it happened The Angels 100% only did one gig – in West Australia for a mining company. However, the barrage of legal mail just intensified.

> **John:** There was a series of letters from Buzz's lawyers sent to me, Rick, Chris, Liberation Records, Harbour and Mick Newton [organiser of Day On The Green]. At one stage Mick Newton withdrew his offer of ten Day On The Green shows. Buzz's lawyer also wrote to the Triple M network, saying they couldn't play any songs by the new line-up. Triple M's lawyers wrote a terse reply, stating, 'No one tells us what we can and can't play on our radio station.' In the end all the letters achieved was to garner more support from the leaders of the Australian music industry for us.

John was at home when the Day On The Green shows were pulled. His wife Sue said, 'This is ridiculous, call Michael Gudinski, he's a director of the company that runs Day On The Green.' John was hesitant:

'He's a friend, but I haven't spoken to him for years.' She said, 'That doesn't matter. He's a friend, call him.'

He rang and spoke to Gudinski's PA, who said she'd let him know that he'd called. With Gudinski's life in a permanent state of high activity, John didn't expect to hear back any time soon, if ever, but next morning the phone rang.

> **John:** It was Michael. He asked me, 'What's the story? Who's behind all this shit?' I said, 'It's Bidstrup.' He said, 'Say no more – I get it.' Then he said, 'Well, let me tell you, you're reinstated in all the Day On The Green shows. Everything goes ahead.' He said, 'Sue' – his wife is Sue – 'Sue and I are both very concerned about you and Rick, what you've been going through. You guys and Chris have done the right thing putting Dave Gleeson in the band. It's a great idea and I'm right behind it. We all know about Doc – it's a shame, but we know about Doc.' He said, 'Anyone that comes after you guys is coming after me.'

In August 2012 a legal letter was sent to Graham Bidstrup and Bernard Neeson, stating that as they had declined to come to work for The Angels for some time now, and as Doc had confirmed in writing that he wasn't available for the foreseeable future, their actions had amounted to a repudiation of the deed and so the three remaining signatories were terminating said deed. When no response was received, the deed then became legally terminated.

Take It To The Streets was released on Liberation seventeen days later and debuted at #24 on the ARIA charts.

CHAPTER SEVENTY-EIGHT
BENEFIT CONCERTS

When The Angels were touring with Chris in 2008–09, he'd occasionally go to hospital to have injections. 'Eventually I'm going to have to have major surgery,' he'd tell them, 'because the radiation from the first bout of cancer has made my jawbones brittle. Little slivers of bone break off and puncture the tissue and start infections.'

In early August 2012 an operation was performed to rebuild his jaw by taking bone from his hip and flesh from his calf. It was major surgery with a long recuperation period and high hopes for a full recovery. There was a small tumour on his jawbone too, which was removed. His doctor gave him reasonable hope for recovery there as well. Sam Brewster was brought into the band prior to the operation as temporary replacement.

> Sam: Nick Norton and I visited him after the operation. He was recovering and was fully expecting to return to work.

On Saturday night, 22 September, the band was to play to a sold-out Bridge Hotel in Sydney. During the afternoon, as they were kicking into their soundcheck, Rick looked up and peered through the empty, dim room. Pushing through the swing doors and shuffling across the threadbare carpet came Chris Bailey on crutches, accompanied by wife

Josie and little Ollie. A surprise visit. John asked if he'd come back for the show and get up for a song or two. He said he'd see what he could do. That night the crew helped him onstage to a huge welcome from the audience. Rather than sit in a chair, Chris, forever the consummate professional, bravely stood and delivered a typically great bass part for 'Devil's Gate' and 'Be With You'.

A couple of weeks later, on Saturday 6 October, the band played a private birthday party for their solicitor Marcus Ahern's brother, Dan, once more at the Bridge Hotel. To everyone's surprise Chris turned up again and played three or four songs. It was a great night that turned out to be Chris's last performance with the band.

Rick: Sam was filling in until Chris got well, and for a long time that was what we all thought. But it gradually became apparent that as far as gigging went, he was never going to come back on the road.

In January 2013, The Angels returned to Alberts and began preliminary work on a new album. Since *Take It To The Streets*, they'd been continually touring and new songs had come to life as they jammed at soundchecks, wrote lyrics in hotel rooms and discussed ideas in the Tarago while it hummed along.

Although Chris wasn't well, he rang John and they discussed whether he might be up for a session or two in the studio.

Sam: He agreed to come in, and I'd be there for when he needed to leave or needed a break.

Once again Chris arrived with Josie and Ollie. He shuffled in, struggled into a chair and tuned his bass while the others attended to their instruments. They discussed each song and tossed about suggestions as they picked through the melodies: 'What ideas do you have for this one?' It was the way they'd always worked in the studio and over the next two or three days Chris played on five songs, all of which landed on the album. These included Rick's reflective 'No Rhyme Nor Reason', largely written about Chris and his illness – although he wasn't aware of it – the final lyrics eventually penned after his passing.

Rick's majestic guitar work weaves though the melancholy as a paean to a fallen comrade.

Nick Norton would later recall, in the album's liner notes he wrote, that Chris 'learnt the arrangements in fifteen minutes flat, then nailed them first take'. 'He had a certain clarity and focus, was very relaxed and just did it . . . I think it was important to him to show up and be part of it. As sick as he was, he did such an effective job.'

But the effort drained him and over the next few sessions Sam stepped in and played on the rest of the tracks.

Cat was at a friend's place on Christmas night when she got a call from Doc's partner, Annie. Doc had felt sick all day and he'd been admitted to hospital. Cat was surprised at her sense of foreboding, how she became unreasonably upset at the news. She visited him over the following days while he was kept under observation and underwent tests. On 4 January, his birthday, she took in a bowl of fruit, a bunch of flowers and a card.

> **Cat:** He handed me a writing pad and I started reading it, thinking these are probably lyrics to a song. Then I read the word 'terminal' and that's when I realised, 'He's written down what the doctor told him.' I just stood there with my mouth open. He said, 'Say something.' That's the first time in my life I've opened my mouth and nothing came out. Eventually I was like, 'This obviously isn't lyrics to a song.'

On 10 January 2013 Cat released a statement announcing that Doc had been diagnosed with an aggressive brain tumour that would require immediate intensive radiation and chemotherapy treatment.

John and Rick Brewster promptly followed up with their own statement: 'Our thoughts are with Doc, his family and others close to him, and we wish him a speedy and complete recovery.'

With medical bills looming and no touring for a while, Cat got to thinking: 'I had this bright idea of organising a benefit to raise some money for him.'

*

On a Saturday morning towards the end of January, Chris Bailey called John.

> **John:** I was at the markets, and he said, 'John, I'm fucked.' I said, 'What do you mean?' He said he had a lump, a tumour on his soft palate, the roof of the mouth. He said, 'I'm fucked.' It was a really hard call.

John found a private place and slumped down, trying to get a handle on Chris's calm voice telling him he was a dying man, that he had three months at the most. He told John he was passing the baton onto Sam, who he considered to be a great player and more than worthy of playing in the band.

> **John:** I managed to pull myself together and said we'd do a benefit concert. It had just been announced about Doc's brain tumour and Chris said, 'Don't worry about me. I own my own house, just worry about Doc.' I said, 'No, you've got a kid.' He said, 'Yeah. Good point.' That's where it started and then it developed from there.

> **Rick:** I called Chris after John gave me the news and he told me the same thing. It was a very sad call. He was still feeling uncomfortable about the idea of a benefit and brought up Doc's situation. Typical Chris, always put others before himself. I told him not to worry, that Cat was organising a concert for Doc. It was little Ollie who would benefit from the concert John was organising in Adelaide.

Meanwhile, Cat's idea for Doc's benefit concert was rapidly developing into an all-consuming project. With the help of a small group of friends and associates, she'd set about pulling together the show. The Enmore Theatre donated the night of 15 April and she began contacting artists and inviting them to play.

> **John:** It's hard to talk about that concert. When Rick and I heard Doc had the brain tumour, we spoke to David Lowy – we were the first to put our hands

up. We said, 'Whatever we can do,' of course, and then we were kept away. A lot of people were pretty upset about that, particularly when they found out that we were purposely kept away, that it wasn't our decision. Initially, there was some bad attitude towards us because we weren't there, and then they found out the truth. It was put to us that Doc was behind banning us from the show. I don't think that's the truth, but I don't know for sure. We didn't fight it, we just thought, 'That's the way it is.' So we focused on organising the Chris Bailey benefit.

John and Rick decided to stage the benefit for Chris back where it all began for him – Adelaide – and started making calls. They contacted Robbie Robertson, who'd been a partner in Sphere, The Angels' agency in the early days. He now owned the Thebarton Theatre with his wife, Carol, and they promptly donated a night, 17 April, two nights after the Rock For Doc show at the Enmore. Then the company that owned the huge sound and stage lighting system in the Thebarton waived their hire fee. John and Rick were stunned at the level of generosity that was unfolding.

John: I got in touch with Jimmy Barnes, Don Walker, Phil Small and Ian Moss. They were from Adelaide and had started out with us. I spoke to them all individually and said, 'We'll bill you under your own names, so there's no suggestion that it's Cold Chisel.' Once Jimmy said yes, we knew we had a show. I spoke to Mark Callaghan of GANGgajang, Chris's other band, and he came up with the title for the concert: 'Adelaide Salutes Chris Bailey'. Everyone I spoke to wanted to join us. Diesel went, 'Absolutely, yeah.' I called Wilbur Wilde and asked him, 'Will you come and be the master of ceremonies and bring your sax?' Then I called James Reyne, who we'd recently befriended. And Dave Gleeson's wife, Katie, who worked in publicity, approached Triple M Adelaide and got them to jump on board by presenting the show.

Promoting and running a show on this level was stretching the Brewsters' many talents and in a masterstroke John rang Brian Gleeson, the brilliant organiser of the concert at the Clipsal 500 car races that took over the streets of Adelaide each year. As it happened, Brian had booked The Angels to headline the 2013 concert in early March. John told him they needed help and Brian unhesitatingly replied, 'Count me in,' and then recruited 'Poster George', one of Adelaide's great wheeler/dealer/hustlers.

Poster George knew the manager of the Hilton and went to see him. 'You've just opened a new bar,' he said. 'We're doing this benefit with Barnes and all these top Australian bands. If we bring everyone back here for the after-show party, how'd you feel about donating a few rooms for the out-of-towners?' Poster George came away with the promise of twenty rooms.

> **John:** At one stage, Chris said, 'John, I can't believe it. Why are all these people putting their hand up for me? I'm an arsehole.' I said, 'No, you're not. They're doing it because you're a good bloke.' He said, 'I just can't believe it.'

On Saturday 2 March, after the roar of the Clipsal 500 races had echoed to a climax, The Angels walked out onto the podium for their performance and used the moment to announce the benefit concert for Chris Bailey. With Triple M broadcasting the show, it was the perfect way to let Adelaide know. When tickets went on sale, with an extra push from the local press, they sold close to 2000 seats within days.

> **John:** About three weeks before the concert Chris was on the phone. He said, 'John, I feel great. I've had the chemo. The doctors are happy and they say I should go to the concert, so I'll come and just play a song with GANGgajang and a song with The Angels.' I went, 'Great, fantastic.' A week later, he made another call and it was a really hard call, because he sounded fucking terrible. Sadly he never made it to the concert.

With the benefit show in a fortnight's time, The Angels were playing a run of dates in Perth when word came through on 4 April 2013 that Chris had passed away at 12.30 am that morning. Sam didn't feel good about playing that night, but John reminded him how Chris had said he was passing the baton to him. He also reminded him that this was his time to uphold one of the great traditions of the entertainment profession: *no matter what, the show goes on.* Chris would have expected nothing less.

Sam: We were all very sad that day. It was difficult that night – I was the guy there because he couldn't be, and there's no joy in that.

He was a great man and a brilliant bass player. He always played for the song, and every bit of melodic embellishment was always very tasteful and never clashed with the other melodies in the song. I spent a lot of time learning his parts and aspired to play them like he did.

Rick: Two days after Chris had passed, we received an email from Monica Saunders, community relations manager at Prince Alfred College, Chris's old school. The school's recording studio was to be renamed the Chris Bailey Studio, and the 'Chris Bailey Project' was to be established to celebrate contemporary arts.

Chris's Sydney funeral pulled a full house at the Macquarie Park Crematorium. The chapel overflowed into the vestibule, standing room only. It was a hot day, the French doors were opened and more stood looking in from the verandah.

It was non-religious with the inimitable Julia Zemiro as master of ceremonies. It was a gig – a celebration of a life much loved – and led by fellow musicians and entertainers. His wife, Josie, told stories of home life with Chris – addressing her words to Ollie who sat in her arms looking around with big eyes. A professional comedienne, red haired, petite and feisty, she effortlessly brought the house to tears one minute, laughter the next, stoic to the end.

Rick: I remember the laughter the most, especially that 'Chris's idea of a great day out was a trip to Bunnings.' Sadly, he never fulfilled his dream of having his own bait-and-tackle store.

GANGgajang stood by Chris's coffin with ukuleles and sang the Rod Stewart song 'Sailing', a salute to Chris's love of yachting – he kept his boat in Rose Bay for years – it was a special song between him and Josie too. Rick and John sang The Angels song 'Love Takes Care', and then others made their way to the front for an ensemble. It came to a poignant finale with a video of a frail Chris sitting with Ollie and singing 'The wheels on the bus go round and round . . .' which brought everyone undone. Right to the end it was music, played live by musicians, that saw him out.

A week later, on 17 April, his friends, family and many fans gathered at the Thebarton Theatre.

> **John:** It made me proud to be from Adelaide. 'Adelaide Salutes Chris Bailey' indeed. The show opened with Peter Head on keyboards. Peter had played with Chris in Headband in the early seventies. Wilbur Wilde was master of ceremonies and played sax with just about everyone. James Reyne performed on acoustic guitar with Tracey Kingsman – brilliant! GANGgajang performed, Swanee with Rob Pippan's band likewise.
>
> Rick and I played with Don Walker and Ian Moss joining us. They, along with Diesel, joined us in The Angels later. My son Tom played drums on a couple of Angels songs with Nick Norton on guitar.

The guys from Cold Chisel played together and did 'Flame Trees'. Don Walker's lyrics were inspired by a combination of his memories of Grafton – on the North Coast of New South Wales – where he had lived as a youth, and his romantic dreams. Walker had once said about the song, 'A lot of people finish up away from where they come from,' and they all surely had that in mind as they sang it for Chris.

All in all it was a wonderful celebration of Chris's life by a close-knit musical community and punters alike.

> **Rick:** There was a feeling of great camaraderie. Everyone there was there for Chris, Josie and Ollie. Very sad, but fulfilling. There's nothing like a tragedy to bring people together.

> The music was outstanding, we all played from the heart and Ollie got to experience it all. Don Walker and Mossie played some BB songs with John and me and that was the highlight for me. Mossie yelled at me to turn up.

During the show Wilbur auctioned a guitar signed by all the artists – $6000. Just over $100,000 was passed on as a gift from Chris Bailey's friends to Josie for their son Ollie's education.

CHAPTER SEVENTY-NINE
SAY ME A PRAYER WHEN I'M GONE

John and Rick knew through mutual friends that things were getting close for Doc and he was constantly on their mind. They discussed the statement they'd release when the time came. John sat in the garden of his home at Victor Harbor thinking about it.

After the less than happy times leading up to New Year's Eve 2000 and all the legal disputes since then, it was now difficult to find the right words. So much time and money had been spent on legal warfare. There'd been accusations, acrimony and recriminations; invective in the press, ex-members and fans writing defamatory comments and mistruths on Facebook. It had been bruising and it had taken a toll. John and Rick had told a journalist that they could never perform with Doc again: 'We've crossed a bridge that can't be re-crossed.' But in the end, it wasn't that simple. There were just too many years together, too many shared dreams, rivers of sweat, the highs and lows, victories and disappointments. There'd been a million miles and *so* many thousands of gigs.

Despite the cabal of gatekeepers surrounding Doc, John and Rick had managed to conduct a friendly if stilted email exchange with him a month back. But it dried up when he stopped responding.

Then just a few days before, Rick had managed to fluke a call to him. He knew he was close to dying and rang the hospital. The switch put him straight through and Doc had picked up. 'Hello?' He sounded terrible. Rick said he wanted to see how he was and maybe have a chat about old times, just reminisce, but Doc said, 'Oh, I can't talk now. I'm about to have my medication. Can you ring back?' Rick rang again and got through to the nurses' station to inquire when would be a good time to call back. He waited a few minutes and then she returned. 'Doc would rather not speak to you,' she said, thanked him for calling and hung up.

John shook his head, remembering the previous Christmas. He'd received a card from Doc, wishing him and his family all the best. At the time they were supposed to have been in major conflict. It made him realise it was probably being generated by certain people around him. It had actually been going on for years – people getting into Doc's ear and manipulating him, using him for their own ends. Or as a trophy friend for a mischievous fan.

John didn't put Lowy in that basket – David had met Doc during the time he was out of the band and had believed in him for all the right reasons. David wanted to do things with Doc and invested in him, but it hadn't worked out. It hadn't worked out for anybody. Doc's success came from being a part of The Angels. He'd never been able to reinvent himself beyond the band.

John went inside, switched on his laptop and began composing, sending words and lines back and forth with his brother as he wrote down his thoughts.

When John and Rick received the inevitable news on 4 June that Doc had passed away at 7.30 that morning, they had this to say:

> I've found myself thinking back to the wonderful days of the Moonshine Jug and String Band when we first met Doc, the residencies at the Modbury Hotel, Adelaide Rowing Club, the Finsbury, all the great gigs that that zany, crazy band performed at, the parties at Doc's rented house in Glenunga, SA. We had so much fun back then.
>
> Somehow that band turned into The Angels, i.e. Doc, Rick, Charlie King and me, and we went out on the road, literally, in my old 1964 EH Holden station wagon. The endless highway, playing every night of the week, mostly

in dives, learning how to do it by live performance and writing better and better songs.

Eventually the band, including Buzz Bidstrup and Chris Bailey, hit it big in 1978 and Doc became one of the great frontmen of all time, a dynamic, demonic, artistic and imposing performer who would give it his all night after night, totally spent at the end of each show.

There was a deep, sensitive and gentle side to Doc. In this sad time of his passing I'll remember him for that and the good times we had together, now and forever more.

John Brewster

Doc stood out as one of a kind, a totally unique performer. His feverish stage presence was unsurpassed yet beneath the public persona was a gentle soul. He leaves behind a wealth of shared memories – good times, hard times and the thrill of creating timeless music together. RIP Doc.

Rick Brewster

The funeral was held on 11 June at Sydney's St Michael's Catholic Church, Lane Cove. It was an invitation-only affair – the family didn't want to risk it becoming a circus.

Rick and John, feeling slightly uneasy, arrived early. They spotted Angry with some familiar faces outside the entrance and joined them. Doc's brother Kevin spotted them and came straight over, shook their hands, and in his Irish brogue thanked them for coming.

John: We were welcomed by all these people we thought were against us – but they were welcoming.

Inside they slipped into a pew and were soon joined by Jim and Jane Barnes, Mark Opitz, and then Peter Garrett as the service began. The place was barely half full but that's what the family wanted, about a hundred or so. It was a Catholic service, a surprise for those who recalled him railing about the way he'd been treated by the nuns at an Irish school, and his views about the Catholic Church as an institution.

A friend from his younger days got up and recalled their friendship and 'man love' for one another. Annie, Dzintra and his three handsome sons read poetry and biblical passages, Aiden hauntingly like his rarely met father. There were prayers and then Jim Hilbun rose with an acoustic guitar and sang 'Love Takes Care', a song Doc and John had written thirty-five years back, while a compilation of Doc footage appeared on two screens.

John and Rick sat among the congregation with their private thoughts, never imagining they'd hear this song floating through a sombre church while a rose-bedecked coffin carrying Doc Neeson lay before them.

As the three young men he'd sired gathered with the pall-bearers and readied for the lift, the original track of 'Be With You' came through the PA. Doc's young voice at its finest whispered through the church, accompanied only by Buzz's tapping drums and Chris's bass notes: 'Your flashing eyes are a beacon light, that guides the jet plane into the night . . .' Then, as he was carried along the aisle, the Irish national anthem swelled up and followed him out to the hearse.

Rick: We weren't invited to the wake, which was probably appropriate. It wouldn't have felt right being there, but it felt right being at the funeral.

CHAPTER EIGHTY
SOMEWHERE OUT THERE TONIGHT

We're in a small white marquee behind an open-air concert in the Hunter Valley. More marquees nearby display handwritten signs: Jimmy Barnes, Badloves, Mark Seymour, Noiseworks, and this one says The Angels. It's the final show of the fifteen-date Red Hot Summer tour.

Musicians and roadies sit round tables and chairs in front of the kitchen tent while their kids race about in the autumn evening. Beyond rows of parked semi-trailers, Mark Seymour and his band start into 'Throw Your Arms Around Me'. In the huge covered stage, their set is coming to an end.

I'm recording an interview for this book with John and Rick, and talking about some recent highlights. We look up as the canvas flap is pulled back and the stage manager leans in.

'Sorry to interrupt, guys, you're on in ten minutes.'

It's sunset as I push past backstage security and slip in amongst the hordes of good-natured punters jostling for positions down the front. There are couples here in their sixties who were married to Angels songs, conceived their kids to Angels songs and brought them up listening to The Angels. Those kids have grown up, married and now bring *their* teenagers to Angels gigs. No generation gap here. And recently there's word of 'Am I Ever Gonna See Your Face Again' being reverentially played at funerals.

On the stage above me, the band is announced. They stroll purposefully out to a roar and a forest of clenched fists rising in a tribal salute. Nick's drums set into a steady beat and as Sam's bass locks in with him, the crowd surges forward. Rick and John's guitars open up and Dave Gleeson takes a breath: 'Who walks on sheets of ice . . .'

As the song draws to an end the guitars seamlessly segue into the nic-nics for 'No Secrets'. Gleeson has his lips on the mic: 'Amanda the actress, waits at the station . . .'

Up on the stage John and Sam range alongside Rick, the three bent over their howling guitars while Dave crouches out on the lip scoping the faces, one hand aloft, the other gripping the microphone. When it comes to an end he yells, 'Good evening, how ya going? It's good to be back home!'

A few songs further along and I recognise the opening bars of 'I Ain't The One'. The song that gave birth to the nic-nics. The song Ray Hawkins had identified as the band's 'tipping point'. The one they'd opened with on the Opera House steps when Doc and Chris were struck down. Thirty-six years back. Two lifetimes ago.

I gaze around the amphitheatre. Twelve thousand people, young and old: laughing, cheering, waving, heads back and singing their hearts out. Home-grown, big-time Australian rock 'n' roll.

The Angels, and their forerunner the Moonshine Jug and String Band, have now been on the road in one guise or another for forty-six years. Other than the associated Brewster Brothers and Hotdog outfits, Rick has never worked in another band. Although John was 'kicked out' for a while, he's still clocked up over forty years of service. They've been in constant motion all that time: rehearsing, performing, composing, releasing albums.

In a country like Australia, if a musician wishes to take up this line of work, they must develop their performance skills and hit the road for a life of one-night stands. It's the nature of the beast and no rock 'n' roll band in this country has ever done it better, and for longer, than The Angels. They follow a tradition that goes back to at least the days of Slim Dusty and his convoy of caravans. Their enduring popularity and ability to win new fans reflects the appeal of the timeless songs they've composed and recorded. It also reflects their impeccable musicianship and stagecraft, acquired during endless tours in their formative years.

And then there's the genius of George Young. His part in their success cannot be overstated. It was George who suggested that Doc, replaced by Chris as bass player, should become their unlikely lead singer. A lead singer who would evolve into 'Doc Neeson', and become one of the greatest Aussie front-men of his era. One of an elite handful.

> John: That late-seventies line-up, everyone gave it their all. Sure, we had arguments, but most were creative ones. The biggest arguments were the ones between Rick and me. That was a creative lens, because we'd scream at each other about what chord should be after this. It was always about the music, but with Rick and me it starts off as a musical argument and then it gets personal. As it only can with brothers.

It was always a rollercoaster ride with this band. Over the years they've had to deal with the fire and rain, but when they mount a stage these days, Dave Gleeson out front, there are no leftover politics simmering beneath the surface.

> John: Everything's easier now. In the studio one of us comes along with an idea for a song, half an hour later we're recording it. You listen to the tape and go, 'It's fantastic.' It's got spontaneity, it's got all the right elements. The reason why is because everybody's so bloody good and there's no funny stuff going on. Nick just plays great, Sam plays great, Dave sings great. We all know our roles.

There's a mysterious force that happens when five compatible and gifted musicians playing different instruments get up in a rock 'n' roll band. Especially with a canon of original music such as The Angels have. It was what set them apart in their heyday.

As for those occasions in later years when they were reduced to trading on former glories, John and Rick are now philosophical.

John: We think back to all the people who've played in the band and just remember the best parts of it. The times we'd throw frisbees around when we were on the road before it all took off and Doc became our great front-man. We had a lot of fun in those days. It's good to remember them.

In 2016 they played the huge Sweden Rock Festival, following an invitation from promoter Johannes Lindstrom. Savvy agent Tony Grace jumped on the phone and before long one of his assistants, Luke, had arranged headline shows at London's Garage club and Paris's Le Forum – where groups of fans milled around with Angels vinyl records, waiting for the band to arrive for the soundcheck. They asked where they've been and why they never returned to France after their early successes.

Back in Australia, they closed doors on a run through the major clubs and pubs, co-headlined a series of Big Day Out festivals, guested on national television shows and were in constant demand for corporate events. They've done a theatre tour of New Zealand with Dragon and the reformed Mi-Sex, promoted by their one-time manager/drummer, Brent Eccles.

The Angels are back!

Rick: The band is re-energised to the extent that I feel like it's a young band again. I feel like I felt when we started out – I really want to be up there. The travel does nothing for me, living in motels . . . the glory went out of that decades ago. The hour and a half onstage is what makes it worthwhile and it's great fun. It's not even the rush. A lot of musicians get the rush of the audience, and I get that to an extent, but to me it's about playing, it's about getting in 'the zone'. It doesn't happen every night, but you hang out for the nights where everything seems to . . . the chemistry of the band, the sound . . . and your fingers just flow in the right spot.

John and Rick have been working on a double CD featuring many of the band's songs that are favourites of theirs, going back to the start.

In their hunt for interesting renditions, they wondered if anything could be salvaged from the disastrous Symphony Of Angels concert, recorded on multi-track tape in 2010 at the Adelaide Festival Theatre.

After listening again to the tape, John rang me in high spirits. Using the latest cutting-edge technology, they'd managed to resurrect six songs from the last recording Doc made with the band, despite the fact that sometimes 'Doc is off-key'.

I couldn't help notice how he'd referred to their former lead singer in the present tense: 'Doc *is* off-key', as well as 'Doc *has* a distinctive voice'. Maybe listening to him for day after day had shifted John's perceptions to another reality, a reality where the old Doc was back in the studio with him – endearing, infuriating, flawed . . . dazzling.

Somewhere out there tonight, an eight-seater will swing off a highway and into a sprawling carpark. John Brewster at the wheel will coast between rows of vehicles as, beside him, Rick dials a number and says, 'We're here.' A few minutes later they'll pull up at the Vegas-like entrance of a licensed club, all smoky glass, stainless steel and water fountains. Two roadies in Angels t-shirts will appear as the side doors slide back and Dave, Nick and Sam alight.

One roadie will help with their bags and guitars and lead the way to the elevators while the other jumps behind the wheel, drives round the back, and parks. As the procession makes its way past throngs of people jostling for the pokies, the restaurants and drinks at the bars, long-standing fans will step forward to say hello. They'll respectfully request selfies and offer CDs and posters for autographs. The group will then push on and arrive at a door guarded by a security guy. He'll step aside as they enter into a private low-lit dressing room where a sideboard of sandwiches, fruit and buckets of cold drinks await.

The club's manager will drop by to say g'day, shake hands, announce they've got a full house and thank them for coming.

Thirty minutes later, tech roadie Falcon will shine his torch on the steps leading up to the darkened stage. A deafening welcome pierced with whistling and chants will erupt as the band walks out, plugs in and prepares for Nick's count.

'One, two, three, four,' he'll yell and The Angels will launch into another show.

ACKNOWLEDGEMENTS

Rick:
Heartfelt thanks to the following –

Hooper Brewster-Jones, our grandfather, who was known to us as Bopo, a gifted musician who planted the seed for us. I never knew him, but I heard him playing his own music on an old 78rpm record and later learnt to play some of his compositions. His wife Gerta (Gran) inspired me to play piano. For that I will be forever grateful. She was a fine pianist and a wonderful teacher.

Mum, who worked in the kitchen right next to the grand piano where I practised for hours every day, always encouraging, and who later came to gigs, danced on tables, never once wavering in her support of me and John.

Dad, a wonderful cellist – his occasional comments (mostly critical) when he heard me practising piano have stayed with me always and influenced my approach to performing: 'Make the melody sing' and 'Let the fingers do the talking'. He loathed 'modern' music, advised us against a musical career and, only after many years, listened critically to *Face to Face* and said, 'Okay, now I get it.' To John and me, that was an enormous compliment.

To my sister, Anne, and her husband, Malcolm, thanks for your encouragement.

My great friends from school and university, Rog Hartley, Greg Baker, Graham Harbord, Laurie Lever, Phil Martin, Maggie Carey, Dave Bartold. Their interest, support and the occasional insightful comment have been invaluable.

Bob Petchell, my school friend, started an acoustic trio with Bitsy and me, and later joined the jug band.

My friend from school, Justin Milne. I played in public for the first time with Justin at a birthday party.

Photographer Phil Morris, who opened his Oxford St developing lab to me in 1979 and taught me all he could about shooting, developing and printing black and white photos. Without his inspiration, my 'private collection' of photos in this book would not exist.

Doc's habitual decisions to leave the band over the years always meant tough times for the rest of us as the touring stopped dead until he decided to return. When he left in 2000, I placed an ad in the local paper as a handyman. Barry Barnes answered my ad and employed me for months to work on his house – thanks, Barry.

Mick McKenna answered another ad I placed in the music mags and employed me for many days to record and produce his songs at my home. He and his wife, Michelle, have become close friends.

When Doc left for good in 2010, we had no work for ages while we re-grouped with Dave Gleeson and Nick Norton (drums). My good friends Craig Swan and Josh Muskett employed me as a builder's labourer for the next year or two. It provided income and gave me an opportunity to soak up valuable knowledge from the tradesmen I worked with.

Many thanks to Craig and Michelle, Josh and Tameka.

Friends – Joe and Stuart Palmer, David and Tania Wedd, Dean and Ali Anderson, Mick and Bridget Belcher, Steve and Chris Page, Tim and Flic Hibberd, Bob Lavis and Michael, Chrissie Thomas, Dave Wilson, Jim and Helen Conway, Joe Matera, John Stephenson, Richard White, Bill Papineau – thank you for your support.

My wife, Michelle, and my beautiful children, Jackie, Charlotte, William, Rhiana and Jody. My love and gratitude to you all.

John:
My special thanks from the heart to the following:

Mum, who would sit with me and listen to Bob Dylan, who kept every article about us, who never had any doubts about our chosen path.

Dad, who, even though steeped in classical music, eventually came to listen to ours and liked it!

My first wife, Robyn, who supported me through the early years and never complained when things looked grim, fantastic mother to my three sons.

My beautiful wife, Sue, who has played such a huge part in my life since 2000. Wonderful evenings spent in that funny Barina with the great sound system playing demos of Brewsters, Angels at massive volume! You have helped give me the confidence to be a singer, a good father when I had my doubts, been right there with me with unwavering support through the good and the bad.

My sons, Sam, Tom, Harry and my stepdaughter Georgia, who so enrich my life. I've watched you grow to be fine young people, played music with all of you and that is amazing! My love to you all.

My friends from surfing days, Pete Thorpe, the late Kim McKenzie, Dave Langdon, Rog and Sal Hartley, and from more recent times, Murray and Denise Golding, Gary and Julie Reilly, David Van Blerk, Greg Annersley and Margaret Mitchell, Paul and Cheryl Leuzzi, Alan and Dale Lancaster, Angry Anderson, Kevin Borich, Rob and Nol Parkyn, Tony and Christine Walsh, Rob Pippan, Swanee, Ian (Polly) Politis, Matt McNamee, Shaun Duncan, Greg and Christine Clifford, Barry Lang and Ian (Ossie) Osbourne.

Wilbur Wilde, my great friend in life, music and in golf. Life would be a little diminished without those wonderful days on the fairways!

Rick and John:
Without our great friend Marcus Ahern the band would probably not exist as The Angels. His legal advice and his collaboration with his friend and lawyer Steven Penglis enabled us to keep the name despite

the opposition we faced through 2011–2013. Hats off to Marcus and Jane, Steven and Vanessa.

Tony Grace, Josh Daly, Dean McLachlan, Warren and Paul Costello were unwavering in their support and belief of the band through this difficult and complicated period, and continue to encourage and inspire us.

David Lowy, whose advice and support helped reunite the original line-up in 2008. And who helped bring about the SOA in 2010.

Blicka Mac Blicka, who toured with us as sound engineer through the reunion 2009–11, became a great friend and, together with Lou Quinlan, built the website which he continues to manage.

Spencer Tregloan and Pete Thorpe, original Moonshine members, who came to live in Sydney in the late nineties while we created our kids band Hotdog.

Bicci Henderson, who went from being our tour manager to running the entertainment at Star City Casino. He gave us our first job as the Brewster Brothers – a Tuesday night residency in the Volcano Bar.

Matt Laverty, our great friend who's been with us through thick and thin, always supportive, generous and funny. Matt, our times at Breakfast Point with you are memorable.

Andy 'Pineapple Head' King, who turns up at any time unannounced to help backstage. Nothing is ever too much for Andy.

Mikael and Jackie Borglund – our great friends who have helped us over so many years. Mikael started as our accountant, became CEO of Beyond International, and produced our documentary in 2008.

Michael Gudinski, the shadowy force behind the scenes who can still turn up at a gig to get it on with the punters . . . it's all about the music, all about the guitars! Thanks for your and Sue's friendship and support.

Angus and Malcolm Young, who with Bon Scott gave us our first lucky break when they introduced us to their older brother George Young and Harry Vanda, and then to the late Ted Albert. It resulted in our first record deal with Alberts and put us in the same stable as AC/DC, Ted Mulry, John Paul Young and Rose Tattoo, working directly with George and Harry, the ultimate mentors who helped shape our songs and our sound.

Harry Vanda and George Young, we couldn't have done it without you guys.

Mark Opitz, the young engineer that George and Harry suggested should work with us: *Face To Face*, *No Exit* and then *Dark Room*. We had great times together.

Fifa Riccobono was the girl in charge at Alberts – a powerhouse who followed us every step of the way, elbowing her way through the packed houses to stand in the front line.

Greg and Chris Clifford have become great friends. Greg is an extraordinary sound engineer, both live and in the studio. His instinct with sound is out of sight.

Jarred Nettle has worked alongside Greg through countless mixing sessions – great engineer!

Bitsy Ackland, Rick's first wife, came to hundreds of gigs and her natural gift for photography produced a huge collection of remarkable shots.

Mick Wordley – his old school recording studio, built by the man himself, tucked away in the Adelaide Hills, is like Alberts Studio 1 revisited. Great engineer, great guitars and amps, great guy.

Eva Roberts, our hard-working publicist, always busy with the next project keeping the band visible. Eva and Jamie – our friends.

Ashley Swinfield (sound engineer), Ray Hawkins (lights) and Bob Daniels (foldback) were our dedicated crew who along with Mark Pope (tour manager) toured the world with us through 1978–81, providing the best production ever. Ashley met his wife Clare when she started the first Angels fan club.

Bob Yates, after initially declining, eventually put up his hand to take the bull by the horns and write this book. He has become a great friend after spending years researching, interviewing hundreds of people, sourcing information online and through chance conversations. Rick's container is the home of most of the archives and Bob has made numerous trips to Tasmania to stay in 'Uncle Bob's Cabin', where he has scoured the material and written much of the story without distraction. Good on you, Bob . . . you deserve a rest!

Rob and Anne Stevens have supported us for more than thirty years with good advice and equipment. Thanks to all at Turramurra Music.

Mick Newton who, with his wife, Anthea, and mate Batesy, showed faith in us when Dave joined the band and booked us on countless 'Day on the Green' gigs.

Duane McDonald, our thanks for all the great 'Red Hot Summer' gigs and your friendship. Our thanks to Paul Taylor too.

Rick Szabo, our Queensland promoter who has showed faith in us throughout – a much-valued friend.

Ross Stapleton, who came on tour with us as a journalist, was there with us in London when he was A&R for Virgin. Thanks for your friendship over many years.

Paul Russell, who was top dog at CBS in the early eighties and gave great support to the *Dark Room* album in particular.

Sam Horsburgh, thanks for all your help in the studio over the years.

Don Bartley, the mastering engineer who has put the finishing touches on just about everything we've ever released.

A big thank you to Ben Nicholls, our friend at Foxtel whose efforts resulted in him producing the brilliant live recording session at Foxtel studio in January 2016, as well as fantastic stage backdrops and merchandise ideas. Dedication does not get any better. We are in your debt, Ben.

Glenn A. Baker, your passion for the music is unbelievable. Thanks for your friendship.

Lee and Jan Simon, many interviews, many crazy nights having fun, always a pleasure to see you.

Charlie King, our first drummer, did so many of the early hard yards with us.

Adrian Townsend (Pud) was our first sound engineer.

Andrew Scott, Al Wright, Jacky Murray and Chipper, the team at Rhinoceros Studio – many great memories!

Rod Chan and the late Craig Upfold, both extraordinary luthiers, who generously provided us with fine guitars which we continue to use and enjoy.

Craig Peihopa (Timeline Photography) – thanks for all your time, effort, expertise and great photos.

Gary Bradshaw and Michael Sims (Rock On Photography) – they can turn up at a gig when least expected and have produced many remarkable shots.

Amanda Gill, who toured widely with us, tirelessly selling merchandise in difficult conditions.

Mal McEwan, Alan, Steve, Mullet and Jeff, our incredibly hard-working production team in NSW. Always reliable, never a complaint.

Rob Pippan, thanks for bringing Symphony of Angels to life.

Rob John, who composed most of the orchestral scores for SOA and conducted on the night.

Jamie Messenger, who composed the remaining scores.

Nick Majcen – film-maker extraordinaire.

Brian and Matt Taranto and all at Love Police.

Chris Bailey's wife, Josie O'Reilly, and their wonderful son, Ollie Bailey – may all your dreams come true.

Adrian Alders, whose enthusiasm and support are unrivalled. Always a pleasure to see you at the gigs with your fine bottles of red!

Rick Harper, Alan Rigg and Clyde from Rock Repairs, who worked on our guitars in the early days.

Jimmy Barnes, thanks for your friendship and thanks for your words – no-one could have put it better!

Jenny Elliot; Joe Konnaris; Ed Thacker; John Boylan; Ashley Howe; Lee de Carlo; Jim Taig; Bill Price; Steve Brown; Terry Manning; Steve James; Reyne Hause; Glenn Mehaffey; Brian Thorpe; Colin Skals; Peter Ward; Tim Bradsmith; Ian Taylor ('Taylie Delaylie'); Mick Richardson; Ben Turner; Falcon; Flea; Acky; Jon Calsley; Derek Bovill; Athol; Johannes Lindström and Inger; Luke Morton; Sean Senett; John Stephenson; Simon Olding; Rosemary and Robin Hill; Rick Nielsen; Paul Hamer; Jol Dantzig; Paul Mineur; Deon Lynde; Steve and Carrie Rawlins; Peter Freedman; Darrel Baird; Cat Swinton; Kathy White; Steve and Lenore Mulry; David Hemming; Peter Head; Joff Bateman; John Bee; Jim Towers; Chris Gilbey; Mark Opitz; Chris Murphy; Richard McDonald; Barry Chapman; Brendan 'Bloss' Keane; Chrystene Carrol; Wendy McDougal; Terry Lee Haefer; Joe the US bus driver; our team, the Hawks under 9s.

RIP Doc Neeson and Chris Bailey

Bob:

This book would have been the half the story if not for the contributions of so many of the people John and Rick have mentioned above. The following should also take a bow.

Charlie King for his scrapbooks and emails covering the KA period! He dedicates his contribution to his daughter Tania. John McGowan for his early days info. Ross Stapleton and Stuart Coupe for allowing me to recycle whatever I wanted from their long-form Angels biographies. I delved into rock magazines of the day; *RAM*, *Juke*, *Roadrunner*, *On The Street*, *Rolling Stone*, and from New Zealand, *Rip It Up*. Miranda Brown's *Penthouse* article on a Europe tour was invaluable. Brent Eccles produced the *Weekly Amatizer* magazine for band and staff which revealed their private antics. New Zealand research by Daniel Phillips, John Dix, Chris Ryder and Mike Corless – thank you. Fans on Angels websites answered my questions, especially Mignonne Immesi, Damian Sharry, Victor Marshall and Dean Soma. Yogi Harrison – respect and thanks. Bjarne Ohlin and Isaiah Brunt for your revelations. My dear friend HO for hers.

My gratitude to the National Film and Sound Archives who commissioned Anthony O'Grady to record interviews with Doc the year before he died. The NFSA's Simon Drake made me very welcome – thank you – NFSA Oral history Title No 1143909.

Murray Engleheart for presenting my early chapters to Alison Urquhart at Penguin Random House. I was stunned next day to receive her email offering a contract to this unknown writer with a story to tell. Heartfelt thanks to my lady Lorraine for her sunlit sanctuary, encouragement, spell-checks, readings and corrections during the final twelve months. Hugs to my sister Sue for IT advice and to Roger and Virginia for always being there.

Patrick Mangan – editor extraordinaire – who, as a teenager, saw The Angels at the Ballarat Civic Hall, and still listens to the music. Thank you for your guidance, invaluable suggestions and cutting my manuscript down to a digestible size.

And finally, to John and Rick. We've travelled through a rock 'n' roll landscape that barely exists anymore. Along the way we've had our highs and lows, laughs and arguments. Whenever I discovered blood on the tracks and asked you uncomfortable questions, to your credit you gulped and answered. It's been an honour, guys, but can I go sailing now?

When I was ten back in '55, my family lived in a boarding house in Scarborough in the UK. A corny song by Kay Starr was a hit on the BBC and the hook line was about 'trying to waltz to a rock and roll song'. My mum used to sing along, asking everyone what a rock 'n' roll song was, but no one knew. Elvis changed that the following year with 'Heartbreak Hotel'. I dedicate this book to Beth, my beautiful mother, long may you run.

We have done our best to remember everyone who deserves mentioning here. There are bound to be some omissions. Our sincere apologies to anyone who feels left out. We thank you anyway.

For the latest band news, visit:
theangels.com.au

ABOUT THE AUTHOR

While recuperating from an operation, **Bob Yates** opened a folk club in a Balmain church hall in 1974, which led to him promoting small concerts and big dances with Skyhooks, Captain Matchbox Whoopee Band, Radio Birdman, Saints, Sports, Ferrets . . . and The Angels. That was followed by organising and promoting two of Sydney's most popular seventies/eighties pubs, the Civic and the Royal Antler. Bob also managed chart-topping NZ band Mi-Sex before moving on from the music business in the mid-eighties and founding the successful pastry manufacturing and distribution company 'Bob & Pete's Croissants' with ex Matt Finish manager Peter Dawson. However he continued an association with the music business arranging charity and benefit concerts.

Bob has been friends with The Angels since the mid-seventies. *The Angels* is his first book.